THE POLITICS OF ADOPTION

THE POLITICS OF ADOPTION

International Perspectives on Law, Policy & Practice

by

KERRY O'HALLORAN

B.A., LL.B., MSc. (CQSW), LL.M.,
Barrister-at-Law (Kings Inns, Dublin),
Ph.D. (Trinity College Dublin) Ireland.
Adjunct Professor, Centre of Philanthropy and Nonprofit Studies,
Queensland University of Technology, Brisbane, Australia

 Springer

A C.I.P. Catalogue record for this book is available from the Library of Congress.

ISBN-10 1-4020-4153-5 (HB)
ISBN-13 978-1-4020-4153-2 (HB)
ISBN-10 1-4020-4154-3 (e-book)
ISBN-13 978-1-4020-4154-9 (e-book)

Published by Springer,
P.O. Box 17, 3300 AA Dordrecht, The Netherlands.
www.springer.com

Printed on acid-free paper

Printed in the Netherlands.

To Molly
More in hope than expectation . . .

CONTENTS

ACKNOWLEDGEMENTS

That *The Politics of Adoption* made it into print owes a great deal to Professor Myles McGregor-Lowndes[1] and to my other colleagues at the Centre of Philanthropy and Nonprofit Studies. For their support and companionship, at a time when this was sorely needed, I remain extremely grateful.

Many academics, senior managers and others voluntarily undertook the task of reading and commenting on particular chapters. Their contributions have spared readers from encountering even more inaccuracies, gaps and inconsistencies. Those that may still be detected, together with all views expressed, are inescapably attributable to the author. While it is not possible to render a full account of the debt owed to so many it would be quite wrong not to acknowledge the particular contribution of a few.

Thanks are due to Deborah Cullen[2] who kindly read and commented on the chapter dealing with the adoption process in the UK, to Geoffrey Shannon[3] for his similar contribution in respect of the chapter on Ireland and to Greg Kelly for his observations in respect of current practice in both jurisdictions[4]. My concerns in relation to the Australian adoption process were allayed by the advice of John Dewar[5] who referred me to Patrick Parkinson[6] and Lee Ann Basser[7]. I'm grateful

---

[1] Professor and Director, Centre of Philanthropy and Nonprofit Studies, Queensland University of Technology, Brisbane, Australia.
[2] Secretary of the Legal Group, British Association for Adoption & Fostering (BAAF), London.
[3] Deputy Director of Education, Law Society, Dublin, Ireland.
[4] Senior Lecturer, School of Social Work, Queens University, Belfast, Northern Ireland.
[5] Professor and Dean of Law, Griffith Law School, Queensland, Australia.
[6] Professor and Associate Dean, Faculty of Law, University of Sydney, Australia.
[7] Associate Professor, La Trobe University, Bundoora, Victoria, Australia.

to the former for his suggested reading list and for putting me in touch with Justice Richard Chisholm[8] who was most helpful. To the latter I am grateful for her comments on draft material relating both to Australia and to the adoption experience among the Indigenous people. The chapter on adoption process in the US received much needed attention from Ann Estin[9] and Charles Putnam[10] both of whom made important improvements.

I am particularly grateful to John Triseliotis for his kind words of endorsement. My thanks also to Springer and in particular to Anne-Marie Blaney for their vote of confidence that resulted in the publishing of this book.

Thanks, Elizabeth, for tolerating this self indulgence.

[8] The Family Court of Australia, now retired.
[9] Professor of Law, University of Iowa, US.
[10] JD and Co-Director, Justiceworks, University of New Hampshire, US.

INTRODUCTION

Adoption has always had a political dimension. Its potential use to achieve political ends has been evident throughout history and in many different cultures. In Roman times an emperor would adopt a successful general to continue his rule.[1] In Ireland under the Brehon Laws the reciprocal placements of children between clans was an accepted means of cementing mutual allegiances.[2] In Japan the adoption of non-relatives was traditionally seen as a means of allying with the fortunes of the ruling family.[3] The willingness of governments to use adoption as a political strategy was apparent, for example, in Australia where it was used to further the assimilation of indigenous people.[4] It is now present in the phenomenon of intercountry adoption where the flow of children, particularly in the aftermath of war, is often politics by proxy and which arguably attracts the involvement of some countries for reasons of economic and political expediency.[5]

Adoption does not function in isolation. It plays a distinct role within the context of family law proceedings. The extent to which it is available as a resource for children in the public care system or as an adjunct to marriage proceedings is essentially politically determined. It is itself susceptible to political influence. In fact direct political leadership, exercised first by President Clinton[6] and then

[1] See, Gibbons, *The Decline and Fall of the Roman Empire*, Harrap, London 1949 at p. 30.
[2] See, Gilligan, R., *Irish Child Care Services: Policy, Practice and Provision*, Institute of Public Administration, Dublin, 1991.
[3] See, Gibbons, *The Decline and Fall of the Roman Empire*, op cit.
[4] See, Bird, C., *The Stolen Children; Their Stories*, Random House, Australia, 1998.
[5] See, further, Chapter 9.
[6] In December 1996, President Clinton issued his Executive Memorandum on adoption and in 1997 the Department responded with the *Adoption 2000* report.

Kerry O'Halloran (ed.), The Politics of Adoption, 1–4.
© 2006 *Springer. Printed in The Netherlands.*

by Prime Minister Blair,[7] introduced fundamental change to the accepted role of adoption in the US and the UK. These changes are now the focus of political attention in countries like Ireland and Australia where adoption law reform is currently underway. They highlight the widening gap between the politically determined role of adoption in countries that share a common law heritage and others of a different tradition such as Denmark, Finland and Sweden.[8] All, however, are also challenged by the more open approach developed and sustained by the Aborigines in Australia, the Maori in New Zealand and the Inuit in Canada.[9]

In a number of common law countries, adoption reform is now giving rise to contentious political issues.[10] The change process underway in England & Wales offers an opportunity and a perspective to explore areas of commonality and difference in the adoption law, policy and practice of other nations. More basically, it also provides a window through which to examine the presumption that within and between cultures there exists a common understanding of what is meant by adoption.

The Politics of Adoption takes an analytical look at adoption. It does so by:

- tracing the evolution of adoption law, policy and practice across many centuries and societies to provide a record of the common pressures that have influenced the development of modern adoption in western nations;
- contrasting this with a consideration of adoption custom and practice as shaped by the social values of indigenous people and allowing adoption to acquire culture specific characteristics;
- analysing the content of adoption law and revealing its essential constituent elements;
- identifying and evaluating the changing balance between public and private interests in adoption law to discern trends with wider policy implications;
- constructing and applying a template of its essential legal functions to facilitate a comparative evaluation of adoption processes in England & Wales

---

[7] In July 2000, the Performance and Innovation Unit of the Cabinet Office, acting under the direction of the Prime Minister, assessed the need for change and published *The Prime Minister's Review: Adoption*.

[8] Adoption in these countries is endorsed by neither law, policy or practice as an option for addressing parental failure.

[9] See, further, Chapter 10.

[10] Adoption law reform concluded in the US with the Adoption and Safe Families Act 1997, in New South Wales, Australia with the Adoption Act 2000 and in England & Wales with the Adoption and Children Act 2002. Ongoing adoption law reviews were launched in Queensland, Australia in 2000, in Scotland in 2002 and in Ireland in 2003. In Northern Ireland, the Department of Health & Social Services and Public Safety published its report *Adopting: Best Care* in 2002 and a full review of the law is expected to commence shortly. In New Zealand the Law Commission published its report *Adoption and Its Alternatives: A Different Approach and a New Framework* in 2000.

and other common law countries, as differentiated from the processes of countries with a different legal tradition;

- assessing the development of intercountry adoption and considering the modern characteristics of this phenomenon;
- examining recent international legislative and judicial developments to demonstrate the extent to which national adoption law, like the wider body of family law, is now becoming subject to certain key principles of international jurisprudence; and
- drawing some tentative conclusions about trends in the law, policy and practice of contemporary adoption in the common law jurisdictions and their implications for the future.

The ten chapters of *The Politics of Adoption* divide into three parts throughout which attention is drawn to an inescapable political dimension in the role played by adoption within and between nations.

Part 1 'Adoption and Society' consists of two chapters which examine the nature of adoption. It looks to the experience of adoption in other societies, ancient and contemporary, for insight into the causes and likely outcome of current trends in adoption in western societies. Chapter 1 'Adoption: Concept, Principles and Social Construct' explores the concept of adoption, the underpinning principles and its history as a social construct, enquiring as to how its use has been variously conditioned by the prevailing pressures on the family. Chapter 2 'The Changing Face of Modern Adoption in the United Kingdom ' tracks changes to the role and function of adoption in the UK with a particular emphasis on developments in England & Wales.

Part 2 'Adoption and the Law', again consisting of two chapters, is central to the book in the sense that it provides material for identifying and measuring the functions of the adoption process within a legal context. Chapter 3 'The Legal Functions of Adoption' constructs a template of the functions typical of the statutory adoption process in most modern western societies, particularly the common law jurisdictions, for use in Part 3. Chapter 4 'International Benchmarks for Modern Adoption Law' considers the provisions and related case law of international Conventions and assesses their significance for adoption practice.

Part 3 'Contemporary Law' in the main applies the template of legal functions (as outlined in Chap. 3) to conduct an analysis and comparative evaluation of the adoption experience in major common law nations. Chapters 5, 6, 7 and 8 examine 'The Adoption Process' in England & Wales, Ireland, the US and Australia respectively. These countries are leading representatives of the common law tradition but perform this function in a variable fashion. They have been chosen for comparative analysis because of their stature as common law jurisdictions and because recent or current engagement in adoption law reform reveals contrasting national approaches to much the same social pressures. Chapter 9 'Intercountry

Adoption' provides an account of this phenomenon and addresses the related issues. Finally, Chapter 10 'Intraculture Adoption' presents a study of the custom
and rules governing adoption practice among the Indigenous people of Australia,
the Maori of New Zealand and the Inuit of Canada. This chapter closes the book
by offering a challenging perspective on adoption law, policy and practice as experienced for centuries within ancient cultures and an opportunity to reflect on the
merits and deficits of the much more sophisticated and highly regulated approach
developed in modern western nations.

Kerry O'Halloran
White Park Bay
Autumn 2005.

Part I

ADOPTION AND SOCIETY

Chapter 1

ADOPTION: CONCEPT, PRINCIPLES, AND SOCIAL CONSTRUCT

1.   INTRODUCTION

Adoption is a complex social phenomenon, intimately knitted into its family law framework and shaped by the pressures affecting the family in its local social context. It is a mirror reflecting the changes in our family life and the efforts of family law to address those changes. This has caused it to be variously defined; in different societies, in the same society at different times and across a range of contemporary societies. It is currently being re-defined in the United Kingdom.

This chapter examines adoption from a developmental perspective drawing largely from law, policy and practice as experienced in England and Wales. It begins with a consideration of definitional matters, the concept and its culture specific determinants. An historical overview then provides some examples to illustrate the different social roles adoption has played in a variety of cultural contexts and to reveal the extent to which its development has been driven primarily by the changing pattern of adopters needs. This leads to a broad consideration of adoption in its English common law context and its gradual statutory transformation into statutory proceedings. The chapter concludes with an introduction to the main elements that emerged to structure statutory proceedings and continue to do so; the 'contract' the parties and the governing principles.

Kerry O'Halloran (ed.), The Politics of Adoption, 7–38.
© 2006 *Springer. Printed in The Netherlands.*

2.   DEFINITIONAL MATTERS AND
RELATED CONCEPTS

It is not possible to frame a definitive statement that captures the meaning of adoption for all societies. The best that can be done is to settle for a legal definition of its core functions within a specific social context.

2.1.   Legal definition

In legal terms, adoption has been defined as:

> ... a legal method of creating between the child and one who is not the natural parent of the child an artificial family relationship analogous to that of parent and child ... [1]

or, more bluntly:

> ... providing homes for children who need them is its primarypurpose[2]

Adoption, however, existed long before it acquired its present form as a legal proceeding and such attempts to reduce it to a stand-alone legal function fail to do justice to its complexity. It can only be properly understood when viewed in the particular social context in which its legal functions are exercised. It must then also be considered against the background of its related legal framework, including, for example: the alternative options available; the consensual or coercive nature of proceedings; and the outcome for all parties involved.

In the UK adoption now exists only as a legal process, delineated and regulated by statute, culminating in proceedings that are judicially determined. Legislation addresses the rights and obligations of the parties concerned, defines the roles of those mediating bodies with roles in the process, sets out the grounds for making an adoption order and states its effect. Statute law also provides the links between adoption and other legal processes; notably child care but also matrimonial proceedings.

2.2.   Concepts

Insofar as it is amenable to a conceptual interpretation, adoption addresses the act of the adopter. It is the voluntary acceptance of the responsibility to protect, nurture and promote the development of the child of another until adulthood that lies at the heart of adoption. It is an act which brings that child into the adopter's family with all the implications for sharing in the family name, home, assets and

---

[1]   See, Tomlin Committee report (Cmnd 2401) 1925.
[2]   See, Houghton Committee, *Report of the Departmental Committee on the Adoption of Children*, (Cmnd 5107), London, HMSO, 1972.

kinship relationships which are thereby entailed. As a corollary, the same act also implies a severance by the adopter of those same links between the child and his or her family of origin. But it remains an artificial and fundamentally a legal relationship. It fails to wholly displace all incidences of the child's pre-adoption legal relationships and fails also to legally subsume him or her fully into the adopter's family. It has attracted some contentious conceptual interpretations.

- The 'gift' relationship.[3] Adoption cannot be properly viewed as the ultimate incidence of a gift relationship though the literature testifies to the attempts of some to do so.
- The 'blood link' relationship. This essentially grounds a presumption that care provided by a child's parent or relative is in the best interests of that child. It can be detected in the prohibited degrees of relationship rule, in the resistance to child care adoptions and in the passive acquiescence given to family adoptions. It underpins traditional rules of inheritance and is also evident in the inference of 'bad blood' that has so often been applied to unfairly discriminate against adopted persons.

The act of the adopter essentially puts in place an alternative legal relationship alongside birth relationships and leaves to time and providence the possibility that a bonding relationship will achieve the attachment between adopter and child necessary to fulfil the needs of both for a family.[4]

As a social construct 'adoption' acquired a common currency definition throughout most modern western societies. It had been shaped to have a specific meaning, imprinted with considerable consistency by the legislatures of common law nations on a range of different cultural traditions, in order to address much the same social problems. In acquiring its identity, adoption became differentiated from alternative child-care arrangements within such societies (e.g. long-term foster care, in *loco parentis* care etc) and from comparable arrangements in other societies.

For example, 'simple' adoption is still common in many African nations and elsewhere while in Islamic countries, under Sharia law, adoption is prohibited but the practice of 'Kafalah', a form of long-term foster care, has long been used. Duncan explains the difference between adoption and Kafalah as follows[5]:

> ... the latter does not have the effect of integrating the child into the new family. The child remains in name a member of the birth family and there are no inheritance rights

---

3 See, for example, Lowe, N., 'The Changing Face of Adoption—The Gift/Donation Model versus the Contract/Services Model', *Child and Family Law Quarterly*, 371, 1997.

4 See, for example, Bowlby, J., *Attachment*, Penguin, London, 1969.

5 See, Duncan, W., 'Children's Rights, Cultural Diversity and Private International Law', in Douglas, G. and Sebba, L. (eds), *Children's Rights and Traditional Values*, Aldershot, Ashgate, 1998 at p. 32.

in respect of the new family. However, Kafalah may if necessary involve delegation of guardianship in respect of the person and property of the child and in an intercountry situation it may result in a change in the child's nationality.

Initially, in the UK and similar western societies, the social construct of adoption broadly conformed to a single generic type. This was the third party adoption of a healthy white Caucasian baby by a couple, unrelated and unknown to the birth mother, who were permanently and irrevocably vested with full parental rights and responsibilities in respect of her child. It involved three sets of needs: those of an unmarried mother wishing to voluntarily relinquish the child for whom she could not provide adequate care; the needs of her child for security of legal status and welfare; and the desire of a married childless couple for a child they could literally afford to call their own. It is unlikely that any society was ever able to quite satisfy the needs of all parties represented by such a providential equation and it is certain that they will be less able to do so in the foreseeable future. That single generic type faded as adoption evolved and permutated to meet certain needs. These included providing for orphaned or abandoned children within the jurisdiction and internationally, responding to the plight of childless heterosexual and same gender couples, reducing the number of children being maintained in public child care facilities and enabling parents to secure the legal cohesion of their re-formed families. Consequently, all modern western societies are now in the process of re-adjusting their use of adoption.

3.   SOCIAL CONSTRUCT

The following brief historical overview of adoption as a social construct reveals that its usefulness, at various times and places, has rested in particular on a capacity to meet the needs of adopters and their range of quite different motives. Adoption, its social role and legal functions, has always been shaped primarily by the needs of adopters.

3.1.   Adoption and the inheritance motive

Adoption has its legal origins in the law relating to the ownership and inheritance of property.[6] The concern of those with land but without children to legally acquire heirs and so consolidate and perpetuate their family's property rights for successive generations, is one which is common to all settled, organised and basically agricultural societies. In China, India and Africa adoption has long served this purpose,[7] but it was the tradition established over the several hundreds

---

[6]   See, for example, Benet, M. K., *The Character of Adoption*, Johnathan Cape, London, 1976.

[7]   *Ibid*, at p. 22. Also, see Goody, E., *Contexts of Kinship*, Cambridge University Press, London, 1973.

of years and throughout the extent of the Roman Empire which laid the European foundations for this social role. A Roman could adopt only if he did not have an heir, was aged at least 60 and the adopted was no longer a minor.[8] This tradition was revived in France by the Civil Code of 1902 which required that the adopter be at least 50 and without legal heirs, while the adopted must have reached his majority.[9] Heir adoption, therefore, owed its origins to an "inheritance" motive and all other factors being favourable found early acknowledgment in law.

3.2.   Adoption and the kinship motive

Closely linked to this property based social role is the practice of kinship adoption.[10] For some agricultural societies, such as those of India and China, these were synonymous as a relative was the preferred adoptee. All the ethnic groups peripheral to American society—Negroes, Indians, Eskimos and Polynesians— have long practiced kinship fostering and adoption as a means of strengthening the extended family, and their society as a whole, by weakening the exclusive bond between parents and children.[11] Though, curiously, the present form of kinship adoptions in the UK, the so-called 'step-adoptions' are for quite the opposite reasons. Elsewhere this occurs as an open transaction between two sets of parents. To the Hindus of India adoption outside the caste is prohibited.[12] For the Polynesians the adoption of anyone other than a relative is an insult to the extended family.[13] Kinship adoptions seem to rest on an 'exchange' motive, whereby the donor nuclear family acquires a stronger affiliation with the wider social group, in exchange for relinquishing parental rights.

3.3.   Adoption and the allegiance motive

The purpose of such adoptions is sometimes to secure social advancement for the adopted.[14] This is not unlike the Roman practice of non-kinship adoption for the purpose of allying the fortunes of two families. A Roman patrician, or even

---

[8]   *Op cit.* As Benet explains: "Full adoption, *adrogatio*, was only possible for a person who was himself *sui iuris*—that is, a member of no family but his own. A minor could not be *adrogated* because a minor *sui iuris* had *tutores* or guardians ... "The adopter "must be 60 or from some cause unlikely to have children" (p. 30).

[9]   *Ibid* at p. 77.

[10]   *Ibid* at p. 14.

[11]   *Ibid* at p. 17.

[12]   *Ibid* at p. 35.

[13]   *Ibid* at pp. 35 and 48–50.

[14]   As Gibbons explains, at the time of the Roman Empire a returning successful adventurer might seek to ingratiate himself "by the custom of adopting the name of their patron" and thereby hope to secure his position in society. See, *The Decline and Fall of the Roman Empire*, Harrap, London 1949 at p. 131.

an emperor, would adopt, for example, a successful general as his successor.[15] In Japan, also, the adoption of non-relatives was traditionally seen as a means of allying with the fortunes of the ruling family.[16] In Ireland under the Brehon Laws much the same ends were achieved by reciprocal placements of children between clans as a demonstration of mutual allegiance.[17] This bears a strong resemblance to the feudal practice of paying fealty and showing allegiance to a lord by placing a child for court service. Again, in 16th and 17th century England, it was quite common for the more wealthy households to take in the sons and daughters of poorer parents on service contracts, for example as pages or servants.[18] Non-kinship adoption, in this form, would seem to be based on an 'allegiance' or 'service' motive.

3.4.   Adoption and the 'extra pair of hands' motive

At a very basic level, adoption has clearly often been valued as a means whereby those with more work than they can manage could enlarge their family and thereby strengthen their coping capacity. This was very evident in the practice of trans-porting children from the United Kingdom to the British colonies throughout the latter half of the 19th and the first half of the 20th centuries. During that period many thousands, perhaps hundreds of thousands, of children were exported by philanthropic societies from the UK and Ireland to the United States, Australia and Canada[19] and elsewhere. There, it was felt, they would have opportunities to lead useful lives[20]; it was also candidly admitted that this would ease the bur-den on English ratepayers. Reputable English child care organizations such as Barnardos, were involved in arranging the safe passage of children who were orphaned, homeless or otherwise uncared for to overseas adopters only too happy to welcome into their family an extra pair of hands to share the work on farms etc. This form of adoption was not unlike the practice of being indentured into a trade.

3.5.   Adoption and the welfare motive

Distinctly different from such historical forms of adoption is the relatively modern practice of non-kinship adoption of abandoned or neglected children for philan-thropic motives. In societies where the functioning of the whole system was

---

[15] *Ibid* at p. 30. Marcus Aurelius being a good example.
[16] *Ibid*.
[17] See, Gilligan, R., *Irish Child Care Services: Policy, Practice and Provision*, Institute of Public Administration, Dublin, 1991.
[18] See, Middleton, N., *When Family Failed*, Victor Gollancz, London, 1971.
[19] See, Bean and Melville, *Lost Children of the Empire*, Unwin Hyman, London, 1989.
[20] See, for example, Tizard, B., *Adoption: A Second Chance*, Open Books, London, 1977.

accepted as being of greater importance than that of each individual family unit, then the modern problem of unwanted children did not seem to arise. An extra pair of hands was always useful in societies tied to the land. But when the economy of a society changed from being land based to industrial, wage earning and mobile, then the nuclear family unit became more independent and children often simply represented more mouths to feed. By the mid-19th century, abandoning their children to the rudimentary state care provided by the workhouse authorities was the only option available to the many poverty stricken parents who had not benefited from the industrial revolution.

By the end of the 19th century, following effective campaigning by voluntary organisations concerned for the welfare of children, there had been a general change in the attitude towards workhouses as suitable environments for children. The better survival rates of children who were boarded-out compared to those consigned to the workhouse and the consequent saving in public expenditure provided convincing evidence that the welfare of children was best assured by transferring responsibility to those who wanted to adopt a child to complete their family life. As Cretney has pointed out[21]:

> Adoption' first appeared in the statute book in the context of the Poor Law: the Poor Law Act 1899 provided that the Guardians could in certain circumstances assume by resolution all the parents rights and powers until the child reached the age of eighteen; and the Guardians were then empowered to arrange for the child to be 'adopted.

The legacy of non-kinship adoption from the Poor Law period established the principle that the state as ultimate guardian should assume responsibility for those children whose parents are unavailable, unable, or unwilling to care for them and then could legally arrange for that responsibility to be vested in approved adopters (see, further, below).

However, the fact that children with welfare needs were available never provided any guarantee of their adoption.

3.6. Adoption and the childless couple motive

Finally, adoption has probably always been seen as a provident answer to the reciprocal needs of a society, burdened with the costs of maintaining children for whom the adequate care of a birth parent was unavailable, and those of settled, married but childless couples able and willing to provide care for such a child. But it is unlikely that any society has ever produced an even numerical match to fully sustain this equation. The probability of this occurring in the future has been dramatically affected by the introduction of readily available means of

---

[21] See, Cretney, S., 'Adoption—Contract to Status?' in *Law, Law Reform and the Family*, Clarendon Press, Oxford, 1998, at p. 186.

birth control. As the traditional source for the supply of unwanted babies dries up, so the childless couples of western societies are being induced to 'widen the market' by looking towards the underdeveloped countries of Asia, South America and Eastern Europe for alternative sources of supply. At the same time public authorities in many western societies are redressing the imbalance in this equation by introducing legislative measures which divert the interest of potential adopters from the few non-marital babies to the needs of the many disadvantaged older, disabled, or children in pubic care in respect of whom full parental rights have been obtained.

4.   ADOPTION IN ENGLAND: HISTORICAL CONTEXT

Adoption in England and Wales has a much longer history as a common law than as a statutory process. That history is one inextricably bound up with the status of the married father and the class system in English society. To fully understand why adoption in this jurisdiction developed the characteristics it did, why it developed some more quickly than others, and why the whole process of its transmutation into statutory proceedings took as long as it did, it is necessary to remember that at the turn of the 19th century England was still a very hierarchically structured and patriarchal society. In this context, these Victorian characteristics were considerably magnified by the gender specific nature of legislators and judiciary; ironically, the female contribution to defining the legal parameters of the adoption process was at best marginal.

4.1.   The common law: parental rights and duties

The common law respect for paternal authority was itself a legacy from Roman times founded on the doctrine of *patria potestas*. The Emperor Justinian in 560 AD had abolished the doctrine and the legal concept of an autonomous patriarchal family unit, but in Britain its hallmarks lived on to underpin feudal society and to become absorbed into the common law. Some of the more characteristic features of this doctrine included: the private autonomous household ruled by the father, the actual or virtual ownership of children, the blood tie, filial piety, the power and limits of corporal punishment, the expectation of maintenance and the diminished relationship between child and state. Parents were guardians of their children as of right, a right which included a custodial authority based on ownership of the child.

    The common law, like that of ancient Rome, was essentially grounded on the rights and duties of the individual. It recognised and placed great importance upon legal status. In the context of the family, this meant a focus on the rights of the father and then to a lesser extent on the legal status of any others involved. The recognition given to the father with marital status was all important. Any actionable rights, in relation to the members of his autonomous marital family unit, belonged to the father. Thus, for example, for centuries he had the right to sue a third party for the loss of services to which he was entitled as father or spouse (e.g., he could claim damages against an adulterer for depriving him of his marital rights).

4.1.1. PATERNAL RIGHTS

By the middle of the 19th century the doctrine of paternal rights was firmly established. The prevailing attitude towards paternal authority and the autonomous marital family unit was reflected in the opinion of a contemporary writer who stated[22]:

> I would far rather see even a higher rate of infant mortality than has ever yet been proved against the factory district or elsewhere . . . than intrude one iota further on the sanctity of the domestic hearth and the decent seclusion of private life . . . "

The *prima facie* right of a father to the control and custody of the children of his marriage, subject to an absence of abuse,[23] was virtually impregnable. It was absolute as against the mother.[24] The approach of the common law was reflected clearly in the judgment delivered by James L J in *Re Agar—Ellis*[25] when, on giving the decision of the Court of Appeal, he added:

> The right of the father to the custody and control of his children is one of the most sacred rights.

In this judgment, which treated paternal authority as almost absolute in the absence of any misconduct, the high water mark was reached for paternal rights. Its principal characteristics concerned the right to custody of a child, the accompanying rights to determine religious upbringing and education and the final right to ensure the continuance of the family estate by bequeathing property to his natural offspring.

---

[22] See, *Transactions of the National Association for the Promotion of Social Sciences* (1874), quoted by Pinchbeck, I. and Hewitt, M. in *Children in English Society* (1973), p. 359. Also, see, Fox Harding *Perspectives in Child Care Policy*, Longman (1997) at p. 35 where he suggests that there was considerable opposition to laws restricting child labour and introducing compulsory education because these were seen as constituting an unwarranted state interference with parental authority.

[23] See *Re Thomasset* [1894] 300.

[24] See, *Ex parte Skinner*, 9 Moo 278; Simpson on Infants, 2nd ed (1908), p. 115.

[25] (1883) 23 Ch D 317, pp. 71–2.

The strength of the paternal right to custody[26] applied only to marital children. Until 1839 the custody of a legitimate child vested automatically and exclusively in the father. As head of the family he had the right to administer reasonable chastisement to his child.[27] His status was also the basis of the action for enticement.[28] Kidnapping a child was viewed essentially as an infringement of the paternal right to custody.[29] Such was the stringent judicial approach to the legal standing of the father that the courts would not permit a father to avoid his parental responsibilities by voluntarily giving up his right to custody and control.[30] The common law prohibited any attempt by a parent to irrevocably transfer all rights and duties in respect of a child to another. As was stated in *Re O'Hara*:

> . . . English law does not permit a parent to relieve himself of the responsibility or to deprive himself of the comfort of his position[31]

and

> . . . English law does not recognise the power of blindingly abdicating either parental right or parental duty.[32]

Parental rights were regarded as inalienable. Parental culpability alone set the threshold for state intervention on behalf of child welfare. No separation agreement—purporting to regulate the future care, custody, education and maintenance of his children—would be enforced by the court against a father as this was viewed as an attempt "to fetter and abandon his parental power" and "repugnant entirely to his parental duty".[33]

4.1.2.   PARENTAL DUTIES

The common law recognised a specific duty particular to the parental relationship: the duty to provide for and adequately maintain a child throughout childhood. As Sir W Blackstone stated[34]:

---

[26] See, *De Mannerville v De Mannerville, op cit.*

[27] See, *Gardner v Bygrave* [1889] 6 TLR 23 DC, *Mansell v Griffin* [1908] 1 KB, 160, *obiter, R v Hopley* [1860] 2F and F 160.

[28] See, *Lough v Ward* [1954] 2 All ER 338; this remained the case until abolished by s 5 of the Law Reform (Miscl Prov) Act 1970.

[29] See, for example, *R v Hale* [1974] 1 All ER 1107 it was alleged that the accused had "unlawfully secreted . . . a girl aged 13 years, against the life of her parents and lawful guardians."

[30] See, *St John v St John* (1805) 11 Vessey 530 and *Vansittart v Vansittart* (1858) 2 De Gex & Jones 249 at p. 256; *Hamilton v Hector* (1872) LR 13 Equity 511.

[31] See, *In re O'Hara* [1900] 2 IR 232, *per* Holmes LJ at p. 253; (1899) 34 ILTR 17 CA. Also, see, *Humphrys v Polak* [1901] 2 KB 385, CA and *Brooks v Brooks* [1923] 1 KB 257.

[32] *Ibid*, per Fitzgibbon L J.

[33] See, *Van v Van*, p. 259, per Turner L J.

[34] See, *Commentaries on the Laws of England*, Oxford, Clarendon Press, 1765.

> The duty of parents to provide for the maintenance of their children is a principle of natural law; an obligation . . . laid on them not only by nature herself, but by their own proper act, in bringing them into the world . . .

This duty was underpinned by the criminal law. The common law evolved a number of criminal offences particular to children and their parents. They were focussed not on the welfare of a child but on the abuse of a parental right; welfare was legally recognised only in an obverse relationship to parental right. A conviction would ensure court removal not just of custody but of all parental rights in respect of the child. The common law was never prepared to concede that a positive welfare advantage to the child would in itself provide grounds for displacing the parental right.

4.1.3. THE SANCTION OF 'ILLEGITIMACY'

The status of the patriarchal marital family in Victorian England was policed by the common law approach to 'illegitimacy'. This term served both to reinforce the 'legitimate' family while simultaneously disenfranchising the non-marital child and father and singling out the child's mother (though not the father) for social opprobrium. All three were firmly and publicly placed outside the law as it then related to the family. The consequences for those tainted by 'illegitimacy' involved serious status constraints not least in regards to rights of inheritance.

4.2. The Poor Laws

From at least the time of the Poor Law 1601, a distinction had been drawn between public and private responsibilities in relation to children. Where family care was not possible—in circumstances of parental death, absence or criminal abuse—then Parliament used the Poor Laws to place responsibility on public authorities for the provision of residential child-care facilities. The Poor Laws significantly extended state interest in parenting standards by making the fact of child need itself, rather than its cause, a sufficient threshold for voluntary state intervention. Parental culpability was no longer a necessary prerequisite for the transfer of a child from private to public responsibility. Parents unable or unwilling to continue caring could voluntarily place their children with the Poor Law guardians. Once in care, parental rights could be assumed by the guardians under s 1(1) of the Poor Law Act 1889,[35] subject to subsequent judicial confirmation, and the guardians could under s 3 be empowered to place the child for adoption.

---

[35] Continued by s 52 of the Poor Law Act 1930 and subsequently by s 2 of the Children Act 1948. This power was regarded by the Curtis Committee as a "very important provision" (para 19) and in 1945 about 16% of children in the care of poor law authorities had been the subject of a s 52 resolution (*ibid.* para 29). This was later echoed by the Houghton Committee (para 153).

Poverty was most often the root cause of parental failure necessitating coercive state intervention, by Poor Law guardians, to remove children from parental care and commit them to the care of the state.

4.2.1. PUBLIC CHILD CARE

The Poor Laws era introduced the formal role of the state as public guardian of child welfare. This role was evidenced by the beginnings of statutory criteria for the state to formally acquire care responsibility for children, schemes for boarding-out orphans and the children of destitute mothers and the provision of residential homes for children permanently separated from their parents.

The influence of various philanthropic societies during the period governed by the Poor Laws was also important. By the end of the 19th century child welfare voluntary organisations such as Dr Barnardo's and the NSPCC began their current specialist services for children by developing a 'child rescue' approach to those abandoned, impoverished or ill-treated in the era of the Poor Laws. However, charitable organisations providing care were often faced with parental demands for the return of their children once they were old enough to be useful and earn a wage. The Custody of Children Act 1891 was introduced to provide a civil remedy for third party carers whose provision for destitute children was opposed by fathers demanding restitution of their custody rights. The rationale for the 1891 Act was explained in the course of the preceding House of Commons debates:

> ... the Bill is intended to deal with ... children who have been thrown helpless on the streets, and wickedly deserted by their parents, and who are taken by the hand by benevolent persons or by charitable institutions ...

Its purpose was to provide a civil remedy to protect abandoned children from their neglectful parents by not enforcing parental rights. As such it was the first piece of legislation to offer protection for children from their parents and to others acting in *loco parentis*.

4.2.2. THE NON-MARITAL CHILD

Under the common law a non-marital or 'illegitimate' child was designated *sui juris* (outside the law) or the child of no-one and received no recognition in law. Parental responsibilities in respect of such a child could, therefore, be transferred. The adoption option in respect of such children admitted to the care of the Poor Law authorities or that of charitable organisations was readily available. This, in effect, confined the practice of adoption as a common law process to the relinquishment of illegitimate children by their unmarried mothers who, given the weight of public approbation and lack of any legal means of securing financial support, were left with little option. The courts took the pragmatic view that, in the circumstances, the decision to terminate parenting was itself a responsible parental act. This sympathetic judicial approach was evident in the ruling of Fitz-Gibbon LJ in *In re O'Hara*[36] when he commented that:

> ... the surrender of a child to an adopted parent, as an act of prudence or of necessity, under the pressure of present inability to maintain it, being an act done in the interests of the child, cannot be regarded as abandonment or desertion, or even as unmindfullness of parental duty within the meaning of the Act.

Where the responsibility for an illegitimate, abandoned or orphaned child could be assumed within the care arrangements of a private family, instead of becoming an additional burden on public rates, then the courts did not interfere.

4.3. Pressures for change; end of the 19th century

In England, at the turn of the 19th century, the prospect of adoption legislation was a contentious matter. Although different reasons have been put forward for this, arguably in the main the resistance to adoption had its roots in the values and ethos that permeated Victorian society at that time.

To those who then constituted the upper echelons of the embedded class structure, matters such as 'blood lines' were important. Maintaining established family lines, and the estates that had survived intact for generations, was viewed as dependant to some degree upon protecting the status quo and with it the ability for families to continue discretely managing opportunities for marriage and eventual succession rights. There were many who considered that adoption would introduce an unknown element into the rules governing inheritance and succession with potential to undermine established rights and thereby threaten the orderly devolution of family property. Victorian England was also a strictly patriarchal society where the male heads of families, whether rich or poor, shared a common law understanding of their rights and duties in relation to children. A view reinforced by the male heads of institutions such as the Church, parliament and the judiciary. Many of those who opposed the introduction of adoption did so in the belief that facilitating it would serve only to condone the actions of feckless parents seeking to avoid their legal, moral and economic duties to provide for the upbringing of their children. At a time when family law was governed by paternal rights and duties, rather than child welfare considerations, adoption was viewed by some with skepticism as a potential licence for continued permissiveness.

Both camps were very alert to matters of status and again, to some, adoption seemed to undermine certain carefully established legal and social distinctions. So, for example, the age old legal distinction between 'legitimate' and

---

[36] [1900] 2 IR 233 at p. 244.

'illegitimate' children and between the social standing of their respective sets of parents had a value for many. Status considerations extended to include matters such as family name, property, religion, residence, domicile etc.

However, there were a number of specific public concerns which steadily added to the pressure for change:

- **Baby-farming**

The practice of 'baby farming', or 'trafficking' in children, whereby unmarried mothers would entrust the care of their children to child minders who would then often neglect, abuse, murder or arrange for the informal adoption of their children, caused growing public disquiet.[37] The Infant Life Protection Act 1872 had sought to extend legal protection not only to the vulnerable young residents of workhouses but also to all those whose care was entrusted by their unmarried mothers to such child minders. This was a period when charitable organisations were very active in rescuing children from such abuse situations.[38]

- *De facto* **adoptions**

Those who undertook responsibility for children, abandoned by parents when they were young and needing care and maintenance, were often faced with parental demands for the return of their children when the latter were old enough to be useful and earn a wage. In an era when the courts were steadfastly defending the principle that parental rights were inalienable, such demands were difficult to lawfully resist. Consequently, by the latter half of the 19th century Parliament was under growing pressure to provide legal protection for persons who cared for the children of others. As explained by Lowe[39]:

"Attempts to introduce adoption legislation were made in both 1889 and 1890. The object of each Bill[40] was to protect both children and adults involved in so-called 'de facto adoptions' (that is, where children were looked after by relatives or strangers either with the parent's consent or following the latter's abandonment of their children) by preventing parents or guardians from removing their children after they had consented to the 'adoption' unless they could persuade the court that such recovery was for the child's benefit."

---

[37] See, the report by the Select Committee on the Protection of Infant Life. This 'baby-farming' scandal resonated with a similar experience in Australia (see, further, Chap. 8).

[38] The Thomas Coram Hospital for Foundling Children, for example, and the Infant Life Protection Society were very active at this time.

[39] See, Lowe, N., 'English Adoption Law: Past, Present and Future' in Katz, S., Eekelaar, J. and Maclean, M., *Cross Currents: Family Law and Policy in the United States and England*, Oxford, Oxford University Press, 2000.

[40] *Ibid.* See, respectively, the Adoption of Children Bill (No 101), 1889 and the Adoption of Children Bill (No. 56) 1890.

- **War orphans**

In the aftermath of the First World War, adoption became a matter of general public concern as families informally undertook the care of very many orphaned children but without any guarantee of legal security for their voluntarily assumed care arrangements. Some of these caring families, like the children concerned, were from influential social backgrounds and were not prepared to passively accept the legal insecurity that accompanied informal adoption arrangements.

It should also be remembered that this was a period when adoption law had already been successfully introduced in some former British colonies[41] to which there was an established practice of sending children for the purposes of their adoption.[42] The issue as to why England should continue to resist introducing legislation to regulate a practice that was good enough for her former colonies and good enough for her to send her children to would not go away.[43]

5. ADOPTION LEGISLATION; EVOLVING PRINCIPLES AND POLICY

Eventually the government established the Hopkinson Committee to examine the case for introducing adoption legislation. In its report[44] the Committee recommended that existing care arrangements be retrospectively secured by legislation but despite several attempts the government failed to do so.[45] Interestingly, as noted by Lowe,[46] the Committee recommended that the courts should have the power to dispense with parental consent not just in cases of parental neglect or persistent cruelty but also 'where the child is being brought up in such circumstances as are likely to result in serious detriment to [the child's] moral or physical welfare'.[47] Instead the government resorted to setting up the Tomlin Committee which did not view adoption as the answer to the problem of unwanted children—"the people wishing to get rid of children are far more numerous than those wishing to receive them".[48] Although not sharing the conviction of its predecessor

---

[41] For example: in Massachusetts, USA in 1873; in New Brunswick, Canada in 1881; in New Zealand in 1881; and in Western Australia in 1896.

[42] See, Bean, P. and Melville, J., *Lost Children of the Empire*, London, Unwin Hyman, 1989.

[43] See, for example, the report of the Royal Commission on the Poor Law (Cmnd 4499), 1909.

[44] See, *The Report of the Committee on Child Adoption* (Cmnd 1254), 1921.

[45] See, Lowe, N., 'English Adoption Law: Past, Present and Future' in Katz, S., Eekelaar, J., and McLean, M. (eds.), *Cross Currents*, Oxford University Press, 2000 at pp. 308–310.

[46] *Ibid*, at p. 311.

[47] *Op cit*, at para 34.

[48] See, McWhinnie, A., *Adopted Children: How They Grew Up*, Routledge & Keagan Paul, London, 1967.

that adoption legislation was necessary to encourage adopters, the Committee was convinced of the need to do so to protect those who had made care commitments to children in *de facto* adoptions. This Committee differed from its predecessor in relation to the proposed power to dispense with parental consent[49] preferring to restrict it to cases of parental abandonment or desertion, where the parent cannot be found or is incapable of giving consent or 'being a person unable to contribute to the support of the minor has persistently neglected or refused to contribute to such support'.[50] It also argued against adoption being a secretive process in which the parties would not be known to each other.

5.1. The Adoption Act 1926

Following publication of the Tomlin Report[51] and further failed Bills,[52] the government introduced the 1926 Act permitting, for the first time in these islands, a formal legal procedure for the adoption of children. This legislation avoided dealing with the thorny issues of inheritance and succession, dispensing with parental consent and the possible rights of an older child to give or withhold consent to his or her adoption[53] and to maintain contact with a birth parent, but it did embody three basic principles:

- all parental responsibilities would irrevocably and exclusively vest in the adopter/s;
- the welfare interests of the child would be independently assessed; and
- the informed consent of the natural parent/s was required unless they were dead, or had abandoned the child, or their whereabouts were unknown or they were incapacitated.

5.2. The Adoption of Children (Regulation) Act 1939

The recommendations of the Horsburgh Committee,[54] set up in 1936 to 'inquire into the methods pursued by adoption societies and other agencies', were incorporated into the 1939 Act. This required the registration of such societies or agencies and prohibited the making of adoption arrangements by any other body. As Lowe notes this legislation established the rudiments of today's adoption service, or

---

[49] See, See, Lowe, N., 'English Adoption Law: Past, Present and Future' *op cit* at p. 311.
[50] See, Clause 2(3) of the draft Bill prepared by the Tomlin Committee.
[51] See, *Report of the Child Adoption Committee 1924–1925*, (Cmnd 2401).
[52] A total of 6 adoption Bills were introduced during 1924–1925.
[53] In Scotland this right has been available to children aged 12 or older from the introduction of the first adoption legislation (the Adoption of Children (Scotland) Act 1930, s 2(3)).
[54] See, *Report of the Departmental Committee on the Adoption of Children*, Cmnd 9248, London, HMSO, 1954.

outlined the remit of the modern Adoption Panel, by empowering the Secretary of State to make regulations to[55]:

(a) "ensure that parents wishing to place their children for adoption were given a written explanation of their legal position;

(b) prescribe the inquiries to be made and reports to be obtained to ensure the suitability of the child and adopter; and

(c) secure that no child would be delivered to an adopter until the adopter had been interviewed by a case committee".

5.3. The Adoption Act 1949

This legislation rectified one omission in the 1926 Act by establishing the principle that adoption changed the child's status and vested him or her with certain succession rights in relation to their adopter's estate,[56] though not to any title, while also empowering local authorities to make and participate in adoption arrangements. Subsequently, both the Hurst Committee[57] and the Houghton Committee[58] recommended strengthening the role ascribed to local authorities and eventually in 1988 a provision was inserted into the 1976 Act making it mandatory for all local authorities to ensure the provision of an adoption service in their areas.

In 1954 the Hurst Committee[59] suggested that the 'primary object...in the arrangement of adoptions is the welfare of the child' and the Houghton Committee in 1972[60] recommended that 'the long-term welfare of the child should be the first and paramount consideration'.

5.4. The Children Act 1975

The 1975 Act introduced a new part for welfare to play in the adoption process. Section 3 stated:

In reaching any decision relating to the adoption of a child, a court or adoption agency shall have regard to all the circumstances, first considerations being given to the need to safeguard and promote the welfare of the child through his childhood; and shall so far as practicable ascertain the wishes and feelings of the child regarding the decision and give due consideration to them, having regard to his age and understanding.

---

[55] See, See, Lowe, N., 'English Adoption Law: Past, Present and Future' *op cit* at p. 322.

[56] Such succession rights were further extended in the Children Act 1975.

[57] See, *Report of the Departmental Committee on the Adoption of Children*, *op cit*, para 24.

[58] See, *Report of the Departmental Committee on the Adoption of Children*, London, HMSO, 1972, Cmnd 5107, paras 33 and 34 and recommendation 2.

[59] See, *Report of the Departmental Committee on Adoption Societies and Agencies*, London, HMSO, 1937, Cmnd 5499, p. 4.

[60] See, *Report of the Departmental Committee on the Adoption of Children*, *op cit*, para 17.

This indicated that the public interest in adoption was to be represented by the welfare principle and was to be considered in all decisions, not just the decision to make an adoption order. The 1975 Act, following recommendations made in the Houghton Report, also introduced custodianship orders[61] which were intended to provide an alternative to adoption for applicants whose circumstances did not merit the absolute and exclusive effects of adoption. Custodianship failed to win any support in the courts and this legal proceeding terminated with the introduction of the Children Act 1989.

5.5.   The Adoption Act 1976

This legislation, which came into effect in 1988, gave effect to most of the recommendations made by the Houghton Committee and incorporated s 3 of the 1975 Act. Protracted delay in implementing the 1976 Act meant that practice developments had outpaced legislative reform by the late 1980s. As Bridge and Swindells comment[62]:

> The legislation had a sense of the past about it almost before it was fully in force and the 1976 Act came to be perceived as meeting the demands of an earlier age while failing to accommodate the changing use to which adoption had been put.

However, the new provisions did provide an improved framework for the judiciary to meet contemporary practice demands. The freeing procedures, for example, together with case law principles stressing the weighting to be given to child welfare concerns relative to parental unreasonableness, facilitated an increase in non-consensual child care adoptions. The scope provided by s 12(6) for the court to attach such conditions as it sought fit, allowed the judiciary to moderate the more extreme effects of adoption by granting orders subject to access conditions that maintained an adopted child's continued relationship with members of their family of origin. Also, the introduction in s 51 of an adopted person's right to obtain a copy of their original birth certificate marked an important break with the traditional veil of secrecy and prepared the ground for more openness in adoption.

5.6.   The Children Act 1989

The 1989 Act affected adoption law and practice and accelerated the general movement towards accommodating more openness in adoption in a number of ways. It made available a menu of family proceedings orders some of which like residence orders and parental responsibility orders reduced the need for adoption while others such as contact orders could be used in conjunction with adoption

---

[61] *Ibid*, at para 121. Custodianship became available in 1985.
[62] See, Bridge, C. and Swindells, H., *Adoption—The Modern Law*, Family Law, Bristol, 2003 at p. 12.

orders. By defining the content of matters held to constitute a checklist of welfare interests it enabled a new, more uniform and objective application of this inherently subjective concept. It also introduced the paramountcy principle to govern judicial decision-making and by doing so sparked off a long period of debate as to why the principle should not be extended to adoption proceedings. More broadly, the flexibility provided by the 1989 Act revealed the absence of this approach in the 1976 Act.

The Adoption and Children Act 2002 (see, further, Chap. 5) now states the law in England and Wales while the adoption law reviews currently underway in Scotland and Northern Ireland will complete the modernising of the legal framework for adoption practice in the UK.

6. LEGAL CONTEXT: EVOLUTION OF A MODERN STATUTORY PROCESS

The Adoption of Children Act 1926 was introduced not to facilitate natural parents nor, particularly, to advance the welfare interests of children but primarily it was intended to provide protection for those third parties who had assumed care responsibility for children. In the aftermath of world war, when very many orphans were receiving such care, this legislative initiative was welcomed. Since then, the volume of annual orders has fluctuated in keeping with changing patterns of need but adoption as a legal process (unlike some other family proceedings e.g., guardianship) has proved its durability. It was conceived and remained as a contractual process that dealt separately with the legal interests of each of the parties.

6.1. The 'contract'

Adoption is a process which, at its most basic, re-distributes the legal interests of the three main participants and, unlike any other orders relating to children, does so on a permanent, irrevocable and usually on an unqualified basis. Some of these traditional hallmarks have been steadily eroded as the process has adapted to fit the contemporary needs of the parties. Like all contracts, the commitments entered into by the parties must be evidenced by their informed consent; though in the UK this requirement has, in relation to older children, been given statutory recognition only in Scotland. The courts have also stressed the importance of ensuring the propriety of the contract by, for example, prohibiting any element of financial reward for the parties involved and any improper practice such as the unauthorised removal of a child from their jurisdiction of origin.[63] In recent years, the contractual standing of the parties to an adoption has been affected not only by

---

[63] Both practices, associated with the traditional abhorrence of 'trafficking' in children, were criminal offences under s 57 and s 11, respectively, of the 1976 Act.

a transformation in the legal weighting ascribed to the role of the natural mother and that of an unmarried father; more recently the legal interests of the child concerned have also undergone a radical change. From being confined to a legal role as merely the object of adoption proceedings, the child has now become fully the subject of such. In England and Wales, the incorporation of the paramountcy principle in the 2002 Act has again altered the balance struck between the parties to an adoption contract (see, further, Chap. 5).

6.1.1.   PRIVATE AND CONFIDENTIAL

From the outset, the statutory process of adoption was viewed and treated as essentially a matter of private family law; in fact, the most private of all family proceedings. The contractual arrangements reflected this in the guarantees of anonymity given to adopters and the natural parent/s, in the court use of serial numbers to identify children, the lack of access to agency files etc. This cloak of secrecy has been steadily lifted in recent years particularly as regards facilitating adopters' rights of access to personal identity information.

6.1.2.   PERMANENT AND IRREVOCABLE

The absolute nature of adoption, relative to other family orders, was apparent from the fact that once made, it retained its binding effect on all parties at least until the child concerned reached maturity. A valid order was not open to challenge by any of the parties, nor by anyone else. In particular, it could not be refuted by the adopters. This characteristic has remained immutable.

6.1.3.   EXCLUSIVE

In keeping with Victorian values, an adoption order was intended to extinguish all parental rights and duties of the birth parents and vest as full a complement of parental responsibilities in named adopters as possible. A quick, clean and absolute break between the child and birth family was the legislative intent; no other form of on going intrusion in the new family was envisaged. For most of its history, adoption very largely met this expectation. However, with increasing awareness of 'attachment theory' has come a willingness to allow adoption orders to be made subject to conditions permitting contact between a child and members of their family of origin with whom a significant relationship has been established. Moreover, as child care adoption increased so too did the frequency of public service commitments to sustaining adoptions through the provision of ongoing professional and other resources. The adoption process has become much more 'open' than could have been initially foreseen.

6.2.   The parties

The legal process of adoption rests on a triangular relationship. In western society this has traditionally been typically represented by the unmarried birth parent/s, their lovingly relinquished healthy baby and the unrelated, married but childless heterosexual couple.

Full party status is usually confined to two of these participants. The relinquishing birth parent/parents or guardian and the person or couple wishing to undertake responsibility have always been parties in any adoption proceeding. The child, the subject of the proceedings, has not usually been awarded party status. Others may mediate, such as statutory and voluntary agencies, in arranging or supervising care arrangements. A range of carers and professionals from foster parents to judiciary will also be involved. An extensive network of family relationships will always be affected. But the legal framework is concerned exclusively with the re-distribution of legal responsibilities within this triangle of relationships. For convenience, these three may be referred to as the parties in an adoption process.

6.2.1.   THE CHILD

Children—their needs, availability and ultimately their acquisition—are of course central to adoption. When children were orphaned or abandoned, when their 'illegitimate' status could be transformed to 'legitimate', where parental consent was available or not withheld and where it was judged to be compatible with the child's welfare interests, then adoption was judicially viewed as wholly appropriate. However, when complications arose, for example in relation to the child in care whose married parents refused consent, then the courts were a great deal more circumspect. In the UK there would seem to have always been an imbalance in the number of children available relative to prospective adopters. For the earliest and longest part of its history as a statutory process that imbalance was evident in an excess of children; resulting in their adoption overseas. In recent decades this imbalance has been reversed; an excess of adopters has resulted in some thousands of children being brought from countries such as Romania for adoption in the UK. While the courts have always required an independent assessment of a child's welfare interests, only in recent years have they been prepared to grant party full party status and rights of representation to older children in adoption proceedings.

6.2.2.   THE BIRTH PARENT/S

The birth parent and/or legal guardian of the child, vested with parental responsibility, have always had full party status in any proceedings for the adoption of that child: the birth mother being inherently vested with such responsibility; the birth father having to legally acquire it. For the purposes of the statutory law of adoption in the UK, the terms 'natural parent' or 'birth parent' have traditionally been interpreted as referring to the mother of a non-marital child whose involvement with the adoption process was solely for the purpose of voluntarily relinquishing all responsibility for that child. In recent years the *locus standi* of an unmarried father has also acquired some salience.

• Birth mother

The forced option of adoption was often unavoidable for an unmarried mother facing social censure, financial hardship and without the means to seek recourse to the courts. Of the three parties, only she held a legal right in relation to adoption; the right to relinquish all future rights. Whether married or not she could consent to the adoption of her child and, until the Adoption Act 1976, could directly place her child for adoption with whomsoever she chose. She thereafter retained, and continues to retain, the right to directly place her child for that purpose with a relative.[64] However, the introduction of the parental responsibility order under the Children Act 1989 together with increased use of adoption by re-married parents in respect of legitimate children transformed the traditional role of the birth parent in the adoption process. The contemporary law of adoption in the UK has broadened that role to include unmarried fathers and marital parents of either gender.

Arguably, in the UK as elsewhere in the western world, the needs of the birth mother had by the final decades of the 20th century become the principal bargaining position around which the needs of the child and those of the adopters had to be fitted. The dominance of the patriarchal model of the autonomous marital family unit had long gone. The legislative and judicial hesitancy to accommodate the paramountcy principle in adoption law had constrained opportunities to give priority to the needs of the child. The needs of adopters, as always the driving force in this dynamic, remained totally dependent upon children being available and all traditional sources were rapidly drying up. But the weighting given to the legal interests of birth mothers had grown to have a powerful impact upon adoption.

A constellation of different factors from financial and housing benefits for unmarried mothers—including a range of birth control methods, increased opportunities for employment, and ease of access to divorce proceedings—to social acceptance of non-marital and serial cohabitation arrangements combined

---

[64] Section 11 of the 1976 Act, following the recommendation in the Houghton Report (*op cit*, para 81), prohibited direct placements by a birth parent with anyone other than a relative of that parent. Exemptions to the application of s 92 of the 2002 Act continue this residual parental right.

to transform the *locus standi* of a birth mother. Not only could she now choose to avoid what had previously been the forced option of adoption but should she decide to opt for her traditional role in that process she could still claim the protection of confidentiality and anonymity that accompanied it.[65] Moreover, the modern use of adoption, as a variant of the long defunct custody order, to secure the boundaries of the increasingly impermanent nuclear family unit, emerged as a significant feature of this change process. The corollary, that it had become the recourse of birth parents for reasons exactly the opposite of those initially intended—to re-assert rather than relinquish their legal responsibilities—is indicative of the fundamental nature of the changes then affecting adoption. Despite a relatively acquiescent judicial practice there had been a long standing unresolved debate as to the nature and extent of a public interest in this use of the law to accommodate the interests of a birth parent applying to adopt his or her own child.[66]

- **Unmarried father**

The traditional and rather dismissive approach towards unmarried fathers without parental responsibility has gradually given way to a more accommodating attitude; as reflected in the Adoption Agency Regulations 1983.[67] In *Re C,*[68] for example, the court at first instance and the Court of Appeal were strongly critical of a local authority that had treated a birthfather in a cavalier fashion and failed to inform prospective adopters of his involvement and his wish to maintain contact with the child placed with them.

Undoubtedly this change in judicial attitude has been influenced by the European Convention on Fundamental Freedoms and Human Rights. In *Keagan v Ireland,*[69] for example, the European Court of Human Rights established the principle that where an unmarried father had previously enjoyed a settled cohabiting relationship with a mother who had decided to place their child for adoption then that father should be informed and consulted because the protection given to 'family life' provided by Article 8 extended to include such a relationship. This principle was upheld in *Re B (Adoption Order)*[70] where a birth father successfully challenged the right of foster parents to adopt his child with whom he

---

[65] See, for example, *Z County Council v R* [2001] 1 FLR 365 where Holman J upheld the right of a relinquishing birth mother to insist that her siblings were neither informed of her decision nor approached to assess whether they would be in a position to undertake care responsibility.

[66] See, the concern expressed by the Houghton Committee in *Adoption of Children* at para 98 (1970), HMSO.

[67] See, Reg 7(3).

[68] [1991] FCR 1052.

[69] (1994) 18 EHRR 342.

[70] [2001] EWCA Civ 347, [2001] 2 FLR 26.

had established a strong and consistent relationship. In *Re R (Adoption: Father's Involvement)*[71] the birth father had neither parental responsibility for nor a consistent relationship with the child relinquished for adoption by the mother with whom he had had an erratic and at times violent relationship. Nonetheless, the Court of Appeal ruled that he should at least be served with notice of the proceedings. *Re H; Re G (Adoption: Consultation of Unmarried Fathers)*,[72] on the other hand, concerned two unmarried fathers neither of whom were to be advised by their respective partners of her decision to relinquish their child for adoption. One had cohabited with the mother and they had an older child in addition to the one she proposed to relinquish. The other had never cohabited. The court ruled that the former but not the latter should be identified and consulted.

The traditional veto, held by a birth mother in relation to disclosure of the identity and the resulting involvement of the child's father in the adoption process, will no longer automatically prevail and will certainly be challenged in the courts if there is evidence of his prior cohabitation with the mother.

6.2.3.   THE ADOPTERS

Thirdly and finally, the changes affecting adoption in the UK can be seen most clearly in the role of the adopters. It is not just that the number of adopters has fallen dramatically it is also increasingly apparent that the legal functions of adoption are now being driven mostly by their needs. Some indication of the extent of that change can be seen in the range of applicants, and the broader span of needs they now represent, when compared with the third party childless marital couple who previously typified adoption applicants.

Birth parents have come to constitute the largest group of annual adoption applicants in the UK: in England and Wales such applications rose from approximately one-third in 1975 to one-half in 2002 though are currently declining somewhat. Adoption by a birth parent acting, jointly with their new spouse to adopt the former's child, marital or non-marital, has emerged as the most pronounced characteristic in the modern use of adoption. In *Re B (Adoption: Natural Parent)*[73] the House of Lords restored the adoption order in favour of the father to the exclusion of the mother, on the grounds of the child's welfare interests, thereby acknowledging that the standard model of family adoption was to continue to form part of modern adoption practice. A trend, originating in a tendency for spouses to jointly adopt the mother's child from a different and non-marital relationship in order to 'legitimate' that child, has extended to become almost routinely applied to children from previous marital relationships.

---

[71]   [2001] 1 FLR 302.
[72]   [2001] 1 FLR 646.
[73]   [2001] UKHL 70, [2002] 1 FLR 196.

Kinship adoptions, whereby a child is adopted by a relative such as an uncle, aunt or grandparent, though of little numerical significance are also increasing as a proportion of total annual applications and so also are adoptions by foster carers (see, further, Chap. 5).

The law has always paid particular attention to the 'worthiness' of third party adopters. Such was the legacy of 19th century 'baby farming' scandals that the legislative intent from the outset was directed towards putting in place the legal functions necessary to test the *bona fides* of would be third party adopters. Ultimately, this led to third party placements made by a birth mother or some person acting at her direction, being prohibited (unless made directly with a relative) because this test was judged more likely to be applied objectively if entrusted exclusively to professionals. The law was concerned to replicate for the child the type of family unit conforming most closely to the approved model prevailing in society at that time. Traditionally, that model was the archetypal childless marital couple of sound health and morals, in secure material circumstances and resident within the jurisdiction. As society became less homogenous, marriage less popular and less permanent, while the population of working age became more accustomed to transient home, employment and relationship ties, so the profile of third party adopters changed. From a position whereby they initially comprised the vast majority of adopters, they are now steadily declining both numerically and as a proportion of total annual applicants. It is probable that the proportion of potential third party adopters in the general population remains at least as high as it has ever been. The fall in the number of children available, however, coupled with changes in the 'type' of child waiting to be adopted, have greatly affected the corresponding pool of potential applicants and considerably reduced the chances of third party applicants successfully adopting a child born within the jurisdiction.

6.3.   The principles

From at least the initiation of adoption as a statutory process the courts were clear that three principles governed the decision to grant an adoption order. Firstly, the court must be satisfied that adoption is in the welfare interests of the child concerned. Secondly, the informed consent of the birth parent/s must be freely given or the need for it dispensed with. Finally, the adopters must be fully vested with the parental responsibilities necessary to safeguard the welfare of the child until he or she reaches maturity.

6.3.1.   THE WELFARE OF THE CHILD

The principle that the welfare interests of a child should be of central importance in any decision taken affecting the upbringing of that child has long permeated all law relating to children. Adoption legislation, like all other family law proceedings, has always required that every application be subject to the 'welfare test', meaning that any decision must be taken only after consideration has been given to ensure its compatibility with the welfare interests of the child concerned. The part to be played by this imprecise term in adoption proceedings has for many years generated much controversy.

Three aspects of 'welfare interests' are relevant in the context of adoption proceedings:

- how is the term's content or meaning defined in statute and case law?
- what role does the law assign to the welfare test i.e. when is it to be applied and over what period?
- and crucially, what weighting is to be attached to the welfare component relative to the withholding of parental consent at time of determination?

While statute law traditionally made many references to 'welfare interests' it made no attempt to define or indicate the meaning to be attached to this term. Not until the 'welfare checklist' was introduced with the Children Act 1989 did legislative intent become specified. Being left with a free hand to develop their own interpretation, the courts have assembled a considerable body of case law illustrating the matters variously construed as constituting 'welfare interests'. They have always needed to be satisfied that the order if made would be at least compatible with the child's welfare interests which could comprise "material and financial prospects, education, general surroundings, happiness, stability of home and the like".[74] Traditionally, the comparative material advantage[75] available in the home of adopting parents would have been judged insufficient justification in itself for severing a child's links with his or her birth parents. So, also, reasons such as 'legitimation',[76] immigration,[77] or simply to change a child's name,[78] have similarly been held to be insufficient. In more recent years the courts have tended to interpret the term in relation to the particular circumstances of the child concerned.

There has always been an issue as to the relationship between the adoption process and the welfare test. The fact that the welfare of children would undoubtedly be improved by their adoption has never been sufficient justification for their admission to the process. For example, before the First World War at any one time there were some 80,000 children in care under the Poor Laws. Afterwards, adoption was a selective service for the benefit of adopters rather than adoptees, as may

---

[74] See, *Re B* [1971] 1 QB 437, per Davies L J at p. 443.
[75] See, *Re D (No. 2)* [1959] 1 QB 229.
[76] See, for example, *CD Petitioners* [1963] SLT (Sh Crt) 7.
[77] See, for example, *In re A (An Infant)* [1963] 1 WLR 34. Also, see, *In re H (A Minor: Non-Patrial)* [1982] Fam Law 121 where an adoption order was granted in respect of an immigrant child despite contrary advice from the Secretary of State.
[78] See, for example, *In re D (Minors)* [1973] Fam 209.

be seen in the fact that in 1929–1930 the National Children Adoption Association arranged 225 adoptions but rejected 550 children. These were also years which saw many thousands of children 'exported' by philanthropic societies from the UK, where they were unwanted, to countries such as Australia and Canada up until the mid 1960s.[79] Subsequently, despite legislative synchronisation of grounds for care orders and grounds for dispensing with parental consent so as to permit adoption, judicial resistance to the welfare test as a bridge between child care and adoption succeeded for many decades in preventing ready access to the process for children in care. In the UK, as graphically highlighted by Rowe and Lambert in *Children Who Wait*,[80] the availability of children needing substitute parental care never provided any guarantee of entry to the adoption process. Only at point of case disposal did the welfare interests of the child have a critical bearing on whether or not an adoption order could be made.

Statute law and case law have always been consistently clear that the welfare test is to be applied not just in the light of the child's current circumstances but also prospectively so as to take into account their welfare interests until he or she attains the age of majority. This approach was extended to suggest that the test be applied with a view to seeking assurance that it can be satisfied into the adulthood of the subject concerned. So, for example, where the Court of Appeal upheld[81] an adoption order granted six days before the subject with a learning disability attained his 18th birthday, it was held that in such circumstances the welfare consideration should extend beyond childhood.

For most of the lifetime of the adoption process, legislators and/or the judiciary have ensured that a measured rather than an overriding weighting was given to welfare interests relative to all other considerations when determining adoption applications. This stand was based on the belief that welfare interests should not have automatic superiority, particularly in relation to the consent of birth parents. As explained by Lord Simon[82]:

> "In adoption proceedings the welfare of the child is not the paramount consideration (ie outweighing all others) as with custody or guardianship; but it is the first consideration (ie outweighing any other)."

As Lord Hailsham had earlier argued, in the debates on the Children Bill in 1975, while the paramountcy principle applied to "care and control, custody and guardianship, it cannot be equally true of adoption". It was strongly felt by many in the judiciary, that to abandon this final parental right—the right to refuse to surrender all parental rights—would be to open the door to 'social

---

[79] As documented by Bean and Melville in *Lost Children of the Empire*, Unwin Hyman, 1989.
[80] See, Rowe, J. and Lambert, L., *Children Who Wait*, London (1973).
[81] See, *In Re D (A Minor)(Adoption Order: Validity)* [1991] 2 FLR 66.
[82] See, *Re D (An Infant)(Adoption: Parent's Consent)* [1977] AC 602 at p. 638.

engineering'.[83] Finally, however, the principle that welfare interests must be the matter of paramount consideration—which had long governed decisions taken in wardship, child care and other proceedings—was extended to adoption with the introduction of the 2002 Act (see, further, Chap. 5).

6.3.2.   CONSENT

The principle that adoption should rest on the full, free and informed consent of the birth parent/s, or the absence of dissent, was the starting point for statutorily regulating the process in the UK. For most of its history, it has in the main been a consensual process resting on the freely given consent of the birth parent/s or on the absence of any need for it due to the child being orphaned or abandoned. While the consent principle has always protected the legal interests of a birth mother and those of a marital couple, in more recent years the law has extended the principle to afford some degree of recognition for the interests of the birth father, particularly if he has acquired parental responsibilities. When dominated initially by third party applicants and latterly by birth parents, adoption was largely consensual. Both forms were facilitated by the legislative intent that the process should enable voluntarily relinquishing birth parent/s to surrender all rights. In consensual adoptions, the law has remained focussed on the evidence necessary to establish the existence of a free and fully informed consent; the fact, its form and the circumstances. In all others the focus has been on whether or not the grounds for dispensing with the need for consent can be satisfied.

As the non-consensual proportion of annual applications has slowly grown, mainly due to an increase in child care adoptions, so too has contention as to the proper balance to be struck between the grounds on which a birth parent may withhold consent and the welfare interests of their child. When should welfare interests prevail over the wishes of a non-consenting parent? What, if any, rights could a non-consenting or indeed a consenting parent retain?

In the UK, the grounds on which a birth parent could rightfully withhold consent to the adoption of their child had been steadily reduced in the last half of the 20th century. The inevitability of the legal balance being struck in favour of

---

[83] See, for example, the leading Northern Ireland case of *In re E.B. and Others (Minors)* [1985] 5 NIJB 1 where, as eloquently explained by Hutton LJ:

> "If the only test was the welfare of the child and the wishes of the natural parents could be disregarded, then there would be some cases where a child, taken into care for a short time because of the illness of his parents or some other family emergency, could be taken away permanently from humble and poor parents of low intelligence, and perhaps with a criminal record, and placed with adoptive parents in much better economic circumstances who could provide the child with greater material care and intellectual stimulation, a more stable background and a brighter future."

welfare as against parental rights had first been signalled with the wardship ruling in JvC^{84} followed by the inclusion of 'paramountcy' in s 1 of the Guardianship of Minors Act 1971. In the Adoption Act 1976 the legislative intent to extend this principle had been evident from the fact that in s 16, the final two grounds for dispensing with parental consent were explicitly child care in nature; ie serious parental ill-treatment of their child would justify this measure. In the Children Act 1989, Parliament firmly directed the judiciary to apply the paramountcy principle to determine all decisions affecting the upbringing of a child in family proceedings. This, together with the explicit child care grounds for freeing orders, should have expedited the flow of children from child care into the adoption process and substantially increased the number of non-consensual adoptions.

Instead of taking the legislative lead, the judiciary steadfastly held to established precedents[85] as the sole justification for dispensing with parental consent; for the last three decades of the 20th century parental 'unreasonableness' was by far the most common ground for dispensing with consent. Simply put, the 'unreasonableness' test required the court to consider whether a reasonable person, in the parent's position, being mindful of the child's welfare interests, would be justified in withholding agreement. It was applied ubiquitously until displaced by the provisions of the 2002 Act.

Such limited rights as were reserved to a birth parent, such as the right to directly place their child with a person for the purposes of adoption, were eventually statutorily removed; except where the placement is with a relative. Whether entering the adoption process on a consensual or non-consensual basis, the only right legislatively left to a birth parent was the right to surrender all parental rights. The statutory power of the courts to attach a condition to an adoption order could be exercised only to further the welfare interests of the child and not to vest rights in the birth parent, whether consenting or otherwise.

6.3.3.   PARENTAL RESPONSIBILITIES

Finally, the law sought to give effect to the principle that adopters should be vested with the rights and duties necessary for them to step into the shoes of the birth parents and thereafter provide for the child as though he or she had been born to them and of their marriage. The legislative intent was that an adoption

---

[84] [1970] AC 668.
[85] See, specifically, *Re W (An Infant)* [1971] 2 All ER 49 where Hailsham LJ emphasised that:

> "The test is reasonableness and nothing else. It is not culpability. It is not indifference. It is not failure to discharge parental duties. It is reasonableness and reasonableness in the totality of the circumstances".

order would create new and permanent legal ties between the child and his or her adopters so that, as expressed by Vaisey J in *Re DX (an infant)*[86]:

> The child looks henceforth to the adopters as its parents, and the natural parents, relinquishing all their parental rights step, as it were, for ever out of the picture of the child's life.

As initially understood, granting an adoption order vested certain common law rights and duties in the adopters. They acquired the right of custody which has been defined as a 'bundle of powers' including not merely physical control but also control of education and choice of religion and the powers to withhold consent to marriage and the right to administer the child's property.[87] Included were such other rights as to determine place of residence, choice of health services, travel and the right to withhold consent to a subsequent adoption. They also acquired the duties of guardianship which included the duties of maintenance, protection, control and provision of appropriate medical care. Excluded to a large extent were rights of inheritance; the common law resolutely protected the traditional rules of inheritance governing the devolution of property from birth parent to child. Since the introduction of the Children Act 1989 and the displacement of the concept of parental rights and duties by that of 'parental responsibilities', the authority vested in the adopters is best understood within the meaning statutorily ascribed to the latter term.

From the outset the courts had some difficulty in accommodating the piece of legal fiction that purported to place a child in exactly the same relationship to 'strangers' as he or she would otherwise have stood in relation to their birth parents. The judicial resistance towards accepting the legislative intent was evident in relation to matters such as inheritance and succession rights while legislation continued the exemption extended to an adopted brother and sister from the laws relating to incest. In more modern times it is evident in the practice of attaching conditions to adoption orders.

Initially, there was a presumption that a clean and absolute break between the child and the birth parent/s was a natural and essential part of UK adoption practice. A meaningful parent/child relationship being judicially viewed as vitiating the welfare ground for an adoption order: adoption and continued contact being seen as mutually exclusive. Since the introduction of the 1976 Act, however, the UK courts[88] have been able to attach such conditions as they think fit to an

---

[86] [1949] CH 320.

[87] See, Eekelaar, J., 'What are Parental Rights?' [1975] 89 LQR 210 and Hall, 'The Waning of Parental Rights' [1972] CLJ 248.

[88] See, in England and Wales, s 12(6) of the 1976 Act and in Northern Ireland, Article 12(6) of the 1987 Order. Note that in Northern Ireland a birth parent also had the right to add a condition of their own volition; the right to determine their child's the religion in which their child was to be brought up (Article 16(1)(b)(i).

adoption order. Most usually this occurs where a pre-adoption relationship exists between the child and a birth parent or sibling, constituting a psychological bond the continuance of which would have a meaningful significance for promoting the post-adoption welfare of that child. This is very often the case in family and child care adoptions where the child concerned is likely to be older and thus to have had the opportunity to form such relationships. In such circumstances, when satisfied that to do so would further the welfare of the child and would be enforceable, the courts are now more willing to attach a contact condition though in fact only rarely do so.[89] The flexibility permitted by the introduction of contact orders under the Children Act 1989, together with the practice of facilitating more 'open' adoptions and the concern expressed about step-adoptions, has led to the present position whereby perhaps a majority of adoptions now accommodate some level of ongoing contact between the child and a member of their family of birth. This development is set to accelerate further under the Adoption and Children Act 2002 (see, further, Chap. 5).

7.   CONCLUSION

Adoption is the most radical of all family law orders. No other order so fundamentally changes the legal status of its subject on a lifetime basis. Its effect is to re-write the relationships between three sets of legal interests with implications for the wider family circles of those involved, the consequences of which will be felt by subsequent generations. Many different societies and the same society at different times, led by the changing motivations of adopters, have shaped adoption to fit the needs of its particular cultural context.

In the UK, adoption is now a creature of statute. This was not always the case. The common law legacy, with its concern to uphold the legal autonomy and privacy of the marital family unit, defend traditional patriarchal social values, and its attention to matters of status, left its mark on the evolving statutory process. Many years later the basic constituent parts of the adoption process remain, to a large extent, as introduced by the first statute. Those recognised as parties, the main governing principles, the elements of their contractual relationship and the effect of an adoption order on their status are all essentially as initially defined. However, the balance then struck between the public and private interests is now undergoing significant change. The key component in this re-balancing has been the welfare interests of the child.

Traditionally, in this jurisdiction, the welfare factor has not played a particularly prominent role in adoption; a point most poignantly demonstrated by the circumstances giving rise to *The Lost Children of the Empire*.[90] Adoption has

---

[89] See, *Re C (A Minor)* [1988]1 AER 712h.
[90] See, Bean & Melville, *op cit.*

never quite shed the political ambivalence that accompanied its eventual arrival onto English statute books, long after the introduction of equivalent legislation elsewhere, because of a reluctance to allow the welfare interests of a child to over-ride all other concerns. This may have been due in part to residual considerations relating to status as evidenced by the continuing attention given in law to matters such as rights of inheritance, implications for rules governing immigration and the *locus standi* of an unmarried father. Until very recently, welfare in law has tended to be treated negatively; the court confining its considerations to ensuring that no consequences adverse to the child's welfare were likely to ensue as a result of it making an adoption order. The paramountcy principle had no bearing on the outcome of the adoption process. Overall, this approach was not inappropriate when adoption was almost exclusively a private family law proceeding in which, typically, the care of a voluntarily relinquished child had been assumed by unre-lated, agency approved and supervised, adoption applicants. Then, the three sets of needs and legal interests neatly dovetailed and the social construct of adoption fitted well with contemporary circumstances.

However, in recent years the triangular relationship of legal interests had become very lopsided. The number of children compulsorily removed had not only vigorously outgrown the number voluntarily relinquished from parental care but were accompanied by a parental veto preventing adoption. The number of prospective adopters unable to satisfy their needs with an indigenous child had also grown. In a social context where birth control, serial parenting and tran-sient family relationships had radically altered the previously prevailing marital, monogamous and nuclear family unit, adoption practice was in danger of being redefined largely as an expedient adjunct to marriage. In particular, the role played by maternal choice was steadily narrowing the interpretation of adoption in the UK. Having emerged from under the patriarchal shadow the legal functions of adoption continued to be susceptible to manipulation to meet the needs of adults.

By the turn of the 21st century, the UK government was faced with the needs of large numbers of children failed by parental care, a judiciary concerned to pro-tect established precedents in the law of adoption from being undermined by the paramountcy principle and practice developments that threatened to entirely pri-vatise the future use of adoption. A new policy was required to redefine the social construct of adoption so that it better addressed the imbalance in the triangular relationship of legal interests between child, birth parent/s and adopters.

Chapter 2

THE CHANGING FACE OF ADOPTION
IN THE UNITED KINGDOM

1.   INTRODUCTION

The role of adoption in contemporary western society is quite different from any
of its historical manifestations as outlined in the previous chapter. This reflects
the nature of changes in the related cultural context. From its historical role in
fairly closed societies with their well defined boundaries, structured roles and
ordered social relationships, adoption has now adapted its functions in relation to
the needs of nuclear impermanent family units within a more fluid cosmopolitan
society. Modern forms of adoption very much reflect the characteristic pressures
on contemporary family life in western society.

    This chapter considers the role and functions of adoption against the context
of unfolding social change in the United Kingdom, with a particular emphasis
on recent developments in England and Wales. It begins with a broad review of
modern adjustments to the traditional form of adoption. This includes a focus on
the nature of change to the process as it becomes more 'open', accommodates a
greater variety of children than formerly and responds to pressure from changes
in the needs of adopters. It examines the causes of such adjustments and their
consequences for the adoption process and for the roles of each of the parties.

    The chapter then deals with each of the three main types of modern adoption:
family adoptions, agency adoptions and intercountry adoptions. It identifies the
different permutations that constitute each type, provides statistical data to reveal
the nature and extent of trends in their use and assesses the capacity of each to
promote the welfare interests of the children involved. In particular, it considers

Kerry O'Halloran (ed.), The Politics of Adoption, 39–69.
© 2006 *Springer. Printed in The Netherlands.*

child care adoption. Because adoption must also be viewed in the context of other options for securing the welfare interests of children it is necessary to trace the modern policy development that now results in increased numbers of children subject to care orders being placed for adoption. This chapter concludes with a brief overview of contemporary models of adoption so as to contrast contemporary UK experience with that of other nations.

2.   MODERN ADOPTION TRENDS IN THE UNITED KINGDOM

A sense of perspective is needed in relation to adoption. Far fewer adoption orders are now made than at any time in the history of this statutory process. While all other family law proceedings continue to generate ever more litigation, adoption continues its steady decline. Adoption has greatly changed since the Adoption Act 1926 first placed this process on the statute books of the United Kingdom. This has not been due to government policy; despite the best endeavours of Houghton and others.[1] In the post-world war period through to the end of the 20th century, while UK society underwent fundamental economic, cultural and other changes, there were virtually no policy led or formative legislative initiatives to adjust the functions of adoption. The considerable changes that have occurred are largely the result of practice developments in response to pressures on the family. These changes have gradually distorted the original functions of adoption.

2.1.   From traditional model to modern variants

The traditional form of adoption in the UK is dying out. Third party adoptions of healthy babies, voluntarily relinquished by natural parents resident and domiciled within the jurisdiction, most probably have no future. This form accounted for the majority of the 875,000 children adopted in England and Wales since 1926. Following a steady rise in annual adoptions between 1927 and 1968, when they peaked at 24,831, they have declined consistently every year since and reached 4,387 in 1998.[2]

The hallmarks of this type, which have endured for most of the statutory lifetime of the process and now colour our expectations of how adoption should be defined, are also fading. It was very much a private family law and 'closed' process, almost always consensual, involving a healthy baby with cultural affinity to the

---

[1] See, the Houghton Committee, *Report of the Departmental Committee on the Adoption of Children* (Cmnd 5107), 1972 which followed on from the report of the Departmental Committee on the Adoption of Children *Working Paper* (HMSO), 1970.

[2] See, the Dept of Health annual statistics.

adopters, conducted confidentially usually by voluntary adoption societies and with guarantees of post-adoption secrecy. The underpinning legislative intent was to facilitate a neatly matching set of needs: relieve birth parents of responsibilities they did not want; provide a means for children to be 'legitimated'; and enable a marital couple to make arrangements for the inheritance of family property. Reflecting the patriarchal values and status considerations of the late Victorian era, the traditional form of adoption primarily served to reinforce conformity to socially acceptable standards represented by the marital family unit. This has now given way to new forms of adoption which have brought with them possibilities for re-interpreting the process and clarifying its functions.

2.1.1. OPEN ADOPTION

The assumption that the traditional 'closed' model of adoption is wholly compatible with the welfare interests of the child has faded in recent years. That approach was rooted in an approach to child development that maintained the importance of allowing a child to form attachments within a clear and consistent set of relationships free from any ambiguity. Any proposed ongoing involvement of members of the child's family of origin was viewed as introducing complicating and confusing factors that might threaten the new and vulnerable family unit. It was also considered likely to impose unnecessary stress on birth parent/s, who needed to come to terms with their loss, and on the adopters who very often wanted to close the door on the facts and relationships associated with the birth history of 'their' child. A clean break and a new start were seen as being in the best interests of all parties.

In recent years, however, research has indicated that adoption arrangements which accommodate a degree of ongoing involvement from members of the child's birth family have been viewed as successful by the parties concerned. In particular, it has been demonstrated that an adopted child has the capacity to make sense of such a relationship framework and form the attachments necessary to ensure healthy emotional development. Increasingly, an adoption that allows for such degree of 'openness' as is compatible with the comfort levels of all parties is now viewed as being in the long-term perhaps healthier and more honest than the traditional closed approach; given the prevailing transparency of the current social context. That arrangements between the parties should be made and maintained in secrecy and information disclosure relating to identity kept to a minimum now contravenes principles well established in international Conventions and case law. The practice of openness[3] is usually associated with family adoptions, where access to information relating to origins and identity is most likely to be readily

---

[3]   See, for example, Triseliotis, J., *Open Adoption: The Philosophy and the Practice*, 1970.

facilitated. In child care adoptions, however, which often involve older children, it has been embraced as an unavoidable necessity unless there is good reason for secrecy such as a background of child abuse or domestic violence.[4] As has been observed, adoption practice reflects social, political, economic and moral changes and the move towards openness in adoption reflects a general trend towards more openness in society.[5] Open adoption is an elastic concept that has been defined by Brodzinsky and Schlechter as follows[6]:

> The practice of open adoption begins with the first contact of both the prospective adoptive parents and the birth parents. It is discussed as an integral part of agency procedure in the adoption of all children. Open adoption is a process in which the birth parents and adoptive parents meet and exchange identifying information. The birth parents relinquish legal and basic child rearing rights to the adoptive parents. Both sets of parents retain the right to continuing contact and access to knowledge on behalf of the child. Within this definition, there is room for greater and lesser degrees of contact between the parties. The frequency and meaning of the communication will vary during different times in the lives of the individuals involved, depending on their needs and desires and the quality if the established relationship.

The concept, and increasingly the practice, of openness brings with it the challenge that if the content of adoption is to be so radically transformed then perhaps the legal form that has housed the traditional interpretation of adoption should also be similarly transformed? Is the complete and permanent severing of the birth parent/s rights and duties in relation to their child, coupled with the equally exclusive vesting of such responsibilities in the adopters, now strictly necessary?

2.1.2.   STEP-PARENT ADOPTION[7]

The attraction of a means whereby a second partner, who has all the day to day care responsibilities but none of the rights in respect of their spouse's child from a previous relationship, may acquire with the latter exclusive parental rights, is an increasingly frequent motive for adoption. A wish to ensure inheritance rights can also be a factor. This use of adoption had not been within the contemplation of initial legislators.

---

[4]   See, for example, *Gunn—Russo v. Nugent Care Society and Secretary of State for Health* [2001] EWHC Admin 566, [2002] 1 FLR 1 [2001] UKHRR 1320, [2002] Fam Law 92, QBD.

[5]   See, Grotevant, H. and McRoy, R., *Openness in Adoption*, Sage Publications, USA, 1998, at p. 196.

[6]   See, Brodzinsky, D. and Schechter, M., *The Psychology of Adoption*, Oxford University Press, USA, 1990 at p. 318.

[7]   In the last years of the 1976 Act, some 50% of adoption applications were from step-parents. Under the 2002 Act, such applicants will be directed towards a parental responsibility order/agreement as an alternative to adoption.

As marriage becomes less popular and less durable and parenting arrangements more fluid so an adoption order has come to be regarded as a useful authority for bolting the door behind a re-formed family unit to the exclusion of previous and now inconvenient relationships.[8] It may also, of course, signify to the child concerned that both birth parent and spouse are wholly committed to making him or her as much a part of the new family unit as is legally possible.

2.1.3. ADOPTION OF CHILDREN WITH COMPLEX OR SPECIAL NEEDS

The term 'special needs' is used inconsistently. In the UK it has been most usually used in reference to children and others with learning difficulties. In the US it refers to all children for whom, for whatever reason (e.g. older, with behaviour problems, with health care needs or members of sibling groups), it may be difficult to identify an adoption placement (see, further, Chap. 7). Practice in the UK, particularly in the context of Adoption Panel determination of eligibility for adoption allowances, is now moving towards acceptance of the US definition.

Again, in all western societies, the reduction in the number of indigenous healthy babies available for adoption has led to adopters broadening their outlook. This has been matched by a commensurate change in the factors governing the availability of children, particularly babies. Previously, the few children with complex health care or special needs, unwanted or inadequately cared for by their birth parents, would have been consigned to long-term institutional care. Due to the advances made in medical sciences, many more vulnerable children are surviving and some need an intensity of care well beyond the abilities of 'average' parents. Such children are now often successfully placed for adoption; though this may necessitate ongoing professional support.

2.1.4. ADOPTION OF CHILDREN BORN AS A RESULT OF ASSISTED CONCEPTION

The introduction of techniques of artificial insemination and the practice of surrogate motherhood have resulted in many children becoming available for adoption by private arrangement. This new form of 'adoption to order' is not without its problems and many court cases have been generated by the withdrawal of consents freely given before birth of the children concerned.[9] It also gives rise to concern for the child's long-term sense of identity and rights of access to information.

---

[8] See, Utting (1995) who noted that 40% of marriages end in divorce, 20% of families are headed by a lone parent and 8% of dependent children live in step-families.

[9] See, *Re MW (Adoption: Surrogacy)* [1995] 2 FLR 789 where the court dismissed a surrogate mother's opposition to an adoption application by commissioning parents in respect of a child who by then had been in the applicants care for two-and-a-half years.

2.1.5.   INTERCOUNTRY AND TRANSRACIAL ADOPTIONS

The acquisition of a child in a foreign country by citizens, resident and domiciled within another jurisdiction, who either adopt the child in his or her country or return with the child and initiate adoption proceedings, is neither a recent nor an unusual phenomenon. For perhaps the last 40 years there has been a flow of children from third world countries into the homes of adoptive couples in western Europe; particularly, from the Philippines and South America towards Scandinavia.[10] However, this is no longer an occasional occurrence. The inward flow of children from foreign countries to adopters in the UK has gradually become a more prominent characteristic of the modern adoption process; although the numbers have only increased slightly (currently approximately 300 annually) in the context of overall declining trends it is now proportionately more significant. There is a clear correlation between intercountry adoption and child care adoption: nations with a high rate of dependency on the former will also have low rates of availability through the latter; while social class (intercountry adoption is expensive), racial bias (white Caucasian prospective adopters tend to look towards Russia, Romania and eastern Europe rather than to Africa for children) and a preference for babies also play their part (see, further, Part III).

This international phenomenon is impacting upon very many countries, involving the annual movement of many thousands of children and is regulated by a Convention drawn up at the Hague Conference on Private International Law in 1993. This Hague Convention has been given effect in the UK by the Adoption (Intercountry Aspects) Act 1999 and has been largely incorporated into the Adoption and Children Act 2002 (see further, Chaps. 4 and 9).

Intercountry adoptions are often transracial, some of the rationale and many of the same tensions prevail in both,[11] and can give rise to identity issues for children removed from contexts of family, kinship, language and culture to be reared in a foreign ethnic environment. In England and Wales, the wisdom of having any formal policy on transracial adoptions—whether to promote or discourage— has been questioned.[12] The Local Authority Circular *Adoption—Achieving the Right Balance*, although not dealing with intercountry adoption, addressed this controversy and concluded with the advice that whereas good practice should

---

[10] See, for example, the account of 20 years of such experience in Dalen, M. & Saetersdal, B., 'Transracial Adoption in Norway', *Adoption & Fostering*, Vol 2, no. 4. 1987. Also Ngabonziza, D., 'Inter-country adoption in whose best interests' *Adoption & Fostering*, Vol 2, no. 1, 1988.

[11] See, Murphy, J., 'Child Welfare in Transracial Adoptions: Colour-blind Children and Colour-blind Law' in Murphy, J. (ed) *Ethnic Minorities—Their Families and the Law*, Hart Publishing, Oxford, 2000.

[12] See, for example, Tizard and Phoenix (1989) who found that transracial placements are not necessarily damaging experiences for the children concerned.

always seek to achieve sensitive racial and cultural matching this must remain conditional upon any such match being wholly in the best interests of the child concerned.[13]

2.1.6. SAME SEX ADOPTERS

The 1976 Act was silent on the prospect of adoption by a same sex couple; it simply was not within the ambit of legislative intent. Indeed, not until very recently would a household consisting of a same sex couple be construed as coming within the definition of 'family'.[14] The possibility of adoption by a single person, however, was and is provided for; the earlier statutory prohibition on adoption of a female child by a single adult male having been removed. An adoption application by a single homosexual male or lesbian, where the applicant is living with a partner of the same gender, has therefore for some time been legally possible[15] but not until recently has it become professionally and socially acceptable. Judicial notice has been taken of research findings indicating that child rearing by same sex couples has not disadvantaged the children concerned.[16] This has led to the current position where judgments emphasise that providing such applicants satisfy the welfare test then their sexual orientation is of little relevance. So, for example, in *AMT (Known as AC) (Petitioners for authority to adopt SR)*,[17] where the subject was a three year old boy and the applicant a male homosexual living with a long-term male partner, the court granted an adoption order. Again, in *Re W (Adoption: Homosexual Adopter)*[18] an application for a freeing order was unsuccessfully opposed by the birth mother who objected to the local authority placement of her child with two lesbian women who intended to adopt. These judgments undoubtedly bring adoption practice more closely into line with the realities of modern family life while the explicit recognition in s 144(4) of the 2002 Act that an adopting 'couple' may comprise "two people (whether of different sexes or the same sex) living in an enduring family relationship" provides confirmation that a fundamental change has occurred in the adoption law of England & Wales following the example set by such other countries as the Netherlands and Denmark (see, further, Chap. 5).

---

[13] See, Department of Health, LAC 20, 1998.

[14] See, *Fitzpatrick v Sterling Housing Association Ltd* [2001] 11 FLR 271 where the House of Lords ruled that a settled homosexual relationship did constitute a 'family' for the purposes of the law relating to landlord and tenant.

[15] See, for example, *Re E (Adoption: Freeing Order)* [1995] 1 FLR 382 where the Court of Appeal, albeit reluctantly, approved the placement of a girl with a single lesbian adopter.

[16] See, Golombok, S., 'Lesbian Mother Families' in Bainham, A., Day Sclater, S. and Richards, M. (eds.) *What is a Parent?* Hart Publishing, Oxford, 2000.

[17] [1997] Fam Law 8 and 225.

[18] [1997] 2 FLR 406. See, also, *Re E (Adoption: Freeing Order)* [1995] 1 FLR 382.

2.2.   Causes of change

The structured homogeneity of late Victorian England has given way to a more fluid, multi-cultural society with permeable boundaries. Family life is now much less likely to be based on marriage, is more impermanent with serial parenting and shared care arrangements not uncommon. It is likely to take the form of a self-reliant fairly mobile nuclear unit, unlikely to be reinforced by an extended kinship network nor by community links and probably transient in nature as families relocate in pursuit of employment opportunities. Against this background the welfare interests and indeed the rights of the child have steadily acquired a more defined salience. This has been partly a consequence of increased knowledge of child development, particularly in relation to theories of attachment and bonding as attested to by a considerable body of research on outcomes for looked after children. It is also attributable to the general withdrawal throughout family law from a defence of the status determined obligations of adults (e.g., marriage) to upholding the principle that the welfare interests of children must prevail in any set of circumstances.

2.2.1.   ADVANCES IN MEDICAL SCIENCE

Advances in medical science have allowed parenting to become more a matter of choice, mostly to be exercised by women. Birth control and abortion services have clearly affected the number of unwanted births and therefore the number of birth parent/s wishing to voluntarily relinquish their babies. Improved techniques for assisting conception (AID, GIFT etc.) and for facilitating surrogacy arrangements have had implications for the adoption process. Indeed, some 500 surrogate births have now occurred in the UK, mostly facilitated by the voluntary organisation Childlessness Overcome Through Surrogacy (COTS). As mentioned above, medical science has also greatly improved the survival rate for babies born with complex health and social care needs resulting in more such children becoming available for adoption.

2.2.2.   WELFARE BENEFITS

Birth parents who choose to provide ongoing care for their child, unlike their predecessors in the more traditional form of adoption, now have access to the range of welfare benefits and public services necessary to undertake and sustain that parental role. This—together with the fading of the social stigma previously associated with that role, access to contraceptives and the growth in equality of employment opportunities—has transformed the relationship between unmarried mothers and the adoption process.

2.2.3.   FAILED PARENTING

Failed family life is becoming more evident as the child care population increases and media reportage of child abuse becomes commonplace. The ever-growing number of child abuse inquiries and paedophilia scandals have generated a level of public concern that is causing the government to formulate new policy initiatives. The failure of community care programmes to provide adequate support for the mentally ill, for those suffering from learning disability, for drug abusers and for refugees has exposed many children to situations of neglect and abuse (see, further, Part III). There is now a recognition that new measures need to be taken to provide both a better level of child protection[19] and also safe and permanent alternative care arrangements for children failed by parental care.

2.2.4.   CHILD DEVELOPMENT KNOWLEDGE

Contemporary knowledge of child development—of what promotes or obstructs healthy physical and emotional growth and of what constitutes the welfare interests of a child—is at a much more advanced stage than in the era of traditional adoption. The importance of 'nurture', physical and emotional, of 'bonding' between child and a significant carer, in contributing towards a child's well balanced psycho-social development have been extensively researched and are now accepted as key concepts in child rearing practice.[20] However, it was 'attachment theory'[21] more than any other aspect of modern child development knowledge, impacting upon child care policy and practice that in turn caused a strategic change in professional attitudes towards the adoption process. Attachment theory suggests that the future psychological wellbeing of every child is dependent upon their experiencing an intimate one-to-one relationship with a caring adult for a crucial period during their formative early years.

---

[19] See, the Department of Health, *The Victoria Climbie Inquiry* ('the Laming Report'), the Stationary Office, London, 2003.

[20] See, for example, Goldstein, J., Freud, A, and Solnit, A.J. *Beyond the Best Interests of the Child*, 1973 which promoted the 'psychological parenting' concept and where the point (contributing significantly to the rationale for permanency planning) is made that "Continuity of relationships, surroundings, and environmental influences are essential for a child's normal development" (pp. 31–32).

[21] See, for example, Bowlby, J. *Attachment and Loss*, London, Hogarth Press, 1969 and Howe, D. *et al.*, *Attachment Theory: Social, Developmental and Clinical Perspectives*, New Jersey, Analytical Press, 1999. Also, see, Harris, G., 'The Human Life Cycle: Infancy' in Davies, M. (ed.) *The Blackwell Companion to Social Work* (2nd ed.), Oxford, Blackwell (2003) at pp. 342—347 where Harris states that 'in extended families, infants might form an attachment to family members other than the main care provider' (p. 343). It is now accepted that an infant child is equally capable of forming an attachment to a male or female carer.

2.2.5. FAILED STATE CARE

The years immediately prior to and following the introduction of the Children
Act 1989, which brought with it the 'partnership with parents' principle' was a
period of professional emphasis on family reunification in which foster care rather
than adoption was the preferred option for children neglected or abused by their
families. This, however, was also a period when the failings of state care became
obvious; the failure of some public child care agencies to satisfactorily provide
for the welfare of some children made the subjects of care orders has been well
documented.[22] The effect of public care scandals, combined with the expense of
state care and influence of the principle that family care is best, led to a period
of intense research focused on evidence based practice to clarify what works
best. The outcomes research[23] for looked after children, together with attachment
theory, suggested that once rehabilitation had been found to be impracticable then
a local authority should institute permanency planning and that adoption rather
than foster care was more likely to produce long-term beneficial outcomes for the
children concerned.

By the end of the 20th century, the 'permanency planning' policy had become
of central importance to local authority child care managers. This requires a plan
to be drawn up for every child accommodated by a local authority showing how a
safe sustainable placement is to be secured that will enable the child to form the
attachment so necessary for his or her welfare (see, further, below).

2.2.6. CHILDREN'S RIGHTS

An important modern development in the law relating to children has been the
relatively recent paradigm shift from a central concern for the protection of welfare
interests to one of asserting their rights. This is largely due to the weight of case
law precedents established under Convention provisions (see, further, Chap. 4).

[22] A number of official inquiries reported on the capacity of the care system itself to permit and
sustain a culture of child abuse. See, for example, Waterhouse, *Lost in Care: Report of the
Tribunal of Inquiry into the Abuse of Children in Care in the Former County Council Areas of
Gwynedd and Clwyd since 1974* (The Stationery Office, London, 2000).
[23] The 'outcomes research', analysing and evaluating the care careers of looked after children, is
comprised of many different reports compiled in the main from within the social work and allied
professions. These include: Triseliotis, J. and Hill, M. *Hard to Place—the Outcome of Adoption
and Residential Care*, Gower (1984); Thoburn, J. *Captive Clients* (1980); Milllham, S. *et al.*,
Lost in Care (1986); Rowe, J., Hundleby, M., and Garnett, L. *Child Care Now—A Survey of
Placement Patterns* (1989); Farmer, E. and Parker, R. *Trials and Tribulations* (1991); Parker, R.,
Ward, H., and Jackson, S. *et al.* (eds.) *Looking After Children: Assessing Outcomes in Child Care*,
London, HMSO (1991); Bullock, R., *et al.*, *Going Home* (1993); Dept. of Health, *Caring for
Children Away from Home: Messages from Research* (1998); *Adoption as a Placement Choice:
Argument and Evidence*, The Maudsley (1999); and Broad, R. *et al.*, *Kith and Kin: Kinship Care
for Vulnerable Young People* (2001).

One effect of this development is that in certain issues, such as disputes regarding contact or parental responsibility, judicial determination will proceed from the premise that the child has a right to whatever arrangement is most conducive to securing and promoting their welfare. A more general effect has been to centre stage children's interests in all family proceedings; the law is now much more for children than about them.

2.3.   Consequences for the adoption process

Radical change in the use of adoption has necessarily impacted upon the process itself. There are now far fewer voluntary adoption agencies involved and many more professional checks and balances[24] (see, further, Chap. 3). In addition to such administrative changes, the content of the process has also undergone a considerable transformation.

2.3.1.   THE PROCESS

Provision for post-adoption support, information rights and reunification services has led to adoption becoming more 'open', less absolute, anonymous, taboo tainted and exclusive. It can no longer be viewed simply as a legal proceeding but must be seen as comprising a comprehensive package of adoption services, governed by statutory regulations and managed, administered and conducted by professionals.

Perhaps one of the more obvious manifestations of the compromises made to the traditional process lies in the fact that it now often accommodates ongoing contact arrangements which are sometimes incorporated as conditions in adoption orders.[25] Where, for example, a relationship already exists between the child and a birth parent or sibling, which may constitute a psychological bond and thus in itself be a determining factor of welfare, then the courts may well see fit to attach a contact condition when making an adoption order.[26] In the past the existence of such a meaningful bond would have been judicially viewed as vitiating the welfare ground for an adoption order: adoption and continued contact

---

[24] The transformation of adoption practice from a patchwork of activities provided largely by voluntary societies to a comprehensive and professionalised adoption service provided in the main by local authorities dates from the recommendations of the Houghton Committee in *Report of the Departmental Committee on the Adoption of Children* (Cmnd 5107), 1972 at para 38.

[25] Under s 12(6) of the Adoption Act 1976, the court was given the discretionary power to attach such conditions as it thinks fit to an adoption order.

[26] See, *Re J (A Minor)(Adoption Order: Conditions)* [1973] Fam 106, *per* Rees J where it was first held that continued contact was not inconsistent with adoption. Also, see, the decision of the House of Lords in *Re C (A Minor)(Adoption Order: Conditions)* [1989] AC 1, HL where it was re-affirmed that there was a power to attach a condition where this was in the welfare interests of the child concerned.

being seen as mutually exclusive. Now, the two factors that determine whether a contact condition (or any other condition) should be attached to an adoption order are the welfare of the child and enforceability.[27] Generally, the new flexibility permitted by the introduction of contact orders under the Children Act 1989, together with the tacit encouragement offered to the practice of facilitating more 'open' adoptions and the concern expressed about step-adoptions, has led to an increasing number of adoption orders being made jointly with contact orders. Most usually, however, contact arrangements are informally negotiated by the parties concerned and do not require a court order.

Another clear development is that the adoption process has come to accommodate a growing number of contested applications. A process, very largely consensual until the 1980s', has since become increasingly non-consensual as child care adoptions are contested and occasionally so also are family adoptions.

Moreover, the modern adoption process no longer necessarily begins with an application for, nor ends with the making of, an adoption order. Pre-adoption counselling services are now available to all parties. In addition, the 1976 Act introduced the requirement that local authorities ensure the provision of an adoption service including post-adoption support services.

Finally, following the introduction of adoption allowances in 1983, the process now allows for considerable state payments to be made to adopters; though these still compare unfavourably with foster care allowances. Local authority Adoption Panels will now, more often than not, recommend the payment of adoption allowances when approving the adoption placements of looked after children. As a consequence the pool of prospective adopters has broadened as foster parents and other carers have opted for financially supported adoption as the preferred means of securing long-term care arrangements.

However, the policy of 'paying people to adopt children' was controversial.[28] It represented a significant shift in the approach of government to what had been

---

[27] See, *Re C (A Minor)* [1988] 1 AER 712h where both factors arose for consideration. However, also, see, *Re S (Contact: Application by Sibling)* [1998] 2 FLR where the court refused an adopted nine year old child leave to apply for a contact order enabling her to resume her relationship with a seven year old half brother with special needs who had been adopted into a different family. The application was resisted by the boy's adoptive parents on the grounds that it would disrupt his life. The court held that the making of an adoption order was intended to be permanent and final and issues such as contact should not be considered after that event; except in the most unusual circumstances.

[28] See, British Association of Social Workers, *Analysis of the Children Bill*, 1975, which states:

> "It would be an intolerable situation if financial resources were made available to subsidise adoption when an allocation of similar resources to the natural parents may have prevented the break up of the family in the first place" at p. 22.

Cited by Lowe, N., 'English Adoption Law: Past, Present and Future' *op cit*, at p. 330. In support of this approach it has to be noted that child care adoption is virtually non-existent in Denmark where the state heavily invests in the family support services necessary to keep vulnerable children at home.

regarded as a private area of family law where the motivation of adopters was expected to be altruistic, above reproach and untainted by considerations of personal benefit.

2.3.2. THE CHILDREN

The profile of today's typical adopted child is very different from the one traditionally placed for adoption. Then the process largely catered for healthy, indigenous, 'illegitimate', white Caucasian babies.[29] Now there are far fewer babies[30] and of those many are likely to be from a different country and possibly from a different race than that of their adopters. The preponderance of family adoptions has naturally raised the average age of children being adopted as has the increase in children adopted by their long-term foster carers. Child care adoptions—often accompanied by very necessary long-term financial, professional and other forms of support—have introduced many children to the adoption process with needs that would not have been within the contemplation of initial legislators. Most contemporary agency adoptions involve children that are the subject of care orders, have some degree of 'special needs', whether suffering from a physical or learning disability, from a behavioural disorder or from 'foetal alcohol syndrome' and may be placed in sibling groups; none of which was envisaged by initial legislators.

The views of the child concerned, age and understanding permitting, will now be sought in relation to their proposed adoption. For example, the decision of a court[31] to dispense with parental agreement was significantly influenced by an 11 year old boy's views on adoption. This judicial approach has been endorsed by an official recommendation[32] that the court should not be allowed to make an adoption order in relation to a child aged 12 years or over unless that child's consent has either been obtained or has been dispensed with. In *Re I (Adoption Order: Nationality)*[33] the court attached considerable importance to the expressed consent

---

[29] In 1968, the peak year for adoptions in the UK and Ireland, one in five of all 'illegitimate' children were adopted in the former jurisdiction compared with four in every five in the latter. See, also, Bridge, C. and Swindells, H., *Adoption: the Modern Law*, Family Law, Bristol, 2003 where it is stated:

> "By 1951, baby adoptions comprised 52% of all adoptions. By 1968 this proportion was even greater—amounting to 76% of all adoptions—and in the same year, 91% of all adoptions were of illegitimate children. Adoption of illegitimate babies had become the primary focus of adoption law" at p. 6.

[30] In 1975, the proportion of children adopted aged 10 years or more was 19% whereas by 1987 it had grown to 27%. In 1998, babies constituted only 4% of total adoptions.

[31] See, *Re B (Minor)(Adoption: Parental Agreement)* [1990] 2 FLR 383. See, also, *Re G (TJ)(An Infant)* [1963] 1 All ER 20 CA; *Re D (Minors)(Adoption by Step-Parent)* [1980] 2 FLR 103, and; *Re B (A Minor)(Adoption)* [1988] 18 Fam Law 172.

[32] See, Interdepartmental Group, DoH, *Review of Adoption Law* , para 3, (1992).

[33] [1998] 2 FLR. See, also, *Re D (Adoption Reports: Confidentiality)* [1995] 2 FLR 687.

of children aged 13 and 16 when approving their adoption despite opposition from the Home Secretary who submitted that the application was a sham intended to defeat immigration controls.

2.3.3. THE BIRTH PARENT/S

The single most radical consequence of modern changes for the adoption process is that adoption came to be used mainly for the opposite reasons for which it was initially legislatively intended. By the early years of the 21st century, more mothers were resorting to adoption, with their new partner, as a means of jointly acquiring rather than relinquishing absolute and irrevocable rights in respect of a natural child.[34] In future, the Adoption and Children Act 2002, s 52(2) will enable the step-parent, or partner, to adopt alone without being joined by the child's birth parent. Where the birth parent/s are otherwise involved in the adoption process, which unlike formerly can now include the unmarried father,[35] it is likely to be on a non-consensual basis to resist the forced adoption of their child. These fundamental changes called into question the continued relevance of legislation constructed on a contrary premise.

Another significant consequence of modern changes to the adoption process is that information rights now mean that the birth parent/s cannot step forever out of the life of their adopted child. The latter will always have access to the information necessary to identify, trace and possibly contact their birth mother if not both parents. In circumstances where a birth father had neither parental responsibility nor given his consent then his name will not appear on the original birth certificate and this will leave an adoptee dependant upon the information sought and recorded by the relevant adoption agency.

2.3.4. THE ADOPTERS

Aside from the above mentioned fact that many of today's adopters are the birth parents of the children concerned, some other changes to the role of adopters have also impacted upon the process. The profile of the typical adopter is now very different from the applicant who would have been involved in the traditional form of adoption. They now may well be older, not necessarily married and perhaps be financially assisted and professionally supported. Occasionally, they may be of the same gender. They may also be of a different nationality and perhaps different race to the child they propose to adopt.

---

[34] See, Bridge, C. and Swindells, H., *Adoption—The Modern Law*, Family Law, Bristol, 2003 at p. 217 where it is noted that under the 1976 Act more than 50% of adoptions in England & Wales were step-parent adoptions.

[35] See, *Re B (Adoption: Natural Parent)* [2002] 1 FLR 196 HL where the House of Lords endorsed an adoption order made by the High Court in favour of an unmarried father as sole applicant.

Arguably, today's adopters may be seen in the main as comprising three distinct groups. Firstly, there are those who adopt children from a child care context. These are likely to be foster parents, or agency approved adopters with similar abilities, who will adopt older children or those with special needs and who may well rely upon and welcome ongoing and intrusive public service support. Secondly, there are those with the motivation, determination and resources to adopt babies from another country. These are more likely to be from a professional or upper middle class background and are unlikely to want any post-adoption public service intrusion. Finally, there are those who adopt children to whom they are related, usually as birth parent or as spouse of the latter. This group is again unlikely to want or welcome any post-adoption public service intrusion. Adoption in the first two groups will be as a result of agency placements involving assessments by an Adoption Panel. A majority of adopters are now likely to have ongoing contact, direct or indirect, with members of the adopted child's family of origin.

3. FAMILY ADOPTION

This term usually refers to first party applicants where the adopter, or one of them in the case of a joint application, is in fact the birth parent of the child concerned. It also includes kinship applications made by other relatives most usually grandparents but occasionally by uncles and aunts who traditionally would have had no *locus standi* in adoption proceedings but under modern family law provisions may acquire legal standing by virtue of an enduring care relationship with the child.

3.1. Trends in annual orders

Family adoptions, though accommodated with some ambivalence by the law in the UK, have grown to the point where they now constitute the single largest category of applicant. Of these, step-parent adoptions have long formed a significant proportion of the total. Although not a new phenomenon[36] this type of adoption has in recent years developed to constitute a large proportion of all annual adoptions. It is explained by Lowe as follows[37]:

> A key element in the increased number of adoption orders during the period 1951–68 was the rise of step-parent adoptions. Such adoptions are essentially of three types:

---

[36] See, Masson, J., Norbury, D., and Chatterton, S., *Mine, Yours or Ours?* HMSO, 1983 where it is noted that in 1951 a third of all adoptions involving 'legitimate' children and just under one-half of those who were 'illegitimate' were step-parent adoptions.

[37] See, Lowe, N., 'English Adoption Law: Past, Present, and Future' in Katz, S., Eekelaar, J. and Maclean, M., *Cross Currents: Family Law and Policy in the United States and England*, Oxford, Oxford University Press, 2000 at p. 317.

so-called 'post-divorce' step-parent adoptions,[38] where the new family comprises a divorced parent, a child of the former marriage and a step-parent; 'post-death' step-parent adoptions, where the family comprises a widowed parent, a child of the former marriage and a step-parent; and 'illegitimate' step-parent adoptions, where the family comprises a formerly unmarried parent, an illegitimate child and a step-parent.

It is the post-divorce adoptions of 'legitimate' children that account for the rise in step-parent adoptions and in turn inflate family adoptions relative to all other types. In 1951 step-adoptions formed 32% of all adoptions and by 1968 this had risen to 34%. The post-divorce adoption of 'legitimate' children more than doubled in the period 1968–1974. As Lowe explains, following the disapproval expressed by Houghton[39] for this type of adoption and the resulting provision in the Children Act 1975 directing the courts to reject such applications where other options were more appropriate, the number of such adoptions fell sharply.[40] However, by 1998, according to the Annual Judicial Statistics, the proportion of all adoption orders made in favour of step-parents still constituted 50% of the total for that year.

3.2.   Adoption by birth parent and spouse

An unmarried mother may adopt her own child.[41] An unmarried father may also do so.[42] Initially, however, the typical such application was made by newly married parents in respect of their child conceived and born in the context of their pre-marital relationship; the purpose being to 'legitimate' that child. More recently it has come to be represented most typically by the re-married parent who applies jointly with their spouse to adopt the former's child from a previous relationship. This use of adoption, which increased considerably after the Divorce Act 1969 came into effect, to legally seal the boundaries of their new family units, has remained contentious. The effect of an adoption order in such circumstances may be to marginalise not only the birth father but also his side of the family. The European Court of Human Rights in *Soderback v Sweden*[43] accepted that such an adoption amounted to interference with the birth father's right to respect for

---

[38]   See, Lowe, *ibid*, where as authority for this definition he cites Masson, J., Norbury, D. and Chatterton, S. *Mine, Yours or Ours?* HMSO, London, 1983 at p. 9.

[39]   See, the Departmental Committee on the Adoption of Children, *Working Paper*, HMSO, London, 1970, paras 92–94. Also, see, *Report of the Departmental Committee on the Adoption of Children* (Cmnd 5107), 1972.

[40]   From 4,545 in1977 to 2,872 in 1983; Lowe cites as his source the Inter-Departmental Review of Adoption Law, Discussion Paper No 3, *The Adoption Process* at p. 9.

[41]   See, *Re D (An Infant)* [1959] 1 QB 229 [1958] 3 All ER 716.

[42]   See, *F v S* [1973] Fam 203 at 207, [1973] 1 All ER 722 at 725 CA. Also, see, *Re B (Adoption: Natural Parent)* [2002] 1 FLR 196 HL above at f/n 31.

[43]   [1999] 1 FLR 250.

family life as it totally and permanently deprived him of the opportunity to enjoy family life with his child (see, further, Chap. 4). But in the UK there has been little evidence of suitability criteria being applied by the judiciary to refer uncontested step-parent applications to marital proceedings. Practice has remained largely unchanged despite the warning in the Houghton Report that an adoption order in such circumstances might be more prejudicial than beneficial to the welfare of the child.[44] The misgivings of Houghton found expression in s 14(3) of the Adoption Act 1976 which required such a judicial referral to custody proceedings, though this was eventually repealed by the Children Act 1989. However the Court of Appeal in a ruling[45] which goes against the normal trend, allowed the appeal of a birth father against an adoption order made in respect of his child and in favour of the child's mother and husband. This decision was based on the grounds that the father had demonstrated the appropriate attachment, commitment and motive to be eligible for a parental responsibility order.

3.3.   Adoption by grandparent

The Houghton Report took the view that adoption by grandparents was not, as a rule, desirable.[46] This reservation rests on the significance of age differentials between adopter and adopted and echoes the warning given by Vaisey J. that 'they should be regarded as exceptional and made with great caution.[47] Adoption by a grandparent has been treated with some caution by UK law but is now becoming fairly common.

3.4.   Other relative adoptions

Being usually grounded on the rationale of extending de jure status to de facto long-term in loco parentis care arrangements, in respect of a consensual parental placement, this type of adoption is now increasingly used by relatives and is referred to as 'kinship adoption'. A characteristic of the modern law as it relates to children is the protection now given to long-term direct care arrangements provided by a person, usually but not necessarily a relative, who has undertaken full responsibility for a child with authority from the parent. Such an arrangement can find ultimate protection in adoption. Also, where a local authority has determined that adoption is in the best interests of a looked after child then, in accordance with the principle of giving first preference to arrangements that retain a child

---

[44] At paras 97 and 103.
[45] See, *Re G (Adoption Order)* [1999] 1 FLR 400.
[46] paras 111–114.
[47] See, *In re DX (An Infant)* [1949] 1 Ch 320 at p. 321.

within his or her family of origin, it will always explore the possibility of kinship adoption.

3.5.   The welfare principle and family adoptions

In the UK, prospective adoption applications from relatives of the child concerned are not subject to scrutiny by the local Adoption Panel. This, in effect, means that perhaps the most important quality control mechanism in the adoption process has no relevance for a very significant proportion of UK adoptions. They avoid this forum for professional assessment on the grounds that this is viewed as a matter of private family law and because there is very seldom a 'placement' consideration as regardless of the outcome the child will almost certainly continue to be retained in the care of the applicants. Although inquiries regarding their suitability will be made by local authority social workers, following the required serving of notice of their intention to apply to adopt, the applicants can choose when to apply and may not do so until several years after making the placement arrangement.

Kinship adoptions (whether by natural parents, grandparents or other relatives) and adoptions by foster-parents and other carers with an established legal relationship with the child concerned, are contentious.

On the one hand a kinship adoption is regarded as problematic because:

- a new and lesser legal status is being substituted for an existing legal and actual relationship;
- purpose and motive can be open to question;
- kinship adopters are usually older than others;
- it can obscure the nature of the actual relationship between child and adopter and be confusing for other children in the family; and
- it can have a divisive effect by alienating other relatives.

On the other hand a kinship adoption is viewed positively because[48]:

- it often retains the child in their home and social environment;
- it always maintains the child within their actual network of relationships (though in some circumstances this can be problematic);
- it facilitates an honest sharing of information between all parties; and
- by retaining the child within their culture of origin it minimises the possibility of long-term identity problems.

---

[48] For further arguments in support of kinship care see, for example, Broad, B. (ed.) *Kinship Care: The Placement Choice for Children and Young People*, Russell House, 2001, Greef, R. (ed) *Fostering Kinship: An International Perspective on Kinship Foster Care*, Arena, 1999 and Hegar, R.L. and Scannapieco, M., *Kinship Foster Care: Policy, Practice and Research,* Oxford University Press, 1999.

4. AGENCY ADOPTION

Third party or 'stranger' adoptions, where the adopters are unrelated in every respect to the child voluntarily relinquished or otherwise consensually available, is the model that has consistently been the subject of legislative intent in the UK. It has also been consistently in decline since the 1970s. In 1982, following the recommendation of the Houghton Committee,[49] such adoptions became the responsibility of adoption agencies as private placements by non-relatives were thereafter prohibited by s 28 of the Children Act 1975. These are now more commonly referred to as 'agency adoptions' because, unlike family adoptions, the critical placement decisions are made by the professional staff of an adoption agency.

4.1. Trends in annual orders

Agency adoptions include consensual placements whether made by registered voluntary adoption societies or local authority agencies and non-consensual placements made by the latter in respect of children subject to care orders (child care adoptions) including placements made with members of the child's family of origin (kinship adoptions). This composite group, though most representative of legislative intent and constituting by far the majority of all orders made, has steadily declined over recent years in the UK. The child care component, however, has remained at a fairly consistent and significant level as a proportion of all adoptions but at a low level relative to the child care population. At the end of the 1980s, only a very small proportion of children in care were subsequently adopted[50] but, as Lowe points out, "whereas in 1968 they accounted for 8.7% of all adoptions, for most of the 1990s they accounted for a third or more of all adoptions".[51] This inverse correlation between child care adoptions as a proportion of all adoptions and between child care adoptions as a proportion of the child care population is explained by the fact that during this period the number of child care adoptions remained fairly constant while annual adoptions steadily fell and the child care population continued to increase.

---

[49] See, *Report of the Departmental Committee on the Adoption of Children*, London, HMSO, 1972, Cmnd 5107, paras 84–90 and recommendation 13.

[50] A survey of six local authorities in England revealed that only 0.8% were eventually placed for adoption (see, Rowe *et al.*, 1989). See, also, review of research into adoption by the DoH, 1999a)

[51] See, Lowe, N., 'English Adoption Law: Past, Present and Future', *op cit*, at pp. 321–322, where he cites the 'Looked After' statistics for England as showing the following child care adoptions: 2,400 in 1997; 2,500 in 1998; and 2,900 in 1999. The Dept of Health annual statistics reveal that in England during the year ending 31 March 2002, a total of 3,400 looked after children were adopted.

4.2.   Voluntary society adoptions

The archetypal triangulation of need—featuring the relinquishing birth parent/s; the child orphaned, abandoned, unwanted or inadequately cared for; and the childless couple selected by intermediaries on the basis of eligibility/suitability criteria—provided the template for adoption law in the UK. It was pioneered and administered for most of the history of adoption as a statutory process, until the 1970s, largely by voluntary adoption societies.[52] Consent for adoption was envisaged and almost always was available, placements were chosen and made by voluntary societies in a confidential manner so as to ensure that all identifying information was held by the society and not shared between the birth parent/s, child and adopters. Record keeping by such societies was a matter for their discretion; many were destroyed in the belief that this was in keeping with the confidential relationship between the society and the three parties. The consequences of this process were legislatively intended to be essentially private, absolute and irrevocable.

The involvement of voluntary societies in adoption has faded as the process became dominated by family applicants, for whom there is no need to provide a placement service, and by child care placements which are usually non-consensual and require to be authorised and managed by local authorities.

4.3.   Child care adoptions

The flow of children from the public child care sector into the private law adoption process has been a relatively recent development. For many generations, when care in the family of origin failed, whether due to criminal abuse perpetrated by a culpable parent or neglect by a well meaning but inadequate parent, children have entered the public care system. This seldom resulted in their becoming available for adoption.[53] Indeed, in 1952 of all children adopted only 3.2% were from public care,[54] rising to 8.7% in 1968, while a survey by Rowe in 1989 of placement patterns in six local authorities discovered that only 0.8% of children in care were eventually adopted.[55] However, the traditional alternatives gradually became less

---

[52] In 1966, for example, of all agency adoptions, 73% were arranged by voluntary societies; by 1971 this had fallen to 60%.

[53] Despite recommendations in the Curtis Report, *The Care of Children*, (Cmnd 6922) 1946 where adoption was advocated for older children in care and subsequently those of the Houghton Committee, *Report of the Departmental Committee on the Adoption of Children*, (Cmnd 5107) 1972 which pressed for adoption to be made available to children in public care where this was in the best interests of a particular child.

[54] See, Lowe, N., 'English Adoption Law: Past, Present and Future' in Katz, S., Eekelaar, J., and Maclean, M., *Cross Currents: Family Law and Policy in the United States and England*, Oxford, Oxford University Press, 2000 at p. 315.

[55] See, Rowe *et al.* (1989).

viable. Long-term residential care in children's homes proved damaging to the welfare interests of thousands of children placed in the care of local authorities by court orders, while the recruitment and retention of sufficient foster carers, became increasingly problematic. A body of research (see, above at f/n 22) convincingly demonstrated that the life chances of a child who had grown up in the public care system compared very badly, across a number of indicators (including employment, mental health, relationships etc), with one who had matured in a safe family environment. Consequently grounds for freeing such children for adoption were eventually legislatively introduced.[56]

The Children Act 1989, however, rested on principles such as that the welfare interests of a child were best served by care in their family of origin and local authorities should work in partnership with parents. The introduction of this legislation saw a change in the trend of child care adoptions. Instead of continuing their steady increase child care adoptions began to decrease from the mid-1990s.

By the beginning of the 21st century, the imbalance between type/volume of child care resources and the needs of children requiring alternative long-term care arrangements had become a matter of acute concern to all local authorities. Residential accommodation for children subject to care orders, where desirable, was difficult to secure. Foster parents were a scarce resource and serial placements for a child in care was the norm. These problems were unfolding in the context of a dramatic decline in the availability of freely relinquished healthy babies and a continued increase in the number of childless couples wishing to adopt. Moreover, the pressure emanating from research findings on the outcomes for looked after children together with the results of evidence based practice utilising attachment theory and implementing the permanency planning policy indicated that traditional approaches to securing care arrangements for looked after children were unsustainable. It seemed that an assertive policy to expedite non-consensual adoption for older and often abused or impaired children might be timely.

4.3.1.   REHABILITATION

The fact that by far the majority of looked after children return to their families and the vast majority of those that do not remain in foster care should not be overlooked in any discussion about child care adoption. Whether the welfare interests of a child committed to long-term local authority care would be best furthered by plans to rehabilitate him or her with their family of origin or extended family, by long-term foster care or by adoption is clearly a matter that must turn on the particular circumstances of the child concerned. The principles and ethos of the 1989 Act, however, exerted an influence, not present in earlier legislation,

---

[56] The concept of 'freeing orders' was first suggested by Houghton, see, *Report of the Departmental Committee on the Adoption of Children*, London, HMSO, 1972, Cmnd 5107, paras 173–186.

towards a preference for the former option. It remains the case that where there are reasonable grounds for optimism, regarding a possible reunification of parent and child, then clearly the local authority must give first preference to pursuing that option. As Munby J remonstrated in *Re L (Care: assessment: fair trial)*[57]:

> ... it must never be forgotten that, with the state's abandonment of the right to impose capital sentences, orders of the kind which judges of this Division are typically invited to make in public law proceedings are amongst the most drastic that any judge in any jurisdiction is ever empowered to make. It is a terrible thing to say to a parent—particularly, perhaps to a mother—that he or she is to lose their child forever.

In the light of the draconian effect of adoption on the future of that parent/child relationship, the guidance from the ECHR is that every effort should be made to explore rehabilitation if subsequent recourse to adoption is to be compliant with Article 8 of the European Convention. In particular, *Gorgulu v Germany*[58] provides authority for the view that the child's welfare must be seen in a long-term context and this may even require terminating an adoption placement, however satisfactory, if local authority intervention is to meet the test of 'proportionality'. The significance of this principle was explained by Hale LJ in *Re C and B*[59] as follows:

> ... one comes back to the principle of proportionality. The principle has to be that the local authority works to support, and eventually to reunite, the family, unless the risks are so high that the child's welfare requires alternative family care. I cannot except that this was a case for a care order with a care plan of adoption or nothing. There could have been other options. There could have been time taken to explore those other options.

In many cases the prospects for safe rehabilitation can be swiftly assessed as unrealisable on the basis of facts grounding the care order, the parent/s track record etc, or the number of years the child has been in care. In those circumstances the principle of partnership with parents and the 'care in the family of origin is best' ethos of the 1989 Act have to give way. A local authority will then apply the policy of permanency planning.

4.3.2.   PERMANENCY PLANNING

A key policy to emerge in recent years in most western societies has been a recognition that public service agencies should strive to secure for every vulnerable child a stable, safe and nurturing environment in which he or she can grow up.

---

[57] [2002] 2 FLR 730.
[58] Application No 74969/01, ECHR, 26.02.2004. Also, see, *P, C and S v UK* (2002) 35 EHRR 31, *K and T v Finland* [2001] 2 FLR 707 and *Johansen v Norway* (1996) 23 EHRR 33; see, further, Chap. 4.
[59] [2001] 1 FLR 611 at para 31.

Where rehabilitation in the family of origin or with relatives is not an option then local authorities must consider how best to secure a permanent placement for a looked after child. 'Permanence' is "a framework of emotional, physical and legal conditions that gives a child a sense of security, continuity, commitment and identity"[60] while 'permanency planning' has been defined as[61]:

> ... the systematic process of carrying out within a limited period a set of goal-directed activities designed to help children and youths live with families that offer continuity of relationships with nurturing parents or caretakers, and the opportunity to offer lifetime relationships.

The term has long played a role as a key concept in American child care legislation and now informs local authority policy in relation to looked after children for whom return to their families of origin is not feasible. The age of the child, the child's wishes and the quality of his or her relationship with their parents may well indicate adoption as the preferred means of securing permanency for that child whether or not parental consent is available. Local authorities will always apply permanency planning to identify the best option for a 'looked after' child, most often this will be either adoption or long-term fostering or by way of such private law measures as a residence order and in the future special guardianship.

A factor of growing significance for local authorities engaged in permanency planning is whether the cost in financial and other terms merits pursuing the adoption option for a looked after child. Purely in financial terms, justifying the investment of scare resources in lengthy contested proceedings often involving QCs, expert witnesses and vast amounts of social work and senior management time in respect of a child (who may in any event remain in the existing care arrangement) can be problematic. The cost in terms of time for the child concerned who needs a settled family environment to form attachments and the insecurity for prospective adopters must also be borne in mind. Then there is the cost to the self-esteem and morale of social workers, often young and inexperienced, exposed to intimidating cross-examination in the gruelling process of contested proceedings. It may be that, despite all the changes in law and policy to facilitate the adoption of looked after children, such practice driven considerations will ultimately weigh in the balance with local authority decision makers.

4.3.3. CONCURRENT PLANNING

In recent years the practice of concurrent planning has been instituted for children accommodated by local authorities in order to reduce the number of changes of

---

[60] See, the Department of Education and Skills, *Draft Regulations and Guidance for Consultation (Care Planning, Special Guardianship)*, London, 2004 at p. 20.
[61] See, Maluccio, A. and Fein, E., 'Permanency Planning: a redefinition', *Child Welfare* 62: 3, pp. 195–201, (1983).

placement endured by such children. This is a practice whereby a local authority will commit to a rehabilitation programme designed to return a child to safe
parental care, while also putting in place a parallel permanent placement plan.
It relies upon foster parents who are chosen for their capacity to engage directly
with the birth parents and facilitate the rehabilitation plan but who, in the event
of that plan failing, are also willing to adopt the children concerned. These two
options will then be played out in tandem with emphasis given to rehabilitation
but the fallback position of adoption is kept alive and preparations for utilising
it are attended to constantly. In very many cases, where the rehabilitation option
has demonstrably failed, children in care have then been successfully and relatively swiftly adopted. This approach avoids the traditional care career of serial
placements and 'drift' in long-term foster care.

4.3.4.   LONG-TERM FOSTER CARE AND ADOPTION

Given the virtual disappearance of residential care provided by voluntary organisations and the influence of the principle that family care is most conducive to
promoting the welfare of a child, permanency planning in practice means a choice
between two forms of placement, long-term foster care and adoption.

Generally speaking, long-term foster care is most often the placement of
choice in circumstances where the probability of successful bonding, the crucial
component in any attempt to replicate in adoption the dynamics of a "normal"
nuclear family, is reduced by some added complication. This may be the case
where the children concerned are older, have been repeatedly fostered, comprise
a multiple sibling group, have complex health or special needs or are children from
a minority culture background. Quite often the choice is made because a child
has close relationships with his or her family of origin which the local authority
want to maintain, and a placement with foster parents rather than adopters is more
conducive to facilitating open-ended contact arrangements. In *Re B,*[62] where such
a relationship existed but a local authority nevertheless chose adoption rather than
long-term foster care, the courts challenged that choice. The court ruled that given
the close and frequent contact between the looked after child and his birth father
and paternal grandmother, all of whom lived locally, adoption was inappropriate
as the child was in fact a secure member of both families.

Also, there are times when an intended short-term placement has been so successful that any change would threaten the welfare interests of the child concerned.
For example, in *Re F (Adoption: Welfare of Child: Financial Considerations)*[63]

---

[62] [2001] 2 FCR 89.
[63] [2003] EWHC 3448 (Fam). Note, also, *R (L and Others) v Manchester City Council; R (R and
       Another) v Manchester City Council* [2001] EWHC Admin 707, [2002] 1 FLR 43 where the
       court ruled that the local authority practice of paying less to kinship carers than to foster carers
       was unlawful.

the local authority sought freeing orders in respect of three siblings whom it proposed to remove from successful but expensive foster care and place for adoption, though an adoption placement had yet to be identified. The foster carers were not in a position to adopt because of the financial loss they would incur on cessation of foster care allowances. The proposal was not supported by the guardian nor by any of the other professionals involved as it was seen as contrary to the children's welfare interests. The court refused the order and rebuked the local authority for not having a child-centred focus in its care plan.

The disadvantages of long-term foster care are that:

- There is intrusion.
- Drift can happen with the child moving from one place to another. It is more likely to lead to breakdown.
- It reinforces impermanence.
- Matters such as surname can be important. Self-image is important as children get older.
- The existence of other children in foster care can increase the insecurity as they come and go.
- Children frequently act out with the other foster children the abuse they have suffered.
- Placements in long-term foster care are more likely to fail than adoption placements.

The advantages of adoption, as stated in the DHSS circular *Departmental Guidance: Permanency Planning for Children: Adoption—Achieving the Right Balance*, are that[64]:

> The importance of family life to a child cannot be overstated. It is the fundamental right of every child to belong to a family and this principle underpins the United Nations Convention on the Rights of the Child which United Kingdom ratified in 1991. Where, for whatever reason, children cannot live with their families, society has a duty to provide them with a fresh start and, where appropriate, a permanent alternative home. Adoption is the means of giving children an opportunity to experience positive family relationships. Adoption continues to provide an important service for children, offering a positive and beneficial outcome. Research shows that adopted children generally make very good progress compared with similar children who are brought up by their parents. Adopted children do considerably better than children who have remained in the care system throughout most of their childhood. Adoption provides children with a unique opportunity to become permanent members of new families enjoying a sense of security and well-being previously denied to them.

---

[64] See, Local Authority Circular (20), 1998. See, also, the government's Green Paper, *Every Child Matters*, published in September 2003.

The government has since firmed up on this approach with an unequivocal policy commitment to prioritising adoption in preference to long-term foster care (see, further, Chap. 5).

4.3.5.   PRIVATE LAW ORDERS

Permanency planning can also result in a looked after child leaving the public care system for private family care not through adoption but under the authority of a private law order. In the past this might have been achieved through use of a guardianship order or the ill-fated custodianship order. Since the introduction of the Children Act 1989, residence orders have been used to discharge a child from a care order and for vesting parental rights, shared with the birth parent/s, in the named holder of the new order. This option has not proved popular with foster-parents because its authority and status is seen as being unduly compromised by ongoing parental involvement. It is hoped that the more authoritative special guardianship order, to be made available under the Adoption and Children Act 2002, will be a more attractive option for foster parents and indeed for kinship carers.

4.4.   The welfare principle and agency adoptions

All prospective agency adoptions are assessed by an Adoption Panel the brief of which is to make recommendations as to:

- whether adoption is in the best interests of a particular child;
- whether a prospective adopter should be approved as an adoptive parent; and
- whether the home of a particular approved prospective adopter would provide a suitable placement for a particular child.

The Panel acts as an independent quality assurance body that makes recommendations to its 'parent' adoption agency on matters concerning adoption as a means of securing the welfare interests of children referred to it (see, further, Chap. 5).

5.   INTERCOUNTRY ADOPTIONS

For some decades the number of babies available for adoption has been declining in all modern Western societies. At the same time, circumstances of war and natural disaster have induced other countries to permit the adoption of orphaned or abandoned children by couples in western societies. The welfare interests of such children can usually only be improved by this modern 'child rescue' approach. However, for some children their availability is conditioned by the social economy of their country of origin and it may be that the dislocation to family and culture resulting from adoption may prove in the long-term not to be conducive to promoting their welfare interests. It may be that intercountry adoption will only satisfy the welfare test where neither rehabilitation in the family of origin nor adoption within the country of origin is possible.

5.1.   Trends in annual orders

The adoption of children from other countries by persons unrelated to them and resident in the UK is slowly becoming a more significant aspect of modern adoption practice. Lowe has drawn attention to the relatively low numbers of such adoptions[65]:

> In the early 1990s, there were a number of adoptions of Romanian orphans. Indeed, in 1992 the *Adoption Law Review* commented that since March 1990 over 400 children from Romania alone had been brought to the UK for adoption. In 1998, however, the total number of intercountry adoptions through official procedures was 258, amounting to 6% of all adoptions for that year.

Currently, some 300 such children are adopted annually in the UK but this now amounts to almost 10% of annual adoptions.

5.2.   Transracial adoptions

The media generated controversy surrounding transracial adoptions has tended to center on a practice by adoption agencies and local authorities to make and break placements on the basis of whether or not there was a racial match between child and prospective adopters. There have been a number of cases where the propriety of this practice has been examined.[66] The emerging consensus is that where possible placement arrangements should reflect a child's ethnic background and cultural identity insofar as such considerations are compatible with the welfare interests of that child which must always have priority. In particular, the courts have upheld the value of preserving established relationships as a key component of welfare interests in transracial as in all other kinds of placements; the duration of current care arrangements and age of the child being of crucial importance. In *Re N (A Minor)(Adoption)*[67] Bush J warned that:

> ... the emphasis on colour rather than on cultural upbringing can be mischievous and highly dangerous when you are dealing in practical terms with the welfare of children.

---

[65] See, Lowe, N., 'English Adoption Law: Past, Present and Future', *op cit*, at p. 333.

[66] See, for example: *Re P (A Minor)(Adoption)* [1990] 1 FLR 96; *R v Lancashire County Council , ex parte M* [1992] 1 FLR 109; and *Re JK (Adoption: Transracial Placement)* [1991] 2 FLR 340. Also, see, Caesar *et al.*, 1993 and Tizard and Phoenix, 1989.

[67] [1990] 1 FLR 58 at p. 63. Also, see, *Re O (Transracial Adoption: Contact)* [1995] 2 FLR 597.

The practice was addressed in the White Paper on adoption.[68] The view then expressed was to the effect that a child's ethnic background and cultural identity should always be factors to be considered by agency staff when making adoption placements but not necessarily to be given any greater consideration than other factors.

5.3.   The welfare principle and intercountry adoptions

All prospective intercountry adoption applicants are professionally assessed and the resulting reports are reviewed by Adoption Panels.

Intercountry adoptions have given rise to eligibility issues. These most often occur in relation to the prohibition on unauthorised payments,[69] unauthorised placements and proof of consents. The first two represent the traditional legal abhorrence of 'trafficking' in children and are criminal offences under s 57 and s 11 respectively of the 1976 Act. Improper payments (e.g. direct or indirect payments to the child's mother) may, if proven, prevent the court from making an adoption order[70]; though much will depend on the circumstances and whether the child's welfare interests are otherwise impaired. Improper placements are viewed more seriously by the courts and are more likely to result in the refusal of an adoption order. The problems in relation to proof of consents refers to the difficulty in establishing, across geographical, cultural and language barriers, the legal status of parent and child and confirming that any consent given was done so freely and with full understanding of the consequences. Any one or combination of these issues may well complicate the court's ultimate application of the welfare test to a particular intercountry adoption application. However, as was illustrated in *Re C (Adoption: Legality),*[71] the fact that there have been irregularities—in adopter approval, payments, matching and introduction of adopter and child—will be insufficient to outweigh the fact that once the placement is made the passing of time steadily dictates the making of an adoption order as the best option available to the court.

5.3.1.   CULTURAL LINKS

Applying the welfare test to the child subjects of intercountry adoptions does of course give rise to some fundamental questions. It must be accepted that the circumstances of war and natural disaster governing the availability of many children are such that their welfare interests can only be improved by this modern 'child

---

[68]   See, *Adoption: The Future*, (Cmnd 2288) HMSO, 1993, para 4.32.
[69]   See, *Re An Adoption Application* [1992] 1 FLR 341, *Re AW (Adoption Application)* [1992] Fam Law 539 and *Re C (A Minor)(Adoption Application)* [1992] Fam Law 538.
[70]   The court may, however, retrospectively authorise payments; see, for example, *Re WM (Adoption: Non-Patrial)* [1997] 1 FLR 132.
[71]   [1999] 1 FLR 370.

rescue' approach of adopters. This rationale, perhaps, lay behind the decision of the court in *Re K (Adoption and Wardship)*[72] which concerned a five year old orphan who as a wounded baby had been removed from Bosnia and then 'adopted' by her English rescuers. The court, when faced with a petition from the child's relatives, set aside the defective adoption order but rather than direct her return to her extended family and her country of origin it ruled that she should remain with the English couple who had become her 'psychological parents'. However, for some children their availability is conditioned by the social economics of their country of origin and it may be that the dislocation to family and culture resulting from adoption may prove in the long-term not to be conducive to the promotion of their welfare interests. This line of reasoning was present in the decision of in the Court of Appeal in *Re M (Child's Upbringing)*.[73] In that case it was held that preserving the Zulu identity of a ten year old boy, reared for seven years by white foster parents, was sufficiently important to order his return to natural parents in South Africa despite his strong wishes to the contrary. While it is admittedly difficult to reconcile the judicial rationale of both cases, it may be that intercountry adoption will only satisfy the welfare test where, as with other adoptions, rehabilitation in the family of origin has become impossible. The consent or absence of dissent, of the child concerned, must also be a factor in meeting that test.

6. A COHERENT LEGAL MODEL FOR ADOPTION PRACTICE

It could be argued that adoption practice in the UK has now outgrown the uniform legal framework which governed its development since its legislative inception. Adoption no longer conforms to the single coherent model that traditionally fitted the social needs of late Victorian England. In fact it has not done so since at least the 1970s.

6.1. Classification of adoption by type

The adoption process in the UK now encompasses several different 'types', usually broadly classified as 'family adoption', 'third party adoption' also known as

---

[72] [1997] 2 FLR 230. See, also, *Re N* [1990] 1 FLR 58 where the adoption application by white foster parents in respect of a four year old Nigerian child, placed with them when 3 weeks old, was successfully challenged by the child's father who lived in the US. The court, attaching considerable weight to the father's assertion that adoption was unknown to Nigerian law and carried resonances of slavery, warded the child giving care and control to the foster parents.

[73] [1996] 2 FLR 441. See, also, *Re B (Adoption: Child's Welfare)* [1995] 1 FLR 895 which concerned an adoption application arising from the informal foster care arrangement made for a Gambian child. In refusing the application, Wall J placed considerable importance upon the child's cultural inheritance as an integral aspect of its welfare.

'agency adoption' which contains a number of quite distinct groups and 'inter-country adoption' which is really a form of third party adoption.

- **Family adoption**

Most usually the applicants are a birth parent of the child concerned and the former's spouse motivated by a wish to legally secure exclusive parental rights and responsibilities. Pre-application professional assessment is not required and counselling is unlikely to be wanted. The child is unlikely to be a baby, their wishes, and their consent if old enough, are likely to be sought and the order may well be compromised by a contact condition in favour of the child's other parent. Post-adoption public support services are not provided.

- **Agency adoption**

The traditional form of adoption, which continues albeit in greatly reduced form, is initiated by a married but childless couple, unrelated to the child and motivated by a need to become parents. They will have been professionally assessed and carefully matched to suit the needs of the child concerned. The child is likely to be a baby or toddler without health or social care difficulties and their views or consent will not be sought. The order is likely to be absolute and post-adoption public services are again most unlikely. Child care adoption, however, is initiated by a local authority seeking carer/s, married or not, with skills appropriate to the needs of the child concerned. The applicants may be motivated by their existing care relationship with the child (although only a minority of such applicants will be foster carers) and will have been professionally assessed, offered counselling and be carefully matched to suit the needs of that child. The subject is likely to be an older child with health or social care problems whose views or consent will be sought. The order may well be compromised by a contact condition in favour of member/s of the child's family of origin and post-adoption public support services will be provided.

- **Intercountry adoption**

The applicants are likely to be an older married couple motivated by a need to parent a healthy baby or toddler without health or social care problems and preferring to do so by looking overseas rather than undergo the waiting and uncertainties associated with agency adoption. They will have been professionally assessed and counselled, will be prepared to pay the considerable costs involved and will not want post-adoption public services. The order will be absolute.

They each conclude, if successful, in an order with a uniform effect on the parties concerned. However, intercountry adoption is different from the others in that it is now regulated by its own quite distinct body of legislation (see, further, Chaps. 4 and 9).

6.2. Social role

The purposes pursued in each type of adoption are often fundamentally differ-ent. In particular, family adoption, child care adoption and intercountry adoption can be clearly differentiated from each other and from the traditional form of third party adoption. The children, their needs and the relative bearing of the welfare principle are also quite different in each context, as are the motives of adopters and the reasons governing the availability of children. The extent to which each type attracts professional and public service intervention differs con-siderably.

6.3. Legal functions

Essentially, the above differentiation in adoption's contemporary social role re-flects the balance respectively struck between public and private interests in each type. The public interest is most strongly represented in child care adoptions while family adoptions are in the main dominated by private interests. All types are also subject to the public interest in safeguarding the welfare of the child.

7. CONCLUSION

Adoption in the UK has greatly changed since the introduction of the first legis-lation. Most change has occurred in the past few years. The traditional form of adoption has largely been displaced by new variants some of which are wholly driven by private interests (e.g., family adoptions, surrogacy associated adoption) and others by the public interest (e.g., child care adoptions). Sustained adopter demand in the face of the shrinking consensual availability of healthy white babies has broadened the adoption 'market'. Intercountry and transracial adoptions, once rare occurrences, are becoming increasingly common as is adoption by same sex couples while many more children with 'special needs' are now being adopted than would ever have been thought possible. A closed, immutable and confidential process has become more open.

All this gave rise to legal complications regarding issues such as consent, application of the welfare principle and post-adoption contact, financial support and information rights. The 'one size fits all' composite legal framework could no longer adequately accommodate the new types of adoption with their associated distinctive problems. Adoption law as a whole in the UK was no longer reflecting a coherent policy nor was it equal to the sum of the parts of adoption practice.

Part II

ADOPTION AND THE LAW

Chapter 3

THE LEGAL FUNCTIONS OF ADOPTION

1.   INTRODUCTION

At each stage of the adoption process a distinct set of legal functions comes into play which are now readily recognised. They have clear roles in a statutorily defined process that, at least in contemporary western societies, is now well established and to a varying degree regulated throughout its sequence of quite different stages. Entry to the process is controlled through the application of threshold criteria to all parties. Placement of the child is subject to an authorised consent. Supervision of the child, after placement and until determination of proceedings, is usually a statutorily ascribed responsibility. The outcome of an adoption application is determined with regard to the rights of the parties but in accordance with the principle of the welfare of the child and may result in the issue of a conditional order or in an order other than the one sought. Finally, the effects of an adoption order, the possible availability of post-adoption support and of long-term services relating to information disclosure, tracing and possible re-unification and the responsibilities of the parties concerned are usually set by statute.

The central focus of this chapter is on identifying the main legal functions of adoption as generally applicable in contemporary modern western jurisdictions. Attention is given to recent changes in emphasis and to the balance now generally struck between public and private legal interests. The chapter goes on to examine the related legislative intent and assesses the consequences of exercising the legal functions for the parties involved in the adoption process. In this way a tool kit is assembled for use in later chapters to assess and track trends in the main operational aspects of the adoption process in other contemporary jurisdictions.

Kerry O'Halloran (ed.), The Politics of Adoption, 73–100.
© 2006 *Springer. Printed in The Netherlands.*

The chapter thereby also provides a template against which the legal functions in the adoption processes of other countries can be compared and evaluated.

The chapter begins with an overview of the adoption process. In particular, it considers:

- the regulatory framework;
- the roles of determining bodies
- the roles of other administrative agencies;
- the sequential stages of the adoption process and the nature and the weighting of different legal functions at each stage;
- the legal criteria governing entry to and exit from the process;
- the legal effects of an adoption order; and
- the outcomes of the process for the parties concerned.

Finally, the chapter concludes with a review of the changing place of adoption within the larger framework of family law.

2.   REGULATING THE ADOPTION PROCESS

While adoption in the UK has been firmly established as a judicial process, closely regulated, successful completion of which is marked by the issue of a court order, this is not necessarily the case in other jurisdictions. In Ireland, for example, proceedings are determined by an administrative body rather than by a court. In the US the process is much less regulated: direct placements with an unrelated third party and placements by private commercial agencies are permitted. Whether or not adoption proceedings are judicial, however, the role assigned to mediating bodies is now almost always professional, intrusive and extensive and the entire process operates within a statutory framework.

This framework provides an important opportunity for influencing the balance between public and private interests. If appropriate standards are to be maintained and good practice promoted then an agency must be positioned to hold an overview of the workings of the adoption process. In the UK jurisdictions, both the local authority and the court undertake this role while in Ireland it falls to an Adoption Board.

2.1.   The adoption process

Until relatively recently in most western societies the adoption process has existed simply as an extreme form of private family law proceedings. It was a process characterised by private initiative, the anonymity of its participants, and by the fact that one or more parties sought to bind the others to permanent secrecy. It aimed to achieve an artificial re-configuration of legal relationships between the participants, sealed by an unconditional adoption order that would be absolute, exclusive and permanent. It was an adoption process wrapped in a distinct aura of taboo. This traditional adoption process usually permitted only one of two possible outcomes: an adoption order was either granted or it was refused; there were no alternative option available to the court.

When being treated as primarily a matter of private law, the adoption process was conducted in a non-intrusive manner. All the important decisions were taken before the application was brought before the court or other determining body. The latter then addressed the public interest dimension by ensuring that the welfare threshold was satisfied. In recent years, instead of the traditional all or nothing, private or public resolution of adoption proceedings, the law in many jurisdictions has developed to provide a longer, broader and more balanced response to adoption applications. An adoption process will now most usually consist of the following stages:

- pre-placement counselling;
- legal procedures regarding availability of child, status of parties, consents, identification of any residual post-adoption rights etc;
- placement of child;
- pre-application supervision of placement;
- legal procedures relating to application;
- the hearing and issue of order/s, with or without attached conditions;
- post-adoption support services; and
- information disclosure, tracing and possibly re-unification services.

As can be seen, the process is now often lengthened at commencement by a statutory pre-placement counselling stage during which adoption agencies are required to provide a counselling service to all birth parents whose consent is available or will be sought for an adoption and to such others as may be necessary. In the context of family adoptions, professional scrutiny is now frequently required. The process has also been extended at the closing stage by procedures governing the disclosure of information, use of contact registers, possible conditions attached to adoption orders and the opportunities for adoption allowances and other forms of ongoing support from government bodies. Moreover, it now encompasses a wide range and uneven mix of participants including: increasing numbers of children from other jurisdictions; children who have special social and/or health care needs; and a growing proportion of parental applications and foster parent applicants.

The sequence of stages constituting the adoption process have become more distinct and are now governed by a mix of some prescriptive rules and large areas of professional discretion but otherwise the continuum has not undergone any substantive change. What has changed most significantly in many jurisdictions is the nature of the process. This has developed from being almost exclusively consensual to becoming increasingly coercive as regards authorising the availability

of children. Although the degree and pace of this change varies from one jurisdiction to another: in Ireland, for example, it affects only a very small minority of
annual adoptions. In general, contention, if not outright adversarial opposition, is
now a not uncommon feature of the adoption process. This has been accompanied
by other changes that have impacted upon the adoption's traditional hallmarks of
absoluteness, exclusiveness, secrecy and permanency. These have necessitated
adjustments to the regulatory role statutorily assigned to the determining body or
agency.

2.2.   Role of the judiciary or other determining body

The consequences of adoption for the legal status of all concerned have always
been viewed in the UK and in the US, unlike some other jurisdictions such as
Ireland, as of such significance as to necessitate the exercise of judicial rather
than administrative authority.[1] This is often also a matter of practical necessity;
as the non-consensual proportion of adoption applications grows so too does the
need to involve the court to adjudicate on contentious legal issues. The role of the
court or other determining body is to:

- ensure that criteria of eligibility/suitability and status are fulfilled by all
  parties;
- ascertain consent or adjudicate on consent issues where necessary;
- check adherence to law, procedures and propriety;
- ensure the welfare of the child; and
- then make such order as may be appropriate.

This role is usually supplemented by the responsibilities of other officials, such as
social workers and a court officer such as the CAFCASS officer. The former will
usually provide reports detailing the circumstances of the adopters and the family
background of the child while the latter will be required to carry out an exhaustive
investigation into all the circumstances of the proposed adoption. The court officer
will interview all applicants and respondents including, where feasible, the child
and ensure that any factor having a bearing on the welfare of the child is brought
to the attention of the court.

2.3.   Role of administrative agencies

The extent to which the law licenses or constrains those in a pivotal position to
influence the finalising of an adoption 'contract' provides a valuable insight into
the legal balance struck between public and private interests.

---

[1]   In Ireland this function is administrative; adoption hearings and the decision to grant or refuse
      the order sought are matters for the Adoption Board. The High Court only has a role where legal
      issues, such as consent disputes, require adjudication; in all cases the final decision in relation to
      an adoption application taken by the Adoption Board not the court.

Adoption legislation generally contains few objective criteria; control over the adoption process has effectively been delegated to adoption agencies. In recent years that process has, in most modern western jurisdictions, become greatly contracted in terms of the numbers of applicants and babies involved while also becoming increasingly professionalised. The fewer children now being adopted, many in the course of contested proceedings and bringing with them complicated legal problems, receive attention from an increasing range of bodies and officials; their bearing on the process differing according to whether an application is 'family', 'agency' or 'intercountry'.

An adoption society or agency is the key professional reference point in the adoption process; in many jurisdictions these are now required to register with a designated government body and such registration is dependent upon ability to satisfy prescriptive standards. The emergence of consortia, umbrella bodies that co-ordinate the work and resources of several adoption agencies, are also beginning to exercise a significant influence on shaping policy and practice. An important development in recent years in the UK, unlike other jurisdictions, has been the extent to which the traditional involvement of voluntary agencies in the adoption process has been displaced by statutory agencies. This reflects three changes in entry to the process: a sharp decrease in the number of babies available for third-party placements; a steady increase in first party applicants adopting a child to whom they are related; and increased access to the process by public bodies placing older children or those with complicated health/social care needs. The key professional functions of an adoption agency are likely to include:

- assessing prospective adopters;
- providing pre-placement counselling for birth parents and where appro-priate, for the children concerned;
- providing information to adopters on health, social care and well-being of children to be placed;
- arranging adoption placements;
- assessing and where appropriate meeting any need for post-adoption support services; and
- providing post-adoption counselling, information disclosure and tracing services.

The actual range of functions undertaken by an agency is a good indicator of whether the adoption process of any given jurisdiction is primarily a public or private process. In the UK, these functions are now much more likely to be implemented by the staff of a local authority than by a voluntary agency. In the US, voluntary or commercial adoption agencies now play a more prominent role at this crucial stage in the adoption process than state agencies. In Ireland, though a number of voluntary adoption agencies continue to practice, some are in fact wholly run as subsidiaries or agents of their local health board.

The local authority in England, or the equivalent public body in other jurisdictions, plays an additional and important role in relation to the adoption process. The statutory powers available to it for the registration and supervision of adoption agencies are again indicative of the public dimension as is the extent to which it acts as a feeder channel to the adoption process. In some jurisdictions that body will manage the child care context for permanency planning on behalf of children in need of long-term foster care but otherwise be positioned alongside and carefully distanced from the adoption process. In others such a body will ensure that the adoption process is firmly embedded and integrated within its child care context.

The Registrar General, or equivalent official in other jurisdictions, has duties with a bearing on the adoption process, though in effect these are tied to a post-adoption role. At a minimum, these will allow for the collection of information sufficient to identify child, adopters, the date and place in respect of every adoption order issued.

3.   THRESHOLDS FOR ENTERING THE ADOPTION PROCESS: ELIGIBILITY AND SUITABILITY CRITERIA

Access to the adoption process is clearly crucial—Who may be a party to adoption proceedings? Who may be prohibited from participation? The conditions under which this may happen—comprise the acid test of how the public/private balance is struck. The eligibility and suitability criteria as applied to natural parents, the child and to the adopters gives effect to this balance. In almost all western jurisdictions, access to the adoption process is now subject to mandatory professional scrutiny to ensure that all parties meet the threshold criteria and that the placement is at least compatible with the welfare interests of the child. In the UK, this role is performed initially by adoption agency staff in relation to all applications including 'family' adoptions and then by Adoption Panels in respect of all third party adoptions whether child care, intercountry or arranged by a voluntary adoption agency.

3.1.   The child

The child is the starting point and in all jurisdictions the law sets prerequisites for his or her entry into the adoption process.

Firstly, the subject must satisfy certain status requirements; traditionally, this focused on his or her 'legitimacy'. Now it is the child's legal status and their welfare interests, rather than the marital status of his or her parents, that are usually the primary determinants of eligibility for adoption; though not, for example, in Ireland where parental marital status is often the key determinant. At its most basic level, status requirements in virtually all modern western jurisdictions include the necessity that the subject of proceedings meets the legal definition of 'child': he or she must be born and be less than 18 years of age; it is not possible to adopt a foetus; nor is it possible to adopt an adult. Additionally, many jurisdictions stipulate that a young person must not have been previously married though a previous adoption is not necessarily prohibited. Moreover, the necessity of obtaining a fully informed and free parental consent imposes a minimum age requirement as some time must elapse from birth before a mother can be considered capable of making such an important decision; most usually the child has to be at least one week old. Where the child is of sufficient age and understanding then there is usually a legal requirement to either seek their views or to obtain their consent in relation to the proposed adoption; in either case this should be preceded by provision of appropriate information and advice as to all relevant rights.

Secondly, the subject must satisfy availability criteria by being amenable to the courts of the jurisdiction in which he or she is resident. It is usually not possible to lodge an application in respect of a child who is resident elsewhere and thus remains subject to the courts of that jurisdiction.

Thirdly, for most of the history of the adoption process, children in this and other jurisdictions have to satisfy explicit suitability criteria before entering the adoption process. Traditionally, in the UK, Ireland, Australia and in the US a suitable child was one who conformed to an archetypal model by being healthy, white, caucasian, illegitimate and a baby. Now the suitability threshold is implicitly higher for a child in the context of 'family' adoptions and lower as regards 'agency' adoptions. The lower suitability threshold is also now apparent in many jurisdictions by the active targeting of special needs children and those with complex behavioural or health needs for adoption coupled with special post adoption allowances and other forms of support. Most jurisdictions now require matters relating to the child's age, gender, religion, ethnic or cultural background and any special health or social care needs to be specifically addressed by the adoption agency involved. In the UK the agency's Adoption Panel is additionally required to be satisfied, except in relation to 'family' adoptions, that all such matters will be appropriately resolved by the proposed adoption.

In summary, for a child to enter an adoption process most contemporary western jurisdictions require the following criteria to be satisfied:

- the child must be a 'person' known to the law i.e., he or she must have been born;
- the availability of the child must be appropriately authorised;
- the child must also usually satisfy minimum and maximum age limits;

- conditions relating to residence/domicile etc must be satisfied;
- a professional assessment must indicate that adoption would be at least compatible with the specific needs and welfare interests of the child; and
- the consent of the child, where he or she is of sufficient age and discernment, must be obtained.

3.2.   The birth parent/s

In most western jurisdictions the appearance of a birth parent in adoption proceedings will be as either donor parent or respondent. In both instances there is usually a statutory requirement that the parent/s be professionally assessed by a registered adoption agency and have access to a counselling service. In the UK, except for 'family' adoptions, the circumstances of the birth parent/s will also be scrutinised by an Adoption Panel.

In the former case, certain threshold requirements must be met by the relinquishing birth parent/s or legal guardian of a child. Eligibility criteria, for example, as demonstrated by being amenable to the courts though not necessarily resident within the jurisdiction, must be satisfied. Also there must be no evidence of illegal practices; in some jurisdictions this means that the selling or smuggling of children for adoption purposes is specifically prohibited. Whether married or not, in most jurisdictions any parent with full parental responsibility is entitled to voluntarily relinquish a child for adoption; though the consent of the other parent must be obtained or the need for it dispensed with. In some jurisdictions, such as Ireland, this is not the case as it is not legally possible for a married parent to abandon all rights and responsibilities in respect of their child; though, in a few extreme circumstances, these may be removed by court order. An interesting permutation, reflecting the different balance struck between public and private interests in modern western jurisdictions, is the nature and extent of any rights which the birth parent/s may exercise or retain when their child enters the adoption process. In some jurisdictions, such as Northern Ireland, the birth parent/s may determine the religious upbringing of their child. In others, such as New Zealand they have the right to choose the adopters. In the UK jurisdictions and elsewhere, although not for example in Ireland, adoption orders may be made subject to a condition granting rights of ongoing contact in favour of the birth parent/s.

In general, the law imposes least requirements where a child is being voluntarily admitted to the adoption process by his or her unmarried mother. The informed consent of the latter is the only absolute necessity; increasingly in modern western jurisdictions the involvement if not the consent of the unmarried father is also sought. Where the adoption is in respect of an overseas child, then evidence of that consent must be available to the court. Where the need for parental consent is obviated by permanent absence, death or by judicial removal of parental rights the court will instead require the consent of the person or body legally charged with responsibility for the child. In some jurisdictions legislation provides for circumstances in which consent may be revoked.

Traditionally 'legitimate' children could not be adopted within the lifetime of either parent, as this was viewed as undermining the legal integrity of the marital family unit. Usually, however, the law no longer draws such an inference. Provided evidence of legal status and the necessary consents are available, then in most jurisdictions any parent or parents, whether married or not, may enter the adoption process on a consensual or coercive basis; Ireland being a notable exception. Where the birth parent is appearing as respondent, for example a divorced father objecting to the adoption of his marital child, the court is usually unable to make the adoption order unless statutory grounds exist for dispensing with his consent.

In summary, the role of the birth parent/s at point of entry to the adoption process will, in most contemporary western jurisdictions, require the following criteria to be satisfied:

- ascertaining legal status regarding marriage, domicile, residence, parental responsibilities etc;
- post-counselling consent of birth mother;
- notice served upon or consent of birth father;
- consent for disclosure of health information on child; and
- ascertaining any pre-conditions for adoption.

3.3. The adopters

Adopters, in particular, must meet the full rigour of threshold requirements; though the onus falls unevenly on applicants according to whether they are first or third party adopters.

Generally, third party applicants, with in the eyes of the law no inherent reason to offer love care and protection to a child to whom they are unrelated, are required to satisfy both eligibility and suitability criteria. The law governing this varies considerably from jurisdiction to jurisdiction. So, for example, in the UK both sets of criteria have traditionally been applied quite prescriptively, in the US they have always been liberally interpreted while in Ireland considerable importance has been attached to an obligation placed upon adopters to ensure the religious upbringing of a child conforms with that of the birth parent/s. In the UK, the responsibility for ensuring that both sets of criteria are satisfied falls in the first instance to the adoption agency involved and then, except for 'family' adoptions, to the relevant Adoption Panel.

Eligibility criteria usually require adopters to satisfy statutory conditions relating to:

- marital status;
- residence/domicile;
- income or financial means;
- no evidence of having procured child by illegal means;
- character, or lack of serious criminal convictions; and
- minimum age.

Suitability criteria are additionally required by adoption agencies and although varying to some degree depending on according to whether they are being approved for a specific child or more generally, these will include matters such as:

- maximum age;
- religious and racial compatibility;
- state of good health;
- appropriate motivation;
- quality and duration of relationships; and
- cultural background and lifestyle.

In recent years certain practice and policy developments have driven some significant changes to the law as in relates to third party adopters. Firstly, a growing volume of intercountry adoptions attracting less rigorous professional scrutiny than other third party applicants led eventually to the Convention on Protection of Children and Co-operation in respect of Intercountry Adoption 1993 which introduced specific legislative provisions that now regulate adopters in this context. Secondly, a policy to maximise the number and range of child care adoptions forced a change in agency perception of adopter eligibility and suitability criteria in application to the often complex health and social care needs of the children in public care. This saw a change in professional emphasis from an 'adopter led' to a 'child led' approach. Instead of responding to applications by identifying 'normal' adopters to be carefully matched—in accordance with characteristics such as race, religion, class and physiological features—to normal 'children' adoption agencies began to sift, sometimes actively recruiting, adopters according to their skills and aptitudes to cope with children with 'special needs'. In many jurisdictions, this has led to a broadening practice interpretation of eligibility and suitability criteria which has come to accommodate adopters who differed from the traditional type by being perhaps older, single, mixed race or of gay or lesbian sexual orientation. Again, in many jurisdictions, the increased availability of post-adoption support services also eased access to the process.

First party applicants, however, have traditionally attracted a relaxed approach: eligibility criteria were viewed as unlikely to be contentious and suitability criteria as unlikely to be relevant as the child would, in any event, almost always remain in the care of the applicants—much the same approach is currently evident as regards applications by long-term foster carers. An increase in the rate of family breakdown and with it the rise in serial parenting arrangements has seen the adoption process in many jurisdictions being used more by birth parents to secure rather than relinquish rights to their children. In response, many such jurisdiction have in recent years been enacting laws requiring first party applicants to demonstrate that adoption, rather than any other order, is a better means of promoting the welfare of the child concerned.

4. PRE-PLACEMENT COUNSELLING

It is a requirement of the law in general that any consent must be informed and given freely with a full appreciation of the consequences. In the context of the adoption 'contract' this often requires a counselling service to be made available to all parties at least for that purpose but most usually also for the purpose of assessing any needs, support or service requirements they may have as they prepare to enter the adoption process. The counselling is not always provided by the agency responsible for placing the child, indeed this would often be unwise, but that agency is usually the one responsible for ensuring its provision. Most jurisdictions now have legislative provisions requiring that pre-placement counselling services be offered to all parties.

4.1. The birth parent/s

Pre-placement counselling services are most usually arranged, if not provided, by adoption agencies and directed towards the birth parent/s of children the agency is considering placing for adoption; traditionally a service associated with the needs of unmarried mothers. In most jurisdictions the provision of this service is now a statutory requirement to be offered to both parents regardless of their marital status; although in relation to fathers, the duty is sometimes restricted to the provision of counselling services to those with legal parental responsibilities. At a minimum the service entails advising the parent/s as to the legal consequences of any adoption decision taken in respect of their child, providing the information necessary and ensuring that this has all been fully understood. It also entails exploring with them all feasible alternative options and, insofar as the law of the jurisdiction permits, establishing whether the parent/s wish to exercise any residual rights in relation to their child such as to maintain a level of contact or determine nature of religious upbringing. It may extend to offering a therapeutic relationship enabling the parent/s to work through their feelings and be reconciled to the decision taken. The duty to provide this service now falls mainly on public care agencies and is most often directed towards the birth parent/s whose child is to be the subject of a compulsory adoption placement by that agency. In such cases parental consent is not always an issue but in all other cases the onus rests on the service provider to satisfy themselves that a fully informed consent has been given and given free from any undue pressure.

4.2.   The child

Where the child concerned is of an appropriate age and level of understanding, then there is usually a statutory requirement that the adoption agency involved at least seeks their views and ensures that a counselling service is provided appropriate to that child's needs. Again, the service is directed as a minimum towards ensuring that appropriate information is made available, that all feasible options are explored and that the child has an understanding of the consequences that will follow from the making of an adoption order. The counselling will take into account any issues arising from the child's age, gender, religion, ethnic or cultural background and any special health or social care needs. In relation to a 'mature minor' the duty may be to establish whether he or she fully consents to the proposed adoption in addition to the obligation to provide a counselling service. The latter may extend to exploring the child's attitude towards maintaining contact with members of his or her family of origin. It will involve advising the child regarding any rights the law of their jurisdiction may provide in relation to matters such as contact conditions and post-adoption access to information. Such work is often viewed as requiring a high level of skill and may necessitate the involvement of specialists.

4.3.   The adopters

Again, most jurisdictions impose a statutory obligation upon adoption agencies to provide such counselling as is necessary to ensure that prospective adopters fully understand and accept the legal consequences that will follow from the making of an adoption order. This duty will usually require the agency to satisfy itself that the prospective adopters appreciate the effects of an adoption order on their rights and responsibilities in relation to matters such as care and protection, inheritance and citizenship. It will entail ensuring that they understand and are willing to comply with any possible conditions that may represent the ongoing legal rights of others in relation to matters such as contact and religious upbringing. It will explore their knowledge of and entitlement to any available professional support services, adoption allowances etc. The counselling should also address issues of willingness to share information with the child as to his or her family and perhaps culture of origin and their acceptance of the child's eventual right to access information held in agency files. The prospective adopters will most usually have counselling opportunities available to them in the context of their relationship with the assessing and/or the placing adoption agency (where, as in intercountry adoptions, these are the functions of separate agencies).

5. PLACEMENT RIGHTS AND RESPONSIBILITIES

In practice, a child enters the adoption process when he or she is placed with prospective adopters. This placement decision must be taken by a person or body with the requisite authority; an initial consent is a legal necessity.

5.1. Placement decision

Traditionally, this decision was a private one taken by birth parent/s or guardian in the belief that it offered the best way of serving the child's welfare interests. It was sometimes implemented by a direct placement or by placement through the good offices of an intermediary. It was most often implemented in favour of a third party or stranger but not infrequently a relative such as an uncle or grandparent was the parental choice for placement. It necessitated a complete change in the child's living environment. In some jurisdictions, such as in New Zealand and certain states within the US, choice of placement may still be determined by the birth parent/s. In the UK jurisdictions and in most other modern western nations, this traditional right has been statutorily removed and replaced by a requirement that the placement decision is taken by a registered adoption agency.

Nowadays, in many jurisdictions, the majority of such decisions are still taken privately, by birth mothers supported by their spouses, but these are decisions to adopt rather than to relinquish the children concerned. Whereas most adoption decisions are still authorised by birth parents, they now do not necessarily entail a change of placement.

In addition, in all jurisdictions a growing proportion of decisions are public policy driven. Most evident are those relating to children in public care. In the UK, following policy developed in the US, specific statutory grounds for dispensing with parental consent and authorising an adoption placement despite parental opposition have been in place for some years (see, further, below). Decisions taken by the courts—subsequent to child care proceedings initiated by health authorities on the grounds of parental abuse, neglect or inadequacy—are now determining the placements of many children. Judicial decisions, however, are preceded by those of child care professionals which in some jurisdictions, such as those of the UK, are in turn based upon the recommendations of an Adoption Panel. To this body falls the responsibility to assess and make recommendations regarding all child care and intercountry adoption placements.

The policy initiatives of foreign jurisdictions have also played a significant role in fuelling the rise in numbers of intercountry placements. For example, in

China the introduction of the government policy to strongly recommend limits to the number and gender of children born to marital couples and the policy of the Romanian government to make available the occupants of its state orphanages to foreign adopters have both directly led to many thousands of placements for children in home environments far removed from their kin and cultural contexts of birth.

5.2.   Placement supervision

In most jurisdictions there is a legal requirement to ensure that an adoption placement is safeguarded until such time as a court or other body determines whether or not an adoption order is to be made in respect of the child concerned. The duties to safeguard the child's welfare interests rest most rigorously upon all placement agencies but apply also, though with less intrusiveness, to family adoptions from notification to hearing. Most usually, once made the placement cannot be terminated without prior approval of the placing agency or court.

6.   THE HEARING AND ISSUE OF ORDER/S

In most jurisdictions, although not in Ireland, the hearing of an adoption application is a judicial process. Whether judicial or administrative, satisfying the statutory grounds relating to eligibility, suitability and consent will itself be insufficient to allow the process to conclude with a granting of the order sought. Whereas any contested application will fail because the statutory grounds have not been met no contested or uncontested application (even where the grounds have been met) will succeed unless the court is assured that the welfare test is also fully satisfied. Applying the test may result in the issue of an altogether different order or no order at all.

6.1.   Where consent is available

Adoption in the UK and elsewhere was traditionally a largely consensual process. Where the necessary consents were available or could be dispensed with and all statutory criteria were met then no obstacle existed to prevent a court or similar body from concluding the adoption process by granting the order sought. Nowadays in most jurisdictions the informed consent of an older child, the subject of proceedings, will also be sought; though this is not always regarded as determinative. In many jurisdictions, the availability of all required consents will not necessarily prevent consideration of whether an order other than the one sought would not offer a more appropriate means of ensuring the welfare of the child concerned.

6.2.   Where consent is not available

In recent decades, non-consensual adoption applications have become a prominent feature of the law in many countries. Adoption law, in modern western
jurisdictions, now often provides specific statutory grounds for dispensing with
parental consent on grounds of child neglect or abuse as well as on the traditional
grounds of parental absence, incapacity or death. Allowance is also generally
made for contested family adoptions.

6.2.1.   GROUNDS IN CHILD CARE ADOPTION

In the context of third party adoptions, the specific synchronisation of some
grounds for dispensing with parental consent with those of child care legislation
is a very significant development in modern family law. The effect of introducing
grounds of parental fault, closely aligned to those already established in public
child care legislation, as justifying an application for freeing or for adoption has finally bridged the gap between the public and private sectors of this law. The rights
of an abusing parent who falls foul of statutory care proceedings may now not only
be qualified by the issue of a care order but may also be abrogated by an adoption
order. From statutory origins based on serving the private parental interests of a
closed nuclear family unit, the legal functions of adoption in most jurisdictions
have now been strategically re-positioned to openly serve a public interest in rescuing a child from parental abuse and providing permanent alternative family care.

6.2.2.   GROUNDS IN CONTESTED FAMILY ADOPTION

In the context of first party adoptions, non-consensual applications also pose
a fundamental dilemma for the policy, law and practice of modern western jurisdictions. As parenting becomes less marriage based and features looser ties
with extended family networks, transient home and locality links and serial care
arrangements, the circumstances in which it can be safely predicted that the permanence and exclusive nature of an adoption order will be an appropriate legal
intervention in private family relationships are decreasing. The use of adoption
as an extreme form of parental custody order is becoming a policy issue in many
countries. Some jurisdictions now provide a statutory power for alternative orders
to be made as indicated by the welfare interests of the child concerned, in either
public or private family law, at judicial discretion.

6.3.   The orders available

Adoption being traditionally regarded as a matter of private family law, it was
often customary to legislatively provide the judiciary with the power to make

an alternative private law order in the rare event of an adoption application not succeeding. Some jurisdictions provide such a power to be used in circumstances where the grounds for adoption have not been satisfied but those for an alternative order in private or public law can be met. Yet again, there are jurisdictions where the matter is left totally to judicial discretion; the order to be made is the one which is most appropriate to the welfare interests of the particular child.

7.   THRESHOLDS FOR EXITING THE ADOPTION PROCESS

There is no general right to adopt or to be adopted. In all modern western juris-dictions, the legal function applied by the court or similar body in concluding adoption proceedings is that of making a determination which is at least compat-ible with the best interests of the particular child. This 'welfare test' universally provides the single over-riding threshold criterion for exiting the adoption process.

7.1.   The welfare interests of the child

Whether an adoption order can be made is determined in accordance with the statutory criteria relating to eligibility, suitability and consent. Whether it will be made is determined by the welfare test. The welfare test in adoption proceedings has three functions:

- it identifies the 'substance' of welfare in relation to the child concerned;
- it indicates the professionals required/permitted to bring welfare related matters before the court; and
- it defines the weighting to be given to such matters in deciding whether or not to make an adoption order.

Firstly, the making of an adoption order is conditional upon a finding that to do so would be at least compatible with the welfare interests of the child concerned; which entails a careful analysis of matters constituting the particular welfare interests of that child. The wishes of an older child regarding his or her proposed adoption have to be ascertained and taken into account. Expert witnesses may be called to give evidence and that evidence may have a determining weight. Whether contested or not, information on matters constituting welfare interests will invariably be required by the court or other such body before any decision is taken.

Secondly, in most jurisdictions the duty to bring welfare considerations be-fore the court rests heavily on a range of specified agencies and/or on such court officers as a guardian *ad litem*. Usually this duty necessitates completion of comprehensive reports detailing the family background and needs of the child, his or her views—where appropriate—regarding the proposed adoption and a professional assessment of the probable outcome for the child if the order is made. In some jurisdictions there are legislative provisions requiring the legal representation of a child's rights and welfare interests before determination of an adoption application can be made.

Thirdly, the weighting given to the welfare factor in adoption proceedings has always been a contentious matter reflecting the balance struck in any jurisdiction between public/private interests and parent/child rights in this area of family law. Traditionally in the UK, both legislative intent and judicial practice have painstakingly differentiated between the paramount weighting given to welfare interests in child care proceedings and a lesser weighting ascribed to such interests in adoption proceedings. While in England this distinction has now been statutorily erased following a government policy initiative to expedite child care adoptions, it continues in Northern Ireland where the law has not yet been similarly amended and it has long prevailed in the Republic of Ireland. The weighting given to welfare interests will also usually differ to some degree in relation to the class of applicant. So, first party applicants may not be subject to the same level of pre-placement scrutiny as third party applicants while non-consensual applicants may find their adoption order qualified by a contact condition imposed to safeguard an aspect of a child's welfare.

8.   THE OUTCOME OF THE ADOPTION PROCESS

In all modern western jurisdictions, legislative intent began by being almost exclusively concerned with regulating the consensual third party applications of indigenous, healthy and in all respects 'normal' non-marital babies. From that common starting point each jurisdiction has steadily adjusted its legislative provisions in response to the pressure from emerging areas of common social need which has inevitably led to a change in the balance struck between public and private interests.

8.1.   Adoption orders and third party applicants

This, the type of order originally legislated for, has everywhere declined both in aggregate and as a proportion of total annual orders.

Unconditional, consensual, third party adoption orders now form a minority of the annual output. This is so despite the fact that orders in respect of children from overseas are of increasing numerical significance and those made in respect of children suffering from learning difficulties, physical disability or behavioural problems are becoming more common. Unconditional but contested adoption orders, where the opposition is from a culpable parent or parents, form a significant and growing proportion of annual orders made. The child concerned will often be the subject of a care order and may well be 'legitimate'.

Conditional adoption orders, usually permitting contact with a member of the adopted child's family of origin but sometimes requiring a specified religious upbringing, now constitute a growing proportion of annual orders. In most jurisdictions, qualified orders are becoming a characteristic of the adoption process in that they represent an increasing public commitment to acknowledge and promote the independent interests of a child, over and above the interests of birth and adoptive parents, before and after the issue of an adoption order. This is also apparent in the statutory provision of post-adoption support services which again indicates a recognition that the long-term welfare interests of an adopted child may well require to be sustained by public resources.

8.2.   Adoption orders and first party applicants

In most modern western jurisdictions, unconditional consensual orders in favour of first party applicants have for some years constituted the main outcome of the adoption process. Except in Ireland, these orders are likely to be in respect of children who are 'legitimate'. They often concern older children and, because such applications are open to professional and judicial challenge on their merits, some are likely to be diverted to other proceedings. A characteristic of such adoptions in many jurisdictions is the fact that some orders will also be made subject to a contact condition.

8.3.   Adoption orders and relatives

A feature of the adoption process in many contemporary modern jurisdictions is the growing minority of orders now made in favour of grandparents. These applications are susceptible to professional or judicial challenge.

8.4.   Other orders

The outcome of a small but growing proportion of adoption proceedings is now likely to be the issue of an order other than the one sought. In the UK and in Ireland, whether contested or not, an adoption application may at judicial discretion conclude in the issue of a different private law order.

9. THE EFFECT OF AN ADOPTION ORDER

In most if not all jurisdictions the traditional outcome of the adoption process for many generations was either no order or a full order with its characteristic permanent, exclusive and absolute legal effects on all parties. This has been dramatically changed in all modern western jurisdictions by the statutory introduction of information rights, contact registers, schemes for payment and support and the possibility of conditions being attached to adoption orders or the issue of alternative orders. In particular, the traditional consequences of an order on the legal status of the parties involved have also changed.

9.1. Effect on the child

Generally, the law in most jurisdictions states the primary effects of an adoption order to be that thereafter the child's legal status cannot be anything other than 'legitimate', he or she will bear the surname of the adopters and in all respects is to be treated in law as their child. Because the child's status is thereafter defined by that of the adopters so also, for the duration of childhood, are all matters of residence, domicile and nationality. The succession rights of an adopted child are usually expressly addressed by legislation and provide that for most purposes there should be no distinction between the inheritance rights of a parent's natural and adopted children. Usually, also, such legislation provides that adoption does not affect the law relating to marriage and incest (i.e. an adopted person may not marry anyone he or she would have been prohibited from marrying if the adoption had not occurred). In short the legal effect of an adoption order on the status of the child concerned will most usually be:

- prevention of 'illegitimacy';
- assumption of the same name, residence, domicile and citizenship as the adopters;
- assumption of the same inheritance rights as an adopter's birth child; and
- the acquisition of such rights as may be attached by condition to the order.

These legal incidences of adoption invariably apply regardless of the type of adoption (e.g. 'open' or intercountry etc.) and will prevail throughout childhood.

9.2. Effect on the birth parent/s

Again, in most jurisdictions the law states the primary effects of adoption on the birth parent/s to be the abrupt, permanent and absolute termination of their rights and responsibilities in respect of the adopted child. It will also operate to extinguish any court order relating to the child and any agency directive requiring payments for the child's maintenance or upbringing. The law is not always as certain regarding the right of the child to inherit from the birth parent/s; in some jurisdictions the adopted child will retain the right to benefit from the estate of the birth parent/s unless specifically excluded. However, for most purposes the birth parent/s will be treated in law as if the child had never been born to them. In summary, the main legal effects of adoption on the birth parent/s are to:

- terminate all parental rights and responsibilities;
- extinguish any court order imposing any liability upon them in relation to the child;
- remove any obligation to provide for the child by will or testament; and
- to grant such rights as may be attached by condition to the order.

9.3.   Effect on the adopters

The law in most jurisdictions states the primary effect of an adoption order on the adopters to be the vesting in them of all parental rights and responsibilities in respect of the adopted child. There is usually a specific legislative provision declaring that in any will, testament or in the event of intestacy, in the absence of any statement to the contrary, the estate of the adopters will devolve to the adopted child as though the latter was their birth child. For most purposes the birth parent/s will be treated in law as if the child had been born to them, though in some jurisdictions exceptions are made to the rules relating to consanguinity so as to permit marriage within degrees of blood relationship that would otherwise be prohibited. The main legal effects of an adoption order on the adopters are to:

- vest in them all parental rights and responsibilities, subject to such constraints as may be specified in any attached condition/s; and
- create a presumption of entitlement to inherit from their estate.

10.   POST-ADOPTION SUPPORT SERVICES

Traditionally, in keeping with the essentially private nature of adoption, once an order was made then the door was closed on the newly formed family unit, professional intrusion in its affairs ended and no further contact with public service agencies was anticipated. However, in recent years there has been a growing recognition that such families should be entitled to call upon the state for ongoing support services as required. As many jurisdictions began to accommodate and give effect to a policy of increased use of adoption as a resource for public care bodies, it has become customary for the latter to facilitate this by providing such short or long-term support services as are likely to sustain the child within that care arrangement. Currently, these support services are usually confined to third party rather than first party adopters and are only occasionally extended to benefit the birth parent/s.

10.1. Child care adoptions

In a child care context, the making of an adoption order marks a double change in the status of the child concerned. He or she is legally transplanted not only from one family to another but also from public to private care. In modern adoption practice and particularly in the context of child care adoption, this transfer is no longer between two necessarily mutually exclusive settings. The child adopted from a public care background is likely to differ from the subject of a traditional adoption by being older, have special health or social care needs and to have formed attachments necessary for promoting his or her post-adoption welfare interests. In all modern western jurisdictions there is now a much greater willingness on the part of adoption agencies, courts and the families concerned to facilitate a carry-over of those relationships, services and professional input deemed important for the welfare of the child in their post-adoption life.

Adoption allowances are the most common form of support service and have a particular significance for child care adoptions. In the main they are used to continue the support provided to carers under the foster care allowance scheme before they elected to adopt the child they previously fostered. Allowances are also important in securing and supporting adoption placements for those requiring particularly high levels of attention, such as disabled children, sibling groups or those with complex health care or special needs. In many jurisdictions counselling services are quite prevalent particularly in the increasing number of cases where ongoing contact arrangements are in place to maintain relationships between the adopted child and members of their family of origin. The provision of other specialist services tends to vary in accordance with the particular needs of the children adopted but may include respite care, the services of psychologists and psychiatrists, occupational therapy, speech therapy and possibly nursing care. At a minimum, however, post-adoption support services will consist of:

- adoption allowances; and
- counselling services.

11. INFORMATION DISCLOSURE, TRACING AND RE-UNIFICATION SERVICES

The traditional guarantee of absolute and permanent confidentiality, given by an adoption agency to a mother voluntarily relinquishing her baby for adoption, has become steadily diluted in all modern jurisdictions in recent years. An adopted person now generally has the right to information about the fact and circumstances of their adoption, the means for accessing that information and an entitlement to related counselling services. The statutory introduction of information disclosure procedures, contact registers, tracing and re-unification services have transformed some of the more traditional characteristics of adoption.

11.1.   Information rights

In most jurisdictions information disclosure is associated with rights of the adopted person rather than with the needs of adopters or the natural parent/s. This right is generally restricted to the adopted adult. For an adopted child, that is where such a young person has not reached the age of 18, it would be most unusual for him or her to have a statutory right to access birth records.

Legislative provisions and procedures enabling an adopted person to acquire by right information relating to the circumstances of the adoption have now been introduced in many countries. So, an adopted person under the age of 18 and intending to be married may apply to the Registrar General, or other such body, for a declaration that the intended spouse is not within the prohibited degrees of relationship for the purposes of marriage law. An adopted person over that age usually has the right to make a similar application for a copy of their original birth certificate and has a right of access to information relating to the circumstances of their adoption. For an adult adopted person seeking to access information about his or her sperm donor father, however, where relevant legislation exists this can vary considerably among modern western jurisdictions.

Prospective adopters are generally entitled to full disclosure of information relating to any child placed with them, or approved for placement with them, for adoption purposes. The birth parent/s generally have no rights to access information relating to the adopters identity nor to the post-adoption circumstances and whereabouts of the child.

11.2.   Information disclosure duties

In addition to the above statutory duties of the Registrar General, or similar government body, it is now also customary to have information disclosure obligations placed upon such other relevant bodies as the courts and public health care agencies. However, it is the adoption agencies that are central to the adoption process and serve as the primary repository for all adoption information.

By virtue of its initial critical role with at least the birth parent/s and child if not also the adopters, the adoption agency will later be the primary source of information relating to the personal history and circumstances of those parties. For the adopted adult seeking access to information and perhaps to relatives associated with his or her birth family, through the statutory procedures available, all avenues will lead back to the relevant adoption agency. The usefulness of the disclosure procedures will be wholly dependent upon the amount and quality of information recorded and held on file by the agency. In most jurisdictions there are now legislative provisions requiring adoption agencies to maintain their records for a specified minimum period; usually not less than 50 years (see, further, Part III).

11.3. Tracing and re-unification services

For some adopted persons access to information is not enough and contact is sought with a relative, most usually a birth parent, who may well have reciprocal needs. Many jurisdictions have introduced 'contact registers' as a means of facilitating the mutually compatible needs of these parties. The purpose of such a register is to hold and co-ordinate information relating to desired contact between adopted persons and members of their family of origin. Right of access to the register is invariably restricted to adopted persons of not less than 18 years of age: any public inspection and search of the registers, books and records are prohibited. The usefulness of this service is restricted to situations where there is matching information in the contact register; many birth parents choose not to be contacted and do not file information.

The next step for many adopted persons is to attempt to meet with their birth parent/s; though the latter may also initiate this process. Most jurisdictions now have a statutory or voluntary procedure whereby the relevant adoption agency will undertake to trace and contact the relative and relay the request for a meeting. Where both parties agree, it is probable that the agency will effect introductions and mediate at least in the initial encounters.

12. ADOPTION WITHIN FAMILY LAW

In modern western societies, being a parent is now largely a matter of private individual choice. Serial parenting arrangements, together with the medical developments which allow adults to choose or reject the option of parenthood, have undone the centrifugal significance that the nuclear marital family once had within the body of private family law. In public family law, an increase in the incidence or detection of child abuse and neglect has led to the development of ever more pervasive interventionist strategies by public child care agencies in relation to families. On both the private and public fronts there has been a retreat from the traditional presumption that the legal integrity of the family should be upheld and a falling back to the safer ground that however families constitute or re-constitute themselves they must ensure the welfare interests of any child involved.

Adoption is intimately linked to the different public and private proceedings that constitute family law. While it has traditionally reflected the principles of private law, in many modern contemporary western societies it now embodies and is being shaped by the more pervasive principles and pressures influencing practice within the broad body of family law. Adoption has come to incorporate principles drawn from the public and private sectors and this enables it to bridge them both and to perhaps play a key role in bringing a new coherence to law, policy and practice in this area.

12.1. Adoption in its traditional family law context

Traditionally, adoption was the ultimate private family law proceeding; no other order in public or private family law had such an extreme effect. It was wholly a creature of private law: initiated by private applicants; allowing for minimum professional intrusion; and concluding in an order that resolutely sealed the private boundaries of the new family unit. Arguably, this was strongly associated with the dominant patriarchical model of the family unit as upheld by Victorian society, entrenched in legislation and vigorously defended in the courts. A legacy that thereafter endured in the legal importance attached to status, to the integrity and autonomy of the family and in the significance of rights of inheritance, perpetuation of the family name etc. The role of adoption and the functions it was initially legislatively established to serve in western society may be viewed as intimately tied to the Victorian legacy of the patriarchical family unit.

In recent years, status in family law has become a much more elastic concept. Illegitimacy, marriage, divorce, residence, 'child of the family' etc are among many examples of designations which have now largely lost their clear and almost immutable capacity to define the status of parties which they held for generations in the family law proceedings of many jurisdictions.

Initially, the law was concerned to recognise and protect the marital family unit as the necessary foundation for society and the essential prerequisite for a body of family law. The private sanctity of this unit was afforded special protection. The law regarded status as emblematic of certain specific sets of rights and duties thereby vested in adults and defining their personal and private legal capacities. Private family law and the statutory processes for conferring or extinguishing status were limited in number, clearly defined, absolute and permanent in their effects and rigorously policed by the courts. Public family law was non-interventionist and largely directed towards policing parental behaviour that threatened or did not conform to the norms represented by the marital family unit.

As times changed the emphasis moved away from protecting the special position of the marital family unit, and the concomitant status of the parties concerned, towards protecting instead the welfare interests of children. Family law is now primarily concerned with giving effect to the public interest in safeguarding the welfare of any child who may be affected by the outcome of status related proceedings whether these are public or private.

12.2. Adoption in the context of modern public law proceedings

In most western jurisdictions, the state as 'guardian of last resort' continues to undertake its traditional duty to provide for the public care of children in circumstances where private care is impossible: usually where parents are dead, missing, cannot exercise proper control; or have been convicted of abuse, neglect or of otherwise failing to exercise adequate care and protection in respect of their children. More recently, in keeping with the ethos of 'partnership' between child care agencies and parents, such care may also be provided with parental consent; usually for reasons of parental respite, training or illness. In either case the law has usually been at pains to ensure that the limited and specific duties of public child care agencies should not be convertible into a power to make a compulsory adoption placement. Parental consent has been upheld as the essential legal passport for a child to pass from public care to private family via adoption.

In many contemporary societies this is no longer the case. Equating the grounds for entry to public care with those of non-consensual third party adoption has been a most significant development for family law as a discipline. This policy is one that now clearly differentiates the family law of modern western jurisdictions.

12.3. Adoption in the context of modern private law proceedings

In most jurisdictions, the legal functions of adoption were legislatively defined and carefully separated from those of such other private law proceedings as guardianship, wardship and matrimonial proceedings; each occupied its own separate well-defined and discrete space within the body of private family law. The legal functions of each were tightly contained, exercised on a once-off basis to achieve permanency in the status awarded by their respective orders. The emphasis was on clarifying the rights and duties of spouses and parents in proceedings initiated by them and in which professional or other agency intrusion was minimal. The legal functions, where they concerned the interests of children, were more about them than for them.

This has greatly changed in most modern western jurisdictions. Adoption is now closely aligned to matrimonial proceedings: the legal functions of the former most often being used as an adjunct to the latter; to assimilate the legal status of either a pre-marital child or one from a previous marital relationship. Other proceedings for broad grants of authority, such as in guardianship and wardship, have largely been displaced by narrower, a range more specific orders that now offer a variety of options dealing with matters such as where and with whom a child is to live, contact arrangements, prohibited conduct etc. Further, the *locus standi* of parents, traditionally central to those proceedings, is being challenged by a new recognition accorded to those who bear direct and continuous care responsibility, whether or not they are related to the child concerned.

Although an adoption order continues to alter the status of the three parties involved, the order itself has changed. Its previous draconian effects have been ameliorated by the statutory introduction of possible qualifications. Instead of vesting/divesting wholly and permanently all incidents of status, an adoption order may now provide for an arrangement which permits a sharing of status attributes. This is indicative of a more generalised and international movement to the same effect in family law as a discipline.

12.4.   Adoption and contemporary family law principles

The contemporary concept of 'family' in modern western society has changed considerably from the Victorian patriarchical model, resting on monogamous marital union for life, on which the family law of such a society was constructed. The UN now defines 'family' as:

> Any combination of two or more persons who are bound together by ties of mutual consent, birth and/or adoption or placement and who, together, assume responsibility for, *inter alia*, the care and maintenance of group members through procreation or adoption, the socialisation of children and the social control of members.

The legal functions of adoption are indicative of those occurring elsewhere in family law as the entire body of law becomes slowly more integrated around certain key principles.

12.4.1.   WELFARE OF THE CHILD

In all modern western jurisdictions, there is now an unmistakable emphasis on ensuring that family law proceedings satisfy a general public interest requirement that all arrangements for the future upbringing of children are subject to much the same controls and supports and are tested against other options before they are legally sanctioned by court order. Mostly, this is evident in the use of the welfare principle to ensure that private and public proceedings are subject to the test that the outcome secures and promotes the welfare interests of the child. This may entail compromises to the order issued by the court that would not have been previously countenanced in neither private nor public family law. From a position where the welfare principle was accorded a paramount weighting in a restricted number of proceedings and in relation to specified matters, it is now gradually permeating all family law in most jurisdictions.

12.4.2. RIGHTS OF THE CHILD

The powerful influence of Convention rights and case law has in recent years made this principle of central importance to the family proceedings of all modern western jurisdictions.

The step from welfare interests to rights is one which has been made in order to equip children to take their place in an adversarial court system where the numbers of adult litigants, the costs and the shortage of court time might otherwise cause their interests to be treated in a cursory, subservient and paternalistic fashion. The fact of party status, entitlement to legal aid, access to a range of professional support and representation and full exposure to the dynamics of adversarial family law proceedings are among the more prominent accompaniments of a rights approach. The balance to be struck between a child's welfare interests and their rights is a contentious issue for many jurisdictions.

12.4.3. PARENTAL RESPONSIBILITY

The increased salience given to the interests and rights of children in the family law of modern western jurisdictions has been accompanied by a corresponding decline in the traditional central importance attached to parental rights. The displacement of rights by the principle of parental responsibility has marked a shift in emphasis in family law from structure to content, from status to protection; parents are legally empowered to re-configure their adult-to-adult relationships but have the duty to do so in ways that enable them to continue being responsible for their children. The new priority given to protecting the welfare interests of children has led to a hardening of the onus on those in a position to afford that protection. Certain concepts such as 'fault' have lost their traditional currency; spouses and parents will in law be held accountable for the consequences, whether intended or not, of their actions or inactions. Other concepts such as 'unreasonableness' now pervade family law as indicators of failure to uphold the responsibilities of spouse or parent and justifying removal of their rights as such.

13.   CONCLUSION

Adoption—law, policy and practice—represents in a particularly intimate and fundamental way the essential characteristics of its society at a specific time and stage in its cultural development. The social functions of adoption reflect the society of which it is a part and are adjusted by it in response to emerging pressures. The legal functions of adoption, being internally referenced and remaining relatively fixed, retain their basic characteristics. This chapter has identified the sequence of stages that constitute the modern adoption process and the range of essential and possible legal functions that are available to give effect to the legislatively determined purposes of each stage. In so doing it has outlined a template to be applied in later chapters to identify and explore the permutations that constitute the legal functions of adoption in other jurisdictions and so permit a comparative evaluation of its social role.

Chapter 4

INTERNATIONAL BENCHMARKS FOR MODERN ADOPTION LAW

1.   INTRODUCTION

National adoption proceedings take place within an overall context of rights, duties and principles set by international legislation. In the UK, when applying the provisions of adoption legislation to the circumstances of any particular case, it will now often be necessary to also have regard not only to relevant domestic legislation, such as the Children Act 1989 and the Adoption and Children Act 2002, but also to Convention law and principles and to a rapidly expanding body of international case law.

'Convention law' is usually taken as a reference to either the United Nations Convention on the Rights of the Child 1989 or the European Convention for the Protection of Human Rights and Fundamental Freedoms 1950[1] or to both. In fact the Hague Convention on Protection of Children and Co-operation in Respect of Intercountry Adoption 1993 together with the United Nations Declaration on Social and Legal Principles relating to the Protection and Welfare of Children with Special Reference to Foster Placement and Adoption Nationally and Internationally 1986 are also very relevant as they provide the framework for regulating intercountry adoption. All these Conventions contribute to the building of an international rights context for the adoption of children. They also further

---

[1]   See, further, http://www.unicef.org/crc/ and <http://www.echr.coe.int> respectively. Also, note that the Council of Europe, on 03.05.02, adopted the Convention on Contact concerning Children; see, <http://convention.coe.int>.

the growing international harmonisation of principles and processes in family law. This chapter is mainly concerned with examining how the development of modern adoption policy, law and practice has been influenced by the Conventions of 1950, 1989, and 1993. Although the effects are considered in relation to the UK, the generic nature of the principles and the remit of the Conventions ensure their equal applicability to other jurisdictions.

2.   THE UNITED NATIONS CONVENTION ON THE RIGHTS OF THE CHILD 1989

The UN Convention on the Rights of the Child was ratified by the UK on December 16, 1991 and has been signed by nearly 200 countries. It lists 42 substantive rights that comprehensively address the needs of children—including Articles 18, 20, 21, and 35 with direct relevance to adoption—and requires the courts in the UK to ensure that decisions broadly comply with the general and specific obligations set out in the Convention. While the Convention has no specifically designated enforcement mechanism, the UN Committee on the Rights of the Child does make recommendations to states, on the basis of reports filed with it under Art. 44, for improvements in national law and practice. For example, in 2002 the Committee's recommendations included:

1. That the legislation governing procedure in courts and administrative proceedings (including divorce and separation proceedings) ensure that a child capable of forming his/her own views has the right to express those views and that they are given due weight.
2. That the State party establish throughout the State party the best interests of the child as a paramount consideration in all legislation and policy affecting children.

The following are some of the more significant provisions of the UN Convention with relevance for adoption law and practice.

2.1.   Article 2—the non-discrimination principle

Article 2 directs that all Convention rights are to apply to children without exception and without discrimination of any kind. This applies irrespective of the child's—or his or her parent's or guardian's—race, colour, sex, language, religion, political or other opinion, national, ethnic or social origin, property, disability, birth or other status. In the latter respect, it therefore prohibits discrimination on the basis of parental marital status. So, for example, in Ireland an effect of the 1988 Act is to facilitate the child care adoptions of children of non-marital parents but to obstruct similar entry by children of marital parents. This would seem to be in breach of Article 2. All appropriate measures must be taken to ensure that the child is protected against all forms of discrimination or punishment on the basis of the status, activities, expressed opinions, or beliefs of the child's parents, legal guardians, or family members. This resonates strongly with the requirement in s 1(5) of the Adoption and Children Act 2002 that adoption agencies give 'due consideration to the child's religious persuasion, racial origin and cultural and linguistic background'.

2.2.   Article 3—the best interests of the child is a primary consideration

Article 3 states the most important principle in the Convention. This Article requires that in all actions concerning children, whether undertaken by public or private social welfare institutions, courts of law, administrative authorities or legislative bodies, the best interests of the child shall be the primary consideration.

2.3.   Article 7—the right of the child to know their identity

Article 7 recognises the right of a child to know the identity of his or her parents. This is a powerful legal acknowledgement that an adopted person has a right of access to information, in the form of agency records etc, that could potentially contribute to their sense of identity. Arguably, this confers on an adopted child the right to have their parents' identity recorded on his or her birth certificate.

2.4.   Article 12—the right of the child to express an opinion in administrative and judicial proceedings

Article 12 states that the child has the right to express his or her opinion freely and the right to have that opinion taken into account in any matter or procedure affecting the child. This is subject to the caveat that the child concerned must be capable of forming his or her own views. Due weight, in accordance with the age and maturity of the child, must be given to his or her views. In particular the child must be provided the opportunity to be heard in any judicial and administrative proceedings affecting the child, either directly, or through a representative or an appropriate body, in a manner consistent with the procedural rules of national law.

The 2002 Act, while not inconsistent with the requirements of this Article, does not take any further forward the established legislative position regarding the child's right to be heard on matters affecting him or her in UK family proceedings. In particular, while it would always be the case that where a child had views in relation to his or her proposed adoption these would be sought and brought before the court by the CAFCASS officer, the child would seldom have the opportunity to express these views either personally and directly or through a solicitor. Moreover, whereas in Scotland consent as well as views is legislatively required, this is not the case in other UK jurisdictions.

2.5.   Articles 13 and 14—the right of the child to self-determination, dignity, respect, non-interference and the right to make informed decisions

Articles 13 and 14 require the state to ensure that the child has the right to freedom of expression and the right to express his or her own views. Again, rights require a mechanism for their enforcement and it is to be noted that the 2002 Act continues the practice of not making provision for automatic representation by a solicitor in private family law proceedings.

2.6.   Article 18—the primary responsibility for the upbringing of a child rests with the parent/s

Article 18 requires the state to render appropriate assistance to parents and legal guardians to facilitate the upbringing and development of their children. It requires the state to ensure that children of working parents have the right to benefit from those child care services and facilities for which they are eligible. Accordingly, the 2002 Act has to be viewed in the context of the family support provisions in the 1989 Act. Preventing children identified as 'in need' from becoming children at risk of 'significant harm' is a central plank in the policy of the latter. However, its frequent failure to achieve this in practice is evidenced by the increase in children coming into public care. In part, the rationale for the 2002 Act is to address the consequences of failure in the preventative intervention mandated by the 1989 Act. Arguably, the need for a new adoption law to expedite the transfer from public care to private care of those children admitted to public care following failed parenting would not have been so pressing if a greater investment had been made in family support services.

2.7.   Article 20—state duty to protect child without family

Article 20. 3 suggests that:

> Such care could include, *inter alia*, foster placement, Kafala of Islamic law, adoption, or if necessary placement in suitable institutions for the care of children. When considering solutions, due regard shall be paid to the desirability of continuity in a child's upbringing and to the child's ethnic, religious, cultural and linguistic background.

Article 20 requires the state to provide care for a child deprived of a family environment and in doing so must have due regard to the child's cultural background.

The local authority interventionist approach to vulnerable families ensures the provision of state care in the circumstances outlined in this Article. However, the quality and permanence of such care arrangements are often jeopardised by forced reliance upon serial foster care placements while the protection afforded to the children concerned cannot be guaranteed as the Waterhouse report[2] and others have convincingly demonstrated. Following extensive debate among the professionals and agencies concerned, there is no doubt that state care is now provided on a culturally sensitive basis and that transracial adoption placements are arranged only after due consideration has been given to the issues involved. However, it could be argued that intercountry adoption in practice is very often undertaken on a culture-blind basis with little concrete allowance made for measures to bridge the usually very significant gap between the cultures of adopters and adopted. Although s 1(5) of the 2002 Act does require that attention be given to such matters it provides no indication of how this is to be done.

2.8. Article 21—adoption shall ensure that the best interests of the child shall be the paramount consideration

Article 21 is of particular significance for adoption as it requires those State Parties that recognise and/or permit adoption to give paramount consideration to the welfare interests of the children concerned when doing so. It requires State Parties to:

(a) ensure that the adoption of a child is authorised only by competent authorities who determine, in accordance with applicable law and procedures and on the basis of all pertinent and reliable information, that the adoption is permissible in view of the child's status concerning parents, relatives and legal guardians and that, if required, the persons concerned have given their informed consent to the adoption on the basis of such counselling as may be necessary;

(b) recognise that intercountry adoption may be considered as an alternative means of a child's care, if the child cannot be placed in a foster or an adoptive family or cannot in any suitable manner be cared for in the child's country of origin;

(c) Ensure that the child concerned by intercountry adoption enjoys safeguards and standards equivalent to those existing in the case of national adoption;

(d) Take all appropriate measures to ensure that, in intercountry adoption, the placement does not result in improper financial gain for those involved in it; and

---

[2]   See, Waterhouse, *Lost in Care: Report of the Tribunal of Inquiry into the Abuse of Children in Care in the Former County Council Areas of Gwynedd and Clwyd since 1974*, the Stationery Office, London, 2000.

(e) Promote, where appropriate, the objectives of this article by concluding bilateral or multilateral arrangements or agreements, and endeavour, within this framework, to ensure that the placement of the child in another country is carried out by competent authorities or organs.

Article 21(d), in conjunction with Articles 8 and 32 of the Hague Convention, requires a State Party to take all appropriate measures to ensure that adoption placements do not result in any improper financial gain for any of the parties involved.

Section 1(1) and (2) of the 2002 Act now ensure that the best interests of the child are treated as the paramount consideration by both court and adoption agency.

2.9.   Article 25—adoption placements must be subject to periodic review

Article 25 requires periodic review of placements of all types, including foster care and residential units, to ensure that no child in state care is overlooked.

Section 118 of the 2002 Act amends the 1989 Act to provide a system of independent review and thereby safeguard children in local authority placements from being allowed to 'drift in care'.

2.10.   Article 27—every child is entitled to a reasonable standard of living

Article 27 requires the state to recognise the right of every child to a standard of living adequate for that child's physical, mental, spiritual, moral and social development. There is now a considerable body of research available to testify to both the enduring level of poverty in the UK and the strength of the correlation between poverty and family failure. There can be little doubt that there would be fewer children coming into public care and out into adoption if the coping capacity of vulnerable families was reinforced by adequate resources.

2.11.   Article 35—prevention of trafficking in children

Article 35 requires State Parties to:

take all appropriate national, bilateral and multilateral measures to prevent the abduction, the sale of or traffic in children for any purpose or in any form.

The UK courts are increasingly referring to this provision in the context of intercountry adoption applications when issues arise regarding improper payments and uncertainty as to consents.

2.12. Article 40—right of child in conflict with the law to dignity and respect for age

Article 40 requires a State Party to respect principles of proportionality and legal certainty when taking decisions in respect of a child. The issue as to whether in a particular case, non-consensual child care adoption is a proportionate response, in a modern democratic society, to a failure in parenting is one which the courts in the UK have frequently had to address. In practice the issue has necessarily been rendered academic in the context of adoption proceedings by the weight given to preserving the attachment and settled home environment provided by the prospective adopters. The 2002 Act will strengthen the probability of such an outcome in the future. In addition, this legislation will also do much to counter the planning uncertainty which in the past condemned so many children to drift in local authority care.

2.13. Articles 44 and 45—every state is required to audit, progress and publish a report

Articles 44 and 45 require a State Party to report on the measures it has adopted which give effect to the rights recognised in the Convention and on the progress made on enjoyment of those rights. The United Kingdom compiles and submits such a report every five years.[3]

3. THE EUROPEAN CONVENTION FOR THE PROTECTION OF HUMAN RIGHTS AND FUNDAMENTAL FREEDOMS 1950

In the UK, the Human Rights Act 1998, incorporating the Convention, came into force on October 2nd, 2000. All public bodies including courts and local authorities have, from that date, been required to ensure that their processes and decisions are compliant with Convention rights. All case law resulting from decisions of the European Court of Human Rights ('ECHR') has since had a direct relevance for the courts in the United Kingdom. However, most breaches never reach the ECHR; they are the subject of proceedings in our domestic courts and the related judgments serve to reshape practice and forestall the likelihood of future similar breaches.

The common law tradition of the UK in relation to the family, evolved with a formal emphasis on parental rights, duties and status accompanied by mandatory

---

[3] See, *e.g. The United Kingdom's First Report to the UN Committee on the Rights of the Child* (HMSO, 1994). The second report was published in September 1999.

court proceedings for sanctioning any permanent changes to the legal relationships between the parties involved (see, further, Chap. 2). This was quite different from the more flexible approach developed elsewhere. Consequently, while there are considerable differences in the law, policy and practice of adoption across the countries of mainland Europe the differences between the latter and the UK are of a more fundamental nature. This has led to certain tensions as the ECHR lays down benchmarks for standards to be upheld by all signatory nations.

The difficulty in setting common benchmarks for human rights is apparent from even the most cursory analysis (which is all that may be ventured in the present context) of contemporary differences between the UK and continental Europe in their approach to adoption. In the Scandinavian countries, for example, the steady decline in consensual domestic adoption and the unavailability of children from public child care has meant that the adoption of babies is now an almost totally intercountry phenomenon (see, further, Chap. 9). In France and more generally in Europe, the absence of statutory powers to remove all parental rights and totally dispense with the need for parental consent means that the adoption experience is virtually entirely a consensual process. The corollary of course is that public child care institutions in those countries have a high investment in family support and long-term foster care services.

In the UK, by way of contrast, the non-consensual use of adoption in relation to children in the public care system has brought with it significant features that are becoming distinguishing characteristics of that nation's adoption experience. For example, the children involved are often: old enough to have their views taken into consideration, for their consent to be relevant and to have a sense of personal and cultural identity; adopted in sibling groups; suffering from significant health and/or social care problems; committed to ongoing post adoption contact with their birth parents/siblings and may be; adopted by persons qualifying for on-going financial assistance.

This somewhat disparate national experience of adoption, particularly between the UK and the rest of continental Europe, has not yet been the subject of international research to identify the difference in outcomes for children failed by parental care but adopted (as in the UK) instead of being retained within alternative public service care arrangements (as in, for example, Sweden). It has, on the other hand, given rise to a range of legal issues with which the ECHR copes by applying the doctrine of a 'margin of appreciation'. This doctrine declares that individual states are entitled to act with a level of discretion in accordance with their particular legal tradition. However, as is illustrated in the case law below, the exercise of discretion is only permissible within the judicial parameters established by principles such as 'necessity' and 'proportionality'.

The following provisions have a particular relevance for family proceedings and therefore also for adoption. They are important and have a potentially direct bearing on the circumstances of those appearing before the court. Accordingly members of the judiciary have cautioned against any inclination to simply refer to them in passing in a routine or ritualistic fashion. In fact, contemporary case law contains constant references to such rights which are treated as essential benchmarks of good practice.

3.1. Article 6—everyone is entitled to a fair and public hearing within a reasonable time by an independent and impartial tribunal established by law

A majority of applications to the ECHR have been generated by alleged breaches of Article 6.

3.1.1. DELAY

Delay in the processes of court or local authority can be harmful to the welfare interests of the children concerned. According to the European Court of Human Rights the following factors should be taken into account when considering whether there has been undue delay in determining a case:

- the complexity of the case[4];
- the conduct of the applicant and the other parties[5];
- the conduct of the relevant authorities[6]; and
- what is at stake for the applicant in the litigation.[7]

In *H v United Kingdom*[8] the parent complained of the "deplorable delay" of almost 2 years in court proceedings concerning her contact application in relation to her child in local authority care. By the time the matter was brought before the

---

[4] See *Glaser v United Kingdom* [2001] 1 FLR 153 where the court recognised that the complexities arising from the case being transferred between jurisdictions required additional reports to ensure that the eventual decision affecting the welfare interests of the child was based on a thorough investigation.

[5] See *Glasser (ibid)*, and *Hokakanen v Finland* [1944] 19 EHRR 139, [1996] 1 FLR 289, where, in both cases, the delay was attributable to the party awarded custody refusing to comply with the terms of contact orders.

[6] See *Bock v Germany* [1990] 12 EHRR 247, where the court held that there had been a breach of Article 6 by the delay resulting from domestic courts seeking an unnecessary number of reports.

[7] See *H v United Kingdom* [1988] 10 EHRR 95, where the court noted that the irreversibility of adoption proceedings was a factor in the adopters' failure to apply promptly. Also, see, *Mikulic v Croatia*, Application No 53176/99, ECHR, 07.02.02 where the court ruled that, given what was at stake for the applicant, the four year delay before hearing did not satisfy the obligation to act with particular diligence to progress the proceedings.

[8] *Ibid.* See, also,*Paulsen-Medalen and Svenson v Sweden* (1998) 26 EHRR 260.

court almost three and a half years had elapsed since she had last seen her child who was by then well settled with prospective adopters. The court stressed that:

> "In cases of this kind the authorities are under a duty to exercise exceptional diligence since ... there is always the danger that any procedural delay will result in the *de facto* determination of the issue submitted to the court before it has held the hearing."

The court held that the time it had taken the parent to pursue a claim for contact with her daughter—from the first application in wardship/adoption proceedings to the rejection of her leave to appeal to the House of Lords—constituted "excessive delay" and thus breached Article 6(1).

Section 1(3) of the 2002 Act, it should be noted, specifically directs that 'the court or adoption agency must at all times bear in mind that, in general, any delay in coming to the decision is likely to prejudice the child's welfare'.

3.1.2.   LEGAL REPRESENTATION

An essential element of a 'fair hearing' is the provision of appropriate legal representation. The court, in *Airey v Ireland*,[9] held that the Irish High Court had breached Article 6 when it failed to provide representation for the applicant who had been left to represent herself. In *P, C and S v UK*[10] the court was clear that the failure to provide parents with legal representation was in breach of their rights under Article 6 because:

> ... the complexity of the case, along with the importance of what was at stake and the highly emotive nature of the subject matter, lead this Court to conclude that the principles of effective access to court and fairness required that P receive the assistance of a lawyer.

3.1.3.   INVOLVEMENT OF PARENT IN DECISION-MAKING PROCESS

In *Re C (Care Proceedings: Disclosure of Local Authority's Decision Making Process)*[11] a mother challenged the local authority for failing to involve her in its decision-making process claiming that she had never been informed that she was required to acknowledge responsibility for the death of her first child as a step towards possible rehabilitation with her second child. The court found that by not informing the mother of the contents of the report, in which an expert witness had raised the responsibility issue, the local authority may have failed to respect her "right to a fair trial" and thereby been in breach of Article 6. The court held that under Article 6 the mother should have had an opportunity to examine and

---

[9]   (1979) 2 EHRR 305.
[10]   (2002) 35 EHRR 31; [2002] 2 FLR 631.
[11]   [2002] 2 FCR 673.

comment on the documents being considered by the expert and to cross-examine witnesses interviewed by the expert on whose evidence the report was based. This is an aspect of the "equality of arms" principle whereby both parties to proceedings must be placed in a position where they have equal knowledge of and be permitted to comment on evidence held by the other.[12]

This issue of the "fairness" of a local authority's process was also raised in *Re C (Care Assessment: Fair Trial)*[13] where again the court stressed that Article 6 rights were not confined to judicial proceedings. In this case the mother had not been properly engaged in the decision-making process, had been excluded from meetings and had not been informed of the contents of certain critical reports. The court ruled that the guarantee of procedural fairness provided by Article 6 was unqualified and could not be compromised (unlike Article 8 rights). Again in *Re M (Care: Challenging Decisions by Local Authority)*[14] parents successfully appealed from a local authority decision that they could not provide care for their child. The appeal was grounded on a failure by the local authority to involve them in the decision-making process which thereby breached their rights under Article 6 and may have done so also under Article 8.

This right is also relevant to the issues of disclosure of documents and other evidence to the court and may have a relevance for the availability or otherwise of legal aid. Alleged breaches of a parent's right of access to their child in care have also been heard under Article 6.[15]

3.2. Article 8—the right to respect for private and family life

This Article requires respect for a person's private and family life, their home and correspondence. It necessitates parental involvement in the decision-making process to a degree sufficient to provide them with the requisite protection of their interests. If they are not, there will have been a failure to respect their family life. Parents are entitled to be involved in the decision-making process relating to the religious education of their children. Essentially this right aims to provide protection for an individual against arbitrary action by public authorities, for example a local authority.[16] It places an obligation on the court to ensure that the rights of an individual are properly secured and are protected against infringements

---

[12] See *P, C and S v United Kingdom, op cit.*
[13] [2002] EWHC 1379, [2002] 2 FLR 730.
[14] [2001] 2 FLR 1300.
[15] See *O v United Kingdom, B v United Kingdom, H v United Kingdom, R v United Kingdom and W v United Kingdom* (1987) 10 EHRR 29.
[16] See, for example, *Re M (Care: Challenging Decisions by Local Authority)* [2001] 2 FLR 1300 and *C v Bury Metropolitan Borough Council* [2002] 2 FLR 868.

by other individuals.[17] It also inherently requires procedural fairness. However, the prohibition on public authority interference is made subject to the exception that where to do so is: (a) in accordance with the law; and (b) is necessary in a democratic society[18] (i) in the interests of national security, public safety or the economic well-being of the country, (ii) for the prevention of crime and disorder, (iii) for the protection of health or morals or (iv) for the protection of the rights and freedom of others.

3.2.1.   RESTRICTIONS ON PRIVATE LIFE

There are limits on a respondent's right to private life under Article 8 of the European Convention; it does not confer upon a litigant an unfettered choice of behaviour. This was demonstrated in *X v Netherlands*[19] where the court dismissed the protest of a 14-year-old girl who objected to being summarily returned by the authorities to her parents. The court held that such action was justified under Article 8(2) in order to protect her health and morals.

3.2.2.   IDENTITY AND ACCESS TO INFORMATION

The ECHR has, in recent years, been exploring the extent of a right to information about matters which have a bearing on an individual's sense of personal identity within the general right to privacy and to family life provided by Article 8. The beginning of this process can be traced to the important decision in *Gaskin v United Kingdom (Access to Personal Files)*[20] where the ECHR endorsed the view of the Commission that:

> . . . respect for private life requires that everyone should be able to establish details of their identity as human beings and that in principle they should not be obstructed by the authorities from obtaining such very basic information without specific justification.

This approach was further reinforced by *Rose v Secretary of State for Health and Human Fertilisation and Embryology Authority,*[21] where it was found that the claimants' request for identifying and non-identifying information relating to their genetic background (both claimants had been born as a result of the AID process) engaged Article 8. The right to establish the details of their identity as

---

[17] See *Airey v Ireland* (1979) Series A No 32, 2 EHRR 305.
[18] See, *Olson v Sweden (No 1)* (1988) 11 EHRR 299 where it is explained that to be justifiable such interference must be "relevant and sufficient; it must meet a pressing social need; and it must be proportionate to the need".
[19] (1974) (Application No. 6753/74) (1975–76) 1–3 DR 118.
[20] (1990) 12 EHRR 36.
[21] [2002] EWHC 1593 (Admin), [2002] 2 FLR 962.

human beings included the right to information about a biological parent; as the court reiterated in *Mikulic v Croatia*.[22]

This right may also prevent a local authority from claiming that its child care records are confidential, to be accessed by the subject only at its discretion. For example, in *MG v United Kingdom*[23] the ECHR found that the applicant had been wrongfully denied full access to social services files and to the information held therein. This information would have clarified whether his name had been entered on the child protection register and whether his father had ever been convicted of child abuse. The court was particularly concerned that the applicant had no opportunity to appeal against the agency's decision.[24]

3.2.3. FAMILY LIFE

Article 8 guarantees the right to respect for family life but the definition of 'family' is not restricted to one based on marriage; it includes unmarried couples, non-marital children and lesbian or homosexual relationships. As the European Court of Human Rights has pointed out:

> ... the notion of 'the family' ... is not confined solely to marriage based relationships and may encompass other *de facto* 'family' where the parties are living together outside of marriage. A child born out of such a relationship is *ipso iure* part of that 'family' unit from the moment of his birth and by the very fact of it.[25]

Article 8 makes no distinction between the "legitimate" and "illegitimate" family:

> ... 'family life' within the meaning of Article 8 includes at least the ties between near relatives, for instance, those between grandparents and grandchildren, since such relatives may play a considerable part in family life.[26]

More recently, in *Salgueiro da Silva Mouta v Portugal,*[27] the ECHR held there had been a breach of Article 8 when a court awarded the mother custody on the grounds that the father's homosexuality was an abnormality and the children should not have to grow up in its shadow. There is an obvious tension between

---

[22] *Op cit*, where the ECHR recognised that the identity of a child's parents is integral to the private life of that child under Article 8. The failure, therefore, to provide a procedure whereby a putative father could be compelled to undergo DNA testing to clarify his possible paternity was in breach of the child's rights under that Article.

[23] Application No. 39393/98, ECHR, September 24, 2002.

[24] The introduction in March 2000 of the Data Protection Act 1998, c 29, provides such an opportunity.

[25] *Keegan v Ireland*: Application No. 16969/90 (1994) Series A No. 290, 18 EHRR 342, at para. 44.

[26] *Marckx v Belgium* (1979) Series A No 31, 2 EHRR 330, at para. 31.

[27] [2001] 1 FCR 653.

this right and the right to non-discriminatory treatment guaranteed by Article 14 (see, further, below).

In *X, Y and Z v United Kingdom*[28] it was held that in determining whether a relationship can be defined as "family life" the following factors are relevant:

> ... including whether the couple live together, the length of their relationship and whether they have demonstrated their commitment to each other by having children together or by other means ....

This approach was taken a step further in *Lebbink v The Netherlands*[29] where the ECHR accepted that cohabitation was not an essential ingredient of 'family life' but, exceptionally, other factors may serve to demonstrate the required constancy of relationships. In this case the father's position as auxiliary guardian and his established pattern of contact, were sufficient to establish family life with the child.

3.2.4. UNMARRIED FATHER

The presumption favouring family life has been extended to include the role of an unmarried father[30] but this is a presumption that can be rebutted. In *Soderback v Sweden*,[31] for example, the applicant unmarried father had never cohabited with the mother and had a tenuous relationship with his daughter whom the mother and her spouse were proposing to adopt. The ECHR ruled that the granting of an adoption order had not breached the father's Article 8 rights.

The ECHR has also ruled the fact that the law disadvantages an unmarried father, unlike either an unmarried mother or a married father, in relation to parental responsibility will not itself constitute a breach of his rights under Article 8. The difference in treatment for married fathers was justified by the ECHR in *McMichael v United Kingdom*[32] on the basis that it was intended to thereby provide a means of identifying "meritorious" fathers.

In *Elsholz v Germany*[33] the ECHR ruled that there had been an unjustified violation of an unmarried father's Article 8 rights. This had occurred when a court had refused to grant him contact, without requesting a report from an expert witness, because of the strength of joint objections from mother and child. He

---

[28] [1997] 2 FLR 892.
[29] Application No 35582/99, ECHR, 01.06.2004.
[30] See *Johansen v Norway* (1996) 23 EHRR 33 and *Rieme v Sweden* (1993) 16 EHRR 155. Note that in *B. v United Kingdom* [2000] 1 FLR 1 the court found against an unmarried father without parental responsibility and held that the UK court had been justifiably discriminatory between his standing and that of a married father as he had no custody rights in respect of the child.
[31] [1999] 1 FLR 250.
[32] (1995) Fam Law 478. See also *B v United Kingdom* [2000] 1 FLR 1.
[33] [2000] 2 FLR 486. But see also *Sahin v Germany; Sommerfeld v Germany; Hoffman v Germany*, [2002] 1 FLR 119.

was entitled to greater involvement and to have had his interests presented more fully before the court.

3.2.5.   PRIVACY OF FAMILY LIFE

Article 8(2) declares that a public authority shall not interfere with the right to respect for family life, the existence or otherwise of which can be determined as a matter of fact. As observed in *Re C and B (children) (care order; future harm)*[34] a state can only legitimately interfere with this right if it satisfies three requirements: that it be in accordance with the law; that it be for a legitimate aim (in this case of the protection of the welfare and interests of the children), and that "it is necessary in a democratic society". However, as indicated by Hale LJ in *Re W and B; Re W*,[35] this right can also be viewed as presenting an opportunity and a challenge to public authorities requiring them to think positively rather than negatively when considering adoption for a child in care.

The presumption underpinning this Article is that the entitlement of parent and child to the mutual enjoyment other's of each others company constitutes a fundamental element of family life and should be protected against arbitrary action by public authorities. This approach has been upheld by the court in *K A v Finland*[36] and *Kutzner v Germany*.[37] In both cases it was made clear that the essential object of Article 8 of the Convention is to protect the right to respect for family life and that any interference with this right violates Article 8 unless the above three requirements can be satisfied. The court must first look at what additional measures of support can be put into place or what alternatives might exist that would obviate the need to make such an extreme intervention as an adoption order.

Article 8(1) also provides a guarantee for a right to respect for home and correspondence.

- **Involvement in decision-making**

In *Buchberger v Austria*[38] the ECHR found that Article 8 rights had been breached by the failure of a local authority to sufficiently involve the claimant in its

---

[34] [2000] 2 FCR 614 at 625. See also, *Kutzner v Germany* [2003] 1 FCR 249, where the court emphasised that any interference with this right will entail a violation of Article 8 unless the three requirements are satisfied. The element of "necessity" implies that the interference must correspond to a pressing social need and in particular be proportionate to the legitimate aim being pursued. An applicant local authority, in such circumstances, must inquire as to what additional measures of support can be given as an alternative to the extreme measure of separating a child from his or her parents.

[35] [2001] EWCA Civ 757, [2001] 2 FLR 582.

[36] (2003) 1 FCR 201.

[37] (2003) 1 FCR 249.

[38] Application No. 32899/96, December 20, 2001. See, also, *Re B (A Child: Non-accidental Injury)* unreported, Court of Appeal, April 24, 2002, where it was held that the judge at first instance had erred in refusing to order disclosure of documents to a sibling of B, the subject of proceedings. The disclosure, if made, would have had a direct bearing on the outcome of the proceedings.

decision-making process (see, also, Article 6 above). The case concerned a mother whose children had been taken into care because she had arrived home 45 minutes late from work having left them unsupervised. When she sought through court proceedings to retrieve her children, the local authority failed to provide a statement of reasons for their action and failed to give her copies of documents upon which it relied but which had not been communicated to her.

A capacity to participate effectively in decision-making is also dependent upon access to all relevant information. The ECHR has made a number of rulings in which it has emphasised the importance of ensuring that defendants are not disadvantaged by a non-disclosure of documents that may have a material bearing on the outcome of their case. In *TP and KM v United Kingdom*,[39] for example, the court ruled that the non-disclosure by a psychiatrist to the defendant of a tape recording adverse to the latter's interests was wrong. A parent must be placed in a position where he or she may obtain access to information relied upon by authorities in care proceedings.

However, the ECHR has also acknowledged that there may be circumstances when there is no right to obtain information held by such authorities. In *Odièvre v France*[40] an adopted person had sought the release of information identifying her birth mother. As the latter had expressly reserved her right to confidentiality, the Parisian Child Welfare Authorities refused her request. The ECHR held that the decision was not in breach of either Article 8 or Article 14 on the grounds that France had a pressing reason to respect the privacy of the mother, namely that mothers might abandon or abort their children if confidentiality on adoption could not be guaranteed. Unquestionably, there are difficulties in reconciling this decision with the approach of the court in cases such as *Mikulic v Croatia* (see, above).

- **Priority of child's interests**

Article 8(2) provides that where there is a conflict between the rights and interests of the child and those of a parent which can only be resolved to the disadvantage of one of them (as in *Hendricks v The Netherlands*[41]), the interests of the child must prevail. The ECHR, for example in *Sahin v Germany, Sommerfield v Germany, Hoffmann v Germany*[42] has stressed the crucial importance of the best

---

[39] [2001] 2 FLR 549. Also, see, *Re M (Care: challenging decision by local authority)* [2002] FLR 1300.

[40] ECHR, 13.02.2003.

[41] (1982) 5 EHRR 223. See also *Kroon v The Netherlands* (1994) Series A No.297–C, 19 EHRR 263 where the court commented that it was a principle of good law to hold that the interests of the child were paramount.

[42] [2002] 1 FLR 119; at time of publication the subject of appeal to the Grand Chamber. See, also, *Scott v UK* [2000] 1 FLR 958 where the ECHR upheld the decision of the court at first instance to dispense with the consent of an alcoholic mother and free her child for adoption because there was no evidence that she would ever be alcohol free and "what is in the best interests of the child is always of crucial importance".

interests of the child in such. Again, in *R v United Kingdom*,[43] where it was held that the parental right of access exists independently of considerations of the child's welfare. In *K and T v Finland*[44] the approach of the court was clearly stated:

> ...a fair balance has to be struck between the interests of the child in remaining in public care and those of the parent in being reunited with the child. In carrying out this balancing exercise, the Court will attach particular importance to the best interests of the child, which may override those of the parent. In particular, the parent cannot be entitled under Article 8 of the Convention to have such measures taken as would harm the child's health and development.

More recently, in *Yousef v The Netherlands*,[45] the ECHR for the first time used the phrase "paramountcy of welfare" when comparing the interests of a child with those of the parent[46]:

> The Court reiterates that in judicial decisions where the rights under Article 8 of parents and those of a child are at stake, the child's rights must be the paramount consideration. If any balancing of interests is necessary, the interests of the child must prevail.

Treating a child's welfare interests as paramount, however, does not mean ignoring the Article 8 rights of their parents; these too must be taken into account and full consideration given to the principle that in general a child's welfare is best assured by parental care.

• Proportionality

Article 8 requires that any intervention of the state between parents and child should be proportionate to the legitimate aim for the protection of family life.[47] This 'principle of proportionality' has emerged as key benchmark and has attracted repeated judicial affirmation of its importance in the context of child care cases as noted, for example, by Wall J:

> Inevitably, however, every order made under Section 8 of the Children Order 1989 represents in some measure interference by a public authority (the court) in the right to respect for family life contended in Article 8. The court's interference must, of course, be in accordance with the powers given to that court under the Children Act 1989 and be proportionate. Every application involves a court balancing the rights of the participants to the application (including the children who are the subject of it)

---

[43] [1988] 2 FLR 445.
[44] [2000] 2 FLR 79.
[45] [2003] 1 FLR 210.
[46] *Ibid* at para 73.
[47] See, *e.g. Re O (A Child) (Supervision Order)* [2001] 1 FLR 923.

and arriving at a result which is in the interest of those children . . . and proportionate to the legitimate aim being pursued.[48]

The principle of proportionality, repeatedly referred to in recent Court of Appeal judgments, is one which will finally see an end to any remnants of the peremptory "child rescue" approach that characterised much social work intervention in families in the last decades of the 20th century and not only in England & Wales. This was most graphically illustrated in the many cases where newly born babies were removed from the care of their hospitalised mothers. For example, in *P, C and S v UK*[49] the newborn child of a woman suffering from Munchausen's Syndrome by Proxy was removed from her care in hospital under an emergency protection order which was followed promptly by the instigation of care and freeing proceedings. The ECHR ruled that[50]:

> . . . the taking of a new-born baby into public care at the moment of its birth is an extremely harsh measure. There must be extraordinarily compelling reasons before a baby can be physically removed from its mother, against her will, immediately after birth as a consequence of a procedure in which neither she nor her partner has been involved.

Draconian intervention of this nature was held to be a disproportionate response to the level of risk presented by the mother and breached the latter's rights under Article 8. Again, in *K and T v Finland*[51] the same court explained[52]:

> . . . when such a drastic measure for the mother, depriving her absolutely of her newborn child immediately on birth, was contemplated, it was incumbent on the competent national authorities to examine whether some less intrusive interference into family life, at such a critical point in the lives of the parents and child, was not possible.

Convention case law clearly indicates that local authorities will now have to exercise great care in determining the degree of authority needed to justify any future such intervention. Sufficient evidence must exist for actions such as the precipitate removal of a child from his or her family home, for justifying a care order rather than a supervision order application, for using a care order rather than any other or no order to supervise home-based parenting and most importantly

---

[48] *Re H (Contact Order)* [2002] 1 FLR 22 at 37. See also comments of Hale LJ in *Re C & B (Care Order: Future Harm)* [2001] 1 FLR 611, at paras. 33–34 and 620–621 and in *Re O. (Supervision Order)* [2001] 1 FLR 923 at paras. 24–28.

[49] *Op cit.* See, also, the similar case of *Venema v The Netherlands* Application No 35137/1977, ECHR, 17.12.2002.

[50] *Ibid* at para 116.

[51] (2003) 36 EHRR 255.

[52] *Ibid* at para 168.

for warranting the permanent severing of parental rights through recourse to non-consensual adoption rather than availing of a lesser statutory power such as a Special Guardianship Order. So, for example, in *Johansen v Norway*[53] the ECHR considered an appeal from a Norwegian court which had directed that a child be taken into care, placed in a foster placement with a view to adoption and refused contact between the child and her applicant mother. The ECHR viewed these measures as "particularly far reaching in that they totally deprived the applicant of her family life with the child and were inconsistent with the aim of reuniting them". It stressed the importance to be attached to the continuing interest of birth parents in the future upbringing of their child. As was subsequently noted in the House of Lords[54]:

> The leading case of *Johansen v Norway* makes clear that deprivation of parental rights and access should only occur in exceptional circumstances. It would be justified if motivated by an overriding requirement pertaining to the child's best interests . . . The opposite of a trivial test.

In England and Wales the courts will need to apply the paramountcy test as determinant of adoption for looked after children with great caution if they are to avoid subsequent ECHR strictures for employing draconian means of intervention compared with the options chosen in similar circumstances by the courts in countries such as France, Norway and Sweden.

Again, in *KA v Finland*[55] the court stressed that, to be compliant with Article 8(2), the making of a public care order must involve a careful and unprejudiced assessment of all relevant evidence held on file and be justified by a recorded statement of specified reasons. The latter should be made available to the parent or guardian so as to ensure that they are in a position to participate in any further decision-making including lodging an appeal.

- **Duty to be proactive in protecting children**

Article 8, together with Article 6, must be construed as imposing on a court not only a duty of watchful vigilance, to ensure that the rights enumerated are properly taken into account when determining family proceedings. They also impose an obligation to be satisfied that any orders then made are given effect in a manner which continues to satisfy those rights.[56] It has been argued[57] that this

---

[53] (1996) 23 EHRR 33.
[54] See, Hansard, Lords, 16.10.02, col 929.
[55] [2003] 1 FCR 201.
[56] See *Re W and B; Re W (Care Plan)* [2001] EWCA Civ 757, as reported in 31 Family Law 581.
[57] See Fortin, J., 'Children's Rights and the Impact of Two International Conventions: the UNCR and the ECHR' in *Delight and Dole: the Children Act 10 Years On* (eds. Thorpe, L.J. and Cowton, C., Family Law, Bristol, 2002).

combination of Articles places a positive obligation on the state (either court or local authority), once it is made aware of abuse to a child, to intervene on that child's behalf and secure his or her safety. In effect it has no discretion once it is put on notice of abuse. This interpretation provides a rationale for following through with proactive steps to expedite permanency placements for the children concerned.

3.3.   Article 12—the right to marry and found a family

Article 12 provides that men and women of a marriageable age have the right to marry and to found a family, according to national law. The right to found a family is absolute and the state cannot interfere with the exercise of this right, though equally it has no legal obligation to provide the services that may be necessary for the right to be exercised. However, the fact that there is no legal right to adopt or to access artificial reproduction treatment was emphasised in *X v Belgium and The Netherlands*[58] where it was held that unmarried persons cannot claim a right to adopt.

3.4.   Article 14—prohibition of discrimination

Article 14 provides that the rights enumerated in the Convention shall be assured without discrimination on grounds such as sex, race, colour, language, religion, political or other opinion, national or social origin, association with a national minority, property, birth[59] or other status. This Article deals only with discriminatory treatment based upon the personal characteristics that distinguish people. As Kennedy L.J. observed in *Southwark LBC v St Brice*[60]:

> In order to establish a claim under Article 14 an individual must show that he has been discriminated against on the basis of 'a personal characteristic ("status") by which persons or groups of persons are distinguishable from each other'.[61]

It must be shown that an applicant is: subject to a difference in treatment from others in a similar situation; in the enjoyment of one of the rights protected by the Convention; which difference cannot be objectively and reasonably justified, having regard to the concepts of legitimate aim, proportionality and margin of

---

[58]   Application No. 6482/147 (1975) 7 DR 75.
[59]   A marital child cannot be accorded prior legal rights over a non-marital child: *Inze v Austria* (1988) Series A No. 126, 10 EHRR 394. See also *Marckx v Belgium* (1979) Series A No. 31, 2 EHRR 330.
[60]   [2002] EWCA Civ 1138, [2002] 1 WLR 1537.
[61]   Citing *Kjeldsen, Busk Madsen and Pedersen v Denmark* (1976) 1 EHRR 711 at para 56.

appreciation. There is no definitive list of matters constituting discriminatory treatment.

In *R & L v Manchester City Council*[62] the practice of a local authority was found to be in breach of Article 14 because it discriminated between payments for family based care and foster care to the disadvantage of the former. Article 14 has no independent validity but operates to complement other substantive rights enumerated in the Convention.

In *Frette v France*[63] the court found that there had not been a breach of Article 14. The case concerned a homosexual man who had been discouraged from proceeding with an adoption application once he had disclosed his sexual orientation. The ECHR found that a State was entitled to draw distinctions between homosexuals and others in the adoption process and held that a ban on adoption by lesbian or gay individuals did not violate Article 14.

4. THE HAGUE CONVENTION ON JURISDICTION, APPLICABLE LAW AND RECOGNITION OF DECREES RELATING TO ADOPTION 1965

As this Convention was only ever ratified by the UK, Austria and Switzerland it never exercised much international regulatory influence. However, although it has since been overtaken by the Hague Convention 1993, it did begin to shape policy. For example.

4.1. Article 32—intercountry adoption fees

Article 32 obliges a state to ensure that the fees charged in respect of an intercountry adoption are reasonable and relate proportionally to actual costs and expenses incurred.

5. THE EUROPEAN CONVENTION ON THE ADOPTION OF CHILDREN 1967

This Convention, now of historical interest only, sought to identify some common principles and standards of practice to serve as international benchmarks for the parties involved in adoption. For example, it established the principle that adoption

---

[62] [2001] 1 FLR 43.
[63] Application No 3651/97.

should be in the interests of the child (Article 8, para 1) and should provide the child with a stable and harmonious home (Article 8, para 2). It gave protection to adopter's rights by emphasising the need for anonymity (Article 20) and to birth parent's rights by establishing that any consent given by a mother to the adoption of her child is invalid if given within six weeks of that child's birth (Article 52, para 3); she can, however, give a valid consent to placement within that period.

6. THE UNITED NATIONS DECLARATION ON SOCIAL AND LEGAL PRINCIPLES RELATING TO THE PROTECTION AND WELFARE OF CHILDREN WITH SPECIAL REFERENCE TO FOSTER PLACEMENT AND ADOPTION NATIONALLY AND INTERNATIONALLY 1986

This UN Convention, though without the force of law and signed by very few countries, provided a starting point for consideration of further international initiatives to regulate intercountry adoption. It states that the best interests of a child should be paramount including the right to affection, security and continuing care.

6.1. Article 3—care outside the family of origin

Article 3 provides that 'the first priority for a child is to be cared for by his or her own parents' but, failing that ' ... care by relatives of the child's parents, by another substitute—foster or adoptive—family or, if necessary, by an appropriate institution should be considered'.[64]

6.2. Article 8—right to name etc.

Article 8 provides for a child's right to name, nationality and legal representation. It also requires signatory states to provide for the supervision of placements.

6.3. Article 24—intercountry adoption

Article 24 requires due weight to be given to both the law of the State to which the child is the national and the law of the respective adoptive parents. In that context it requires due regard to be given to 'the child's cultural and religious background and interests'.

---

[64] See, Article 4.

7. THE HAGUE CONVENTION ON PROTECTION OF CHILDREN AND CO-OPERATION IN RESPECT OF INTERCOUNTRY ADOPTION 1993

Replacing the Hague Convention on Jurisdiction, Applicable Law and Recognition of Decrees relating to Adoptions 1965, the 1993 Convention was signed by the UK in 1994 and ratified by it in June 2003.[65] The aims of the 1993 Convention are:

- to establish safeguards to ensure that intercountry adoption takes place in the best interests of the child and with respect for his or her fundamental rights as recognised by international law[66];
- to establish a system of co-operation amongst Contracting States to ensure that the safeguards are respected and thereby prevent the abduction, the sale of or traffic in children[67]; and
- to secure the recognition in Contracting States of adoptions made in accordance with the Convention.[68]

The Preamble to the Hague Convention explicitly states that it is to be read in conjunction with the UN Convention on the Rights of the Child (UNCROC).[69] The 1993 Convention, as Duncan has pointed out, provides a "set of minimum standards and procedures, which may be supplemented by additional safeguards thought appropriate or necessary by individual states".[70] It is underpinned by principles, sometimes explicitly stated sometimes not, that are intended to guide international practice.

7.1. Principle that the welfare interests of the child are paramount in adoption law and practice (see, also, UNCROC)

This clear statement, intended to guide the decisions of all bodies involved in the adoption process, usefully reinforces the firming-up of the paramountcy principle in recent ECHR case law.

---

[65] As of June 2003, some 53 Contracting States had ratified this Convention.
[66] Article 1(a).
[67] Article 1(b).
[68] Article 1(c).
[69] The Preamble also refers to its links with the 1986 UN Declaration.
[70] See, Duncan, W. 'Regulating Intercountry Adoption—an International Perspective', in Bainham, A., Pearl, D.S. and Pickford, R. (eds) *Frontiers of Family Law* (2nd ed), John Wiley and Sons, 1995 at p. 51.

7.2.   Principle that intercountry adoption is only justified after in-country placement options have been eliminated

This principle is expressed in the Preamble and in Article 4(b).

7.3.   Principle that adoption is a service for children, rather than for an adult seeking to acquire a child (see, also, UNCROC)

This principle recognises that no person has an automatic right to adopt a child.

7.4.   Principle that children requiring adoptive placements are entitled to know and have access to information about their family background and cultural heritage and maintain or develop cultural identity (see, also, UNCROC)

This principle recognises that due regard must be given to a child's ethnic, religious, cultural and linguistic background when considering adoption. It also recognises that intercountry adoption must respect the child's fundamental rights which include the foregoing.

7.5.   Principle that the natural parent/s have an entitlement to make decisions about their child's future care (see, also, UNCROC)

This principle recognises that both parents are entitled to make decisions about their child, including consenting to the child's adoption and participating in the selection of approved prospective adopters. Article 4(b) provides that a Convention adoption 'shall only take place if the competent authorities of the State of origin have determined, after the possibilities of placement within the State of origin have been given due consideration, that intercountry adoption is in the child's best interests'.

7.6.   Principle that the child is entitled to be involved in decision-making (see, also, UNCROC; Article 12)

This principle recognises that the child's views must be sought, must be taken into consideration and may be determinative depending upon their maturity.

7.7. Principle that the parties are entitled to negotiate mutually agreed adoption arrangements (not explicitly stated)

This principle recognises that parties to an adoption are, with mutual agreement, entitled to participate in ongoing information exchange and/or contact after an adoption order is made. The child's views must be sought and must be taken into account.

7.8. Principle that adoption should safeguard and promote the welfare interests of the child throughout his or her life (not explicitly stated)

This principle recognises the lifelong nature of adoption and the need to ensure that the interests of the adopted person are always given priority over those of other parties.

7.9. Principle that Adoption Authority should 'promote the development of adoption counselling and post-adoption services' (Article 9)

This principle requires, under Article 9C, the accreditation of bodies established to provide adoption services. The responsibilities in relation to such bodies are addressed in subsequent Articles.

- **Article 10**

Accreditation shall be granted to and properly maintained by bodies demonstrating their competence to carry out the tasks with which they may be entrusted.

- **Article 11**

An accredited body shall—

(a) pursue only non-profit objectives according to such conditions and within such limits as may be established by the competent authorities of the State accreditation;
(b) be directed and staffed by persons qualified by their ethical standards and by training or experience to work in the field of intercountry adoption; and
(c) be subject to supervision by competent authorities of that State as to its composition, operation and financial situation.

- **Article 12**

A body accredited in one Contracting State may act in another Contracting State only if the competent authorities of both States have authorised it to do so.

- **Article 22**

1. The functions of a Central Authority under this Chapter may be performed by public authorities or by bodies accredited under Chapter III, to the extent permitted by the law of its State.
2. Any Contracting State may declare to the depositary of the Convention that the functions of the Central Authority under Articles 15–21 may be performed in that State, to the extent permitted by the law and subject to the supervision of the competent authorities of that State, also by bodies or persons

who—

   (a) meet the requirements of integrity, professional competence, experience and accountability of that State; and
   (b) are qualified by their ethical standards and by training or experience to work in the field of intercountry adoption.

8.   CONCLUSION

International Conventions and related case law are now rapidly promoting a harmonisation of principles, policy and practice in the adoption law of many countries. They provide a framework of established principles and standards within which more refined benchmarks for good practice are gradually emerging. This facilitates the analysis of national adoption processes and a comparative assessment of national differences in law and practice which is addressed in the following chapters.

Part III

CONTEMPORARY LAW, POLICY AND PRACTICE

Chapter 5

THE ADOPTION PROCESS IN ENGLAND & WALES: THE ADOPTION AND CHILDREN ACT 2002

1.   INTRODUCTION

The Adoption and Children Act 2002 repealed the Adoption Act 1976 and significantly amended the Children Act 1989. It marked an important change in the government's policy towards adoption, particularly in the use made of it by local authorities in respect of looked after children, and follows very closely the same process of change implemented in the US.[1] The 2002 Act provides a strong lead for the adoption law reviews currently underway in Scotland and Northern Ireland. This legislation was the product of a decade and more of debate and now provides a strategic consolidation of policy, principles and the law in adoption and child care practice.

This chapter is in three parts, the first two of which update the developments in policy and law outlined earlier (see, Chap. 2). The first part gives a brief account of the background to the Adoption and Children Act 2002 which now provides the legal framework for modern adoption practice in England & Wales. It considers the policy and legal issues that arose at different stages in the reform process. The second identifies the main changes introduced by this legislation. The third and main part applies the template of legal functions (see, Chap. 3) to detail the current law and practice of adoption in England & Wales.

---

[1]   See, Sargent, S., 'Adoption and Looked After Children: a comparison of legal initiatives in the UK and the USA', *Adoption & Fostering*, BAAF, vol. 27, no. 2, 2003, at pp. 44–52.

Kerry O'Halloran (ed.), The Politics of Adoption, 129–164.
© *2006 Springer. Printed in The Netherlands.*

2. BACKGROUND TO THE ADOPTION AND CHILDREN ACT 2002

The roots of the 2002 Act lie in the 1992 review of adoption law conducted jointly by the Department of Health and the Law Commission.[2] This resulted in the Consultation Document[3] which led in turn to the publication of the government's White Paper *Adoption—the Future*[4] and its sequel the Bill *Adoption—A Service for Children.*[5] However, despite a gestation period of thirteen years, it was not until the pressure generated by child care scandals became acute that the government was finally prompted to prepare new legislation.[6]

2.1. Policy review

At the heart of this policy review lay the fundamental question—What was to be the function of adoption in the 21st century? Practice had transformed the use of adoption since implementation of the 1976 Act, while the principles governing child care and adoption had become increasingly conflicted since the introduction of the 1989 Act. It was becoming steadily less clear where adoption fitted within the context of other family proceedings: where should the dividing line be drawn between adoption and residence orders or between adoption and other forms of care available to looked after children?

2.1.1. ADOPTION LAW REVIEW: CONSULTATION DOCUMENT

The consultation document emphasised the importance of adoption's traditional characteristics as "a way of making a child legally part of a new family and severing any legal relationship with the birth family".[7] It advocated a clarification of existing law so as to retain and reinforce the distinctiveness of adoption. It recommended that certain traditional features be retained. Applications should

---

[2] The working party, drawn from the two agencies, was established in 1989. Constituted as the Inter-departmental Review of Adoption Law, it published four preliminary discussion papers: *The Nature and Effect of Adoption* (1990), *Agreement and Freeing, The Adoption Process*, and *Intercountry Adoption*; and three background papers: *International Perspectives* (1990), *Review of Research Relating to Adoption* (1990), followed by *Intercountry Adoption* (1991–1992).

[3] See, the Department of Health, *Adoption Law Review: Consultation Document*, 1992.

[4] (Cmnd 2288), 1993.

[5] See, *Adoption—A Service for Children*, HMSO, 1996. Also, note the current consultation process in relation to the Children Bill particularly the Green Paper *Every Child Matters*, 2003 and *Every Child Matters: Next Steps* published by the Dept. of Skills and Education, 2004.

[6] See, in particular, the Waterhouse Inquiry, *Lost in Care: Report of the Tribunal of Inquiry into the Abuse of Children in Care in the former County Council Areas of Gwynedd and Clwyd since 1974*, The Stationery Office, London, 2000.

[7] *Op cit* at para 3.6.

continue to be restricted to married couples and extended to single persons only in exceptional circumstances. The consent of unmarried fathers without parental responsibility should remain unnecessary. However it questioned the necessity for rigid and inflexible age limits, and the priority given to matched racial placements, while acknowledging that post-adoption contact and greater openness[8] in accessing information should have a part to play in adoption in the future.

This consultation document also addressed the long-standing concern that step-adoptions had the effect of legally guillotining the interests of all members of one side of the child's family in maintaining relationships with that child.[9] It suggested that other orders, such as a residence order, would be more appropriate in this context. Underpinning this document and the resulting 1993 White Paper was the need to put clear blue water between the permanency of adoption and the lesser and more specific care responsibilities of other proceedings.

2.1.2. ADOPTION—ACHIEVING THE RIGHT BALANCE[10]

Following the review of adoption services,[11] this local authority circular represented an important reformulation of the policy governing child care adoptions. It firmly stated that henceforth the governing aim was to "bring adoption back into the mainstream of children's services". It contained detailed sections dealing with issues such as race, culture, religion, language and avoiding delay and stated that where:

> ... children cannot live with their families, for whatever reason, society has a duty to provide them with a fresh start and where appropriate a permanent alternative home. Adoption is the means of giving children an opportunity to start again; for many children, adoption may be their only chance of experiencing family life.

This circular has to be viewed in conjunction with the research findings published at much the same time in *Adoption Now*.[12] The message from research was that the fall in child care adoptions during the period 1992–1998 was largely attributable to the local authority emphasis on attempting to rehabilitate looked after children with their families of origin. This was due to social workers earnestly struggling to give effect to the principles of 'partnership with parents' and 'family care is best care' that underpinned the 1989 Act. In so doing, it was argued, local authorities were undervaluing the adoption option.

---

[8] See, *Review of Adoption Law, op cit*, at para 4.2.
[9] *Ibid*, at para 19.2.
[10] Local Authority Circular (20) 1998.
[11] See, the Department of Health, *For Children's Sake: An SSI Inspection of Local Authority Adoption Services*, 1996 and *For Children's Sake—Part II: An SSI Inspection of Local Authority Adoption Services*, 1997.
[12] See, the Department of Health, *Adoption Now: Messages from Research*, 1999.

As Lowe points out, the approach in *Adoption Now* was subsequently endorsed by the *Quality Protects* programme which aimed to "maximise the contribution that adoption can make to provide permanent families for children in appropriate cases". It also required local authorities "to reduce the period children remained looked after before they are placed for adoption".[13]

2.1.3.   ADOPTION: PRIME MINISTER'S REVIEW[14]

This policy initiative, under the Prime Minister's personal leadership, firmly placed child care adoption on the political agenda. Too few children were being adopted from public care and those that were had to wait too long; adrift in care was not an acceptable option. It unequivocally asserted the need to make available the best form of permanent care to children failed by parental care and otherwise destined to experience a transitory sequence of residential and/or foster placements. There was considerable evidence that such children suffered poor educational attainment and a greater likelihood of eventual exposure to unemployment, homelessness and prison. The proposed use of adoption was to be viewed as distinctly different from the traditional form because[15]:

> ... adoption from care is not about providing couples with trouble-free babies. It is about finding families for children of all ages, with challenging backgrounds and complex needs.

It was accepted that local authorities would have to undertake more assertive recruitment campaigns, unrestricted by former preconceptions of ideal adopters, in order to find such families and achieve a much higher rate of adoption for looked after children. This was not a question of recruiting more of the same but rather of recruiting prospective adopters with the capacity to provide care appropriate to the complex needs of those looked after children who might be adoptable; the criteria for selecting appropriate adopters would have to be revised. The policy articulated in this review was responsible for the decision to apply the National Standards to local authority adoption practice and for driving forward the new approach to child care adoption. It was also a policy that owed a great deal to a similar initiative launched earlier in the US (see, further, Chap. 8).

---

[13] See, the Department of Health, *The Government's Objectives for Children's Social Services*, 1999, at para 1.3.
[14] See, Department of Health, Consultation Report by the Performance and Innovation Unit, *Adoption: Prime Minister's Review*, Cabinet Office, London, 2000.
[15] *Ibid*, at p. 14.

2.2.   Law review

Preparations for new legislation began with the White Paper, *Adoption: A New Approach* in December 2000, followed in March 2001 by the Adoption and Children Bill being introduced in Parliament and concluded in November 2002 when the Bill received the Royal Assent. This was a period of much debate in relation to such key issues as:

- the introduction of the paramountcy principle;
- the substitution of a form of guardianship for family adoption and for some foster carer adoptions;
- an increased adoption service;
- provision for post-adoption contact; and
- permitting unmarried and same sex applicants.

However, the political climate in the aftermath of the Waterhouse report meant that the focus was on the potential of the new legislation to reduce the number of children spending long periods in public care, often in a series of disrupted foster care placements, and to increase child care adoptions. In that context, where child welfare was the primary concern, such other traditional hallmarks of the process as the legal presumption favouring married applicants eventually gave way. This was also a period in which the principles and case law of the Human Rights Act 1998 were beginning to make their influence felt; apparent, for example, in a changed approach to unmarried fathers without parental responsibility whose involvement in decision-making was now to be sought.[16]

2.2.1.   THE WHITE PAPER, ADOPTION: A NEW APPROACH

The White Paper proposed that the 1976 and 1989 Acts should be brought into alignment to make the welfare interests of the child, interpreted in the light of the welfare checklist, the matter of paramount importance in all decisions throughout the adoption process. The application of this principle would be determinative of all issues including those relating to such matters as transracial placements and placement with unmarried or same gender couples. It would also, in effect, override the principle of 'partnership with parents' that had been such a cornerstone of the 1989 Act. There was much concern about the policy of allowing the paramountcy principle alone to so decisively and irreversibly extinguish all rights of birth parents but despite suggested caveats it prevailed.

The White Paper set out the government's expectation that there would be a 40% increase in adoption orders over the next 5 years in respect of looked after

---

[16] See, for example, *Re B (Adoption Order)* [2001] EWCA Civ 347, [2001] 2 FLR 26. See, also, Chap. 4.

children.[17] It also prepared the ground for the introduction of National Standards to govern matters such as the length of time such a child should expect to wait before a decision is taken regarding his or her eligibility for adoption and before a placement is found. These goals echoed recent US government initiatives.

The White Paper noted that post-adoption contact and 'openness' in general had become an established part of modern adoption policy and practice. Acknowledging that 'links with birth families are very important to children',[18] it refrained from including any provisions to address this matter. The White Paper did focus on the issue of information disclosure to adopted persons. It proposed that new legislation should include the right of both birth parents and adopted persons to register a wish for 'no contact' in the Adoption Contact Register.[19] It also stated that 'all adopted people should be able to discover their family history if and when they wished to do so'.[20] It suggested that new legislative provisions should facilitate this by placing duties upon adoption agencies to compile and retain the necessary information and provide counselling and assistance to those wishing to access records.

2.3.   The Adoption and Children Bill

The contents of the Bill largely followed those of the White Paper but differed from it in some important respects. For example, it sought to remove the established and automatic right of an adopted adult to obtain a copy of his or her original birth certificate. Instead it proposed making this conditional upon the relevant adoption agency being satisfied that disclosing the information necessary to obtain the certificate was compatible with the wishes of the birth parents. However, this attempt to restrict rather than broaden existing rights was defeated and the government reinstated the initial provision.

3.   THE ADOPTION AND CHILDREN ACT 2002

The Adoption and Children Act 2002 became partially operational early in 2004 with the remainder expected to come into effect by September 2005. In conjunction with the Children Act 1989, the 2002 Act provides the legislative framework for adoption in England & Wales. It introduced some important changes to the

---

[17] According to adoption statistics released by the Department for Education and Skills some 3,700 children were adopted from care in the year ending March 2004 (an increase of 6% on the previous year) bringing the level of increase to 37%.

[18] *Op cit*, at para 2.6.

[19] *Op cit*, at para 4.22.

[20] *Op cit*, at para 6.44.

principles, parties, process, the order and its consequences and made specific adjustments in relation to intercountry adoption.

3.1.   Principles

In a development tenaciously resisted by the judiciary for several decades[21] (see, further, Chap. 1), the principles governing child care and adoption in England & Wales have now to a large extent been harmonised.

3.1.1.   THE PARAMOUNTCY PRINCIPLE

In particular, the paramountcy principle of the 1989 Act now governs all decisions, relating to any matter affecting the child throughout his or her life, whether taken by adoption agency or court at any stage of the adoption process.[22] The principles of no delay[23] and non-intervention[24] are also incorporated.

3.1.2.   THE WELFARE CHECKLIST

A customised version of the welfare checklist in the 1989 Act has been embodied in the 2002 Act[25]; some items are deliberately calibrated across both statutes to ensure consistency of interpretation.[26] The adoption specific items on this list include:

- the likely lifelong effect on the child of becoming an adopted person;
- his or her relationship with relatives and other significant individuals;
- the ability and willingness of relatives, including birth parents or others to provide care; and
- the value of any ongoing relationship the latter may have with the child.

---

[21] See, for example *Re D (An Infant)(Adoption: Parent's Consent)* [1995] 1 FLR 895 where Wall J remarked that it is " ... logical that a different test needs to be applied to the making of an order which extinguishes parental rights as opposed to one which regulates their operation" at p 898. A view endorsed by the DoH in its *Review of Adoption Law* 1992 at para 7.1. Note also *Re W (An Infant)*[1971] AC 682 where Hailsham LJ remarked that " welfare per se is not the test" endorsed by MacDermott LJ in the same case " ... the mere fact that an adoption order will be for the welfare of the child does not itself necessarily show that a parent's refusal to consent to that adoption is unreasonable" at p 706. More recently, however, perhaps in response to decisions of the ECHR, the judiciary in this jurisdiction have been demonstrating an increasing willingness to recognise that the paramountcy principle has a bearing on consent issues.

[22] Section 1(3).

[23] Section 1(6).

[24] *Ibid.*

[25] Section 1(4).

[26] For example, provisions s 1(3)(a), (d) and (c) of the 1989 Act are replicated in s 1(4)(a), (d) and (e) respectively of the 2002 Act.

In keeping with the child care checklist, the items listed in the 2002 Act are neither exhaustive, prioritised nor uniformly applicable to all cases.

3.2.   Parties

There are a number of changes to the law as it relates to the parties. Many of these are changes that apply in an incidental fashion, for example by diverting step-adopters to alternative orders.[27]

3.2.1.   THE CHILD

Issues relating to transracial and cross-cultural adoptions are addressed in a provision requiring adoption agencies to consider religious, racial, cultural and linguistic factors when placing a child for adoption.[28]

3.2.2.   THE BIRTH PARENT/S

The consent of both birth parents, with parental responsibility, is now required before the placement of their child for adoption[29] and before the making of an adoption order.[30] Consent can no longer be withdrawn after an application has been lodged.[31] For the first time in UK law, the paramountcy principle now applies to dispensing with parental consent.[32]

3.2.3.   THE ADOPTERS

The eligibility criteria have been broadened to include a new category of applicant—the 'partner of a parent'[33]—and to permit joint applications from an unmarried couple and from a same sex couple.[34] Provision is made for establishing an Adoption and Children Act Register to promote the recruitment of adopters and facilitate the matching process.[35]

---

[27] Section 112 of the 2002 Act amends s 4 of the 1989 Act to allow step-parents to acquire a parental responsibility order.

[28] Section 1(5). There was no equivalent requirement regarding racial considerations in the 1976 Act.

[29] Section 19(1).

[30] Section 47(2).

[31] Section 52(4).

[32] Section 52(b).

[33] Section 144(7).

[34] Section 49; c/f s 144(4).

[35] Sections 125–131. See, also, the National Standards and Practice Guidance.

3.3.   Process

There has been a firming up of agency responsibilities at various stages of the adoption process.

3.3.1.   THE ADOPTION SERVICE

The previous statutory requirement governing provision of an adoption service has been considerably reinforced by the 2002 Act and by other legislation.[36] Local authorities are now required to ensure the availability of such a service for all parties whether they are involved in an agency, intercountry or family adoption.[37] There is also a right to an assessment of needs for adoption support services (but no duty on a local authority to provide the services assessed as being necessary) for adoptive families and others[38] which can be undertaken on a pre-adoption basis. Adoption support service providers are required to be registered.[39] The first phase of provisions under the 2002 Act governing adoption support services for adoptive families was implemented on October 31, 2003. From April 2004, the Commission for Social Care Inspection assumed responsibility for regulating and inspecting adoption agencies, adoption support agencies and the services provided.

3.3.2.   THE PLACEMENT

An adoption agency may now make a placement either with consent[40] (including 'advanced consent')[41] or by placement order.[42] In the former instance, the child may be placed with prospective adopters identified either in the consent form or by the agency.[43] In the latter, application must be by a local authority as voluntary adoption agencies are not permitted to use this procedure. The child concerned will be a party to the application and must be the subject of a care order or the court must be satisfied that the grounds for such can be met[44] and that either parental

---

[36]   See, the Care Standards Act 2000 (Commencement No 17 (England) and Transitional and Savings Provisions) Order 2003; the Voluntary Adoption Agencies and the Adoption Agencies (Miscellaneous Amendments) Regulations 2003; the National Care Standards Commission (Fees and Frequency of Inspections)(Adoption Agencies) Regulations 2003); and the Local Authority Adoption Service (England) Regulations 2003. Also, see, the Department of Health, *Providing Effective Adoption Support*, 2002

[37]   Section 3(2)(b).

[38]   Section 4.

[39]   Under Part II of the Care Standards Act 2000.

[40]   Section 52 of the 2002 Act.

[41]   Section 20.

[42]   Section 21(1).

[43]   Section 19(1)(a) and (b).

[44]   Section 21(2)(a) and (b).

consent is available (and has not been withdrawn) or can be dispensed with.[45] Parental responsibility is vested in the agency[46] and in the prospective adopters[47] for the duration of the placement. While a placement order is in force the child may not be removed[48] except by the local authority.[49] After an adoption application has been made, removal requires the leave of the court.[50] Before making the order the court must consider whether contact arrangements are necessary.[51] It may then, or at any time during the placement, make a contact order[52] subject to such conditions as it sees fit[53] or authorise the agency to refuse contact. A placement order can be revoked.[54]

3.4.   The order

There are no significant changes to the preliminaries for an adoption order. Specified criteria relating to applicants' age and domicile etc (see, above, for marital status) must be satisfied; though habitual residence (of both applicants in a joint application) is now an alternative basis of jurisdiction even if they are not domiciled within the jurisdiction. All prospective adopters must provide care for the child for a stated minimum period, and assessment reports are still required in respect of all agency adoption applicants. The most noticeable change is in the criteria for making a non-consensual order. For the first time there are no grounds based on parental conduct—whether of fault, default or unreasonableness—to justify dispensing with consent. Instead, making an order simply requires three alternative conditions to be satisfied: consent[55]; placement[56]; or the existence of a freeing order (in the case of a child from Scotland or Northern Ireland).[57] The main consequences of making an adoption order are also very much as before, the terminology traditionally associated with the effects of the order having been deliberately incorporated into the new legislative provisions.[58]

---

[45] Section 21(3).
[46] Section 25(2).
[47] Section 25(3).
[48] Section 30.
[49] Section 34.
[50] Section 37(a).
[51] Section 27(4).
[52] Section 27(3).
[53] Section 27(5).
[54] Section 24.
[55] Section 47(2).
[56] Section 47(4).
[57] Section 47(6).
[58] Section 67; including, for example, 'an adopted person is to be treated in law as if born as the child of the adopters or adopter'.

3.4.1. CONDITIONAL ORDER

The 2002 Act, unlike any of its predecessors, is prepared to facilitate adoption orders subject to contact conditions. As noted above, the court is specifically required before making an adoption order to consider whether that order should allow for contact arrangements between the child and another person[59]. In addition, the natural parents retain their right to have an application for a s 8 contact order heard in the course of adoption proceedings.[60] The National Adoption Standards also contain provisions explicitly addressing the need for possible post-adoption contact to be explored with the child, his or her birth parent/s and other members of the birth family. In practice, however, the judiciary is likely to maintain the established practice of encouraging arrangements to be made by the parties rather than issuing adoption orders subject to conditions.

3.4.2. ALTERNATIVE ORDERS

In an important adjustment to the previous law, the 2002 Act extends the range of alternative permanency orders so as to reduce inappropriate recourse to adoption. The introduction of alternative orders is reinforced by a directive requiring the court to 'always consider the whole range of powers available to it' under both the Acts of 1989 and 2002.[61]

- **Special guardianship order**

    By amendment to the 1989 Act, the 2002 Act has added the special guardianship order to the menu of orders available to regulate the care arrangements for children in circumstances where the absolute and exclusive powers of adoption are unwarranted.[62] It is strategically significant as it offers a compromise between long-term foster care and adoption. The court must first consider whether it should couple this order with a contact order.[63]

- **Extended residence order**

    Also, by amendment to the 1989 Act, the 2002 Act has made available to anyone (other than a parent or guardian) a long-life residence order that will endure in respect of the child concerned until his or her 18th birthday.[64]

---

[59] Section 46(6).
[60] Section 26(5).
[61] Section 1(6).
[62] Section 115; amending s 14 of the 1989 Act.
[63] *Ibid.*
[64] Section 114; amending s 12 of the 1989 Act.

- **Parental responsibility for step-parents**

Again, by amendment to the 1989 Act, the 2002 Act has enabled step-parents to acquire parental responsibility with the agreement of the parent spouse (or both parents, if both have parental responsibility)[65]. It also provides a power for the court to make a parental responsibility order in favour of the step-parent.[66]

- **Orders for foster parents**

Finally, by amendment to the 1989 Act, the 2002 Act facilitates the right of local authority foster parents to apply for any s 8 order[67] or an extended residence order or a special guardianship order.[68] Although available before the introduction of the 2002 Act, this right was then subject to conditions, including leave of the court and a three year period of care where the foster parents wished to apply without the agreement of the local authority and those with parental rights. This right applies in respect of a child who has lived with their foster parents for a minimum period of one year.

3.5.   Disclosure of information

The statutory provisions governing the duties of the Registrar General to maintain certain registers and facilitate access to the information therein, continue much as before. In this context, the main change effected by the 2002 Act is that adoption agencies are now the designated gatekeepers to information and are required to meet certain standards in relation to collating, storing and disclosing such information.[69]

3.6.   Intercountry adoption[70]

The 2002 Act basically replaces the Adoption (Intercountry Aspects) Act 1999. Subsequently, the Intercountry Adoption (Hague Convention) Regulations and the Adoption (Amendment) Rules were introduced to provide for the incorporation of the 1993 Hague Convention into English law and the Dept of Health issued the Adoption (Bringing Children into the United Kingdom) Regulations; all of which took effect from 1st June 2003 (see, further, Chap. 4).[71] Intercountry adoption in

---

[65] Section 112; amending s 4 of the 1989 Act.
[66] *Ibid.*
[67] Section 10 of the 1989 Act as amended by Sched 3 of the 2002 Act.
[68] Section 14A(5)(d) of the 1989 Act as amended by the 2002 Act.
[69] Sections 54, 56–65.
[70] Section 1 of the Adoption Bill 1996 first made explicit reference to intercountry adoption.
[71] See, also, Dept of Health, Intercountry Adoption Guide, May 2003.

the UK, now tightly regulated and restricted to adoption agencies, exists in three different forms.

3.6.1. CONVENTION ADOPTIONS

Most intercountry adoptions will be conducted between parties resident in countries that are signatories to the Hague Convention and will be regulated in accordance with Convention rules and procedures (see, further, Chaps. 4 and 9).

3.6.2. DESIGNATED COUNTRY ADOPTIONS

Some intercountry adoptions will be in respect of children listed in the Adoption (Designation of Overseas Adoption) Order 1973.[72] This is a process whereby the UK authorities will extend recognition to a valid adoption order made in another country.

3.6.3. NON-CONVENTION ADOPTIONS

There will be a few cases where the circumstances are such that neither of the above two legislative frameworks apply. The prospective adopters, having arrived in the UK with a child from another country (designated a 'private foster placement'), must within two weeks notify the relevant local authority and must, before bringing the child in, have submitted to the usual adoption assessment process by that or another agency. Failure to obtain prior agency approval is a criminal offence.

4. THE LEGAL FUNCTIONS OF CONTEMPORARY ADOPTION

Under the Adoption and Children Act 2002, as under all previous legislation, adoption in England & Wales remains firmly a judicial process the successful completion of which is marked by the issue of a court order. However, although adoption proceedings are judicial, the role assigned to mediating bodies has become more intrusive and extensive and while the adoption process now has more features of 'openness' it nevertheless continues to operate within a tight regulatory framework.

---

[72] The list includes China, most countries in the Commonwealth and some in Europe. New statutory provisions relating to adoptions with a foreign element are currently being prepared under authority of s 87 of the 2002 Act.

4.1.   Regulating the adoption process

In this jurisdiction both local authority and court retain their traditional regulatory roles. The court also acts as a watchdog in relation to agency practice and the High Court will use its powers of judicial review to intervene when alerted to possible improper practice.

This tightly regulated approach, resting on a body of specific requirements with definite sanctions for non-compliance, underpinned by Court Rules (currently in draft form), has been and continues to be a distinctive characteristic of the adoption process in England & Wales and elsewhere in the UK. In England & Wales it has been further reinforced by the introduction of two separate sets of standards: the National Adoption Standards, given the force of statutory guidance from April 2003; and the National Minimum Standards for adoption imposed under the Care Standards Act 2000 and against which agencies will be inspected by the Adoption and Permanence Taskforce. The efficiency of the process has also been facilitated by the introduction of the National Adoption Register to expedite the matching of child and adopter/s. The net result is a very formal adoption process subject to highly prescriptive statutory and administrative rules—specifying targets, timescales and quality standards—raising fears in some quarters that this leaves very little scope for the discretion that is necessary if professionals are to hold focus on the particular welfare interests of each individual child.

4.2.   The process

In England & Wales, the introduction of the Adoption and Children Act 2002 has changed the character of the adoption process from being in the main a form of private family law proceedings to instead being on balance more a creature of public law. The proportion of children entering the adoption process who are legitimate and/or whose eligibility has been determined by coercive intervention of the state has grown to become a particularly distinctive characteristic of adoption in the UK. In addition, the number of children who originate from overseas and/or who have special needs continues to grow. Other distinctive characteristics include the consistently high proportion (though perhaps not as high as it has been) of parental applications and the growing proportion of foster parent applicants.

The stages of the adoption process remain much as before the introduction of the 2002 Act. It commences with a statutory pre-placement counselling stage and concludes with the statutory availability of disclosure procedures, use of contact registers, possible conditions attached to adoption orders and the opportunities for adoption allowances and other forms of ongoing support from government bodies.

4.3. The court

Adoption proceedings are heard in family proceedings courts, or most often in county courts (some of which have been designated Adoption Centres) or occasionally in the High Court.

4.3.1. THE ROLE OF THE JUDICIARY

The court continues to ensure that eligibility/suitability criteria are fulfilled by all parties, ascertains or adjudicates on consent requirements, confirms that the proposed arrangements are compatible with the child's welfare and then issues or refuses the order sought. However, the 2002 Act has added some refinements such as:

- flexibility in relation to marital status of applicants;
- application of the welfare checklist;
- obligation to check whether post-adoption contact arrangements are necessary;
- determine whether a conditional adoption order would be appropriate; and to
- consider the appropriateness of an alternative order.

4.3.2. CAFCASS

The judicial role is supplemented by the Children and Family Court Advisory and Support Service[73] which will appoint CAFCASS officers (previously a guardian *ad litem* and a children and family reporter) who are assigned vital roles in adoption proceedings. They will carry out an exhaustive investigation into all the circumstances of the proposed adoption, interviewing all applicants and respondents including, where feasible, the child and ensuring that any factor having a bearing on the welfare of the child is brought to the attention of the court. In particular, s 102 of the 2002 Act requires the CAFCASS officer to advise parents on the implications of giving consent and to witness any consent then given. Unlike under the 1976 Act, however, current draft rules do not envisage the appointment of a CAFCASS officer in all future cases. This will mark a significant change to long established practice whereby the appointment of a guardian *ad litem* was mandatory in all adoption proceedings.

---

[73] Established in April 2000, CAFCASS brings together the role, functions and staff of the Probation Service in private law proceedings, the Guardian *ad Litem* Panels in public law proceedings and the child section of the Official Solicitor's Department. This non-departmental body now provides welfare reports and other support services in family proceedings throughout the three tiers of the court system and is accountable to the Lord Chancellor.

The court will also receive a report from the adoption agency or local authority in all cases.

4.4.   Role of administrative agencies

The steady growth in the space occupied by mediatory bodies, and the reliance placed upon their findings at the adjudication stage, has become a conspicuous feature throughout all UK family law processes. In England & Wales the role of administrative agencies in the adoption process has been enlarged by the legal requirements in the 2002 Act to provide a more comprehensive adoption service and by the good practice requirements of the National Adoption Standards. The Adoption and Children Act Register, now underpinned by s 125 of the 2002 Act, expedites the workings of the adoption process by providing a national data bank of information relating to children waiting to be adopted and approved adopters.[74]

4.4.1.   ADOPTION AGENCIES

An adoption agency is defined as a "local authority or registered adoption society".[75] The latter includes voluntary adoption societies, which unlike local authorities are required to register, and both are subject to the inspection of the CSCI/National Assembly for Wales against the regulations and minimum standards. The crucial professional functions of such an agency are likely to be borne by the staff of a local authority as voluntary agencies now very rarely get involved in the consensual placement of children for adoption, although they do approve large number of adoptive families with whom looked after children are placed on interagency placements.

Each agency is required to set up at least one Adoption Panel.[76] This must take all referrals relating to whether: adoption is in the best interests of a particular child; a prospective adopter should be approved as an adoptive parent and; if the home of a particular approved prospective adopter would provide a suitable placement for a particular child. Although it does not have a role in relation to family adoptions it does screen all assessments made of prospective intercountry adopters.[77] The Panel provides a vital and discretionary function by matching

---

[74] By March 2004, the Adoption Register had compiled a database of records relating to more than 10,000 children and approved adopters and had facilitated the adoption placements of 50 children.

[75] See, s 2(1) of the Adoption and Children Act 2002.

[76] See, Department of Health, *Adopter Preparation and Assessment and the Operation of Adoption Panels: A Fundamental Review*, 2002.

[77] The Adoption of Children from Overseas Regulations 2001 require prospective intercountry adopters to submit to the same assessment process as prospective domestic adopters; since

prospective adopters with available children. Although it makes recommendations rather than decisions for its agency, the latter is prevented from taking decisions in those areas without first inviting recommendations from the Panel and must make its decisions before the child is placed for adoption. The draft Adoption Agency Regulations and the Suitability of Adopters Regulations 2004 in the main continue the previous provisions but make some important additional changes to practice. The prospective adopters, for example, are now to be given relevant information relating to the child in question before referral to the Panel and this must include any plans relating to post-adoption support services and contact arrangements.

4.4.2.   LOCAL AUTHORITIES

The local authority also plays a more structural role in the adoption process. An onus is placed on each agency to justify itself in terms of its contribution to the needs of the adoption process. The adoption responsibilities of local authorities rest on four planks. Firstly, they must contribute to forming and maintaining local adoption services. Secondly, they must link adoption to their other child care services. Thirdly, they must manage their own work as adoption agencies. Fourthly and finally, they must carry out certain supervisory duties in relation to placements. The adoption service requirement entails each local authority ensuring the provision within its area of services (including, for example, residential, assessment and counselling services) appropriate to the needs of all parties to an adoption.

4.4.3.   THE REGISTRAR GENERAL

This official has statutory duties with a direct bearing on the adoption process being obliged to maintain an Adopted Children Register and keep an index of this in the General Register Office. The duty imposes a further requirement that records are kept which provide a link between an entry in the Register of Births marked 'adopted' and the corresponding entry in the Adopted Children Register (a link not publicly accessible). This allows for the collection of information sufficient to identify child, adopters, the date and place in respect of every adoption order issued. The Registrar General is required to maintain an Adoption Contact Register which enables adopted persons and their natural parents who want to contact each other to do so.

---

reinforced by the provisions of s 83 of the 2002 Act. Intercountry adoptions do not constitute a significant proportion of total annual adoptions in England & Wales; it is estimated that perhaps 300 such orders are made every year.

5.   THRESHOLDS FOR ENTERING THE ADOPTION PROCESS

The Adoption and Children Act 2002 has introduced significant changes to the threshold requirements for all parties entering the adoption process.

5.1.   The child

The child must be a 'person' known to the law i.e. he or she must have been born. It is not possible to adopt a foetus. That parties may enter into a contract in respect of a foetus to be carried to full term by a surrogate mother for the purposes of adoption is beside the point. Such a contract could well collapse as the pregnancy may not reach full term or one or more of the parties may decide not to proceed with the adoption etc.[78] The child must also satisfy minimum and maximum age limits by being not less than six weeks old and not having attained their 18th birthday before the application is lodged.[79] Where of sufficient age and discernment, their views must be sought and taken into account; he or she will be made a party to placement order proceedings.

The child must be subject to the courts of this jurisdiction. Children from overseas who are to be adopted in this jurisdiction must cease to be subject to the courts of their country of origin and come within the jurisdiction of our courts. This is achieved by being resident if not domiciled within the UK and by not being excluded by any provision of international law. In the latter context, however, for Convention adoptions it is of no consequence that the 'habitual residence' of the child is in another country provided that of the adopters is within the jurisdiction.

In addition, in all adoptions but perhaps mainly in relation to 'family' adoptions, suitability criteria may now either prevent an adoption by diverting applicants (either self initiated or by judicial discretion) from the adoption process to an alternative and more appropriate order or it may result in an adoption order subject to a contact condition in favour of a natural parent or sibling. The availability of alternatives to an absolute adoption order is an important and characteristic feature of the adoption process in this jurisdiction which demonstrates the leverage available for judicial assertion of the public interest to compromise the private interests represented by an adoption order. In relation to 'agency' adoptions the provision of a more comprehensive adoption service including post-adoption allowances has facilitated the adoption option for children with particular needs. As very many agency adoptions involve children with special needs or complex

---

[78] See, however, *Re Adoption Application (Adoption: Payment)* [1987] 2 FLR 291 where it was recognised that such a contract was in itself valid.

[79] See, s 47(9) and 49(4) of the 2002 Act which introduce a new rule permitting the adoption after a child's 18th birthday provided the application was lodged in court before that birthday.

health/behavioural problems, a multi-disciplinary assessment will now more often than not be necessary to ascertain a child's post-adoption needs for health, social care or educational services.[80]

5.1.1. THE WELFARE THRESHOLD

The introduction of the 2002 Act has significantly altered the balance between legal status requirements and welfare interests. In what, perhaps, has been the most radical adjustment ever made to the law of adoption in the UK, the availability for adoption of a looked after child in England & Wales may now be determined by his or her welfare interests.[81] This point is arguable.

There are those who would say that the change from "first consideration" in the 1976 Act to the present "paramount consideration" is not so huge. They might add that the application in practice of the "unreasonable withholding" ground for dispensing with consent under the 1976 Act was more or less decided on welfare grounds. Their position is reinforced by the probability that when the courts apply the checklist, the no order principle, and the consideration of other options in the context of the European Convention, it may not be that much easier to dispense with consent. In particular, application of the Convention's proportionality principle may well make it harder to get an adoption order as special guardianship will offer a less draconian but nevertheless reasonably secure option.

On the other hand for many decades UK legislators and judiciary have been at pains to draw a line between the public and private law proceedings of child care and adoption respectively. The difference between "first" and "paramount" consideration, however tenuous, had come to represent that line and many judicial pronouncements laboured the point that they would not countenance the "unreasonable withholding" ground being deployed as a Trojan horse to undermine it. The grounds for a child care order could not be used to passport a child into the adoption process. To concede would be to open the doors to accusations of 'social engineering' (see, further, Chap. 1).

However, whether or not it represents a paradigm shift in UK adoption law, the 2002 Act has now bridged the gap between child care and adoption proceedings.

5.2. The birth parent/s

Whether married or not, any parent with full parental responsibility is entitled to voluntarily relinquish a child for adoption and, following the introduction of

---

[80] See, also, the National Adoption Standards.
[81] Unlike the law in other UK jurisdictions and in stark contrast to adoption law in Ireland where factors such as parental consent and marital status of parents continue to be largely determinative of a child's availability for adoption.

the 2002 Act, such consent may be given on an 'advanced' basis. The consent of the other parent, if he or she has parental responsibility, must be obtained or the need for it dispensed with. This right is only exercisable via an adoption agency. Parents may have their rights restricted by a care order under the 1989 Act and then further abrogated by a placement order under the 2002 Act which authorises an adoption placement against parental wishes. Where this occurs it is now almost inevitable that subsequent adoption proceedings will result in the granting of the order sought as the paramountcy principle will apply as the test of whether or not an adoption order should be made.

Section 1(2)(f) of the 2002 Act directs the agency/court specifically to have regard to relationships with relatives (which, in this context, includes parents). This will result in agency social workers exploring the possibility of kinship care and/or the appropriateness of ongoing contact with relatives, possibly using a family group conference to do so, before referring the case to its Adoption Panel.

As before the 2002 Act, the voluntary relinquishing of a child to the adoption process by his or her unmarried birth parent vested with parental responsibilities presents the least difficulties. The informed consent of the latter together with that of the other birth parent, if he or she has parental responsibility, is the only absolute necessity. Unlike the situation before the 2002 Act, an unmarried father may now acquire parental responsibility by registering the birth jointly with the child's mother. While the consent of an unmarried father without parental responsibility continues to be unnecessary, he must where possible be served with notice and his views ascertained. The situation is no longer any more complicated in respect of marital children. Where the subject is an overseas child, then evidence of parental consent must be brought before the court.

5.3.   The adopters

All adopters must satisfy eligibility criteria—such as the statutory conditions relating to age, domicile/habitual residence and duration of placement—though these have always been most stringent in relation to third party prospective adopters. Since the introduction of the 2002 Act, adopters no longer have to meet the traditional requirement relating to marital status. Not only may unmarried couples now satisfy the eligibility criteria but so also may same gender couples.[82] In addition, the suitability criteria consisting of administrative conditions as applied by adoption agencies and relating to factors such as maximum age, health, quality and duration of relationships, cultural background and lifestyle must also be satisfied but these are now governed by the National Standards and/or the Regulations.

---

[82]   See, s 144(4)(b) of the 2002 Act which permits applications from 'two people (whether of different sexes or the same sex) living as partners in an enduring family relationship'.

5.3.1.   THIRD PARTY ADOPTERS

Those who are local authority foster carers and can satisfy residence, suitability and notice criteria now have stronger statutory rights in relation to adoption. The 2002 Act, in the provisions regarding notice/time for child to have lived with such applicants, recognises their singular position and facilitates their applications. In an agency case (designated by the local authority as an adoption placement) the foster carers can now lodge an adoption application on completion of the statutory 10 week care period. In a non-agency case (where the placement has not been so designated) the foster carers can apply to adopt after one year of continuous care without local authority consent, though only after serving at least three months notice.

Capacity to meet criteria of eligibility and suitability is determined in the first instance by the Adoption Panel of the relevant adoption agency. The availability of adoption allowances eases the access of third party adopters to the process.

5.3.2.   FIRST PARTY ADOPTERS

These have traditionally received relaxed legislative treatment as regards eligibility and suitability criteria. While this broadly continues to be the case, since the introduction of the 2002 Act parents and relatives are now required to demonstrate that adoption, rather than any other order, is a better means of promoting the welfare of the child concerned. A step-parent is now enabled, under s 51(2), to make application alone without the necessity for this to be accompanied by an application from the birth parent partner; regardless of whether that partner is their spouse. Adoption orders issued to such applicants may be made subject to conditions of contact.

Because adoption is often inappropriate in circumstances where it can obscure the true nature of blood relationships, special guardianship orders now offer relatives an alternative. Relatives applying to adopt must now have cared for the child for three years within the last five unless exempted by the court.[83]

5.3.3.   INTERCOUNTRY ADOPTERS

The Adoption (Intercountry Aspects) Act 1999 gave effect to the Hague Convention 1993 and introduced a new framework to govern the adoption of overseas children by UK citizens. It requires prospective adopters to be assessed, approved and authorised in the UK before children are brought into the jurisdiction[84]; reinforced by the Adoption of Children from Overseas Regulations 2001. It also

---

[83]   See, s 42(5) and (6). Previously the care period for such an applicant was only 13 weeks.
[84]   See, *Re C* [1998] 2 FCR 641 and the case of 'the internet twins'.

requires all local authorities to include services to intercountry adopters within the general duty to provide an adoption service; a provision reinforced by s 2(8) of the 2002 Act.

6.   PRE-PLACEMENT COUNSELLING

Adoption agencies are now required, under s 3 of the 2002 Act, to ensure the availability of services to all parties involved in arrangements for a prospective adoption.[85] Such services necessarily include counselling,[86] which is specifically addressed in s 63 where provision is made for the relevant regulations to be drawn up, and in the National Adoption Standards.

6.1.   Adoption support services

Section 3(4) of the 2002 Act places a duty upon a local authority to respond to a request from any of the parties to a prospective adoption by carrying out an assessment of their needs for such a service which may include counselling.

6.1.1.   WISHES, WELFARE AND SAFETY OF THE CHILD

The National Standards require the needs, wishes, welfare and safety of the child to be placed at the centre of the adoption process. Every child is to have a named social worker who will be responsible for that child and will be required to explain to him or her the matters arising at every stage throughout the process. The child must be listened to and their views taken into account and where his or her wishes are not complied with this must be recorded and an explanation given to the child.

6.1.2.   ADOPTION PANEL

In practice the issue of whether or not counselling services have been provided, or will need to be, in relation to all parties to a prospective adoption (except family adoptions) will be raised by the Adoption Panel. The 2002 Act requires the Panel to make its recommendations to the local authority in advance of any such placement.

Providing information to prospective adopters, regarding the child to be placed with them, will be an important matter to be addressed at this stage. The adoption

---

[85]   The Houghton report, *op cit*, had first recommended that such services be available and this was subsequently given effect by s 1 of the Children Act 1975.

[86]   Reg 7(1) of the Adoption Agencies Regulations 1983 specifically required adoption agencies to provide counselling services to relinquishing mothers.

agency is required to ensure that prospective adopters have information relating to the child's family background, health and personal history.[87] Where insufficient or wrong information is provided, the placing agency may find itself liable to a compensation claim by the adopters.[88] This duty has been supplemented by requirements in the National Standards.

7. PLACEMENT RIGHTS AND DUTIES

The 2002 Act states minimum and maximum periods for all adoption placements; differences in duration and in the rights and duties of those involved, particularly birth parents and local authority, vary according to the type of adoption.

7.1. Placement decision

The law governing placements is to be found in sections 18–29 of the 2002 Act. Basically, this legislation makes a clear distinction between the public and private law contexts of placement decisions. In relation to the former, it removes the previous discretionary authority of a local authority to place a looked after child in a foster care placement 'with a view to adoption'. This practice, relying on the passage of time to strengthen the child's attachment to the carer while eroding it with the parent, thereby created a de facto adoption arrangement.[89] It positioned many foster carers to successfully claim that parents were being unreasonable in withholding consent to an adoption that by then had become the only feasible means of securing a child's welfare interests.

The 2002 Act requires instead that the placement decision is specifically authorised and thus open to challenge at that stage.[90] It designates two different decision-making routes for agency adoption placements: either under s 19, with parental consent and by an adoption agency or local authority; or under s 22, with a placement order and by a local authority. In relation to the latter, it largely avoids regulating placement decisions relating to family adoptions and leaves those in respect of intercountry adoptions to be regulated, where possible, by Convention provisions. In either case, as sections 18 and 19 of the 2002 Act make clear, once

---

[87] Reg 12(1) of the Adoption Agencies Regulations 1983. Also, see, s 54 of the 2002 Act.

[88] See, for example, *W v Essex County Council* [2000] 1 FCR 568 and *A and Another v Essex County Council* [2002] EWHC 2707 (QB).

[89] See, Department of Health, *Review of Adoption Law*, 1992 at para 27.2 for criticism of the injustice of this practice in relation to natural parents. Also, see *Gorgulu v Germany*, Application No 74969/01, ECHR, 26.02.2004 and further at Chap. 2.

[90] Section 18(2) of the 2002 Act directs an adoption agency to first satisfy itself that an adoption placement should be made after applying the paramountcy principle, the checklist and other s 1 considerations.

the child is six weeks old parental consent for the placement must then be formally obtained or the need for it dispensed with. Once placed, parental responsibility for the child is vested in the prospective adopters but must be shared with the placing agency and the birth parent/s until such time as the proceedings are determined.

7.1.1.   FAMILY ADOPTION

In the context of step-parent adoptions, the 2002 Act has ended the necessity for a birth parent to adopt their own child; the application will now be made by the step-parent alone but not before the completion of a six-month period of care. Whereas most adoption decisions are still authorised by birth parents, they seldom entail a change of placement except where a natural parent with parental responsibility exercises their right to place with a relative. This exemption is available under s 92(3) of the 2002 Act which continues the right previously available under the 1976 Act; a right not extended to an "intercountry" placement with relatives. Under s 144(1) a 'relative' for this purpose is defined as a grandparent, brother, sister, uncle or aunt (whether full blood, half blood or by marriage).

Notice of intention to commence adoption proceedings[91] must be served on the local authority which will then assess and report to the court as to whether the order sought, an alternative or no order would be in the best interests of the child.

7.1.2.   AGENCY ADOPTION

When considering the adoption option for a looked after child, an adoption agency is required to consider the child's relationships with relatives; including the natural father even if he does not have parental responsibility.[92] This provides an opportunity for practitioners to examine the merits of securing permanency through care arrangements, not necessarily but possibly by way of adoption, within the child's family. However, this may be dependent upon maternal consent.[93]

Following referral to the Adoption Panel, the recommendation and the agency decision, the adoption agency must then draw up a 'placement plan'.

A growing number of placement decisions are public law in nature. Indeed, as has been noted[94]:

> The UK is closer to the US in the extent to which it is willing to over-rule parental wishes in order to place children for adoption. Elsewhere in Europe there is a much greater reluctance to over-rule the wishes of parents.

---

[91] Section 44 of the 2002 Act.
[92] Section 1(4)(f) of the 2002 Act.
[93] See, *Re R* [2001] 1 FCR 238 where the court upheld a natural mother's veto on any such overtures being made to her siblings or other relatives by the local authority.
[94] See, Performance and Innovation Unit, *Prime Minister's Review of Adoption*, London, Cabinet Office, 2000 at Annex 4.

These may be made with or without parental consent but this must now be determined prior to placement. Where, following counselling, a parent has given their written and witnessed (by CAFCASS officers) consent or 'advanced consent' to an adoption agency in respect of a child more than six weeks of age, then the agency may make an adoption placement in respect of the child concerned. The placement may be chosen by the consenting party or by the agency. Otherwise only a local authority can make an adoption placement and only if it first obtains a placement order having established that the consent of both parents is available or can be dispensed with, and the child is the subject of a care order or that the grounds can be met for such an order. Where a consenting parent withdraws their consent before the prospective adopters lodge their application, then too the local authority must obtain a placement order if the adoption placement is to be maintained. The court must give due consideration to the welfare checklist before determining an application for a placement order and placements made by adoption agencies are also governed by the checklist.

Section 1(5) of the 2002 Act requires agency placements to be made after giving due consideration to the child's religious persuasion, racial origin and cultural and linguistic background. This new legislative directive has been reinforced by the National Standards which require preference to be given to ethnic matching as a determinant of placement choice, all other factors being equal.

7.2.   Placement supervision

There is a legal requirement to ensure that adoption placements are safeguarded and the duties to safeguard the child's welfare interests are statutory, specific, prescriptive and comprehensive. They rest most rigorously upon all adoption agencies but apply also, though with less intrusiveness, to family adoptions from notification to hearing. During this period parental responsibility remains at least partially vested in the birth parents.

7.2.1.   REMOVAL OF CHILD

Where a consensual placement, made within six weeks of child's birth, is terminated by parental retraction of consent within that period then the child must be removed and returned to the parent within seven days; unless a placement order is in effect or an application has been lodged. Otherwise, a parent may withdraw consent at any point up until the application has been lodged[95] in which case the child must be returned to the parent within 14 days; subject to the former caveat. In such circumstances, if it has not already done so, the local authority may apply under s 22 for a placement order if it considers the grounds can be satisfied.

---

[95]   Section 52(4) of the 2002 Act.

However, from time of lodging an adoption application in court, all consensual placements and those made in respect of children subject to placement orders cannot be terminated without prior approval of the court.

8. THE HEARING AND THE ORDER/S AVAILABLE

Adoption in the UK remains a judicial process and the judicial role is still largely as traditionally defined. If the hearing establishes that certain grounds relating to eligibility, suitability, duration of placement[96] and consent are satisfied then an adoption order can be made. Whether it is made will depend not upon the availability or otherwise of consent but on whether the paramountcy principle applied in conjunction with the welfare checklist indicates that it is the most appropriate order, and better than no order, for the child concerned. Evidence on welfare matters will be submitted to the court by the adoption agency involved. The making of an adoption order requires a predictive assessment of welfare and allows for legal compromises to be made to condition the future exclusiveness of the order. The 2002 Act also makes some significant changes to the powers and options available to the judiciary in England & Wales.

8.1. Where consent is available

The adoption process in the UK is gradually becoming less consensual. In England & Wales, as before the 2002 Act, the consent of an unmarried father without parental responsibility is not strictly required though notice should be served on him and where feasible his views sought. The consent of an older child, the subject of proceedings, is also not required under the 2002 Act; although his or her views will be sought these will not be regarded as determinative. However, even where all necessary consents are available the court may well make an order other than the one sought. There is now a statutory requirement that court and agency consider whether an alternative order under either the 1989 or 2002 Act would be more appropriate and/or whether ongoing contact arrangements will be necessary to promote the welfare interests of the child concerned.[97]

---

[96] Ten weeks in relation to a looked after child (s 42(2) of the 2002 Act).
[97] See, Performance and Innovation Unit, *Prime Minister's Review of Adoption, op cit*, where it is stated that "at least 70% of adopted children have some form of contact with members of their birth families" (para 3.141).

8.2. Where consent is not available

In England & Wales, under s 52(1) of the 2002 Act, there are now only two grounds for dispensing with parental consent whether in the context of agency or family adoptions. This may occur either (a) on the traditional statutory ground that the parent or guardian cannot be found or is incapable of giving consent or (b) on the new ground that 'the welfare of the child requires the consent to be dispensed with'. Section 1(7) of the 2002 Act applies the paramountcy principle of s 1(2) to the issue of dispensing with parental consent; thus consigning to history many decades of complex jurisprudence regarding 'the unreasonable withholding of consent'.

Once the court makes a finding that adoption is in the child's best interests, gives this finding the weighting required under s 1(2) and considers the matters specified in s 1(6), then the outcome in the context of s 52(1) is in reality a foregone conclusion.

8.3. The orders

Apart from granting the adoption order applied for, or granting it subject to conditions, the court may instead make any of the public and private family law orders now available under the 1989 and 2002 Acts. These include residence order, extended residence order, parental responsibility order, care order, supervision order or special guardianship order.

9. THRESHOLDS FOR EXITING THE ADOPTION PROCESS

Since the introduction of the 2002 Act, the decision as to whether the court makes the order applied for, with or without conditions, or any other order or no order will be determined by applying the paramountcy principle in conjunction with the welfare checklist.

9.1. The welfare interests of the child

The welfare interests of the child are determined by the 'welfare checklist' which serves to identify the 'substance' of welfare in relation to the child concerned while the paramountcy test defines the weighting to be given to the sum total of such matters relative to all other considerations. The 'no-delay' and the 'no-order' principles must also be applied. The no-delay principle is reinforced by the provisions of s 109 which require a timetable to be drawn up and steps specified to expedite it.

Whether an adoption order can be made is determined in accordance with the statutory criteria relating to eligibility, suitability and consent. Whether it or some other order will be made is determined by the particular welfare interests of the child concerned after applying the 'welfare checklist'.

9.1.1. THE WELFARE CHECKLIST

Section 1(4) of the 2002 Act provides a list of considerations to which, among other matters, the court must have regard.

(a) *The child's ascertainable wishes and feelings regarding the decision (considered in the light of the child's age and understanding).* This conservative restating of the law relating to the capacity of a child to influence decisions taken concerning their welfare clearly avoids addressing consent issues. However, the wishes of an older child regarding his or her proposed adoption have to be ascertained and taken into account and case law indicates that good reason will have to shown if an order is to be made contrary to those wishes.[98]

(b) *The child's particular needs.* This clause implicitly refers to the 'physical, emotional and educational needs' in s 1(3)(b) of the 1989 Act and its associated case law which must be interpreted in relation to the particular circumstances of the child concerned. The need to retain the child in the care context in which he or she has formed safe attachments and which offers the best chance of permanency will be crucial to addressing their emotional needs.

(c) *The likely effect on the child (throughout his life) of having ceased to be a member of the original family and become an adopted person.* This novel requirement imposes on the court the duty to take a long-term view of whether adoption will continue to meet the needs of the subject throughout their adult life. Established case law indicates that even if adoption could only promote welfare in adulthood, this would be sufficient justification for making the order.[99]

(d) *The child's age, sex, background and any of the child's characteristics which the court or agency considers relevant.* This catchall provision gives the court absolute discretion to determine the welfare factor most relevant to the circumstances of the child concerned.

(e) *Any harm (within the meaning of the Children's Act 1989) which the child has suffered or is at risk of suffering.* Again, correlating the provisions of the 1989 and 2002 Acts strategically strengthens the child care context of

---

[98] See, for example, *Re D (Minors)(Adoption by Step-parent)* (1981) 2 FLR 102.
[99] See, *Re D (A Minor)(Adoption order: validity)* [1991] 2 FLR 66.

modern adoption practice and maximises consistency of interpretation. It is to be noted that the definition of 'harm' in the 1989 Act has been broadened by the 2002 Act to include 'impairment suffered from seeing or hearing the ill-treatment of another'[100] to, in effect, allow for the possible non-consensual adoption of children who have suffered harm from witnessing domestic violence.

(f) *The relationship which the child has with relatives, and with any other person in relation to whom the court or agency considers the question to be relevant, including—*

  (i) *the likelihood of any such relationship continuing and the value to the child of its doing so;*

 (ii) *the ability and willingness of any of the child's relatives, or of any such person, to provide the child with a secure environment in which the child can develop, and otherwise to meet the child's needs;*

(iii) *the wishes and feelings of any of the child's relatives, or of any such person, regarding the child.*

This provision places a statutory duty upon court and local authority to assess the ability and willingness of relatives to undertake care responsibility for a child and also requires that an assessment be made of the value to that child of any ongoing relationship with a relative. It is likely to be used particularly to safeguard established sibling relationships.

9.1.2. THE PARAMOUNTCY PRINCIPLE

The rights and reasonableness of the case presented by a contesting birth parent will not deflect the court from now looking to the best interests of the child as the overriding determinant. Even where all parties satisfy eligibility/suitability criteria, relevant consents have been provided, the child is available and it would be demonstrably to his or her material advantage, the court may still determine that disposal options other than adoption would better serve the interests of the child concerned. The fact that the child, the birth parent/s, prospective adopters and/or others (including expert witnesses[101]) have a clear and positive view as to what constitutes 'best interests' will not prevent the court from imposing its own contrary decision. It is for the court to decide, after objectively applying the

---

[100] Section 31(9) of the 1989 Act as amended by s 120 of the 2002 Act.

[101] See, *Re B* [1996] 1 FLR 667 where an appeal by a local authority, supported by the guardian *ad litem*, argued that the judge at first instance had erred in law in not acting on the unanimous opinions of the experts, all of whom urged that the child be placed for adoption. The court dismissed the appeal, citing with approval the comment of Lord President Cooper in *Davie v Magistrates of Edinburgh* 1953 SC 34, 40 that "the parties have invoked the decision of a judicial tribunal and not an oracular pronouncement by an expert" *per* Ward LJ at pp. 669–670.

welfare checklist, on a projected basis in relation to considerations throughout the child's life, what order if any satisfies the test of the paramountcy principle.

9.2.   Representing the child's welfare interests

In the UK, the welfare interests of a child in adoption proceedings will be represented by a CAFCASS officer accompanied by a social work report from the relevant agency. In England & Wales, however, as before the introduction of the 2002 Act, there is no provision for automatic representation of a child's legal interests by a solicitor, though in contested cases such interests will be asserted by the court making the child a party and enabling him or her to be represented by a solicitor. The 2002 Act explicitly requires that a child's wishes be sought and taken into account but it remains the case that his or her consent is not required. Expert witnesses may be called to give evidence. All family adoptions are subject to prior mandatory professional screening the results of which are judicially taken into account in determining welfare.

10.   THE OUTCOME OF THE ADOPTION PROCESS

Section 1(6) of the 2002 Act requires the court to consider the whole range of powers available under both that legislation and the 1989 Act before making any order. The same provision adds that the court should not make any order under the 2002 Act unless convinced that doing so is better for the child than not doing so.

10.1.   Adoption order

In the UK the traditional unconditional, consensual, third party adoption order is becoming increasingly rare and in England & Wales will become more so following the full introduction of the 2002 Act. Adoption orders made in favour of parents and relatives had grown to form the major proportion of annual orders but had decreased and will decrease further when the 2002 Act makes alternatives available which the court is obliged to consider.[102]

10.2.   Conditional adoption order

Perhaps in most adoptions there is now some form of ongoing contact between the child and their birth parent or with other members of their family of origin.

---

[102] Section 1(6) of the 2002 Act requires the court to be satisfied that adoption is a better option than any other available to the court while s 44(2)–(6) requires certain conditions to be met.

Most often this results from arrangements voluntarily entered into by the parties concerned. However, the issue of an adoption order subject to a condition, most usually directing specified contact arrangements between the child and members of his or her family of origin, though still relatively rare has also become more common in recent years as the courts strive to ensure that each order fits the particular welfare interests of the child concerned. This development will accelerate in the wake of the 2002 Act because of the requirement in s 46(6) that the court consider the necessity for post-adoption contact arrangements. The authority to attach a condition, however, must now be sought from s 8 of the 1989 Act as there is no longer any equivalent to s 12(6) of the 1976 Act. Conditional orders are likely to remain firmly associated with child care adoption with a strong focus on maintaining links between siblings.

10.3. Alternative private family law order

The requirement that the court consider alternative orders available under the 1989 and 2002 Acts provides an opportunity to choose any one or combination of private family law orders. Those most likely to be selected include the following.

- **Special guardianship order**

Available under s 14 of the 1989 Act (as amended by s 115 of the 2002 Act), this order appoints a named person as 'special guardian' of the child. It vests in that guardian the degree of parental responsibility necessary to safeguard the welfare interests of the child to the exclusion of others. This order may be accompanied by a s 8 contact order and is likely to be particularly relevant for older children or those being cared for by foster parents (the order discharges the care order) or relatives, for whom the draconian effects of total legal separation from birth family would be inappropriate.

- **Extended residence order**

Available under s 12 of the 1989 Act (as amended by s 114 of the 2002 Act), this order may be made in favour of any person who is not a parent or guardian of the child concerned and may continue until the latter attains adulthood.

- **Parental responsibility order**

Available under s 4 of the 1989 Act (as amended by the 2002 Act), this order may be made in favour of a step-parent as an alternative to the more informal means of acquiring parental responsibility through agreement with the birth parent/s. It provides for an ongoing sharing of parental responsibilities with birth parents.

10.4.   Alternative public family law order

The 1989 Act removed the traditional discretionary judicial option of making a care order, where necessary, when rejecting an adoption application; instead there was a power to require the relevant local authority to conduct an investigation into the child's circumstances. This has been continued by the 2002 Act. If the court should consider, during the course of adoption proceedings, that grounds of significant harm may exist then it can as before refer the matter to the local authority. On a subsequent application from the local authority, the court may in turn issue a care order or a supervision order where the significant harm grounds are satisfied and where it considers this to be more appropriate than any other order or no order at all.

11.   THE EFFECT OF AN ADOPTION ORDER

A full adoption order remains, after as before the introduction of the 2002 Act, the most absolute and irrevocable of all orders affecting children; as before there are no provisions relating to any possible variation or revocation. However, not all its legal characteristics in relation to the parties concerned are as immutable as they were traditionally.

11.1.   The child

An adoption order confers upon the child concerned the status attributes identified in s 67 of the 2002 Act and traditionally associated with adoption. This requires that he or she 'is to be treated in law as if born as the child of the adopters or adopter' and as 'the legitimate child of the adopters or adopter'[103] (which in the case of same gender adopters introduces equity at the price of logic). It also entails acquiring the nationality,[104] domicile and residence of the adopters and an entitlement to inherit from their estate.[105] The distinctions traditionally made by the law between an adopted and a 'natural' child have been maintained.[106]

---

[103] See, further, Chapter 4, sections 66–76, *Status of Adopted Children*, the Adoption and Children Act 2002.

[104] See, s 1(5) of the British Nationality Act 1981. Although not always: only if the adopters, or one of them, are British citizens and the order is made in this country, will the child acquire British citizenship. In the light of the rules regarding habitual residence, this could give rise to future difficulties (e.g., French citizens habitually resident in this country adopt a child who, although born here, is not a British citizen). The author is grateful to Deborah Cullen for this observation.

[105] See, sections 69–73 of the 2002 Act.

[106] See, para 30 of Sched 4 of the Sexual Offences Act 2004, which amends the 2002 Act to continue the legal exception to incest where sexual relations occur between an adopted brother and sister

11.2.   The birth parent/s

The effects of a full adoption order on the legal standing of the birth parent/s are largely as traditionally defined. Section 46 of the 2002 Act states that the order operates to extinguish 'the parental responsibility which any person other than the adopters or adopter has for the adopted child immediately before the making of the order' and any other order or duty unless specifically exempted. However, unlike traditional orders, adoption may now be qualified by conditions providing for ongoing contact arrangements between the child and the birth parent/s.

11.3.   The adopters

Again, as before the 2002 Act, the effect of an adoption order is to vest the adopters with all parental rights, duties and responsibilities in respect of the adopted child. The traditional absolute and exclusive nature of the order may now, however, be compromised by a condition permitting post-adoption contact arrangements while its traditional privacy characteristic may equally be compromised by ongoing public health and social care support services.

12.   POST-ADOPTION SUPPORT SERVICES

The 2002 Act introduced a concept of support services, more comprehensive and with wider applicability than that previously available since 1988 from local authorities. These are to be available at any time (ie both pre and post-adoption) and for all parties or others involved in any type of adoption.[107] In relation to adoption services for looked after children, the provisions of the 2002 Act are reinforced by the National Standards which apply quite specific requirements in relation to matters such as timescales for service provision, extent of information to be provided etc.

The impact of these services and the necessary accompanying professional intrusion will over time accelerate the changing character of adoption as it becomes more a public and less a private family law proceeding.

---

aged 18 or more. Also, s 74(1) leaves intact the traditional rule relating to consanguinity and prohibited degrees of relationship.

[107] Following the 2002 Act, the Dept of Health issued a consultation paper entitled *The Draft Adoption Support Services (Local Authorities)(Transitory and Transitional Provisions)(England) Regulations and Draft Accompanying Guidance*, December 2002. See, also, Dept of Health, *Providing Effective Adoption Support*.

12.1.   Adoption support services

Section 3(2)(b) of the 2002 Act places a duty upon all local authorities to ensure the availability of specified adoption support services. Section 4 of that Act requires all local authorities to respond to any request for assistance from a party to an adoption by carrying out a needs assessment, though the provision of related services is a matter that has been left to their discretion depending upon available local resources. It is envisaged that this will be a multi-agency and interdisciplinary assessment resulting in possible long-term resource commitments from a number of agencies.

12.1.1.   ADOPTION SUPPORT AGENCY

This is defined by s 8(1) of the 2002 Act as 'an undertaking, the purpose of which, or one of the purposes of which, is the provision of adoption support services'. Section 8(3) of the 2002 Act amends the Care Standards Act 2000 to permit the registration of independent adoption support agencies in addition to those established by adoption agencies.

13.   INFORMATION DISCLOSURE, TRACING AND RE-UNIFICATION SERVICES

The right of one party to access information given in confidence by another has always been a fraught issue in law and has certainly been so throughout the statutory life of the adoption process. The 2002 Act has introduced some changes to the law previously governing this sensitive matter.

13.1.   The Registrar General

The Registrar General continues his responsibilities much as before in relation to compiling information in the Adopted Children Register and the Adoption Contact Register. However, as regards the disclosure of that information, the role of an adoption agency has now become of central importance.

13.1.1.   THE ADOPTED CHILDREN REGISTER

This register is maintained by the Registrar[108] who uses an index to cross-reference entries marked 'adopted' in the main register of live births with entries in the

---

[108] This facility has a history of being very popular; by 1999 some 70,000 people had sought adoption related information from the Registrar General.

Adopted Children Register. Access to the information necessary to connect corresponding entries made in the two registers is governed by s 79 of the 2002 Act which performs a dual function. It requires an adoption agency to request the Registrar General to make available that information in respect of a named adopted person. It also permits the Registrar General to divulge on request to any adopted person (i.e., who has attained their 18th birthday) information identifying the adoption agency involved in their adoption.

13.1.2. THE ADOPTION CONTACT REGISTER

Again, this register[109] is maintained by the Registrar General in the same way as before the 2002 Act to record the wishes for contact of relatives of adopted persons and to provide the information necessary to facilitate contact.

13.2. The adoption agency

The 2002 Act places the adoption agency in the driving seat for all post-adoption information disclosure and contact purposes including adoptee access to original birth certificate. Sections 54 and 56–65 of that Act govern the role of an adoption agency in relation to record keeping, information disclosure, making contact arrangements and providing counselling. Section 60 enables an adopted person to obtain the following:

- the information necessary to obtain his or her birth certificate;
- any information given to the adoptive parents on placement; and
- a copy of any 'prescribed document' held by the court.

Section 61 outlines the four stage process whereby an adoption agency responds to a request from an adopted person for information other than that governed by s 60:

- application made;
- adoption agency considers whether application is appropriate;
- if so, then it must take all reasonable steps to contact and ascertain the views of any other person to whom the information relates; and
- in the light of the particular circumstances, the adoption agency must decide whether or not to disclose the information sought.

The right to disclose or refuse disclosure rests with the adoption agency although its decisions will be subject to possible review by an Independent Review Panel to be established by the government. Regulations will further specify the details regarding matters such as type of information, conditions for disclosure etc while

---

[109] Established by Sched 10 of the Children Act 1989.

the National Adoption Standards also provide guidance relating to the provision of information disclosure services.

13.3.   Adoption support agencies

Under s 98 of the 2002 Act, a registered adoption support agency is authorised to seek access to the information held in registers or in court or adoption agency records necessary to advise parties to a pre-1975 adoption on matters relating to identity information and possible contact.

14.   CONCLUSION

Adoption in England & Wales now sits, uncomfortably, at the crossroads of public and private family law. This is a juncture at which parental responsibilities may be consensually relinquished by birth parents and assumed by others or coercively removed and transferred. Adoption is intimately linked into the family law framework leading to that point and reflects many of the more pervasive principles and pressures currently influencing practice within the broad body of family law. In particular, changes to the legal functions of adoption are indicative of those occurring elsewhere in family law. There is now an unmistakable emphasis on ensuring that adoption satisfies a public interest requirement that this means of providing for the future upbringing of children is subject to much the same controls and supports, and is tested against alternative welfare options, as are other statutory means of doing so. This is evident in the threshold criteria marking each stage of the adoption process. It is evident also in the types of bodies, forums and rules to which the participants are subject. Mostly, it is apparent in the use of the welfare principle to ensure that private purposes pursued by parents and adopters and public purposes pursued by a local authority now respect the best interests of the child as the paramount consideration. This may entail compromises or additions to the order issued by the court that would not have been previously contemplated in adoption proceedings.

Chapter 6

THE ADOPTION PROCESS IN IRELAND

1.   INTRODUCTION

In Ireland the law of adoption, now consisting of seven pieces of legislation,[1] has provided the legal framework for a practice that has seen 41,618 children adopted[2] since the Adoption Act 1952 first introduced a legal means for making this possible. As elsewhere, this period has seen a steady annual decline in adoption orders—from 1,115 in 1980 down to 263 Irish adoption orders in 2003. It has also been a period in which there has been an uncoupling of the traditional association between unmarried mothers and adoption as the latter has gradually ceased to be used almost exclusively as a means of regulating the non-kinship placements of voluntarily relinquished illegitimate babies. Instead it is increasingly becoming a means of sanctioning the private family arrangements of birth parents, almost always mothers, in respect of their own children. Adoption as a public child care resource, legislatively expedited elsewhere, is not encouraged by government policy in this jurisdiction which partially explains the steady increase in intercountry adoptions.

This chapter begins with a brief history of the adoption process in Ireland and an account of the main influences that have combined to shape its current social role. This leads into an overview of contemporary law, policy and practice

---

[1]   The Adoption Acts of 1952, 1964, 1974, 1976, 1988, 1991 and 1998; two further Acts are imminent.

[2]   The annual reports of the Adoption Board (or An Bord Uchtála), available from Government Publications, Molesworth St. Dublin, provide a useful and comprehensive source of information on adoption in Ireland

Kerry O'Halloran (ed.), The Politics of Adoption, 165–195.
© 2006 *Springer. Printed in The Netherlands.*

including a guide to the complicated set of statutes that now constitute the legal framework for adoption. Account is taken of the results of the adoption consultation process completed in January 2005 but, in the absence of anticipated new legislation, the legal framework is assessed as it stands in the summer of that year.

The chapter then applies the template of legal functions (see, Chap. 3) to outline the adoption process, identify and assess its distinctive characteristics and facilitate a comparative analysis with other jurisdictions. In conclusion, some observations are made about the representativeness and significance of the characteristics of the adoption process in Ireland.

2.   BACKGROUND

Adoption as a statutory process has a particularly short history in Ireland. It began fifty years ago, on 1st January 1954, when the Adoption Act 1952 came into effect. However, it did play a part in ancient Irish history as a practice intimately linked to the clan system and governed for hundreds of years by the Brehon laws.[3] Arguably, modern adoption law and practice remains rooted to some degree in ancient practices when clans and kinship networks were central to the social infrastructure of this jurisdiction.

2.1.   Traditional use of adoption

A thousand years ago, under the Brehon laws, a form of kinship adoption had long been practiced whereby members of a child's extended family or clan would undertake to rear him or her as a means of binding the clan group into a stronger more cohesive unit. Much the same ends were achieved by reciprocal placements of children between clans as a demonstration of mutual allegiance.[4] In both, adoption or *fóesam* simply meant "taking into protection" and was seen as a means of allying with the fortunes of others. It had clearly defined legal consequences for the adopted person. As has been explained: "rights of inheritance may be acquired by a person adopted into a kin-group, either through payment of an adoption fee *(lóg fóesma)* or through invitation".[5] Such a person is then described as *fine thacair* or "kinsman by summoning". An adopted son who failed to carry out his filial duties *(goire)* could be disinherited and another adopted in his place.[6]

---

[3]   See, for example, Kelly, F., *Early Irish Law*, Dublin Institute of Administration Studies (1988).
[4]   See, Gilligan, R., *Irish Child Care Services: Policy Practice and Provision*, Institute of Public Administration, Dublin (1991).
[5]   See, Kelly, F., *Early Irish Law*, *op cit.*
[6]   *Ibid,* at p. 105 where the author explains that adoption was originally a contract bound by sureties and ratified by the head of the kin. See also pp. 86–90 for an interesting account of the importance of 'fosterage' in early Irish society and the respective duties of foster child and foster parent according to their rank in society.

Eventually, the gap left by the fading authority of social systems based on feudalism, the Brehon laws and the extended agricultural family was filled by the state through the provision of basic containment and shelter as required by the Poor Laws.[7] The Irish Poor Law Amendment Act 1862 enabled young children who would previously have been consigned to the workhouse to instead be "boarded-out" with state approved caring families; an official approach which outlived that legislative framework to become a key component in the 20th century public child care system. However, the non-kinship adoption of such children was not encouraged. The Poor Law administrators feared that the existence of a means whereby parents could be totally relieved of their responsibilities would amount to condoning immorality and encourage the production of more children to become a further burden on the rates of the parish. Kinship fostering, where a family would take in its own rather than let, or be seen to let, relatives go to the workhouse, was both common and encouraged by the Poor Law authorities.[8]

2.2. Modern influences on the development of adoption

In Ireland, during the 50 year period since the introduction of adoption legislation, considerable economic and other social changes occurred, as elsewhere in the western world, which led to a loosening of the legal relationship between the family unit and the state. In all western nations at much the same time, adoption was required to accommodate a similar generic set of problems and to fit in with new emerging social norms governing parenting arrangements. In particular, the period separating the 1974 and the 1988 Adoption Acts saw a number of influences converging to shape the modern use of adoption.

2.2.1. DECLINE IN THE MARRIAGE RATE

Marriage became less popular: the annual rate of marriages decreased from 7.0 per 1,000 of the population in 1970 to 5.1 in 1988; the number of people seeking sepa-ration, annulment, or a foreign divorce increased dramatically during this period.[9]

2.2.2. INCREASE IN RATE OF NON-MARITAL BIRTHS

Childbirth became less dependent upon marriage: the annual number of non-marital births multiplied from 968 in 1960 to 1,708 in 1970, 4,517 in 1983[10] and

---

[7]   See, Robbins, J., *The Lost Children: A Study of Charity Children in Ireland 1700–1900* (1980).
[8]   See, Benet (1976) at p. 60. Also, Eekelaar, J., *Family Law and Social Policy* (1984) and Gilligan, R., (1991).
[9]   The following categories of separated persons were recorded in the 1986 census: deserted (11,622): marriage annulled (983); legally separated (7,187); other separated (13,062); divorced in another country (4,391).
[10] See, Central Statistics Office.

reached 16,461 in 1999. In 2001, they accounted for 31% of annual births as opposed to 2.14% in 1953.

2.2.3.   WELFARE BENEFITS FOR SINGLE PARENTS

Since 1973 preferential welfare benefits have been available for single parents thereby allowing those with low incomes to consider child rearing as a financially viable option. This also resulted in a lessening of the social stigma traditionally associated with the role of a single mother, reducing the pressure previously felt by many in that position to surrender a child for adoption. Consequently, whereas in 1967 some 96.9% of non-marital births resulted in adoptions, this was true for only 16.74% of such births in 1985 and for a mere 1.93% in 1999.

2.2.4.   MATERNITY BY CHOICE

Developments in medicine and law in the neighbouring jurisdictions increased the extent to which maternity for some in Ireland became a chosen option. Pregnancy could be either avoided, through the use of improved contraceptives, or terminated by abortion.[11] Pregnancy for the infertile became a stronger possibility due to the introduction of techniques of artificial insemination and the practice of surrogate motherhood.[12]

2.2.5.   INCREASE OF CHILDREN IN CARE

Finally, increasing numbers of children entered the public child care system. The child care population increased from 1,717 in 1970 to 2,614 in 1988. The proportion in residential care was more than half in 1978 but only 26.9% in 1988, the balance being almost exclusively in foster care. By 2001, the care population had increased to 3,600 of which 3,200 were in foster care. Because of the limited access to adoption for children from marital families, provided by the 1988 Act, a far higher proportion of the Irish child care population remain in long-term foster care than is the case in other modern western jurisdictions.[13]

---

[11]   Annually published statistical data reveal that many thousands of young women, with addresses in Ireland, undergo abortion operations in the United Kingdom.

[12]   Note that some such options, for example surrogate motherhood, would be illegal in this jurisdiction.

[13]   See, further, *Foster Care—A Child Centred Partnership*, Stationery Office, Dublin, 2001 and Gilligan R, 'Children Adrift in Care-Can the Child Care Act rescue the 50% who are in care five years or more', *Irish Social Worker*, Vol. 14, No. 1.

2.3. Resulting trends in types of adoption

The adoption of babies by third parties or 'strangers', where the adopter is un-related in any way to the adoptee was until very recently, in Ireland as in many western nations, the most prevalent form of adoption. In the latter half of the 20th century, much the same set of generic problems in those countries triggered a change in their use of adoption. In Ireland, however, this transformation had a significantly different twist.

2.3.1. THIRD PARTY ADOPTIONS

The traditional adoption model now known more simply as 'non-family adoptions', grew from and remained rooted in the concept of a Christian family unit, based on lifelong and monogamous marital union and defended by the Constitution. The child of such a union, unless orphaned, could not be available for adoption; this legal process was exclusively reserved for non-marital children[14] and indeed in 1967 a total of 96.9% of those born that year were adopted. By 2001, when Ireland had become a quite different society, the total had fallen to 1.6%.

The Catholic Church played a pivotal role in this process being initially responsible for arranging institutional care for unmarried mothers,[15] the placement of their children and the selection of suitable adopters; it also facilitated the overseas placement of Irish babies, mainly in the United States.

The total children adopted by third parties far outnumber those adopted through a combination of all other forms; only in the last decade have family adoptions come to constitute an annual majority in a decreasing total.[16] However, whereas in the past third party adoption conformed to a very definite model, it now accommodates a number of variations.

- **Adoption of children with special needs**

Children with 'special needs' are defined in this jurisdiction as those suffering from learning or physical disability, or both, with significant social and health care needs. Whereas this variation of third-party adoption has been successful in Northern Ireland, as in the UK generally and in the United States, there is little indication that it attracts potential adopters in Ireland. In 1993 10 orders

---

[14] The Adoption Act 1952 confined the use of adoption to: orphans and non-marital children aged between 6 months and 7 years; adopters who were married couples living together, widows, the child's birth mother/father and certain relatives (on the mother's side); and to adopters who were of the same religion as the child.

[15] See, the 'Magdalene Sisters' etc.

[16] For example, whereas in 1991 family adoptions constituted 43.6% of the total of 590 orders, in 2000 they constituted 68.32% of 303 orders.

were made in respect of such children; 6 in 1995; 2 in 1996; 3 in 1997; and 1 in 1998.

• Child care adoption

The increase in numbers of children in care has not, unlike comparable cir-cumstances in the UK and elsewhere, resulted in a proportionate increase in child care adoptions. Access to the adoption option for a child in care is very largely de-termined by the marital status of his or her parents which results in very few such adoptions. The Adoption Act 1988 provided for the possibility of non-consensual adoption for children in long-term foster care, whether from marital or non-marital families. Under s 36(1)(c) of the Child Care Act 1991 a health board can place a child who may be eligible for adoption "with a suitable person with a view to his adoption". Also, under s 6(3), a board may "take a child into its care with a view to his adoption and maintain him . . . until he is placed for adoption". But the boards' capacity to utilise the adoption option for a child in its care has remained virtually unaltered by the 1988 and 1991 Acts. For example, in 2000 the Board made only 5 adoption orders under the 1988 Act, none concerning children from a marital family background. In 2003, of the 68 agency placements only 20 were in respect of children in long-term foster care.

• Open adoption

This form of adoption has no specific standing in law, although the practice[17] has developed to become a significant characteristic of adoption in Ireland and is permitted under the 1991 Act (as amended by the 1998 Act) in relation to the adoption of children from overseas. In many family adoptions the adopting birth mother and her spouse make a voluntary agreement with the child's father to facilitate post-adoption contact arrangements between him and the child. In *Northern Area Health Board v An Bord Uchtála*[18] McGuinness J noted this trend:

> Adoption practice in general has become more open in recent years. The old insistence on secrecy and a complete exclusion of the natural mother has virtually gone and it is not uncommon for adopted children to continue to meet their birth parents from time to time.

• Same sex adoptions

Co-habiting couples, however, whether or not of the same gender, may not adopt. Should one partner in a same sex relationship choose to make an adoption

---

[17] Note that in *W.O'R v E.H.* [1996] 2 IR 248 the Supreme Court held that any order allowing the non-marital father (or any other person) access is deemed to have lapsed upon the making of the adoption order. For a broad definition, see Triseliotis, J., 'Open Adoption' in Mullender, A. (ed.) *Open Adoption: The Philosophy and the Practice*, British Agencies for Adoption and Fostering, London, 1991 at pp. 17–35.

[18] [2003] 1 ILRM 481. Also, see, *J.B. and D.B. v. An Bord Uchtála*, (1998).

application this will prove difficult as the law only permits this in "particular circumstances". Since 1991, some 1,766 adoption orders have been granted to married couples but only 29 to single applicants. The National Census of 2002 recorded 2,580 gay or lesbian couples in settled domestic relationships.

- **Intercountry adoptions**

In recent years this type of adoption has been proportionately more significant in Ireland than in neighbouring jurisdictions. Its development is usually traced to the altruistic surge of Irish interest in the very many children found to have been abandoned in Romanian orphanages in the post-Ceausescu period in the early 1990s. However, that interest was also stimulated by the lack of alternative forms of third party adoption. In fact intercountry adoption existed in an inverted form during the years 1948–1968 when as many as 2,000 children born to un-married mothers were discretely removed by religious organisations from Ireland for adoption overseas, usually in the United States.[19]

The number of children adopted from overseas has increased every year since the introduction of the Adoption Act 1991 (see, further, below). A total of 2,124 were adopted between 1991 and 2003: 782 (36.82%) from Romania; 489 (23.02%) from Russia; 164 (7.72%) from China; 148 (6.97%) from Vietnam; 146 (6.87%) from Guatemala; the remainder being largely from South America, India. Thailand and from countries that formerly constituted part of Russia. In 2003, the Adoption Board made 468 declarations of eligibility and suitability to adopt outside the State and it made 341 entries in the Register of Foreign Adoptions (in 2001 the figures were 391 and 163 respectively, which represented an increase of almost 40% on the previous year).[20]

2.3.2.   FIRST PARTY ADOPTIONS

The adoption of a child by a person or persons related to him or her is referred to as a 'family adoption' and has become the most common type of adoption in Ireland. It is a relatively modern phenomenon in this jurisdiction unlike, for example, in the United States. In the latter jurisdiction some 50% of all adoptions in 1970 were by relatives whereas in Ireland at that time the corresponding proportion was approx 10%. In Ireland family adoptions increased from 126 in 1975 to 196 in 2001 when 180 were made in favour of step-parents, almost invariably in respect of a non-marital child. In 2002, 167 of the 266 domestic adoptions were step-parent adoptions family adoptions and of the 171 family adoptions in 2003, 164 involved step-parents. However, in Ireland neither parent can shed their guardianship duties in respect of a child of their marriage and therefore cannot be held to have 'abandoned' that child as the term is construed under the 1988 Act.

---

[19]   Milotte, M., *Banished Babies*, New Island Books, Dublin, 1997.
[20]   See, *Report of An Bord Uchtála*, Stationery Office, Dublin, 2000, at para 3.1.

This presents an insurmountable legal block to an application from a remarried widow/widower in respect of the child of their previous marriage.

3.   OVERVIEW OF MODERN ADOPTION LAW, POLICY AND PRACTICE

The above influences and trends resulted in significant changes in adoption practice in Ireland and were accompanied by adjustments to the legal framework and challenges to policy. These developments were necessarily constrained by constitutional imperatives.

3.1.   Adoption and the Constitution

In Ireland there is a constitutional presumption that 'the best interests of the child' are to be found within his or her family and only the most compelling reasons will justify the removal of a child from their marital family unit.[21] The state, in Article 42, section 1 of the Constitution, acknowledges that the primary and natural educator of the child is the family and guarantees to respect the inalienable right and duty of parents to provide, according to their means, for the religious and moral, intellectual, physical and social education of their children. The parents' right and duty to educate their child can only be displaced by state care in circumstances falling within section 5 of Article 42. This provides that, in exceptional cases, where the parents for physical and moral reasons fail in their duty towards their children, the state as guardian of the common good by appropriate means shall endeavour to supply the place of parents, but always with due regard for the natural and imprescriptible rights of the child.

3.1.1.   THE NON-MARITAL FAMILY

In keeping with the religious ethos (specifically, that of Roman Catholicism) pervading the Constitution, there is a strong implication that in law the term 'family' refers to a marital family unit. Article 41 of the Constitution, while not explicitly so defining the term, clearly establishes a preferential status and protection upon such a family.[22] For that reason, in Ireland the non-marital family

---

[21] See, *Re JH (An Infant): KC and AC v An Bord Uchtála* [1985] IR 375 and Duncan, W., *The Constitutional Protection of Parental Rights in Parenthood in Modern Society*, Eekelaar, J.M., and Sarcevic, P., (eds), (Dordrecht, 1993 and reproduced in the *Report of the Constitutional Review Group*, Dublin, Stationery Office, 1996, pp. 612–626.
[22] See, for example, *The State (Nicolaou v An Bord Uchtála* [1966] IR 567; *G v An Bord Uchtala* [1980] IR 32; and *WO'R v EH (Guardianship)* [1996] 2 IR 248.

has always and continues to attract less protection in law than the family based on marriage. While an unmarried mother has a guaranteed right, under Article 40.3.1, to the care and custody of her child, there is nothing in the Constitution to prevent her from relinquishing all her parental rights through adoption.

3.2. Adoption law

The Adoption Act 1952 (the 'principal Act') together with subsequent amending statutes (in 1964, 1974, 1976, 1988, 1991 and 1998) and the ancillary Adoption Rules constitute the legislative framework for adoption law and practice in Ireland. This considerable body of law has recently been the subject of consolidation and re-statementing.

3.2.1. THE ADOPTION ACT 1952

The 1952 Act introduced adoption as a statutory process in Ireland. It provided for the complete termination of the birth parent's parental rights and responsibilities and for the vesting of all such in the adopters. It also established the Adoption Board, or An Bord Uchtála, to consolidate, regulate and administer the procedures for adoption.

3.2.2. THE ADOPTION ACT 1964

The 1964 Act provided for the adoption of children who had been 'legitimised' by the subsequent marriage of their parents but whose births had not been re-registered.

3.2.3. THE ADOPTION ACT 1974

This statute empowered the High Court to authorise the Adoption Board to dispense with the need for the consent of a birth mother at time of hearing, in circumstances where she had already consented to placement, where this was justified by the welfare interests of the child. It also provided for adoption by a couple of mixed religion on condition that the birth mother knows the religion of the applicants and does not object.

3.2.4. THE ADOPTION ACT 1976

This Act was introduced to retrospectively secure adoption orders that might have otherwise been vulnerable to challenge on the grounds that birth parents had perhaps not been advised of, and given every possible opportunity to exercise, their right to withdraw consent up to the making of the order.

3.2.5.   THE ADOPTION ACT 1988

This legislation introduced two important changes to the adoption process in Ireland. Firstly, statutory powers authorised non-consensual adoptions in certain circumstances. Secondly, the children subject to such powers could be from marital family units. However, these opportunities were confined to the small minority of children of married parents who had so totally abandoned their rights as to permit the possibility of non-consensual adoption from care. For the far greater numbers of children whose married parents had neglected, abused or otherwise failed to care for and protect them—but not to the point of total abandonment— the option of non-consensual adoption was unavailable.[23] The very stringent and rigorous requirements to be satisfied under the Adoption Act 1988, imposed to ensure that the Act passed constitutional scrutiny, together with the excessively lengthy and cumbersome procedures required by the Act, have undermined the initial legislative intent. Consequently, many children remain in long-term foster care and a disproportionate number of those are from marital families.

When processing applications under the 1988 Act, the Board is required to refer the substantive issue of parental consent to the High Court where authority lies to determine whether or not the Board can make an adoption order.

3.2.6.   THE ADOPTION ACT 1991

The 1991 Act was introduced to retrospectively validate all those 'foreign' adoptions that might otherwise have been found to be void due to issues relating to 'simple' forms of adoption, residence and domicile in other jurisdictions.[24] It provided prospective adopters of a foreign child with a statutory entitlement to an adoption assessment and put in place a related statutory procedure. It enabled Irish adopters of foreign children to be placed in the same legal position as Irish adopters of Irish children.

3.2.7.   THE ADOPTION ACT 1998

This legislation provided for circumstances where a birth father wished to be consulted in relation to the proposed adoption of his child.[25] Section 7D of the

---

[23] See, however, *Northern Area Health Board and WH and PH v An Bord Uchtála* (December 17, 2002) where McGuinness J held that a failure of parental duty and abandonment of rights while not being the same concepts in law are and will be related in the facts of any particular case.

[24] Following the ruling in *MF v An Bord Uchtála* [1991] ILRM 399.

[25] Following the ruling in *Keegan v Ireland*, Application No 16969/90 (1994) Series A No 290 (1994) 18 EHRR 342. Note, also, *J.B. v D.B.* (1998) where the consent of the father in respect of a child conceived as a result of rape was obtained which would seem to indicate that consent of the father in such circumstances should be obtained where possible. I am grateful to Shannon, G., for drawing this case to my attention.

principal Act (inserted by the 1998 Act) enabled such a father to serve notice of his interest on the Board in which case the Board is required to notify the relevant adoption society accordingly. The latter must then consult with the father prior to placing his child for adoption. It also introduced new pre-placement adoption procedures to be followed by adoption agencies and prohibited direct placements by a birth mother with a non-relative.

3.2.8.   CONVENTION LAW

The Irish government ratified the European Convention on the Adoption of Children in 1968 (currently under review), subscribed to the United Nations Convention on the Rights of the Child 1989[26] and to the European Convention for the Protection of Human Rights and Fundamental Freedoms 1950. The latter was given effect by the European Convention on Human Rights Act, 2003, which became part of Irish law on 31 December 2003 and now requires the decisions of the European Court of Human Rights be taken into account by the Irish courts.

3.3.   Adoption policy

In June 2003, the government launched a review of adoption law to make it:

> ... more compatible with life in the 21st century by ensuring that it takes account of the huge changes in society as well as changing trends and practices that have taken place since the 1952 Adoption Act.[27]

The review was a two-part process. Part 1 consisted of a written consultation, attracting some 300 submissions, which formed the backbone of Part II, an oral consultation held in the form of a conference and workshops in October 2003. The consultation process suggested that the following guiding principles should inform proposals for change—

- That the best interests of the child are paramount.
- That the child has the right to be heard in every action taken concerning him or her and to have those views taken into account in accordance with his/her age and development.
- That the child has the right to know and be cared for by his/her parents and to preserve his or her identity, including name and family relations.
- That the child has the right to continuity of care where possible and—

---

[26] In Ireland the United Nations Convention on the Rights of the Child is given effect by the National Children's Strategy, launched in 2000, responsibility for the implementation of which rests with the National Children's Office.

[27] See, Minister for Children, Mr Lenihan, B., TD, in foreword to Shannon, G., *Adoption Legislation Consultation: Discussion Paper*, Dublin, June 2003.

- That efforts must be made to ensure that adoption legislation and service provision are characterised by clarity, consistency and fairness where possible, while retaining the necessary flexibility to meet individual needs.

On January 5, 2005, the Minister, announced the outcome of the consultation process. He reported that certain specific legislative proposals had emerged from the 18 month consultation process, had received government approval and appropriate bills would now be prepared for enactment in Autumn 2005. In addition, a number of significant administrative changes would also be introduced.

3.3.1.   PROPOSALS FOR LEGISLATIVE CHANGE

- *The Hague Convention on Protection of Children and co-operation in Respect of Intercountry Adoption 1993 is to be ratified.* This will include a provision making 50 the upper age limit of eligibility for assessment.
- *An Adoption Authority is to be established.* This will replace the present Adoption Board and will include adopted people, natural parents and adoptive parents as well as other people with appropriate expertise. The Authority will take on role of central authority under the Hague Convention and develop best practice and set down guidelines for adoption services nationally. It will monitor adoption services in line with guidelines and carry out and commission research.
- *A Tracing and Reunion service is to be established.* To progress this service a National Records Index and a Contact Preference Register are to be set up on a legislative basis.
- *Legislation is to be introduced to address a range of other adoption issues.* There is to be an adoption option for people who are over 18 and who have been in foster care with the same family. The Adoption Authority will have a power to attach conditions to an adoption order, allowing for ongoing contact with birth family, where this is in the best interests of the child. There is to be an adoption option for a step-parent without requiring adoption by the mother, and the adoption option is to be made available to children of a marital family unit where a parent has died.
- *Guardianship.* The option of guardianship will be made available for step-parents and will also be available for foster parents of children in long-term foster care.

3.3.2.   PROPOSALS FOR ADMINISTRATIVE CHANGE

Many of the deficits identified were of a service provision nature and accordingly certain administrative proposals were approved.

- *A National Adoption Information and Tracing Service is to be set up.* This is to be based on recommendations from an advisory group including

representatives of adoption service users. National protocols and standards will be developed
- *A National Voluntary Contact Preference Register is to be established.* This will be managed by the Adoption Authority and will be open to adopted people, to natural parents and to any natural relative.
- *A National Adoption Records Index is to be established.*
- *Research into Intercountry adoption is to be undertaken and*
- *The delay in Intercountry adoption assessments is to be addressed.*

However, these changes do not address the legal obstacles to child care adoption. Although the paramountcy principle is to be given legislative recognition, the fundamental issue still stands as to how this is to be balanced against the 'inalienable and imprescriptible' parental rights principle enshrined in the Constitution. Until greater clarity is achieved, probably through a prolonged period of Supreme Court elucidation, it is difficult to predict how the paramountcy principle will effect decision-making not just in relation to the right of a non-consenting marital parent to resist an adoption order but also at other points in the process where the principle and rights are in conflict e.g. authority for placement, contact conditions and post-adoption access to identifying information. Resolving the tension between Convention and Constitution principles remains the central challenge for the adoption process in Ireland. The law and policy in this jurisdiction will therefore be left on a fundamentally different and diverging track from that taken by the UK, converging instead with the adoption model developed in New Zealand and in such mainland European countries as France, Norway and Sweden.

4. REGULATING THE ADOPTION PROCESS

In Ireland, the Adoption Board or An Bord Uchtála is the only agency positioned to hold an overview of the workings of the adoption process and of the contribution made to it by a total of some 20 statutory and voluntary agencies. The main functions of this body are: making/refusing adoption orders; granting declarations for eligibility and suitability to adopt abroad; and formally recognising foreign adoptions. Its regulatory function, however, is restricted to one of minimalist intervention: monitoring practice and registering and de-registering adoption agencies at their initiative.

4.1. The process

The adoption process, as statutorily defined, now consists of the following stages:

- legal procedures regarding availability of child, status of parties and consents,
- placement of child;

- legal procedures relating to application;
- the hearing and issue of order/s; and
- certain information disclosure and entitlements.

In addition to the above legislatively required components, some agencies have voluntarily developed services that are now accepted as part of the adoption process in Ireland. These include pre-consent counselling, post-adoption support services and tracing and possibly re-unification services. In Ireland, the adoption process has significant jurisdictional characteristics. Most obviously the statutory process is both shorter and narrower than in other modern western jurisdictions. Also of significance is the fact that adoption proceedings are administrative and the role of mediating bodies is less intrusive and less extensive in nature than elsewhere. Finally, there is no regulatory framework governing the entire adoption process in this jurisdiction.

4.2.   Length and breadth of process

In the context of family adoptions, the process does not start until an application is lodged; which may be several years after the care arrangements were assumed. This is a singular characteristic of adoption in Ireland.[28] The waiving of preliminary professional scrutiny, and with it any opportunity for public service support in this context, emphasises the process's distinctively private characteristics. The reverse is true in the context of adoption in a public care context where the process cannot begin for at least a year after placement with foster parents. At the end of the process closure occurs abruptly with the making of an adoption order. The absence of any statutory post-adoption allowances or support scheme, any statutory possibility of ongoing contact arrangements, or access to statutory information disclosure procedures effectively terminates any rights or duties in respect of ongoing services.[29]

In Ireland, the adoption process does not encompass as wide a range nor as uneven a mix of participants as elsewhere. The very small proportion of children entering the adoption process who are either 'legitimate' or the subject of a care order continues to be a particularly distinctive characteristic of adoption in this jurisdiction.[30] Intimately related to that fact is the relatively large proportion of

---

[28] See, s 10(1) of the 1991 Act. This may not occur until several years after placement by which time the adoption is a virtual *fait accompli* as there can be no reasonable alternative.

[29] Some such opportunities may be available through private or agency based practice but not as a statutory service.

[30] The Adoption Board's report for 1989 shows orders having been granted in respect of: 3 children who were legitimated under the 1964 Act; 3 whose availability was determined under s 3 of the 1988 Act; and 9 declarations made by the Board under the latter Act. In addition, 3 orders were made under s 3 of the 1974 Act. By way of comparison, the 1998 report gives the

adopted children who originate from overseas.[31] Other distinctive characteristics include: the proportion of parental applicants, for decades very low in Ireland, now constitute by far the single largest source of applications[32]; the relatively high proportion of applications from grandparents[33] and the low proportion from single third party applicants and from foster parents.

4.3.   Role of the determining body

In Ireland, adoption proceedings are heard in an administrative rather than a judicial setting with hearings held by the Adoption Board and orders made or refused by it. Nonetheless, the High Court plays a significant role in the Irish adoption process as the Board passes disputed legal issues, including disputed parental consent matters and in particular all such matters arising in applications made under the 1988 Act, to the High Court.[34]

4.4.   Role of adoption agencies and other administrative agencies

The traditional involvement of voluntary agencies in the adoption process has not been entirely displaced by statutory agencies. There is no statutory duty upon adoption societies to ensure that all placement decisions are taken by formally constituted adoption panels but the assumption of such responsibilities by appropriate bodies is a notable characteristic of the adoption process in this jurisdiction. A similar situation exists in relation to the provision of an adoption service. There is a statement of broad principle that a service for the adoption of children should be available but its actual provision is entirely at the discretion of the health boards and that of such voluntary organisations as may have the necessary resources.

---

following statistics for the respective groupings: 0; 1; and 16; with an additional 0 under s 3 of the 1974 Act.

[31] The Board's annual reports give the following percentages: 1991, 7.49%; 1992, 36.98%; 1993, 6.51%; 1994, 5.41%; 1995, 6.39%; 1996, 8.85%; 1997, 10.32%; and 1998, 18.06%.

[32] For example, in 1987 the proportion of parental applications amounted to some 22.6% of the total rising to 63.23% in 1998.

[33] In Ireland, the proportion has remained stable at approx 3.5% of the total. Elsewhere, professional caution, judicial discretion and the statutory availability of alternatives would result in few successful applications.

[34] But, see Walsh J., in Binchy, W., *Casebook on Irish Family Law*, Professional Books, Dublin, 1984, at p. viii for a critical analysis of the Board's authority to make adoption orders without judicial endorsement.

4.5.   Registrar General

To this official falls the duty, as stated in s 22 of the 1952 Act, of recording in the Adopted Children Register the particulars of every child in respect of whom an adoption order has been issued. These must include details of date and place of birth, the date of the adoption order, the child's first name and sex, and the name, address and occupation of the adopters. In addition the Registrar General must also maintain an index, linking this information with the corresponding data recorded in the Register of Births. Unlike the latter the index is inaccessible to the general public and the information it contains, or provides access to, may not be disclosed to any person unless the Board or court directs that to do so would be in the best interests of the child concerned.

5.   THRESHOLDS FOR ENTERING THE ADOPTION PROCESS: ELIGIBILITY AND SUITABILITY CRITERIA

The eligibility and suitability criteria determining entry to the adoption process have certain singular characteristics in relation to all three sets of participants.

5.1.   The child

In Ireland, the twin criteria, normally determining the availability of a child for adoption, are non-marital parental status and parental consent. There is no evidence to show that child welfare (as represented by factors such as the child's wishes, the 'blood-link', degree of bonding, complex health or other special needs) is itself a matter attracting a determinative weighting at point of entry to the adoption process. So, for example:

- a marital child can only become available for adoption on a coercive basis as it is not possible for a marital parent to voluntarily relinquish a child of the marriage;
- the consensual adoption of children by relatives, most usually the child's birth mother and her spouse—in which the welfare factor has a nominal role—is a particular feature of adoption in this jurisdiction;
- evidence of criminal abuse or neglect of a child is in itself insufficient grounds for the compulsory placing of that child for adoption, there must also be evidence of an 'abandonment' of parental responsibilities;
- an adoption application in respect of a child subject to a care order must come from foster parents i.e., it is a private rather than a public initiative;

- suitability criteria are not weighted in favour of welfare interests as evidenced by the very few children with special needs or subject to care orders being placed for adoption and the considerable numbers of healthy babies and young foreign children[35] being adopted;
- the lack of adoption alternatives is an important and characteristic feature of the law in this jurisdiction; and
- the lack of adoption orders subject to a contact condition in favour of a birth parent or sibling is also a significant feature.

These features very clearly illustrate the lack of any leverage available for judicial assertion of the public interest represented by the welfare principle to compromise the private interests represented by an adoption order.

5.2.   The birth parents

In Ireland, only an unmarried mother is entitled to voluntarily relinquish a child for the purposes of adoption. This she may do in favour of a relative and, until the introduction of the 1998 Act, she could have done so in favour of a complete stranger. She is not legally obliged to serve advance notice on any professional or government agency nor is their approval for the placement required. The only legally operative criteria is that her decision to relinquish is accompanied by her full and informed consent given both at time of placement and at time of hearing. The consent decision, given at time of placement for adoption but subsequently rescinded, is by far the most common reason for natural parents to subsequently appear in court as respondents.

The unmarried father of the child in question has limited rights relative to those of the mother. This remains the case despite improvements to his *locus standi* provided by the Status of Children Act 1987 and the Adoption Act 1998. He must, where feasible, be consulted and may appear as a respondent to challenge the mother's decision but only if he has first acquired guardianship rights.[36] Finally, one or both married parents of a child subject to a care order, may appear as respondents in adoption proceedings lodged by the child's foster-parents. While the birth mother's donor role receives very strong legal recognition the role of parent respondent is comparatively weak and seldom succeeds.

---

[35] In 1998, of the 400 orders made, only one adoption order was made in respect of a child with special needs, one in respect of a child subject to a care order, but 27 adoption orders were made in respect of children from overseas.

[36] The Adoption Act 1998 introduced a requirement that such a father be consulted prior to placement so that he may be advised of his right to apply for guardianship, access and/or custody of the child.

5.3.   The adopters

In Ireland there is a legislative minimum age requirement of 21 years but no stated maximum age limit.[37] The eligibility criteria are in general framed to ensure that third party applicants closely conform to the constitutionally approved marital family unit. Only in exceptional circumstances, under s 10(2) of the 1991 Act, will applications from anyone other than a married couple be accepted. All third party applicants must also satisfy a statutory requirement that they be of the same religion as the natural parents or be of a different religion and that is known to the birth parents. The only third party applicants eligible to adopt a marital child are the foster parents of that child who have to satisfy carer tenure criteria which, unlike other jurisdictions, provides them with a power rather than a right to apply to adopt.[38] In contrast, family adopters in this jurisdiction do not have to satisfy rigorous eligibility and suitability criteria.[39] There is an assumption that the welfare of a child can only be enhanced by family adoption. There is no requirement to serve notice of an intention to make a family placement, no opportunity for professional assessment prior to application and no possibility of a discretionary judicial decision to issue an alternative order on the grounds that such would be more compatible with the child's welfare.

In this jurisdiction, the legal standing of parents or other relatives does attract preferential treatment in law.

In short, access to the adoption process is considerably restricted in Ireland for all prospective parties. A common restraining factor is marital status. For applicant, subject and relinquishing parent, access is very dependent upon whether or not the individual is from a marital family unit. There are also characteristics affecting each class of participant. Applicants such as birth parents and relatives attract little professional scrutiny while foster parents comprise a low proportion of total annual applicants. Few children subject to care orders and/or with special needs are eligible for adoption. Intimately related to all the foregoing is the fact that the proportion of birth parents who are unwilling participants in adoption proceedings is very low. These, unarguably, are all the consequences of a markedly protectionist policy towards marital family units.

---

[37] However, it has been recommended that, in the context of intercountry adoptions, there should be a lower age limit of 25 years and an upper limit of not more than 42 years for the older of the applicants at time of placement. See, further, *Towards a Standardised Framework for Intercountry Adoption Assessment Procedures: A Study of Assessment Procedures in Intercountry Adoption*, Stationery Office, Dublin, 1999.

[38] In Ireland, foster carers must provide a minimum of 12 months continuous care and be supported by the health board before they can be considered as applicants. In the UK jurisdictions, for example, the foster carers have the right to apply independently of the views of the relevant public authority.

[39] However, one of the applicant parties must be at least 21 years of age; Adoption Act 1991; s 10(5)(b).

6. PRE-PLACEMENT COUNSELLING

In Ireland there is as yet no statutory requirement to provide pre-placement counselling. Part 11 of the Child Care Act 1991 includes provisions requiring an adoption service to be established and maintained. Under s 6 of this Act the health boards are required to provide or ensure the provision of "a service for the adoption of children". They are empowered to do so by entering into arrangements with any registered adoption agency. Characteristically, in keeping with the significant non-statutory dimension to the adoption process in this jurisdiction, pre-placement counselling services are available from some voluntary agencies.

7. PLACEMENT RIGHTS AND RESPONSIBILITIES

In practice, a child enters the adoption process when he or she is placed with prospective adopters. This placement decision must be taken by a person or body with the requisite authority; an initial consent is a legal necessity.

7.1. Placement decision

This decision may still be taken on a private basis by the birth parent/s who remain entitled to place their child directly with a relative.

7.2. Placement supervision

In Ireland there is no specific statutory provision that gives rise to any protective duties owed to a child placed for adoption.[40] Ultimately, all placements must be notified to the Adoption Board, but this does not trigger any specific protective duties.

8. THE HEARING AND ISSUE OF ORDER/S

In Ireland the hearing of an adoption application is conducted by the Adoption Board and is administrative rather than judicial in nature.

---

[40] As regards 'family' placements, the care and maintenance provisions of s 56 and s 57 of the Health Act 1953 require advance notification of placement to be served on the local health board. As regards placements made by child care agencies, these are subject to the boarding out regulations. All adoption agency placements must be notified to the health board within 7 days.

8.1.   Where consent is available

Adoption in Ireland was traditionally based on consent and this very largely remains the case; the parent/s whose consent is required must be informed of their right to withdraw consent at any time prior to the making of the order. In recent years, the disproportionate increase in family adoptions, which are seldom contested, has itself served to strengthen the consensual nature of the process.

8.2.   Where consent is not available

In Ireland, the law provides for the possibility of non-consensual adoptions in only two sets of circumstances. Firstly, where it can be shown that the initial placement decision was authorised by an informed parental consent which was subsequently withdrawn.[41] Secondly, where there is compelling evidence of parental abuse or neglect amounting to an abandonment of parental responsibilities.

8.2.1.   DISPENSING WITH CONSENT; PRIVATE LAW

In a private law context no statutory grounds exist for dispensing with parental consent at the time of placement.[42] Much, if not most, case law has been focussed on the contractual grounds for affirming or discounting the consent already given by young unmarried mothers to the placement of a child for adoption. Even if given within 6 weeks of the birth of the child concerned, such consent will be upheld by the courts. It is a telling irony that such grounds as exist under the 1974 Act to provide for the possibility of non-consensual adoption do so only in respect of an unmarried mother and become operative only if she has already given a valid consent to placement.

Also, in this jurisdiction there is no judicial discretion in relation to first party applicants to make a different order to the one sought (e.g. a residence order or parental responsibility order). The use of wardship, with its reliance on the principle that the welfare interests of the child are of paramount importance, has not played a key role in supplementing statutory powers and authorising non-consensual placements.

8.2.2.   DISPENSING WITH CONSENT; PUBLIC LAW

The Adoption Act 1988 introduced parental failure due to 'physical or moral reasons' as grounds for dispensing with parental consent to adoption, regardless

---

[41] The Adoption Act 1974, s 3.
[42] Except under s 14(2) of the Adoption Act 1952 which is restricted to circumstances where the parent/guardian either suffers from mental infirmity or their whereabouts are unknown.

of the marital status of such a parent. However, these grounds are not synchronised with those that constitute criminal fault or default in child care legislation. Case law has shown that parental inaction will be sufficient to convince a court that parents have 'failed in their duty towards the child' within the meaning of s 3(1)(I)(A) of the 1988 Act.[43] The grounds may be satisfied even if the parent concerned is without blame and the failure is attributable to their suffering from a learning disability.[44]

Mere parental culpability, however grave, is insufficient; the conduct must be such as to amount to an 'abandonment' of parental responsibilities[45] and it must be attributable to both parents; failure by one parent but not the other will not satisfy this requirement. The court will require evidence that the parents, by fault or default, have behaved in a manner constituting an abandonment of all responsibilities in respect of the child; whether or not this was intended or involved actual physical abandonment.[46]

Moreover, the 'abandonment' must have already lasted for a minimum of 12 months and be likely to continue without interruption until the child reaches the age of 18. The courts have looked to past conduct as evidence of probability of continued parental failure and have had no difficulty finding that where conduct has satisfied the grounds of s 3(1)(I)(A) of the 1988 Act then it is likely to continue to do so throughout childhood.

The grounds also require, under s 3(1)(I)(D) of the 1988 Act and in compliance with Article 42.5 of the Constitution, the court to be satisfied that the state, as guardian of the common good, should supply the place of the parents. This places an onus on the court to examine firstly whether it can do so and then whether in the circumstances of the particular child, it should make an order providing for permanent alternative care; which may in either instance indicate an alternative to adoption.

Finally, it is not the fact of parental culpability which triggers a public agency initiative to place for adoption but the fact of foster care tenure which may or may not give rise to a private initiative to apply to adopt the child in question.[47]

---

[43] See, for example, *The Southern Health Board v An Bord Uchtála* [2000] 1 IR 165 where the court was satisfied that while the father had actually committed the acts of abuse the mother was also culpable as she had failed to protect her child.

[44] See, *NAHB v An Bord Uchtála* [2003] 1 ILRM 481.

[45] See, s 3(1)(I)(C) of the 1988 Act: the degree of parental failure must be such as 'constitutes an abandonment on the part of the parents of all parental rights'.

[46] See, for example, *The Southern Health Board v An Bord Uchtála, op cit,* and also *The Western Board, HB and MB v An Bord Uchtála* [1995] 3 IR 178.

[47] In the UK jurisdictions, for example, the freeing process has for decades clearly placed a statutory responsibility upon the public child care services to initiate the process whereby a child in care may become available for adoption. In Ireland, this is left to the discretion of a child's foster carers.

In short, the formulation of the grounds for dispensing with parental consent has been worded so as to ensure compatibility with and subservience to constitutional principles with their emphasis on the 'inalienable and imprescriptible rights'[48] of parents. The result is that the grounds for non-consensual adoption are confined to a narrow definition of parental failure and to private rather than public responsibility for commencing relevant proceedings.

9.   THRESHOLDS FOR EXITING THE ADOPTION PROCESS

There is no general right to adopt or to be adopted but in this jurisdiction the few alternative options available to the determining body result in a higher proportion of applications concluding with the issue of an adoption order than would be the case in most modern western jurisdictions.

9.1.   The welfare interests of the child

The making of an adoption order is conditional upon a finding that to do so would be at least compatible with the welfare interests of the child concerned. The wishes of an older child regarding his or her proposed adoption have to be ascertained and taken into account; but there is no evidence that determining weight can be attached to those wishes.[49] Whether or not proceedings are contested, the duty to bring welfare considerations before the Adoption Board rests lightly and on comparatively few professionals in this jurisdiction. There is no guardian *ad litem* or equivalent professional statutorily charged with the duty to act as 'court officer' and represent the wishes or welfare interests of a child before the Board. No specific information on matters constituting 'welfare' as itemised in a statutory report form are required to be brought before the Adoption Board. There is no statutory requirement to take into account the likely effect of an adoption order on the welfare of the child throughout childhood; welfare is a factor relevant only at the time of hearing.

Family adoptions are not subject to prior mandatory professional screening, the results of which could be taken into account in determining welfare.

In Ireland, the 'blood-link' factor has gained considerable judicial endorsement and has the capacity to transform welfare into the determining factor in third-party non-consensual applications.[50] In other jurisdictions it is the 'bonding'

---

[48] See, Articles 41 and 42 of the Constitution.
[49] See, however, *NAHB v An Bord Uchtála, op cit,* where the clear informed wish of the 12 year old child to be adopted was taken into account by the court when granting the order.
[50] See, for example, *RC & PC v An Bord Uchtála & St Louse's Adoption Society* (8th February, 1985), unreported, HC.

rather than the 'blood-link' factor which is often determinative; as apparent, for example, in the availability of contact conditions to license the continuation of relationships which would otherwise be legally terminated by adoption.

The lack of a more holistic long-term approach to welfare interests is also evident in the absence of statutory disclosure procedures. In short, the welfare factor as a statutory consideration has a less specific, comprehensive and significant impact upon adoption in Ireland than in other contemporary western societies.

10. THE OUTCOME OF THE ADOPTION PROCESS

In this jurisdiction, legislative intent began by being almost exclusively concerned with regulating the consensual third party applications of indigenous, white, healthy and in all respects 'normal' non-marital babies. The extent to which it has moved away from this baseline may be seen in the present diversified outcome of the adoption process.

10.1. Adoption orders and third party applicants

This, the type of order originally legislated for, has declined in Ireland both in aggregate and as a proportion of total annual orders. Placements are almost always religion specific (i.e. Catholic child with Catholic adopter, Protestant child with Protestant adopter).

Consensual applications have traditionally been associated with 'illegitimate' children and this very largely continues to be the case; the majority of applications concern children under the age of two years.[51] However, the adoption process in this jurisdiction now includes a small but increasing number of children born within marriage and a similar small number who, having been the subject of care orders, have subsequently been adopted by their foster parents.[52] There has also been a relatively recent but significant and sustained increase in the number of

---

[51] For example, the Board's annual report reveals that in 1989 the number of children aged 24 months or less at time of placement with third party adopters amounted to 358 out of the total of 366; in 2000, they constituted almost 73% of the total 96. The proportionate decrease in annual orders made in favour of third party applicants has been accompanied by a similar decrease in the number of orders made in respect of children aged 24 months or less.

[52] For example, in 1989 the same report shows 4 such children who were subject to declarations made by the Board in favour of their foster parents under the 1988 Act and 3 who were adopted as a consequence of High Court proceedings taken under that Act. The comparable figures in the 1998 report are 16 and 1 respectively; and in 2000 only 5 orders were made under the 1988 Act while 9 declarations were made of which one concerned a marital child. Effectively, the only children born within marriage and available for adoption (as opposed to those who having been legitimated are then adopted) are those in the care of foster parents.

overseas children adopted.[53] The proportion of third party applications which are contested has always been very small and invariably arises in circumstances where a birth mother withdraws her consent to the adoption of her non-marital child. In this jurisdiction, there is no legislative provision for conditions to be attached to adoption orders.

10.2.   Adoption orders and first party applicants

The number of orders granted in favour of birth mothers and their spouses has grown rapidly in recent years and now constitute the most significant character-istic of the adoption process[54]. Other types of first party application—by a birth mother acting alone or by a natural father and his spouse—have remained con-sistently low[55]. The application is seldom contested or unsuccessful, the subject is almost invariably a non-marital child and the order granted will always be full and unconditional.

10.3.   Adoption orders and relatives

A consistent characteristic of the adoption process in Ireland has been the signif-icant minority of orders made in favour of grandparents. In other jurisdictions, such applications may be open to professional or judicial challenge.

10.4.   Other orders

In Ireland guardianship orders have been the main private law statutory alternative to commencing adoption proceedings and a failed adoption application may well result in the issue of a guardianship order or possibly a wardship order. This well established use of guardianship instead of adoption, particularly as an option for discharging a child from the public care system, is very similar to practice in New Zealand.

11.   THE EFFECT OF AN ADOPTION ORDER

In this jurisdiction the outcome of the adoption process is as it always has been either no order or a full order with its characteristic permanent, exclusive and

---

[53] The Board's annual reports provide the following data: 1996, 54; 1997, 51; 1998, 120; 1999, 176; and 2000, 209.

[54] From 59 of the 1,115 orders granted in 1980 to 188 of the 615 granted in 1989, 252 of the 400 orders made in 1998 and reaching 199 of the 303 orders made in 2000.

[55] For example, the Board's report for 1989 shows that out of a total of 226 family adoptions, only 2 orders were in favour of 'natural mother alone', 0 for 'natural father and wife' and 2 for 'natural father alone'. More recent comparable figures are: 1998–0, 0 and 1; 2000–0, 2 and 1.

absolute legal effects on all parties. That an adoption order continues to have its traditional effect was reaffirmed by the Chief Justice in *I.O'T. v B. and the Rotunda Girls' Aid Society and M.H. v Rev. G.D. and the Rotunda Girls' Aid Society*[56]. He then stated that "the effect of an adoption order is that all parental rights and duties of the natural parents are ended, while the child becomes a member of the family of the adoptive parents as if he or she had been their natural child".

The statutory availability of information rights, contact registers, schemes for payment and support and the possibility of conditions being attached to adoption orders or the issue of alternative orders are as yet unknown in this jurisdiction.

11.1.   Effect on the child

For the one participant who has no statutory right of consent and, generally speaking, no say in the proceedings, the legal consequences of adoption are particularly far reaching. They may be seen in terms of the changes made to his or her legal status and the rights retained despite such changes:

- the rules of 'legitimation' apply and s 24(a) of the 1952 Act prevents the subject from being treated in law as a non-marital child—thereafter he or she is regarded as the marital child of the adopters;
- the rules of consanguinity apply and the child is instantly endowed not only with the name and social standing of his or her adopters but also with a complete set of new relatives—but there is no statutory bar on marriage or sexual relationships between the adopted person and a "sibling" of their new family;
- the rules of domicile apply and thereafter the child's domicile of origin is held to be that of the adopting parents rather than of the natural parents; and
- the rules of succession as stated in s 26 of the 1952 Act apply providing equality of succession rights between a testator's adopted and natural children.

11.2.   Effect on the birth parent/s

The effect of an adoption order on the rights and duties of a birth parent is necessarily absolute and irrevocable. This was confirmed by the Chief Justice in *IOT v B*[57] when he held that no familial relationship can survive between a legally adopted person and his or her birth mother. For a new family unit to be vested with the full complement of parental rights necessary to attract the protection of the Constitution the previous holder of those rights must first be

---

[56] [1998] 2 IR 321.
[57] *Ibid.*

equally thoroughly divested of them:

- they are divested by s 24 of the 1952 Act of all parental rights and freed from all parental duties with respect to the child[58];
- all previous orders in respect of that child are automatically quashed[59];
- a natural parent, under s 4 of the 1974 Act, retains the right to know the religion, if any, of the prospective adopters where this is different from her own[60]; and
- the traditional practice of a placing agency to guarantee permanent secrecy to the natural parents has given way to rights and professional practices in relation to information disclosure, tracing and re-unification.

11.3.   Effect on the adopters

The legislative intent, to fully vest the adopters with the rights of marital parents in respect of the child, is evidenced by the nature of the parental responsibilities vested in them and in the reluctance to accept any attempt to condition the effects of an adoption order. The parental rights and duties transferred to the adopters include:

- the custody and physical possession of the child;
- entailing control of education and choice of religion together with powers to withhold consent to marriage and to administer the child's property;
- the duties of a guardian as understood in common law and as stated in s 10(2) of the Guardianship of Infants Act 1964 such as maintenance, protection, control and provision of appropriate medical treatment;
- also rights to determine place of residence, choice of health and social services, travel and the right to withhold consent to a subsequent adoption; and
- the full legal status of a parent within the terms of Articles 41 and 42 of the Constitution also thereby vest in the adopter.

These transferred rights cannot be qualified in any way. So, the granting of an adoption order operates to extinguish any restriction on an adopter's full enjoyment of parental rights imposed by a guardianship, custody or child care order which may have been in effect up to the time of hearing. This also operates to prevent the attachment of a condition to an Irish adoption order.

---

[58] The unmarried father, under existing Irish legislation, does not inherently possess any such rights.
[59] An affiliation order, however, or any voluntary agreement to the same effect, will not be cancelled if the adopter is the child's birth mother.
[60] The constitutional validity of s 12(2) of the 1952 Act was successfully challenged in *J McG & W McG v An Bord Uchtála & AG* (1974) 109 ILTR 62 (High Court) which led directly to the introduction of the 1974 Act.

12. POST-ADOPTION SUPPORT SERVICES

Traditionally, in keeping with the essentially private nature of adoption, once an order was made then public intrusion ceased and in the absence of any statutory provision for ongoing post-adoption support and counselling for adopters[61] this largely continues to be the case. However, the development of some such services by both voluntary agencies and health boards has been given added impetus by the requirement in Article 9C of the Hague Convention that every Adoption Authority should promote 'the development of adoption counselling and post-adoption services'.

In practice very few adopters receive post-adoption support. Perhaps the only consistent exception arises in the context of child care adoptions. An important point of difference between the standing of child care and all other adopters is that the former may qualify for a continuation of boarding-out payments. Section 44 of the Child Care Act 1991 made specific provision for the continuation of boarded-out payments in respect of an adopted child who, prior to adoption had been in the care of a health board and fostered by the subsequent adopters. This is a purely discretionary matter for the health board. As there are very few child care adoptions the proportion of adopters receiving support from the health boards is small.

13. INFORMATION DISCLOSURE, TRACING AND RE-UNIFICATION SERVICES

Irish law has never provided a right for adopted persons to have automatic access to their birth certificates, neither has there ever been a legal right to access agency records for information[62] on an adopted child's family of origin, nor a reciprocal duty to disclose such information.[63] There is no legislative provision for tracing and re-unification services. However, in recent years, voluntary agencies sometimes in conjunction with health boards have sought to provide such services.

---

[61] See, Eekelar, *What are Parental Rights'?* [1973] 89 LQR 210; Hall *The Waning of Parental Rights* [1972] CLJ 248; and Bevan and Parry *Children Act 1975* pp. 208–239.

[62] However, a High Court judgment in 1993 determined that, where an adopted person is seeking information under Section 22(5) of the Adoption Act, 1952, then the Board is obliged to inform itself about the circumstances of the individual case and to decide whether to release or withhold the information sought.

[63] Section 22(5) of the 1952 Act generally prohibits public access to the Adoption Index. The prior permission of the Adoption Board is required before any information is released from the Index. Section 8 of the 1976 Act prevents a court from ordering the release of any such information unless satisfied that this is in the best interests of the child in question.

13.1.   Information disclosure

Articles 7 and 8 of the UN Convention established the important guiding principle that every child is entitled to the information necessary to form their sense of personal identity. The Supreme Court in *I.O'T. v B. and the Rotunda Girls' Aid Society and M.H. v Rev. G.D. and the Rotunda Girls' Aid Society*[64] found this to be compatible with the constitutional right to know the identity of one's birth mother as guaranteed by Article 40.3 of the Irish Constitution. This case considered consolidated actions brought by two women informally adopted before legal adoption became available. The applicants had sought an order directing the agency that facilitated the placements to disclose the identities of their birth mothers. While these cases concerned informal adoption, the Supreme Court made a number of references to legal adoption. Keane J, in considering the right to privacy, stated:

> I find it difficult to imagine an aspect of human experience which falls more clearly into the constitutional area of privacy ... than the circumstances of the natural mothers in the present case.

Barron J held that secrecy "has always been a paramount consideration in adoption law" and while "the public attitude to absolute secrecy has been weakened ... there [does] not appear to have been any cases where communication has taken place against the wishes of the mother".

In short, the Supreme Court recognised a person's unenumerated constitutional right to know the identity of his/her birth mother, but said that this had to be balanced against the birth mother's right to privacy. It stated that neither set of rights was absolute. While the Court implied that access to adoption records might be appropriate in certain cases, this, it held, would depend on many factors including:

- the circumstances surrounding the birth mother's loss of custody of the child;
- the current status and circumstances of the birth mother and the potential effect upon her of the disclosure of her identity;
- the birth mother's own wishes and attitude regarding the disclosure, and the reasons behind these wishes and the aforementioned attitude;
- the current age of the birth mother and child respectively;
- the attitude of the adopted child, including the reasons why he or she wishes to seek disclosure of his or her birth mother's identity;
- the present circumstances of the adopted child; and
- the opinion of the adoptive parents or other interested persons.

[64]   [1998] 2 IR 321.

Considerable judicial emphasis was placed on the birth parent/s privacy rights in this case which concerned the rights of persons informally adopted. It is probable that even greater importance would be accorded to privacy in circumstances where an adoption order had been granted and the links between the birth mother and adopted child were legally severed.

This case generated considerable public debate. As a consequence the Adoption Information Post-Adoption Contact and Associated Issues Bill, as it now stands, is unlikely to be enacted.[65]

The issue of access to adoption records is currently being addressed in the context of the government's review of the European Convention on the Adoption of Children. If, as proposed, the relevant provisions are incorporated in Part 11 of the Convention this will require the confidentiality of the adoption and the birth mother's identity to be safeguarded under Irish law.

13.2.   The Register of Foreign Adoptions

Under s 6 of the 1991 Act, the Board is required to maintain a Register of Foreign Adoptions. In this it enters all details relating to those foreign adoption orders obtained by Irish couples who have complied with the procedure as outlined in the 1991 Act. By April 1997, some 750 entries had been made in this Register. In 2000, the Board made 323 entries.

13.3.   Tracing and re-unification services

The lack of any statutory rights or duties in respect of tracing and re-unification services has led to the present position where these are provided on an ad hoc basis as resources permit by some voluntary agencies and some health boards.[66] The Adoption Board also receives many direct inquiries, which it welcomes and which are rapidly increasing. In 2000, the Board dealt with 1,422 search and reunion enquiries compared to 1,010 in 1999 though the numbers have since decreased somewhat to 966 such enquiries in 2003.

Legislation is to be introduced in the immediate future to authorise and regulate relevant service provision.

---

[65] This draft legislation provided for information disclosure services, the safeguarding of records, establishing and maintaining contact registers and provision of a counselling service for both adopted persons and birth parents.

[66] Search and reuniting services have generally been left to voluntary societies, many of which have been forced to close in recent years. For example, St Anne's Adoption Society in Cork, which provided such services, closed in September 2003 but the Southern Health Board was unable to assume responsibility for maintaining service provision.

14.   CONCLUSION

Adoption in Ireland, in its brief legislative history, can be seen to have acquired certain characteristics; some of which may be attributable to the Brehon law legacy and its reliance upon formal reciprocal kinship care arrangements within and between clans. In its relative openness, its weighting towards family applicants, marginal relevance to children in care, comparatively high recourse to intercountry adoption and its long-standing reliance upon the alternative of guardianship (and to a lesser extent wardship), the characteristics of adoption in this jurisdiction now more closely resemble those of New Zealand[67] than of its neighbouring jurisdictions in the UK.

Most obviously adoption in Ireland is essentially a consensual process, regulated by a disparate series of statutes, involving many voluntary organisations, presided over by an administrative rather than a judicial body that makes or refuses unconditional adoption orders. The special position of the Roman Catholic Church, religion in general, the legal integrity of the marital family unit, an established non-interventionist child care policy and a strong tradition of reliance upon extended family networks to supplement or substitute for parental responsibilities can all be seen to colour the law, policy and practice of adoption. Certain traditional legal presumptions favouring, for example, the marital nuclear family, Christianity and the maternal bond continue to exercise considerable influence. However, the main distinguishing characteristic of this process, as clearly revealed in its output, is a rapidly increasing trend towards the privatisation of adoption.

The use of adoption by a birth parent and spouse to jointly acquire maximum rights and full parental status and thereby deny rights and status to others is very evident in Ireland. This reversal in the traditional role of the birth parent from donor to applicant is a striking example of the extent of change in the social functions of adoption. The assertiveness with which private applicants now use adoption can also be seen in the increase in applications relating to children, usually healthy babies, from other countries. This choice is to some extent a forced one because of the sharp and continuing decline in numbers of children voluntarily relinquished in Ireland. However, it is a choice quite often made despite the availability within this jurisdiction of children from the public child care sector and/or with special needs.

The lack of use of adoption by public child care agencies is very evident from the annual statistics which show a steady divergence in the correlation between the annual statistics for children in care and adoption orders. In Ireland, the law will

---

[67] See, Law Commission, *Adoption and its Alternatives—A Different Approach and a New Framework*, Wellington, New Zealand, 2000. This report draws attention to the particularly high rate of intercountry adoption (116 per million in 1998 compared with 26 per million in Sweden and 117 per million in Norway) at p. 119.

have to change considerably if it is to facilitate the government's aim to "ensure that adoption is an option available to all children who might otherwise be denied a permanent home and stable relationships".[68] In the period 1988–2001 while the care population increased by a third the number of adoption orders made fell by more than one-half. The just completed adoption law review is clearly a positive step towards fulfilling the Minister's promise to make adoption "more compatible with life in the 21st century" but it remains to be seen whether in fact this will be achieved by the resulting legislation.

[68] See, Report of the Review Committee on Adoption Services, *Adoption*, Dublin, Government Publications, 1984 at p. 10.

Chapter 7

THE ADOPTION PROCESS IN THE US

1.   INTRODUCTION

The United States of America is a federation of 50 individual states each of which is a separate geographic jurisdiction with independent responsibility for enacting legislation, providing a judicial system and for managing programmes of service provision. Included within the range of authority of a state administrative system are matters relating to children and the adoption process.

The federal government has responsibilities in relation to funding service programmes across all states and an accompanying oversight role as regards monitoring the effectiveness of such programmes. This power, exercised under the Spending Clause, provides it with considerable authority to shape state policy. The federal government also provides an overarching framework of law that sets out the parameters for state legislation and a federal judicial system that considers issues with a constitutional dimension.

This chapter begins by examining the social and legal contexts that shaped the development of the adoption process in the US and traces the legislative steps that produced the present framework of adoption law. A consideration of the emerging characteristics of adoption practice leads into an overview of contemporary adoption law and policy. The chapter then applies the template created earlier (see, Chap. 3) to reveal the legal functions of the adoption process and concludes with some comment on the more distinctive aspects of adoption in the US.

Kerry O'Halloran (ed.), The Politics of Adoption, 197–227.
© 2006 *Springer. Printed in The Netherlands.*

2.   THE SOCIAL CONTEXT FOR ADOPTION

In the US as in the UK and more generally in the western world, the increase in adoption in the 1950s and 1960s was largely conditioned by the same set of prevailing social values, fuelled by the considerable numbers of relinquishing unmarried mothers and absorbed by the many infertile married couples who wished for the child that would pass as their own. To some extent this can be viewed in terms of public status. At that time the pressures on adopters as much as on unmarried birth parents to achieve social conformity—in terms of private, marital family units with children, all subscribing to much the same value system—were considerable.

2.1.   The birth parent/s

For most of the legislative history of adoption in the US, the term 'birth parent' meant in effect an unmarried mother.

2.1.1.   UNMARRIED MOTHERS

The stigma of 'illegitimacy' and with it the complications for any entitlement under the laws of inheritance and succession presented a very real burden for the child of an unmarried mother and one which the latter was naturally anxious to avoid for her child. Unmarried mothers were encouraged to view relinquishment as the reasonable decision of a responsible parent acting to secure her child's future.

The postwar boom in pregnancies saw a change in the demographic profile of such relinquishing mothers. Whereas previously it had been primarily married or divorced working-class women who relinquished their usually older children for economic reasons, after the war it became common for younger, more broadly middle-class unmarried women to relinquish their children in infancy. From the late 1950s until the mid-1970s, the social stigma and financial hardship accompanying the role of single parent made adoption a forced option for many unmarried mothers in the US as elsewhere. More recently, while the stigma reversed and attached to relinquishment rather than to single parenthood, poverty or relative poverty continued to significantly influence the decisions of unmarried mothers. As Patricia Strowbridge of Adoption Professionals has recently explained[1]:

> Take Florida, which has 5,000 to 7,000 adoptions a year. Over 80% of them are private and most of these involve young women. In many cases they simply can't afford to keep their babies because income is so low and welfare is so poor. So they get in touch with an adoption agency.

---

[1]   See, *The Independent Review*, 5th January, 2005, as cited by Hilpern K. in her feature article 'The Daddy of All Game Shows' at p. 3.

2.1.2. UNMARRIED FATHERS

Until the early 1970s, the unmarried father of a child relinquished by his or her mother had no legal standing in adoption proceedings; his consent was not required and he was not even entitled to formal legal notice of such proceedings. This situation was irrevocably altered by the case of *Stanley v Illinois*[2] which marked a fundamental change in American adoption law. The decision was confined to the issue of an unmarried father's lack of status in dependency proceedings affecting his children who lived with him. However, the Supreme Court in a footnote to its judgment—added that such a father should also be given the opportunity to be heard in adoption proceedings. Nonetheless, unless they are aware of and assert their legal rights, unmarried fathers continue to be largely peripheral to the adoption process.

2.2. The adopters

Married couples with fertility difficulties and a need for a home with children have always provided the primary driving force in adoption. Whereas initially the motivation may have had more to do with public status and the need to acquire an heir, it has since become associated simply with the private psychological need to parent and create a home for the nuclear family.

2.2.1. INFERTILE MARRIED COUPLES

In the recent past the needs of such couples were addressed by agency practice in the US, the UK and elsewhere that carefully sought to fit the child to be adopted with the characteristics of the prospective adopters. Children were matched to adopters in accordance with criteria such as race, class, physical and genetic attributes with the clear intention of providing a couple with the baby that would most readily approximate the child that could have been born to them. This practice, resting on in-built denial, was reinforced by the issue of an altered birth

---

[2] 405 US 645 (1972) at footnote 9 where in reference to "custody or adoption proceedings" it is stated that:

> "Extending opportunity for hearing to unwed fathers who desire and claim competence to care for their children creates no constitutional or procedural obstacle to foreclosing those unwed fathers who are not so inclined" (p. 657).

As cited by Katz, S. 'Dual Systems of Adoption in the United States', in Katz, S., Eekelaar, J. and Maclean, M. (eds.), *Cross Currents: Family Law and Policy in the United States and England*, Oxford University Press, Oxford, 2001, at p. 279. For further Supreme Court rulings positively affecting the *locus standi* of unmarried fathers see, *Quilloin v Walcott*, 434 US 246 (1978), *Caban v Mohammed*, 441 US 380 (1979) and *Lehr v Robertson*, 43 US 248 (1983).

certificate and the lack thereafter of access by any party to identifying information. In the 1950s and into the 1970s, as Katz points out[3]:

> Agencies tended to prefer married couples of childbearing ages, who were well educated, financially secure and who could provide a child with all the necessities of life in order for her to mature into a productive adult. In addition, agencies tried to match the child with the adoptive parents so that the new family would look like it had been created through biology not the law. If a religiously affiliated private agency placed the child, that agency would require the adoptive couple to be a member of its religion or, in certain instances, to promise to raise the child in the religion associated with the agency.

By the 1990s this had all changed. In the wake of the new American led emphasis on the psychology of the individual and the importance of psycho-social relations, instead of the previous focus on socio-economic models of the family unit, adoption practice had reversed its approach towards matching adopters and child. The starting point was to be the child. The suitability of prospective adopters came to be measured by the fit between their attributes and the needs profile of the child regardless of any physical resemblance between them. However, although the emphasis on facilitating religious congruity had faded, it was to some extent replaced by a similar approach towards racial matching.

3.   THE LEGAL CONTEXT FOR ADOPTION

In the US, all law—whether statutory, judicial or administrative—occurs within and can be tested against the overarching principles of the Constitution. Family law including adoption, being replete with tensions between public and private rights, has always had the potential to generate work for constitutional lawyers.

3.1.   The Constitution

The Constitution, particularly the 13th, 14th, and 15th Amendments, together with the Bill of Rights, has influenced the development of adoption law as it has all aspects of family law. To some extent this can be seen in the careful balance it strikes between the powers of state and Congress to enact legislation and control the spending of public revenue. Mostly it is evident in the capacity of certain principles, underpinned by rulings of the Supreme Court, to shape a degree of uniformity in law and practice across the country.

[3] See, Katz, S., *ibid*, at p. 294.

A first principle is, perhaps, the right to privacy. In general terms, this confers on individuals and other entities the right to be protected from government intrusion. There is a legal presumption that the conduct of persons or businesses is a matter for self-regulation unless or until the law is infringed. Its effect can be seen, for example, in relation to the laws governing access to personal information in the form of adoption records, in the private parental placement rights and in the independence of commercial adoption agencies.

Secondly there is the right to due process, both 'procedural' and 'substantive', as enshrined in the 5th and 14th Amendments. Basically, procedural due process requires that the legal system, its processes and protections, are available to all and perform their functions with the utmost propriety. Substantive due process, in this context, has been interpreted to establish a protected interest for parents to raise their children and for those children to be safe.

The effect of this due process principle can be seen, for example, in:

- the requirement that all persons (such as unmarried fathers) are served with notice of proceedings affecting them;
- that representation be provided to those (such as children) whose interests are being determined; and
- that full and informed consents (unless statutorily dispensed with) are available.

Finally, although the 14th Amendment with its due process guarantee is usually associated with the protection of fundamental rights (such as the right to free speech or the right to practice one's religion) it also declares the principle that all persons are entitled to equal protection before the law. Its effect can be seen in relation to the rules governing trans-racial placements, the availability of adoption to special needs children and the non-discriminatory requirements in agency assessments of adopter suitability.

These principles have formed a backdrop to the development of adoption law, policy and practice in the US. Throughout its legislative history and across all states, adoption practice has been measured against these and other constitutional principles and continues to be adjusted in the light of emerging case law.

3.2.   Adoption law

Adoption as a formal statutory procedure was introduced in the US by the Massachusetts Adoption of Children's Act 1851. Thereafter, adoption became exclusively a judicial process the successful conclusion of which resulted in the issue of an adoption order.

3.2.1.   STATUTORY ADOPTION

In the US, adoption law is largely state law. However, while each of the 50 states have statutes governing adoption, the consequences for the legal status of the parents and children involved are such that adoption is necessarily also affected by federal law addressing matters such as entitlement to social security payments etc.

3.2.2.   EQUITABLE ADOPTION

In some states, the doctrine of "equitable adoption" allows courts to give formal recognition to de facto adoptions in addition to those resulting from statutory procedures. Equitable adoption usually applies in circumstances where the parties have a well-established set of relationships which approximates adoption in all respects except that the statutory procedures have not been completed. In equitable adoptions the parent(s) must support the child and may be ordered to pay child support if the adult and child no longer live together.

3.2.3.   ADOPTION WITH CONSENT

Adoption in the US, as in the UK, has for most of its history been an essentially consensual process. Unless the consent of the parent/s was available or the need for it could be dispensed with (due, for example, to the child being abandoned or orphaned) then adoption of their child was not possible.

3.2.4.   ADOPTION WITHOUT CONSENT

In the mid-1960s, faced with an increase in the number of children entering the care system, many states moved to simplify the process of terminating parental rights in circumstances where children had been abandoned in foster care.[4] A development which may well have been motivated in part by recognition of a child's legal interest in having a parent. If parents had shown no consistent interest in their child and there was no reasonable or foreseeable likelihood that the parents could, or would, resume care responsibility for their child then new legislative provisions enabled parental rights to be terminated. One of the earliest examples of this process occurred in New York in 1959 when legislation was introduced to free the 'permanently neglected' child for adoption. The term 'permanently neglected' was defined as a child in foster care whose parents "failed substantially and

---

[4]   In the period 1964–1970 the number of children in foster care increased from 192,300 to 326,000; see, further, Fanshel, D., and Shinn, E.B., *Children in Foster Care* 29 (1978) as cited by Katz, S., 'Dual Systems of Adoption in the United States', *op cit* at p. 300.

continuously or repeatedly for a period of more than one year to maintain contact with, and plan for the future of the child, although physically and financially able to do so . . . ".[5] The net effect of the New York reform was that termination of parental rights without the birth parents' consent was made possible in circumstances where the birth parents had surrendered their rights to the child by a failure to discharge the obligations of parenthood.[6] This approach was replicated in many other states.

3.2.5. POST ADOPTION INFORMATION RIGHTS

In the aftermath of World War II, laws were passed throughout the US permanently sealing all adoption information relating to birth certificates and families of origin. While most states sealed their records in the 1940s and 1950s, some did not do so until much later.[7] These laws have been criticised as "a relic of the culture of shame that stigmatised infertility, out-of-wedlock birth and adoption".[8] Most state legislation, however, usually included provision for records to be opened by court order.

4. HISTORY OF ADOPTION LEGISLATION

In the US, the Constitution reserves to individual states all powers not specifically delegated to the federal government, though some umbrella pieces of legislation and judicial decisions bring a degree of commonality to law and practice across all states. Family matters, including child welfare laws, have historically been reserved to the state. The Constitution, however, as interpreted by the Supreme Court, requires a state to show compelling reason for infringing rights of family privacy and for overriding parental autonomy as these fundamental liberties are protected by the 14th Amendment and its guarantee of due process.[9] Further, Congress exercises considerable influence over state child care and other family related programmes through its control of central funding sources. In practice,

---

[5] See, Polier, 'Amendments to New York's Adoption Law: the Permanently Neglected Child' in 38 *Child Welfare* 2, 1959.

[6] See, Pennypacker, 'Reaching Decisions to Initiate Court Action to Free Children in Care for Adoption', in 40 Child Welfare, 1961; also Polier, *Parental Rights*, Child Welfare League of America, New York, 1958.

[7] Pennsylvania sealed original birth certificates in 1984 and Alabama in 1991; by 1998 only Kansas and Alaska still allowed unconditional adoptee access.

[8] See, Bastard Nation: The Adoptee Rights Organisation, 'A History of Sealed Records in the US', *The Basic Bastard*, www.bastards.org (2003).

[9] See, for example, *Meyer v Nebraska* 262 US 390 (1923), *Stanley v Illinois* 405 US 645 (1972) and *Wisconsin v Yoder* 406 US 205 (1972).

therefore, the autonomy of individual states in matters relating to the welfare of children is balanced by constitutional, judicial and budgetary constraints.

In the US, to a much greater extent than in other western societies, the development of adoption legislation must also be viewed in the context of evolving child care provision.

4.1.   State legislation

The 1851 Act in Massachusetts, preceding the introduction of similar legislation in England and Wales by 70 years, sets out for the first time some of the more basic functions of the law relating to adoption. Since then each state has enacted and updated much the same body of legislation.

4.1.1.   THE MASSACHUSETTS ADOPTION OF CHILDREN'S ACT, 1851

The 1851 Act was a legislative response to public concern regarding the practice of distributing children from state institutional care, where they had been abandoned by parents or placed by voluntary organisations (including many children transported from England) to long-term foster care placements with farming families. This legislation put into place several foundation stones for the subsequent development of adoption by requiring that all future adoptions were to be:

- judicially sanctioned by an adoption order (until then it had generally been left to the parties to formalise the arrangements by deed, contract or private statute);
- conditional upon the court being satisfied as to the consent of the parties involved;
- conditional upon the court being satisfied that, if made, the adoption order would be in accordance with the welfare interests of the child[10]; and
- conditional upon the court being satisfied that the suitability of prospective adopters had been assessed.

4.2.   Federal and Uniform legislation

Increasingly, in recent years, model statutes are drawn up to provide a template of that which the federal government, at any point in time, considers to be a body of core provisions for US wide legislation. States are free to enact such legislation in whole or in part, or to ignore it. In addition, 'uniform' statutes

---

[10] See, *Curtis v Curtis* 71 Mass (5 Gray) 535, 537 (1856) where the court ruled that "adoption is not a question of mere property . . . the interests of the minor is the principal thing to be considered". Cited by Katz, S., 'Dual Systems of Adoption in the United States', *op cit* at p. 283.

(providing recommendations for removing obstructive inconsistencies between states in areas of similar legislative provision) are prepared within states which may then attract federal government endorsement and pressure to adopt such legislation.

4.2.1.   THE UNIFORM ADOPTION ACT, 1953

The National Conference of Commissioners on Uniform State Laws, a nation-wide non-governmental organisation, was established in 1892 to promote uniformity in the law of the states in certain areas. Its two attempts to introduce legislation to regulate consensual adoption practice were unsuccessful. This legislation, produced by the National Conference, was enacted by Oklahoma (without revisions), and by Alaska, Arkansas, Montana, North Dakota and Ohio. It was revised in 1969.

4.2.2.   THE MODEL ACT TO FREE CHILDREN FOR PERMANENT PLACEMENT, 1978

This legislation provided a procedure for the termination of parental rights and the non-consensual placement of children for adoption in circumstances where rehabilitation within their family of origin was not feasible. It incorporated and applied the concept of 'permanency planning'.

4.2.3.   THE INDIAN CHILD WELFARE ACT, 1978

As the title implies, this legislation related only to Native American children and restricted placement to the child's family, tribe or other Native American families.

4.2.4.   THE ADOPTION ASSISTANCE AND CHILD WELFARE ACT, 1980

Initiated by Congress, the 1980 Act focussed state intervention on preventing the removal of children from parental care and on facilitating rehabilitation in circumstances where removal had been necessary. It set out a hierarchy of options for children requiring alternative permanent care arrangements directing that preference be given to placements in 'the least restrictive environment'. In practice this meant reunification or formal kinship care arrangements; the latter increased considerably following the introduction of the 1980 Act. In the 1980s, the number of children in foster care dropped from a high of nearly 500,000 to a low of about 275,000 as a result of a vigorous implementation of the permanency planning provisions in the 1980 Act (as reiterated in the 1997 Act).

The 1980 Act authorised the channeling of federal funds to those states that implemented child welfare laws emphasising family preservation and reunification and made 'reasonable efforts' to prevent the removal of children from their families or to reunite them as appropriate. It also funded state initiatives to provide post-adoption support for adopters of hard to place children. It was reinforced by the decision of the Supreme Court in *Santosky v Kramer*[11] which ruled that states must have 'clear and convincing evidence' that parents would be unable to care for their child before terminating parental rights or such action would be in breach of the Fourteenth Amendment. It inaugurated an era characterised by public service investment in family reunification.

Nearly twenty years later, however, as Woodhouse has pointed out, this policy was clearly failing[12]:

> An over emphasis on 'reasonable efforts' was preventing children who would never realistically be reunited with their parents from moving on to find safe, permanent families through adoption.

The reason for failure was identified by the Department of Health and Human Services as due to[13]:

> ... well-intended but misguided practices to preserve families through prolonged and extensive reunification services without adequate consideration of the permanency needs of children.

Accordingly, in 1997 Congress passed the Adoption and Safe Families Act in order "to move abused and neglected kids into adoption or other permanent homes and to do it more quickly and more safely than ever before".[14]

4.2.5.   THE MULTIETHNIC PLACEMENT ACT, 1994

Again initiated by Congress, this Act permitted a state agency to take racial matching into account when placing a child if this was a relevant factor in promoting the best interests of the child. Two years later it was replaced by the Small Business and Job Protection Act 1996 which introduced regulatory requirements governing all individuals and agencies involved in adoption or foster care and in receipt of federal funds. Such persons or bodies were prohibited from refusing any person the opportunity to become an adopter or from delaying or denying the placement of any child solely on grounds of the race, colour or national origin of either party.

---

[11]   455 US 755 (1982).
[12]   See, Woodhouse, B., 'The Adoption and Safe Families Act: a Major Shift in Child Welfare Law and Policy' in Bainham, A. (ed.), *The International Survey of Family Law, 2000 Edition*, Family Law, Bristol 2000 at p. 380 citing in support Gelles, R., *The Book of David: How Preserving Families Can Cost Children's Lives*, New York, Basic Books, 1996.
[13]   See, US Department of Health and Human Services, *Adoption 2002: A response to the Presidential Executive Memorandum on Adoption*, Washington, DC, 1997.
[14]   See, Senator Rockefeller of West Virginia, 143 Cong. Rec. 12199.

4.2.6. The Uniform Adoption Act, 1994

The 1994 Act, again drafted by the National Conference, was even less successful than its 1953/69 predecessor; Vermont was the only state to comply. This legislation has been described as follows[15]:

> It seals adoption records for ninety-nine years, potentially criminalises searching, does not define non-identifying information and creates a muddled mutual consent registry that virtually ensures that no exchange of information, even between willing parties, will be made. The act allows a birth mother to relinquish a child without the consent of a birth father if she states that his whereabouts are unknown or that she does not know the birth father's identity, and establishes revocable consent periods of a dismal eight days from the birth of the child. The sections on pre-placement evaluations of prospective adoptive parents are clearly intended to make it easier for couples to adopt rather than ensure that the best interests of the child are being served.
>
> In fact, the entire UAA is clearly meant to expedite adoptions by increasing the number of babies available through shorter consent periods and lack of adequate birth father notification controls, removing barriers to transracial adoption, terminating former contact agreements between original families and their children, and providing for easier home studies that are effective for eighteen months rather than the now-standard thirty days. Critics describe it as defining adoption as a near-contractual agreement among consenting adults regarding newborns. All reference to special needs adoption, including older children, and the placement needs of foster children, the initial concerns of the Model State Act, is gone, leading to its being perceived as facilitating the business of adoption rather than regulating a social service to provide families for children.

4.2.7. The Personal Responsibility and Work Opportunity Reconciliation Act 1996

This legislation impacted upon adoption by requiring states to give preference to kinship placements rather than to 'stranger' foster care placements thus preparing the ground in many cases for subsequent kinship adoptions. It introduced specific requirements in relation to the assessment, management and support of such placements.

4.2.8. The Adoption and Safe Families Act, 1997

This legislation amended but did not repeal the 1980 Act. It was initiated by Congress, came into effect in 1998 and, because it was strongly tied to federal

---

[15] See, Bastard Nation: The Adoptee Rights Organisation, "A History of Sealed Records in the US", *The Basic Bastard*, www.bastards.org (2003).

funding programmes, it immediately prompted individual states to review their legislation to ensure compliance. It had four main goals: making children's safety and health the paramount concern; moving children more rapidly out of foster care and into permanent homes; removal of barriers to adoption; and fast tracking into adoption the children of severe or repeat abusers.

5.   EMERGING CHARACTERISTICS OF ADOPTION PRACTICE

In the US, contemporary adoption law, policy and practice very much reflect the value context of that society. In keeping with 'open society' principles featuring minimum regulatory constraints on the freedom of individuals and businesses to act independently and for private gain, consensual adoption has been largely treated in law as just another enterprise that should largely be allowed to find its own niche in the marketplace. Non-consensual adoption, however, where court rather than parent takes the operative decision, is to some extent treated differently.

Professor Sanford Katz, who for some decades has been a leading authority on adoption law and practice in the US, explains that a twin-track approach, involving either a voluntary relinquishment or an involuntary termination of parental rights, each with its own systems has developed in the US.[16] He defines the first as "consensual and private, involving non-governmental, non-profit or profit-making agencies or individuals" and the second as "non-consensual and public, involving state agencies". Each, in his view, has its own distinctive goal. In the former this may well be "to provide a childless couple with an infant so as to continue the adopters family name". In the latter it is "to protect children and the disposition of adoption is a vehicle for providing a child with a permanent attachment to a family".[17] He adds that they are further differentiated by class association: "infants voluntarily relinquished . . . tend to move into the middle class"; but "children who are the subject of termination proceedings tend to be the offspring of poor parents from deprived backgrounds . . . for the most part, couples who adopt these children are their foster parents".[18]

The Katz typology, however, may not be quite so clinically distinct in practice. While it is true that so far most non-consensual (or child care) adoptions have been made in favour of foster parents, this might have been partially circumstantial due to the backlog of adoptable children in the public care system following

---

[16] See, Katz, S., 'Dual Systems of Adoption in the United States', in Katz, S., Eekelaar, J. and Maclean, M. (eds.), *Cross Currents: Family Law and Policy in the United States and England*, Oxford University Press, Oxford, 2001.

[17] *Ibid*, at pp. 280–281.

[18] *Ibid*, at p. 281.

implementation of new procedures under the 1997 Act. In future there could be a degree of convergence between his two strands as a greater proportion of non-consensual adoptions feed directly into the private system (as in the UK). State agencies, applying the concurrent planning approach, may directly recruit adopters for specific children at point of entry to care.

5.1.   Adoption trends

In 1992 there were a total of 126,951 adoptions of which: 42% were by step-parents; 23% by non-relatives following placement by a not for profit or by a for profit agency; 20% by non-relatives following placement by a birth parent or an intermediary (e.g. doctor, priest etc.) and 15% were arranged through public service agencies (i.e. special needs children).[19]

5.2.   Private adoption

As the statistical data clearly demonstrates, by far the largest proportion of all children adopted annually in the US are simply the subjects of a formal process intended to legally consolidate their position within a new configuration of previous parenting arrangements. Usually, as in the UK, adoption agencies are not required to assess step-parent applicants. Although their eligibility and suitability remain to be judicially assessed, completion of a home study report and a mandatory period of care are not normally required in respect of step-parents. For the children concerned their adoption signifies a minimal adjustment rather than a complete change in home and family life. Typically, the child remains with one birth parent, sometimes accompanied by one or more siblings, often in the family home where he or she has perhaps lived with the step-parent for some years before being adopted. Most significantly, such private adoptions do not entail a change of placement.

In some states[20] where, following the death of a spouse, the other parent re-marries and both adopt the child of the first marriage then the legal relationship between that step-child and the family of their deceased natural parent (e.g. grandparents) continues. This is not the case in many other states nor in countries such as the UK.

5.2.1.   KINSHIP ADOPTIONS

Arguably, 'kinship adoptions', whereby children are placed with members of their extended family, are a variation of private adoption. Initially this practice was

---

[19] See, National Centre for State Courts, 1992.
[20] For example Arkansas, Alaska, Montana, New Mexico, New York, North Dakota, Ohio and Wisconsin; as cited by Bridge, C. and Swindells, H. *op cit*, 2003, at p. 300.

most strongly associated with African American culture but it is now promoted by public child care agencies as it provides for minimal disruption to a child's sense of belonging within the family, class, culture and locality of their birth. The recent and significant growth in kinship adoptions has been a direct consequence of drug abuse, particularly the rise in addiction to crack cocaine.

5.2.2. PARENTAL PLACEMENTS

In marked contrast to practice in other western societies, most states continue to permit private adoption placements; only four restrict placement to agencies in non-relative adoptions. Private adoption placements may be made 'direct' by parents, on a not-for-profit basis, in a final exercise of their parental rights with persons of their choosing, or by a person (e.g. clergyman, doctor or lawyer) to whom the parent has delegated that responsibility. Private adoption enables prospective parents to make a direct personal approach to a birth mother or to do so through the mediation of a third party or perhaps by placing an advertisement in local, national or international journals or on the internet. Adoptive parents are generally permitted to recompense the birth mother for reasonable expenses incurred during pregnancy but are otherwise prohibited from making any payments by way of inducement or reward for relinquishing a child.

5.2.3. INDEPENDENT AGENCIES

A distinguishing characteristic of adoption in the US is that by far the majority of non-family adoptions are arranged by private, independent agencies that usually operate on a commercial or for-profit basis. These agencies are very lightly regulated. Livingstone in her 1994 report to the US Dept of State noted that very few of the 50 states regulate the profit status of individuals or organisations involved in adoption ... "as adoption has become a business, a sense of competition has developed. Professional co-operation and efforts towards internal monitoring are hard to find". As expressed by Katz[21]:

> In the past thirty years, an adoption industry has developed. The private placement of children has taken on the characteristics of a business, in effect trading in children ...

Some of these independent, for-profit agencies, such as 'All God's Children, International' operate on a global basis placing children from sending countries (e.g. Russia) with adopters from anywhere in the western world (e.g. Northern Ireland).

---

[21] See, Katz, S., 'Dual Systems of Adoption in the United States', *op cit* at p. 285. But also see (as cited by Katz) the positive findings of Somit, J., 'Independent Adoptions in California: Dual Representation Allowed' in 1 Adoption Law and Practice (eds., Hollinger, J.H., and Leski, D.W.), 1988, para 5.01–5.09.

5.3.   Public adoption

The US now has a very high proportion of children in care, some 74 per 10,000 compared with 47 per 10,000 in England.[22] But being in care does not ensure children's safety; 48% of child abuse deaths in 1995 involved children previously known to the authorities.[23] In order to facilitate the adoption of such children, US public service provision for children is so organised that a separate department deals specifically with planning adoption from care.

Between 1985 and 1995 the population of children removed from home and placed in substitute care almost doubled from 276,000 to 494,000. As explained by Selwyn and Sturgess[24]:

> Between 1986 and 1995 there was a 72% increase in the number of children in care, associated with a rise in the number of child abuse referrals.[25] This trend was most apparent for younger children and the median age of entry to care reduced from 12.6 years in 1982 to 8.0 years in 1999.[26] The rise threatened to overwhelm the child welfare system and kinship care was encouraged whenever possible. By 1999, 547,000 American children were in care with most looked after in foster care placements.[27] The goal for the majority of these children was reunification with their birth families.

During this period the public service tradition of placing children in foster care homes declined[28] as kinship placements became steadily more numerous.[29]

5.3.1.   SPECIAL NEEDS CHILDREN

The United States House of Representatives has defined a 'special needs' child as one "to whom the State determines there is a specific condition, such as age, membership of a minority or sibling group, or a mental, emotional or physical handicap which prevents placement without special assistance". The Adoption and Safe Families Act, 1997 was introduced to address a worsening situation in

---

[22] See, Performance and Innovation Unit, 2000.

[23] See, National Committee to Prevent Child Abuse, *Current Trends in Child Abuse Reporting and Fatalities: the Results of the 1995 Fifty-State Survey*, Chicago, NCPCA, April 1996 at p. 3. Cited by Besharov, D., *The Future of Children: Protecting Children from Abuse and Neglect*, 1996.

[24] See, Selwyn, J. and Sturgess W., 'Achieving Permanency through Adoption: following in US footsteps', *Adoption & Fostering*, London, BAAF, vol. 26, no. 3, 2002 at p. 40.

[25] *Ibid*, citing *National Adoption Information*, 2001.

[26] *Ibid*, citing Children's Bureau, 2001.

[27] *Ibid*, citing *Adoption and Foster Care Analysis and Reporting System*, 1998–1999.

[28] See, General Accounting Office, 1989 as cited by McFadden, E., 'Kinship Care in the United States, in *Adoption & Fostering*, BAAF, vol. 22, no. 3 p. 8 (1998).

[29] The number of foster homes available decreased from 137,000 in 1984 to 100,000 in 1989. By 1993, kinship care accounted for approximately one-third of placements in New York and about one-half in Illinois.

which ever increasing numbers of such children were living out their childhood in the public care system. In 1992 these 'special needs' children accounted for approximately 15% of total adoptions (a far higher proportion than in the UK).

The 1997 Act significantly increased the funds available for special needs children.[30] It also provided a system of 'adoption incentive payments' to the states whereby a bounty is payable for every additional adoption above a set quota and it promotes the provision of post-adoption support services.

The new approach initiated by the Adoption and Safe Families Act 1997 has since been implemented by replicated state legislation across the US. Children in the public care system and unable to return to their birth families are now, whenever possible, placed for adoption; most often adoption is by the child's foster parents with ongoing financial support.[31] In such circumstances, adoption is the preferred option and all alternatives are discouraged. In particular, and unlike practice in countries such as Ireland, long-term foster care is now positively discouraged. In the US, the non-consensual adoption of children from the public care system into private family care has become an established characteristic and one that is now being emulated in the UK but is rejected by such other modern western countries as Sweden, Denmark, France, Australia and Ireland. In terms of the international political context of adoption, this practice whereby state responsibilities for neglected and abused children are privatised and often accompanied by on going financial payments, has emerged as something of an ideological fault line.

5.3.2.   PERMANENT LEGAL GUARDIANSHIP

This order was introduced because[32]:

> ... the emphasis on legally secure permanent placement is meant to provide the child with psychological stability and a sense of belonging and limit the likelihood of future disruption of the parent-child relationship ... traditional adoption does not meet the needs of children in public foster care. Legal options for permanent and legally secure placement should be broad enough to serve the needs of all children in care who are not able to return to their homes of origin ...

A permanent legal guardian has the legal custody and control of a child including powers to make decisions concerning that child's care, education, discipline and

---

[30] See, Barth, R.P., Yoshikami, R., Goodfield, R.K. and Carson, M.L. 'Predicting Adoption Disruption' in *Social Work*, 1998, pp. 227–33 for evidence that post-adoption subsidies mitigate adoption disruption.

[31] See, the Children's Bureau report (1999) which noted that one half of all children adopted from foster care were adopted by their foster parents and that 86% of those received adoption subsidies.

[32] See, Department of Health and Human Services, *Adoption 2002: The President's Initiative on Adoption and Foster Care; Guidelines for Public Policy and State Legislation Governing Permanence for Children* (1999).

protection. Both birth parents may retain some ongoing rights of contact and access and responsibility for maintenance. This order is intended for use by those relatives who may not wish to see a complete severance of ties between child and family and is particularly appropriate in relation to older children who object to adoption because of an established attachment to their parents.

In 1998, of the 248,000 children exiting the public care system, 5,836 did so by way of permanent legal guardianship.

5.3.3. THE ADOPTION AND FOSTER CARE ANALYSIS AND REPORTING SYSTEM

The Adoption and Safe Families Act, 1997 established the Adoption and Foster Care Analysis and Reporting System (AFCARS), a mandatory data collection system, which provides evidence that the policy drive to use adoption to secure permanency for children unable to return to their birth families is indeed working.

5.4.   Open adoption

From the mid-1970s into the 1990s, the practice of 'open adoption'—allowing adoption orders in respect of newborn infants to be made subject to the visiting rights of the birth parent/s—became more common. The rationale for this lay in the realisation that for many birth parents who were failing to provide adequate parental care, the finality of adoption was a barrier which could be overcome by ongoing contact arrangements. In 1992 Washington State enacted 'co-operative adoption' provisions, followed by similar initiatives by Oregon in 1993 and Indiana in 1994. Open adoption[33] is now permitted in several US jurisdictions including Minnesota and New Mexico. Many models of open adoption (e.g. in Oregon) allow for an agreed level of contact to be maintained between the child and their birth parents and other family members.

5.5.   Intercountry adoption

By the 1990s, the rapid fall in the number of babies voluntarily relinquished for adoption in the US led to a steady increase in adopters prepared to look overseas for a healthy baby. In 1992, approximately 8.9% of all adoptions were intercountry.

The US Congress has decreed that only orphans (children orphaned, abandoned or where the sole or surviving parent is unable to provide care) can be brought into the country for adoption.

---

[33] See, Mullender (ed.) *Open Adoption* (BAAF, 1991).

214 *Contemporary law, policy and practice*

5.6.   Transracial adoption

Native Americans, and to some extent African Americans, are well-established socio-political entities in the US. However, while African American children are over represented in the care system,[34] there is a scarcity of available African American foster parents and adopters. Against that background, the question whether transracial adoption is compatible with the welfare interests of the children involved was inevitably going to be more seriously contentious in the US than elsewhere. Proponents and opponents of transracial placements defend their case with such ideological conviction that it is impossible to do justice to their concerns in this context. Transracial adoption in the US has been and continues to be a difficult policy matter.

5.7.   Surrogacy

When, in New Jersey, the surrogacy case of *In re Baby M*[35] came to court there was no precedent in the US or elsewhere to which the court could turn for guidance. Since the 1990s, surrogacy has become quite common and the legal issue of the enforceability of a surrogacy contract has become accepted as an ancillary aspect of the adoption process. In all states surrogacy can now be the subject of proceedings. Individual states have legislated differently in response to the legal difficulties. For example, in some states, surrogacy contracts are valid if the surrogate is not compensated while in others such contracts are invalid. Many states allow for the revocation of consent within a certain timeframe. For example, Alaska allows birth parents to revoke their consent within ten days after consent if the court finds it to be in the child's best interests. In New Jersey, once a birth mother relinquishes her child to an agency she cannot revoke her consent but in a private placement she can change her mind within twenty days of receiving notice of the adoption proceedings.

5.8.   Same sex adopters

Adoption applications by same gender couples are an established if minor aspect of the US adoption process. Since the leading Hawaiian case of *Baehr v Lewin*[36] the judiciary in most states where the issue has arisen have accepted that adoption

---

[34] See, Stehno, S., 'The elusive continuum of child welfare services: implications for minority children and youth', *Child Welfare* 69, pp. 551–562 (1990). Also, Tatara, T., *Characteristics of Children in Substitute and Adoptive Care: A statistical summary of the VCIS national child-welfare database*, Washington DC, American Public Welfare Association (1993).

[35] 537 A 2d 1227 NJ (1988).

[36] 852 P 2d 44 Haw (1993); though this was not a 'same-sex' case.

by same-sex couples can be compatible with the welfare interests of the children concerned. As Justice Ruth Abrams has stated[37]:

> An increasing number of same gender couples, like the plaintiff and defendant are deciding to have children. It is to be expected that children of nontraditional families, like other children, form parent relationships with both parents, whether those parents are legal or de facto ...

5.9.   Adoption orders

The total of annual adoption orders in the US decreased from 125,000 in 1970 to 104,000 in 1986. Child care adoption orders, however, have in recent years increased. The AFCARS data system reveals that in relation to children in public care "the estimated number of children adopted annually from 1998 to 2002 increased dramatically from 37,000 in 1998 to 51,000 in 2000, declined to 50,000 in 2001 and increased to 53,000 in 2002".[38]

Between 1990 and 1999 the number of care adoptions by relatives doubled, 66% of orders were in favour of married couples while 30% were granted to single female applicants.

5.10.   Post-adoption access to information

Access to identifying information has been a long-standing and very controversial issue in the US. The privacy rights of individuals, as enshrined in the Constitution and protected by the Supreme Court, have provided an effective obstacle to any legislation granting blanket rights of access to records held by adoption agencies or other bodies.

In 1978 President Carter convened a panel of independent experts in the field of child welfare to address the issue of "special needs" adoption and to draft an appropriate model for related state legislation. The panel instead formulated a Model State Adoption Act that would open records to adult adoptees and instruct adoption agencies to serve as intermediaries in searches by birth parents for their adult relinquished children. This draft legislation was abandoned, in the face of effective lobbying from adoption agencies and adopters. Subsequently, President Regan's government substituted the Uniform Adoption Act that made no reference to the open records provisions nor to many other proposed reforms. However, during the period 1979–1999, several states began introducing

---

[37] See, *E.N.O. v L.M.M.* 711 NE 2d 886 Mass. (1999) at p. 891.
[38] See, AFCARS, annual report, 2004 at http://www.acf.hhs.gov/programs/cb/dis/afcars /publications/ dlinkafcars.htm.

legislation facilitating access to adoption information.[39] Now, as Katz has noted:

> At least seven jurisdictions allow identifying information to be released by the court either because of the consent of the adopted child and her birth parents or for good cause. About the same number of jurisdictions allow access to an adopted child's birth certificate when she is an adult, and twenty-four States have statutory provisions that set up mutual consent registries.[40]

6.   OVERVIEW OF MODERN ADOPTION LAW AND POLICY

In the US, there is no national legal framework governing the adoption process. Adoption law is represented by 51 different pieces of legislation, one for each state and one for the District of Columbia. However, Congress, through exercise of the Spending Power, is able to induce some degree of conformity by formulating broad policy initiatives leading to model legislation intended to frame new laws and guide practice across all states.

6.1.   Adoption policy

The development of modern policy in the US has been marked by a sea change with regard to children in the public care system due to parental fault or default. The Adoption and Safe Families Act 1997 consolidated a policy shift away from public service resource investment in family reunification and towards the promotion of adoption as a private resource for the care of children by non-relatives together with support for kinship care. As expressed by Woodhouse[41]:

---

[39] Following the decision in *ALMA Society Inc. v Mellon* 601 F2d 1238 (2nd Cir), cert denied, 100 S Ct 531 (1979); as cited by Katz, S., 'Dual Systems of Adoption in the United States', *op cit* at p. 292. The Supreme Court then held that the adult adopted applicants did not have a right of access to identifying information. Adoptees now have an unconditional right of access to their records in Alaska, Kansas, Oregon and Alabama. However, as Julia Feast (co-author of *The Adoption Reunion Handbook*) has commented:

> "Legislation lags far behind the UK with most states not allowing adopted adults the most basic information about themselves—in some cases, not even their original name. This can make it nearly impossible for adopted adults and birth relatives to find each other, unless they can afford private investigators. Even then it can be difficult."

As cited by Hilpern K. in her feature article 'The Daddy of All Game Shows' in *The Independent Review*, 5th January, 2005, at p. 2.

[40] *Ibid* at p. 292.

[41] See, Woodhouse, B., 'The Adoption and Safe Families Act: a Major Shift in Child Welfare Law and Policy' at p. 383.

In essence, ASFA shifts money and services from biological families and foster families to adoptive families.

This policy change was initiated by President Clinton when, on 14th December 1996, he issued his Executive Memorandum on adoption directing the Secretary of the US Department of Health and Human Services to outline a national plan to expedite permanency placements for children entering the care system. In 1997 the Department responded with the *Adoption 2000* report in which it detailed the obstacles to permanency planning in law and practice and set out an agenda for effecting change that would double the number of child care adoptions by 2002. As a direct consequence, the provisions of the Adoption and Safe Families Act 1997 were drawn up and signed into law by President Clinton on November 19, 1997.

6.2. The contemporary legislative framework

The Adoption and Safe Families Act 1997, in conjunction with the amended Adoption Assistance and Child Welfare Act 1980 and other statutes of lesser importance together provide the contemporary legislative framework for adoption in the US. This is supplemented by the provisions of international Conventions and by the International Adoption Act 2000.

6.2.1. THE ADOPTION ASSISTANCE AND CHILD WELFARE ACT 1980

This statute, a legislative response to concerns that too many children were being removed from parental care only to disappear into the public care system, established the modern legal framework for child care in the US. It introduced and positioned within statute law the formative concepts of 'permanency' and 'reasonableness' and provided the basis for a generation of professional intervention focussed on rehabilitating children within their families of origin. It was because this approach was largely unsuccessful, resulting in many children being left to drift in foster care, that an alternative strategy was mandated by the Adoption and Safe Families Act 1997.

6.2.2. THE ADOPTION AND SAFE FAMILIES ACT 1997

This legislation introduced two new concepts: the duty of a state to make reasonable efforts at 'permanency planning' once adoption or permanent guardianship becomes the goal; and the concept of 'concurrent planning'.[42] To qualify for federal funds a state scheme must show that 'in determining reasonable efforts ... to be made with respect to a child, and in making such reasonable efforts, the child's

---

[42] 42 USC Section 675 (E). See, further, Chapter 2.

health and safety shall be the paramount concern'.[43] This shifted the legal emphasis from family preservation to the priority of child safety. It requires:

- a clear statement made in court when a care order is issued of the changes to be made by the parents within a 12 month period after which the child will either be returned to parental care or placed for adoption;
- a permanency hearing to be held 12 months after the issue of a care order;
- mandatory concurrent planning; and
- after a child has been in care for 15 out of 24 months, good reason must be shown as to why a petition to terminate parental rights should not be filed.

A principal aim of the 1997 Act is to promote the adoption of children in foster care, facilitated by a timetable for expediting the termination of parental rights. In particular, there is provision for fast-tracking cases where there is a record of a parent having killed, abused or had their parental rights terminated in respect of another child. In such cases there is a maximum of 30 days to a permanency hearing. The 1997 Act also introduced 'legal guardianship' which provides authority for the transfer of parental rights to a relative enabling them to assume permanent care responsibility for a child failed by parental care.[44] The legislative intent is to speed up the process of removing children from the care system and placing them in permanent alternative care arrangements by use of adoption or legal guardianship. States are eligible to claim financial bonuses from federal funds if they exceed their set quota of annual adoptions. In effect the 1997 Act imposes a 15 month time limit on the use of financial resources to achieve family reunification after which resource allocation switches to supporting permanency through adoption. This is seen by some as a worrying development[45]:

> This shift of resources into promoting adoption, as opposed to state-managed foster care, as a solution for children in 'dysfunctional' families can be seen as a form of 'privatising' child welfare.

6.2.3.   THE MULTI ETHNIC PLACEMENT ACT 1994

This legislation and its 1996 successor prohibits discriminatory practices by banning the denial or delay of a foster or adoption placement solely on the basis of race, colour, or national origin of carer or child. It also compels states to make diligent efforts to recruit and retain foster and adoptive families that reflect the ethnic diversity of 'waiting' children.

---

[43]   42 USC 671 Section 15.

[44]   A 'legal guardianship' order bears a strong resemblance to the English 'special guardianship' order. Both offer a strategic half-way-house between long-term foster care and adoption that does not require the extinguishing of birth parents rights.

[45]   See, Woodhouse, B., *op cit*, at p. 375.

6.2.4. THE SAFE HAVEN LAWS

Since 1999 over forty states have passed 'safe haven' laws in an attempt to prevent unsafe abandonment of babies and neonaticide. While statutes vary from state to state, most include the following provisions:

- Parent(s) or those designated by the parent(s) may anonymously leave an "unwanted infant" at a Safe Haven center (hospital emergency room, fire station, police station).
- No questions are asked. No identification of parent(s) is required. No social or medical history of baby is required.
- Age of Safe Haven babies range from birth to five days; some states permit up to thirty days (South Dakota permits anonymous abandonment up to one year).

In about half of the states immunity from prosecution for abandonment is granted to parent(s) if there is no evidence of abuse or neglect; the remaining states allow an affirmative defence to prosecution.[46] Safe haven laws have been criticised because they[47]:

- deny the right of identity to infants abandoned 'legally' and strip the infant of all genetic, medical and social history;
- include few or no safeguards against third party intervention (for example, a father who doesn't want responsibility, embarrassed grandparents etc);
- ignore established birth parent revocation timeframes that permit a birth parent—usually the mother—to reclaim her child in a reasonable amount of time;
- deny birth fathers due process;
- contravene sections of the Indian Child Welfare Act which give tribes preferential custody rights in cases of child relinquishment;
- deter adoption through traditional legal channels and replaces standard practice with what some Safe Haven advocates call 'non-bureaucratic placement';
- discourage women from seeking pre-natal and post-natal medical care and counseling, thus endangering the health, well being, and even life of both the mother and the baby (in Florida receiving centers are prohibited from even asking women if they need care);

---

[46] Safe haven laws were a response to public concern regarding the abandonment of babies: in 1992 sixty-five infants were found abandoned (fifty-seven live and eight dead) and in 1997 out of 3,880,894 births in the U.S. (including 18,507 neonatal deaths) only 105 newborns were abandoned (seventy-two live and thirty-three dead).

[47] See, Bastard Nation: The Adoptee Rights Organisation, 'Legalized Anonymous Infant Abandonment/Safe Haven Laws', *The Basic Bastard*, www.bastards.org (2003).

- create legislative band-aid solutions instead of addressing the root socioeconomic causes of baby abandonment and neonaticide (for example, poverty, substance abuse, physical abuse, shame and mental illness); and
- reject long-standing best child welfare practice.

It is suggested that such laws do not just provide opportunities for women to avail of a life-saving option by anonymously taking their baby to a hospital or other safe place. They are also seen as a tool to endorse secret relinquishment and thereby enable birth parents to avoid professional involvement and eventual disclosure obligations.

6.3.   International law

The US has signed but not yet ratified the Convention on the Rights of the Child 1989. In 1994 the US signed the Hague Convention on Protection of Children and Co-operation in Respect of Intercountry Adoption 1993. The US Congress has since enacted legislation to implement the Hague Convention and the State Department is currently in the process of certifying agencies to perform the various required functions after which it will be ratified.[48] The US Constitution's Bill of Rights together with the 13th, 14th, and 15th Amendments, may be considered to provide a body of provisions equivalent to the European Convention on Human Rights.

7.   REGULATING THE ADOPTION PROCESS

A distinguishing feature of adoption in the US is that, in keeping with the prevailing 'free-market' ethos, consensual placements are not subject to the type of tight regulatory systems that characterise the way in which other nations, such as the UK, manage the adoption process. Non-consensual placements, however, attract regulatory provisions across the US.

7.1.   Judicial process

In all states, adoption is a judicial process set within a statutory framework.

7.2.   Adoption agencies

In the US, adoptions are most usually arranged by adoption agencies that are either public child care agencies or private independent commercial organisations.

---

[48] Intercountry Adoption Act of 2000, codified at 42 U.S.C. sec. 14901 *et seq*. The Hague Convention is expected to be ratified by the US by the end of 2004.

All private agencies are required to be licensed and to submit to monitoring, periodic inspection and state regulatory systems. As an alternative to making a direct placement, a parent may place their child through an agency after having formally relinquished all rights and this may be done on a for-profit basis. The child may then be advertised for adoption through nation-wide media outlets. This commercial component to private placements is a distinctive and long-standing characteristic of the adoption process in the US.

Adoption agencies provide the link between children in need of a home and prospective adoptive parents. They assess prospective applicants, arrange suitable placements and process court applications. They often provide pre and post support services for birth mothers and usually have very long waiting lists. The pivotal position of such agencies in the adoption process is accompanied by legal responsibilities. An adoption agency may be liable to adopters for 'wrongful adoption' i.e., a failure to disclose facts about a child's history, including genetic information, that could have had a bearing on their decision to accept a particular placement.[49]

7.2.1.   ADOPTION COMMITTEE

The functions of an Adoption Panel in the UK are usually performed in the US by an adoption committee which comprises much the same mix of executive officers, specialist professionals and some independent members. A licensed adoption agency will normally ensure that tasks of confirming the availability of particular children, selecting approved adopters and agreeing matched placements are assigned to such a committee.

7.3.   Registrar

All states have laws that provide a formal process for the registration of an adoption order by the state Registrar in a Registry of Births. The Registrar will also be responsible for the issue of a birth certificate naming the adopters as parents of the child, for recording in a separate register the facts relating to the birth parents and for determining rights of access to identifying information.

---

[49] See, for example, the Ohio case of *Burr v Board of County Commissioners* 491 NE2d (1986) where the tort of 'wrongful adoption' first attracted judicial notice and *Meracle v Children's Service Society* (1986) where an agency was prosecuted for wilful negligence. Also, see, Blair, D.M., 'Liability of Adoption Agencies and Attorneys for Misconduct in the Disclosure of Health-Related Information' in Hollinger, J.H., and Leski, D.W., (eds.), 2 *Adoption Law and Practice* (1998) at para 16.01-08.

8.   THRESHOLDS FOR ENTERING THE ADOPTION PROCESS: ELIGIBILITY AND SUITABILITY CRITERIA

In the US, the criteria governing entry to an adoption process are set by similar statutory requirements in all states and would seem to broadly conform to the adoption typology suggested by Katz.[50]

8.1.   The child

The availability of a child for adoption is determined by either the existence of parental consent, the absence of any need for it (i.e., being orphaned or abandoned) or the presence of grounds for dispensing with it (i.e., judicial removal of parental rights) as set out in the Adoption and Safe Families Act 1997. Where the child is of an age to give a full and informed consent, then this is often an additional statutory requirement. Whether or not articulated in statute law, the right of a 'mature minor' to assert their views, identify matters constituting their welfare interests and often to determine their future care arrangements is well established in the courts of the US.

8.2.   The birth parent/s

Where the parents of the child to be adopted are or have been married to each other then the consent of both is required, or grounds for dispensing with this must be shown, if the child is to be regarded in law as available for adoption. In relation to intercountry adoption, evidence is required that the birth parent/s are dead or have abandoned the child (including abandoned to institutional care).

8.2.1.   UNMARRIED MOTHER

The consent of an unmarried mother, or grounds for dispensing with it, must always be available. Most states have laws stipulating a minimum time period following birth of a child before the mother can give a valid consent to adoption.

8.2.2.   UNMARRIED FATHER

All states require, as a minimum, that an unmarried father be notified where feasible that adoption proceedings in respect of his child have been, or will shortly be, commenced. Most states, in compliance with developing international law, now also require that the consent of such a father be obtained or that grounds for dispensing with it be shown.

---

[50] See, above, under 'Emerging Characteristics of Adoption Practice'.

8.3. The adopters; eligibility and suitability criteria

Where a birth parent is also an adopter, as in step-parent adoptions, and the consent of the other parent is available, the courts generally find that eligibility and suitability criteria are readily satisfied. In the case of kinship adopters, the courts have shown a willingness to be flexible in relation to age and health criteria.

8.3.1. THIRD PARTY ADOPTERS

Eligibility criteria as set out in statute law and suitability criteria as applied by adoption agencies are much the same in the US as in the UK. Some issues such as the upper age limit of adopters, same sex applicants, willingness to accommodate contact arrangements and the availability of state financial support have generated the same level of controversy. Trans-racial adoption has been and continues to be a particularly sensitive matter for policy and practice in this jurisdiction.

In the majority of cases the suitability of adopters is decided by the birth mother. This is most obviously the case in step-parent adoptions. It is also, in effect, the reality in agency adoptions when prospective adopters are encouraged to prepare a videotape—in which they relate their qualities—for distribution to birth mothers. The decision of the latter may well be influenced by financial considerations as brokered by the agency.

9. THE PLACEMENT

The placing of a child for adoption is the most crucial decision in any adoption process. In the US, to a much greater extent than in the UK, that decision is taken by a birth parent.

9.1. Pre-placement counselling

In most if not all states, both public and private adoption agencies are now required to provide counselling to the birth mother and to the birth father, if he is involved, regarding their legal rights and the options available. Counselling must also be offered to prospective adopters.

9.2. Authority to make an adoption placement

The right of a birth mother to place her child for adoption with whomsoever she chooses, or to authorise another person to do so on her behalf, has been embodied in the laws of all but four states which restrict the right to placement with a relative.[51] In a private adoption context, placement decisions are mostly made by adoption agencies at their discretion following formal parental relinquishment of the child to the agency. In a public child care context, the placement is made by the relevant government agency following judicial termination of parental rights. Many but not all states also permit independent persons, such as lawyers, to make placement arrangements.

9.2.1.   PLACEMENT SUPERVISION

The Interstate Compact for the Placement of Children, endorsed by all states, provides procedures to safeguard children in pre-adoption placements.

10.   THE HEARING AND ISSUE OF ORDER/S

A judicial hearing, held in camera and subject to the usual reporting restrictions, but managed in a more relaxed manner than other court proceedings, provides the context for determining all adoption applications across the US.

10.1.   Role of the determining body

In all states, the court, in response to proceedings commenced by prospective adopters, will determine whether or not an adoption order should be made. This decision rests on that which the court construes to be the best interests of the child concerned.

10.2.   Representation

The 'due process' and 'equal protection' requirements, of the 5th and 14th Amendments respectively, necessitate legal representation for all parties to adoption proceedings. The arrangements for representing the interests of the parties are much the same in the US as in the UK and the court will have the benefit of the same type of professional reports from the agencies involved.

10.3.   Where consent is available

The availability of a valid parental consent places the court in a position to make the order sought, whether or not it does so will be determined by the welfare test i.e.—Are there any contraindications to the suggestion that adoption is in the best interests of the child? Would any other order or no order be more appropriate given the particular circumstances of the child?

---

[51] Colorado, Connecticut, Delaware and Massachusetts.

10.4. Where consent is not available

In the context of child care adoptions, the child welfare laws of all states provide grounds for the termination of parental rights in circumstances of parental neglect or abuse within the parameters as set out in the Adoption and Safe Families Act 1997. Where parental rights have been so terminated and the child successfully placed by the relevant public service agency with selected prospective adopters, the latter will then commence adoption proceedings. On the matter coming before the court it will rule that it can dispense with the necessity for parental consent and accede to the application if satisfied that this is compatible with the welfare interests of the child.

In the context of private adoptions, where an application by a parent or relative is contested by a birth parent who withholds consent, the court must proceed to a full hearing, receiving evidence from the parties and perhaps from expert witnesses, making findings of fact, ruling in favour of the rights of the parties and ultimately making a determination on the merits of the case and in accordance with the welfare principle. In contested private adoptions, the rights of the parties under the Constitution will play a significant role in what will be more adversarial proceedings than is normally the case in other modern western nations and the outcome is more likely to be an order other than adoption; guardianship being a probable option.

11. THRESHOLDS FOR EXITING THE ADOPTION PROCESS

The established priority given to 'permanency planning' in law and practice, together with the policy not to regard long-term foster care as a viable option and the absence of a range of alternative orders, have elevated adoption to become the judicial disposal option of choice where family reunification is impractical.

11.1. Adoption order

In the US, as in other western jurisdictions, the granting of an adoption order with attendant if qualified rights of access to information and to ongoing support is the most usual outcome of the adoption process. This order will be for 'full adoption' which, as in the UK and elsewhere, terminates the parental rights of birth parents and effects the permanent and exclusive vesting of parental responsibilities in adopters. The child assumes the name, residence and citizenship of the adopters and will have the same legal rights as a child by birth. After the order is granted by a court, the adopters will receive an official decree and a birth certificate with the adopters' name listed as the parent. However, in a number of states, statute law still allows adopted children to inherit from biological parents.[52]

11.1.1. ADOPTION ORDERS WITH CONTACT

Where all parties agree, including the child concerned (if aged 12 years or more), then an adoption order can be made subject to a contact condition. There is a judicial duty to enforce such a condition in those states where the law specifically recognises post-adoption contact and a judicial power to do so in circumstances where this is indicated by the welfare of the child concerned. Failure of the contact condition will not invalidate the adoption.

11.2.   Other orders

Unlike other jurisdictions such as the UK, the alternatives to an adoption order are limited. In the US, in order of preference, the judicial options to secure permanency are either safe reunion with parent/s or family of origin, adoption or permanent legal guardianship.

11.2.1. PERMANENT LEGAL GUARDIANSHIP ORDER

This is recommended in circumstances where reunification with parent/s or family of origin is not possible and adoption is inappropriate. The order does not terminate parental rights but instead transfers custodial rights to a named guardian leaving intact other legal rights such as those relating to inheritance. Permanent legal guardianship is the next preferred option to adoption and is intended for use by relatives of the child. Long-term foster care is the least preferred option. It has been noted that "there seems to have been a more recent shift in emphasis from regarding adoption as the only option for securing permanence to embracing guardianship by relatives and long-term foster carers".[53]

12.   POST-ADOPTION SUPPORT SERVICES

The involvement of an adoption agency in placement ensures that it is thereafter available to offer support and that its records and counselling services can be made available at a later stage should the parties seek identifying information.

---

[52]   Including, for example, Alaska, Arkansas, Connecticut, Montana, New Mexico, New York, North Dakota, Ohio and Wisconsin.

[53]   See, Selwyn, J. and Sturgess W., 'Achieving Permanency through Adoption: following in US footsteps', *Adoption & Fostering*, London, BAAF, vol. 26, no. 3, 2002 at p. 75.

12.1. Support services to adopters

Ongoing post-adoption support services were not necessarily available in the US before the introduction of the 1997 Act. The only definite financial and professional support scheme for permanency placements was then in relation to long-term foster care. Since state implementation of legislation conforming to the 1997 Act, the proportion of child care adoptions receiving financial subsidies has grown to 88% of all annual orders.

13. INFORMATION DISCLOSURE, TRACING AND RE-UNIFICATION SERVICES

In the US, there is no national law, policy or practice framework governing access to adoption records. State legislation on this matter has tended to focus on the protection of rights to privacy. So, for example, the Uniform Adoption Act 1994 contains a general provision prohibiting access to closed adoption records.

13.1. Information disclosure

State laws passed many decades ago to seal adoption records remain largely in place. However, nearly all states have provisions for opening adoption or birth records for good cause without the consent or even notification of the birth parent. Many adoptive parents routinely obtain records with the names of the birth parents, or can obtain them by request.

Nevertheless, the continued strong resistance to open access from organisations representing the interests of birth parents means that most adult adoptees in the US are currently denied unconditional access to their original birth certificates. This general denial of a right of access to information with a bearing on personal identity, typical of the traditional 'closed' model of adoption in western societies, is another distinguishing feature of modern adoption practice in the US.[54]

13.1.1. CONDITIONAL ACCESS

Conditional access includes provision for disclosure vetoes, contact vetoes and other intermediary systems. Disclosure vetoes, by which an adoptee may access their original birth certificate only if their birth parent does not object, would seem to vest the latter with a privacy privilege.[55]

---

[54] Nations currently facilitating access to records include the UK, Sweden, The Netherlands, Germany, South Korea, Mexico, Argentina and Venezuela.

[55] Delaware passed a disclosure veto law in 1998.

In *Doe v. Sundquist*[56] a Tennessee semi-open records law (containing both contact and disclosure vetoes) was challenged on the grounds that it violated the privacy of birth parents. The Sixth Circuit Court of Appeals ruled that "if there is a federal constitutional right of familial privacy, it does not extend as far as the plaintiffs would like." The opinion also cited a 1981 decision in which the appeals court found that "the Constitution does not encompass a general right to nondisclosure of private information."

The case concluded in 1998 when the United States Supreme Court rejected the plaintiffs' claim that their right to privacy was infringed and upheld the Appeal Court's ruling in favor of the defendants and open records.

In *Does v State of Oregon*[57] the legislature in Oregon approved provisions to permit the unconditional opening of original birth certificates to adult adoptees upon request but was immediately challenged in court by six anonymous birth mothers with support from the National Council For Adoption, an anti-open records lobbying organisation. The plaintiffs claimed that open records violated contracts of anonymity made at the time of relinquishments as well as their right to privacy. The case was dismissed in mid-1999, a decision subsequently upheld by the Oregon Court of Appeal and affirmed by the Supreme Court in May 2000.

13.2.   Tracing and re-unification services

Independent agencies providing services for all parties to an adoption—on a continuum from counselling, through information gathering and tracing to possible re-unification—are now well established in the US with many operating on an inter-state and for profit basis. The fact, however, that the law governing access to birth records is shrouded in controversy and varies from state to state results in an uneven patchwork of services.

14.   CONCLUSION

Adoption as a legal process has been in existence for nearly twice as long in the US as in the UK. At first glance, there are strong similarities in the adoption experience of the two jurisdictions. Both are statutory processes, administered by the courts, providing much the same legal protection for the parties involved, regulating the same set of legal functions and concluding, in the main, with similar permanent and absolute adoption orders. They have both evolved in much the same way and at the same pace from the traditional 'closed' model to the present more 'open' form of adoption. In doing so, their practice has shared common contentious

---

[56]   943 F. Supp. 886, 893–94 (M.D. Tenn. 1996).
[57]   164 Or. App. 543, 993 P.2d 833, 834 (1999).

issues in relation to matters such as intercountry and transracial placements, post adoption allowances and information rights, special needs children, surrogacy, same gender adopters, the rights of birth fathers and the roles of step-fathers. Most obviously, led by the US, both have recently developed very similar policy and legislative initiatives in relation to child care adoption.

There are points of difference, however, of varying significance, which reveal distinctive and representative characteristics of the adoption process in the US. Perhaps most obviously the private placement rights of parents, the role of commercial adoption agencies, the extent of intercountry adoption and the lack of open access to birth records together indicate the relative strength of legal protection given to the private rights of individuals to act independently. Where independent action violates public law, as in the context of child protection, then the rates of admission to public care and subsequent recourse to adoption demonstrate a much greater willingness to resort to coercive intervention in family affairs than is the case elsewhere. However, the recent increased reliance on kinship care and a higher tolerance for step-adoption would seem to indicate a greater readiness to use adoption and guardianship to facilitate permanency through family care than has been evident in the UK.

Adoption in the US very much reflects the values of its social context. The Constitution, in particular, the 5th and 14th Amendments, provides a rights framework for the parties and bodies in the adoption process and generates a tendency towards adversarial proceedings.

Chapter 8

THE ADOPTION PROCESS IN AUSTRALIA

1.   INTRODUCTION

Adoption as a formal statutory procedure began with the Western Australian Adoption of Children Act 1896 and has always been restricted to 'full' rather than 'simple' adoptions. Since the 1920s some 200,000 Australian born children have been adopted there, of whom one-third were adopted by birth parents or relatives. In keeping with the experience of the UK, the US and other western societies, the rate of annual adoptions increased in the 1960s, peaked in the early 1970s, and has been in decline ever since.[1]

   This chapter begins by providing some background on the social and legal contexts and the emerging characteristics of adoption in Australia. It then identifies the significant trends in modern adoption practice, considers the main elements of current policy and outlines the prevailing legislative framework. The template of legal functions (see, Chap. 3) is then applied to reveal the actual mechanics of the process in action. The chapter concludes with a summary and assessment of the more distinctive and significant characteristics of the contemporary adoption process in Australia.

---

[1]   In 1971/2 annual adoption orders peaked at 9,798; by 1989/90 they had fallen to 543 (Australian Institute of Health and Welfare, 1999).

Kerry O'Halloran (ed.), The Politics of Adoption, 231–261.
© 2006 *Springer. Printed in The Netherlands.*

2.   BACKGROUND

Adoption legislation has always been enacted at state rather than federal level and, with the exception of Queensland, has been and continues to be administered as a judicial process throughout Australia.[2]

2.1.   The social context giving rise to adoption

In Australia, as in the UK and elsewhere, the introduction of a formal legal adoption procedure was a legislative response to public concerns regarding both the social circumstances of unmarried mothers and the vulnerable position of those who voluntarily undertook the care of children in the late 19th century. From the outset it was also intimately linked to the public child care system.

2.1.1.   UNMARRIED MOTHERS

There is much evidence of the inequitable treatment of young single mothers in Australia at the close of the 19th century.[3] The stigma and financial hardship accompanying that role resulted in the voluntary and private relinquishment of many children into the non-kinship, informal care provided by baby minders and foster parents while the public child care system absorbed the victims of failed parental care. Reported incidents of young destitute unmarried mothers being driven to crimes of abandonment or infanticide[4] generated a growing public concern. In 1889, the Society for the Prevention of Cruelty to Children was founded largely in response to the circumstances of such unmarried mothers and accompanying 'baby farming' scandals. By the latter half of the 19th century a patchwork of largely unregulated private and public arrangements was in place providing care for children for whom parental care was unavailable.

2.1.2.   INFORMAL FOSTER CARE

Australia, in the latter half of the 19th century, was a 'new frontier' for immigrants from Europe seeking to create a new life. A continuous labour supply was needed

---

[2]   However, the Queensland Government in *The Adoption Legislation Review: Public Consultation*, (Dept. of Families, 2003) accepted that a majority of respondents indicated a preference for adoption orders to be made in future by the Children's Court.

[3]   See, Swain, S. and Howe, R., *Single Mothers and Their Children*, for an account of the degrading experience of unmarried mothers and the prevalence of 'baby farming' and infanticide in the period 1850–1975.

[4]   See, for example, the successful prosecution for infanticide of John and Sarah Makin in 1893. Also, see, Allen, J., *Women, Crimes and Policing in New South Wales* (Ph.D thesis), Macquarie University, Sydney, 1984, as cited by Marshall, A. and McDonald, M., in *The Many—Sided Triangle, op cit* at p. 22.

to construct roads, houses and build the necessary social infrastructure. Well into the 20th century, the arrival of many boatloads of orphaned and abandoned children from the UK and elsewhere were welcomed into Australian homes. Any child aged 12 years or more could be contracted for employment and paid wages accordingly. Many children were placed by their parents in families for employment purposes and were reared in informal 'adoption' situations. This was a period when the future of the country depended on the contribution of every additional pair of hands.

Against that background all Australian states and territories experienced protracted legal disputes between birth parents and the foster parents to whom the former had entrusted the care of their young dependent children. Informal adoption arrangements were quite common but once their children reached an age to be employed then many birth parents sought re-possession.

2.2.   The legal context for adoption

The Western Australian Adoption of Children Act 1896 was introduced very largely to protect long-term foster parents from the claims of birth parents. Its purpose was "to provide for the adoption of children and to see that when they are adopted they cannot be taken away from those who have adopted them when, perhaps, they are becoming useful".[5] It provided for the adoption of children under the age of 15, thereafter "deemed in law to be the child born in lawful wedlock of the adopting parents".[6] This was eventually followed by the introduction of broadly similar legislation in Queensland[7] and gradually to all Australian states and territories.

2.2.1.   PUBLIC CHILD CARE

Traditionally, each state and territory provided care for children who were orphaned, abandoned, neglected or abused in institutional accommodation where conditions closely resembled those of the English workhouse.[8] Legislation, such as the Orphanages Act 1879 in Queensland, sought to regulate the standards of care provided in state facilities or by charitable organisations for such children

---

[5] *Ibid*, citing WA PD 1896, p. 335.

[6] In 1920 Tasmania introduced similar legislation.

[7] The Infant Life Protection Act 1905 made provision for the adoption of 'illegitimate' children in Queensland, was amended in 1921 to provide for the adoption of children aged less than 10 years and replaced by more comprehensive legislation in 1931; in South Australia statutory adoption was introduced by the Adoption Act 1926. See, further, Boss, P., *Adoption in Australia*, National Children's Bureau, Melbourne, 1992 at p. 211 as cited by Marshall, A. and McDonald, M., in *The Many—Sided Triangle, op cit* at p. 25.

[8] See, the Royal Commission into Public Charities in New South Wales, 1873/74 for a record of the inadequacies of this system.

under the age of twelve years. Public concern regarding these facilities and 'baby farming' practices, coupled with lobbying from the Society for Prevention of Cruelty to Children, led eventually to the introduction of the Children's Protection Act 1892. The Royal Women's Hospital in Melbourne, established in 1856, was among the first to establish a policy of providing assistance to unmarried mothers[9] and from 1929 it developed an adoption service.

2.2.2. WARDS OF THE STATE

Adoption practice in Australia has been facilitated by the fact that the statutory child care framework did not and does not always apply to the children for whom placements are being sought. The legal status of many children in the care of the state was and is that of a 'ward' rather than the subject of a child care order. The decision as to whether to retain a child in wardship rather than seek a care order is one for the relevant state department. This contrasts with the equivalent situation in the UK where wardship is not a discretionary option for local authorities which must instead look to the statutory framework for designation of the legal status of a child for whom parental care is not available or is inappropriate. For many such children in Australia the full complement of parental rights and duties are vested through wardship in the state. Indeed, it has been observed that the authority of the Family Court of Australia is very similar in scope to the *parens patriae* jurisdiction of the Court of Chancery in England as devolved to the High Court when exercising its inherent wardship powers.[10]

2.2.3. EARLY ADOPTION LEGISLATION

The common experience in all Australian states in the late 19th century, of poverty induced private and public care arrangements for children outside their families of origin, led to the policy of introducing adoption legislation. This was seen as the most appropriate legal means of regulating private parental decisions to relinquish children, protecting the homes voluntarily provided by long-term foster parents and opening up the possibility of secure family based care for many children languishing in the public care system.

The State Children's Relief Act 1881 was introduced to provide a public care 'boarding out' service for orphaned, abandoned, neglected or abused children. This marked an important policy shift in the public child care services by substituting family based care for the former reliance on institutional provision. As explained by Marshall and McDonald[11]:

---

[9] See, McCalman, J., *Sex and Suffering: Women's Health and a Women's Hospital*, Melbourne University Press, p. 9.

[10] See, *AMS v AIF; AIF v AMS* (1999) 199 CLR 160 *per* Gaudron J at p. 189.

[11] See, Marshall, A. and McDonald, M., *The Many—Sided Triangle*, Melbourne University Press, Victoria, 2001 at p. 24.

The State Children's Relief Act also authorised a form of adoption by which a person could apply to have a child placed in their care. Parents who applied in this way to adopt were subject to the same process of supervision as other boarding out parents, and to the same risks of the child being removed from their care. The difference was that they were not paid the boarding out allowance. Similar forms of adoption were practiced in all states . . . In all states some form of boarding out provided the pathway to later adoption legislation.

In this way a statutory adoption procedure, set within but differentiated from child care procedures, was introduced in Australia. The 1881 Act was subsequently amended to permit a child to be boarded out in his or her own family with allowances paid to the parents.[12] This measure, which sought to prevent family poverty and thereby reduce the large numbers of children admitted to public care due to parental destitution, also became available in the state of Victoria under the Child Welfare Act 1916 and in New South Wales under the New South Wales Act 1923.

2.3. The emerging characteristics of the adoption process—(a) 1930s–1960s

By the early 1930s, all states had introduced adoption legislation broadly sharing the same characteristics which, with some variations between states and territories and with some amendments, provided the legal framework for regulating adoption practice in Australia until the 1960s.

2.3.1. JUDICIAL PROCESS

All states, with the exception of Queensland[13] (see, further, below), chose to embed adoption proceedings within the judicial process. This was primarily because of the importance attached to ensuring that the legal requirements governing consent could be properly addressed before all parental rights of the birth parents were extinguished by adoption. The ancillary issue of the level of court most appropriate to deal with adoption proceedings was determined differently by individual states. Responsibility was confined to the Supreme Court in New South Wales, Western Australia, the Australian Capital Territory and the Northern Territory, in Victoria it was allocated to both the Supreme Court and the county court, it was assigned to a judicial panel in South Australia while in Tasmania a magistrate was deemed sufficient.

---

[12] The amendment in 1896 also increased the boarding out allowance from 2 to 10 shillings per week per child.

[13] See, the Adoption of Children Act 1935 which, interestingly, required the consent of any child over 12 years of age; subsequently amended in 1941 and 1952.

2.3.2. PLACEMENTS

In some states such as Queensland and New South Wales the responsibility for placing a child for adoption was assigned to a government body while in others such as Victoria it was left to charitable organisations. In practice, adoption placements most often fell to be privately and discretely arranged by whichever professional or other intermediary was most closely involved with the natural parent/s (usually an unmarried mother), at the time of birth. So, adoptions were organised through the agency of doctors, nurses, hospitals, mother and baby homes or clergymen and also often resulted from direct placements made by the natural parent/s or their relatives with persons of their choosing.

2.3.3. CLOSED, CONFIDENTIAL PROCESS

Initially, adoption in Australia was probably characterised by a fairly open practice: in South Australia, for example, an adopted child would have kept their birth parent/s surname and had access to their original birth certificate. However, by the 1960s, the adoption process in all states had become shrouded in secrecy with assurances of confidentiality and with hearings invariably held in private. The emphasis on restricting access to identifying information was evident also in the use of separate registers not accessible to the public for recording birth information relating to adopted children.

2.3.4. CLOSELY LINKED TO PUBLIC CHILD CARE SYSTEM

The advantages of utilising adoption procedures as an option for securing permanent care for children in the public child care system had been openly debated during the various legislative processes. The benefits were seen in financial terms as well as in terms of promoting the welfare interests of children. As noted by Marshall and McDonald[14]:

> Governments were quick to recognise the very considerable saving to budgets which adoption represented. During the 1928 Victorian debate, it was pointed out, quoting a report from New South Wales, that the 800 adoptions already completed in that state would result in a saving over fourteen years of £300,000.

2.3.5. CONSENSUAL AND NON-CONSENSUAL

The voluntary relinquishment of a child by the birth parent/s was the normal circumstance catered for in all adoption legislation. However, from the outset it would seem that all states also legislated for situations where children had been

---

[14] See, Marshall, A. and McDonald, M., *The Many—Sided Triangle, op cit* at p. 30.

abandoned or where parents had been found guilty of child neglect or abuse. Provision was then made for the court to supply the necessary consent.

2.3.6. THE WELFARE OF THE CHILD

In all states the legislation required that the welfare interests of the child be taken into account in adoption proceedings but none required a particular weighting to be attached to such interests relative to other considerations.

2.3.7. FULL AND EXCLUSIVE VESTING OF PARENTAL RIGHTS AND DUTIES IN ADOPTERS

The legal abolition of all parental rights vested in the birth parent/s, followed by the exclusive vesting of those rights together with the associated duties in the adopters, were common features of the adoption processes enacted in all Australian states. This was primarily to assure adopters that their care arrangements would be absolutely secured against any possible future attempt by the birth parent/s to reclaim possession of the child. The surname of the adopted child was changed to that of the adopters and registered as such in the Registry of Births, Deaths and Marriages. The inheritance rights of adopted children was a problematic issue in Australia as in other common law jurisdictions but New South Wales led the way with provision for inheritance rights for such children in respect of the property of intestate adopters.

2.3.8. ADOPTION ORDERS

In Australia, unlike the UK (see, further, Chap. 2), the introduction of statutory adoption proceedings proved immediately popular.[15] In New South Wales, for example, some 58,000 adoptions occurred between the first legislation in 1923 and the Adoption of Children Act 1965.

2.4. (b) 1960s–1980s

Whereas the 1960s in the UK marked the onset of a more liberal attitude towards sex, Australia at this time remained a very conservative society. The continuing social approbation accompanying the role of unmarried mother served to maintain adoption as a popular if forced option for such mothers and focussed legislative intent on measures to professionalise the adoption process. A more or

---

[15] See, New South Wales Child Welfare Department, *Annual Report 1921–25*: "rich and poor alike are vying with each other to open their hearts and homes to these derelict children", at p. 5 as cited in Marshall, A. and McDonald, M., *The Many—Sided Triangle, op cit* at p. 30.

less common baseline of adoption legislation was gradually introduced through-out Australia following a co-ordinated approach by the Attorney-Generals of all states and territories in 1961 to regulate practice.[16]

2.4.1.   LICENSED ADOPTION AGENCIES

Privately arranged adoptions, except with relatives, were prohibited under the new legislation in all states and territories; instead placements had to be made by registered adoption agencies with couples who had been professionally assessed and approved.

2.4.2.   CONSENT

In New South Wales, the Adoption of Children Act 1965 introduced for the first time in Australian adoption law a procedure for ensuring the validity of a consent to adoption by the birth parent/s and outlining the latter's right to retract such a consent within 30 days.

2.4.3.   CONFIDENTIALITY

In keeping with the times, measures to shroud the adoption process in secrecy increased as this was seen as being for the benefit of all parties. The prevailing ethos was that adoption provided for the complete vesting of all attributes of a child's identity within that of the adopters as though the child had 'been born to them in lawful wedlock'. Any contra-indicators were willingly suppressed by all parties. So, for example, after the 1960s adoption orders no longer bore the names of the birth parent/s and similarly the birth certificates of adopted children were altered to remove unnecessary information referring to the birth parent/s.

2.4.4.   THE BIRTH PARENT/S

During this period the role of the birth parent/s in the adoption process was almost exclusively confined to unmarried mothers. As far as the putative fathers were concerned, the law focussed on their liability to pay maintenance rather than on any rights or duties they might have in relation to the proposed adoption of their child. At a time when all states and territories were collaborating to formulate a common regulatory framework for adoption, the alternatives for unmarried women in Australia were restricted and remained so until the reforms of the early 1970s. The introduction of welfare benefits for unmarried mothers[17]

---

[16]   See, Turner, N., 'Adoption or Anti-Adoption? Time for a National Review of Australian Law', 2 JCULR 43 (1995) for an analysis of the relative conformity in adoption law across all jurisdictions in Australia in the 1960s.

[17]   This was effected, for example, in New South Wales by the introduction of the Child Care Act 1972 and subsequently throughout Australia by the Supporting Mother's Benefit in 1973.

made government supported child care services available to single parents thereby allowing those with low incomes to consider educational or employment opportunities while continuing to bear parental responsibilities. As in the UK and elsewhere, the provision of financial support also resulted in a lessening of the social stigma traditionally associated with the role of a single mother, reducing the pressure previously felt by many in that position to surrender a child for adoption. Abortion remained an illegal procedure throughout the 1960s.[18] Contraception did not begin to become widely available in Australia until 1974 when the Family Planning Association introduced the guidance and treatment available in the UK for most of the previous decade. The stigma of 'illegitimacy' did not begin to fade until after the legal removal of this term by the Status of Children Act 1974 in Victoria and Tasmania, followed thereafter in all other states.

Against this background it is remarkable that in Australia many, indeed most, unmarried mothers retained their children. The advocacy and support services provided by the Australian Relinquishing Mothers Society (ARMS) undoubtedly played an important role. During 1959–1976, the peak period for adoptions, 60% of such mothers continued to care for their children; an interesting contrast to their counterparts in Ireland (see, further, Chap. 6).

2.4.5.   ADOPTION ORDERS WITH CONTACT

The Victorian Adoption Act 1984 first made legislative provision for adoption orders subject to a condition permitting contact, direct or indirect, between the relinquishing birth parent/s and child but only with the agreement of the adopters.

2.4.6.   INFORMATION AND POST-ADOPTION CONTACT

The question of access to birth records had become a contentious issue in the 1970s but in 1976 the New South Wales Review Committee recommended retaining the existing restrictions on adoptee access to their original birth certificates. The Association of Relinquishing Mothers (ARMS), an Australia-wide organisation, successfully campaigned for access to information[19] and in 1984 both Victoria and New South Wales finally made legislative provision for such access. In 1976 the Adopted Persons Contact Register in New South Wales was established providing a means whereby adopted persons and their birth parent/s could, with mutual consent, register their wishes for contact. Two years later similar provision was made in South Australia. During 1984–1994 all states and territories enacted adoption information legislation opening up adoption records for adult adopted persons and their relatives and the availability of non-identifying

---

[18] Not until the judicial decisions in *Menhennit* (1969) in Victoria and *Levine* (1971) in New South Wales did prosecutions for abortion gradually cease in all states.

[19] See, Winkler, R. and Van Keppel, M., *Relinquishing Mothers in Adoption*, 1983.

information rapidly became a standard feature of the adoption process throughout Australia.

3.   EMERGING TRENDS IN ADOPTION PRACTICE

By the late 1970s, adopting a 'normal' healthy baby born in Australia had become an unlikely prospect for most infertile couples.[20] To satisfy their wishes for a family, such couples found they often had to consider either Australian children with 'special needs' or intercountry adoption. This new and broader interpretation of a traditional practice was accompanied, often necessarily, by a move towards greater openness in adoption. In addition, family adoptions continued to grow as a proportion of the total.

3.1.   Family adoptions

Throughout Australia, s 98 of the Marriage Act 1961 provided, and continues to provide, that the subsequent marriage of a child's parents to each other 'legitimated' that child. However, adoption was the only legal means whereby a birth parent who married someone other than the child's parent could 'legitimate' their pre-marital child. Generally, the use of adoption by birth parents or relatives to change the nature of an existing relationship with a child is now discouraged. Many such arrangements are informally agreed between the parties or are formalised by written agreements or through recourse to other more appropriate private family law orders.

3.1.1.   STEP-PARENTS

From the early 1980s adoption by step-parents and other relatives sharply and consistently declined.[21] This is largely due to the availability of alternative orders coupled with a general acceptance of the principle that adoption is seldom the most appropriate order in such circumstances.

All Australian jurisdictions continue to retain legislative provisions for step-parent and other forms of family adoption but access is now subject to a 'best interests' or exceptional circumstances test.[22] An assessment of a step-parent's

---

[20] See, Marshall, A. and McDonald, M., *The Many–Sided Triangle, op cit* at p. 106.

[21] See, Turner, N., 'Adoption or Anti-Adoption? Time for a National Review of Australian Law', 2 JCULR 43 (1995) for evidence that applications from step-parents and relatives, during the 1970s and early 1980s, dominated adoption proceedings in Australia.

[22] In 1999/00, only 114 children were adopted by step-parents in Australia.

attitudes and understanding is now required together with the exploration of matters such as motivation, the alternative options, and the understanding of all parties regarding the effect of adoption on relationships within the family and extended family. The quality and duration of an applicant's relationship with the child concerned will be of crucial significance.[23]

3.2. Child care adoptions

A distinctive characteristic of adoption in Australia, relative to other modern western societies, is the comparatively low rate of child care adoptions due to a policy emphasis on family reunification. Whenever statutory intervention is necessary, the preferred policy has been to work towards family reunification rather than countenance the permanent severance of non-consensual adoption. As a corollary, it has been recognised that maintaining contact arrangements between a child in care and their family of origin is crucial to successful reunification.

In the 1980s and 90s, the emphasis in child care public service provision was on prevention. In the period 1983–1993 the number of children in care decreased by 29% but in more recent years this trend has been reversed following a sharp increase in reported cases of child abuse in the early 1990s.[24] In 1998 there were 14,470 children in the public care system of which 87% were in home based rather than institutional arrangements. At that time, over 40% had been in care for two or more years. The Children's Services Act 1986 introduced the requirement for compulsory reviews of court orders to be held in respect of each child within 12 months; every state and territory had the discretion to determine its own time limits.

The annual percentage of adoptions from the public care system currently stands at 6.6% in the US and at 3.8% in the UK, but it is only 0.8% in Australia.[25]

3.3. Children with special needs

Initially, adoption was not seen as applicable to children with special needs—defined as being more difficult to place due to emotional, health or behavioural difficulties, membership of a sibling group, being an older child or aboriginal or belonging to a minority group or any combination of the foregoing. Instead

---

[23] See, for example, the Adoption Act 2000 (NSW) which makes an adoption order in favour of a step-parent conditional upon an established three year care relationship between applicant, birth parent and child and requires that the child be at least 5 years of age. In addition, relevant consents must be available and it must be proven that adoption is better than any other legal option for promoting the child's welfare interests.

[24] Between 1988 and 1994 there was an annual increase of approx 9% in substantiated child abuse cases.

[25] See, AFCARS at www.acf.dhhs.gov/programs/cb/dis/afcars.

such children were placed in specialist foster care or group care facilities.[26] However, adoption was in due course extended to benefit disabled and other 'hard to place' children. From the late-1970s the state child care departments began to successfully place for adoption increasing numbers of children with special needs who had been relinquished by their parents and had become wards of the state; parental consent in such circumstances was not an issue. In Queensland, for example, a Special Needs unit was set up in the early 1980s specifically to facilitate such adoptions. Attracting appropriate prospective adopters, however, could not be achieved by simply diverting the traditional type of applicant but most often necessitated actively recruiting people with relevant skills and providing them with ongoing support. While some government agencies established specialised units to further this work, many voluntary adoption agencies also contributed.[27]

In recent years the number of children with special needs available for adoption has decreased[28] due, it has been suggested, to the development of specialist foster care services to cater for such children.[29]

3.4.   Intercountry adoption

The airlift of some 300 orphans from Vietnam in the mid-1970s marked the beginning of what has become a significant trend—the adoption in Australia of children born elsewhere. The numbers of such children adopted in Australia peaked at 420 in 1989/90 and thereafter steadily decreased until 1992/3 when only 227 were adopted.[30] However, in total it has been estimated that some 5,000 children arrived in Australia as a consequence of intercountry adoptions over a 20 year period ending in 1999.[31] By far the majority of children came from Korea.

A working party, established by the Council of Social Welfare Ministers, reported in 1986 with a set of guidelines to govern future intercountry adoptions which was endorsed for implementation throughout Australia. Since then in all states and territories, with the exception of South Australia,[32] the welfare

---

[26] See, Barth, M. (1998) who documents a clear trend towards the development of specialist foster care services to cater for children with special needs.

[27] Barnardos in New South Wales, for example, established a 'Find-a-Family' Centre in 1985 which focussed exclusively on finding placements for children with special needs.

[28] Whereas in 1990/91, 28 infants with special needs in Queensland required adoption, in 1999/00 there were none and only 1 required such a placement in 2000/01.

[29] See, Barth, M.,1998, *op cit.*

[30] See, Australian Institute of Health and Welfare, *Child Welfare Series: Adoptions Australia 1994–95*, No 14 (AGPS, Canberra) at p. 21.

[31] See, report by the Post Adoption Resource Centre of New South Wales as cited in Marshall, A. and McDonald, M., *The Many—Sided Triangle, op cit* at p. 196.

[32] This is the only state or territory with its own specialist, private and registered intercountry adoption agency, *Australians Aiding Children*, which undertakes all home study reports.

department takes responsibility both for the preparation of the required home study report and for the application to the court for an adoption order. The government agencies are heavily reliant upon the information and support offered by local parent groups which have always played a prominent role in Australian adoption services.

3.5.   Surrogacy

In Australia, as in other modern western nations, surrogacy arrangements are now not uncommon and have introduced much the same complications for adoption law as experienced elsewhere. In this jurisdiction, *Re Evelyn*[33] emerged as the leading case at a time when surrogacy arrangements were illegal throughout Australia. The Family Court of Australia upheld the ruling of the court at first instance which had broadly decided in favour of the biological mother who had reneged on the surrogacy arrangement; though both parties were ordered to share responsibility for long-term decisions regarding the child's health, welfare and development. The decision was based squarely on the paramount welfare interests of the child and the court reiterated its ruling in *Rice v Miller*[34] that there could be no presumption favouring a birth parent.

3.6.   Same sex adopters

As in other countries, adoption law in Australia neither facilitated nor obstructed adoption by gay or lesbian couples; it had nothing to say on the matter as this was simply outside the contemplation of legislators at that time. So, in particular, the definition of 'parent' in s 60H of the Family Law Act 1975, as amended in 1996, understandably makes no allowance for the possibility of a sperm-donor father. Gay or lesbian couples were left in a situation whereby only a single applicant could apply under traditional legislative provisions while more modern legislation such as the Adoption Act 2000 (NSW) placed them in the same position as other applicants with the requirement that they satisfy the 3 year co-habitation rule. In response to the lack of any legislative provisions specifically addressing the issue, the Australian Capital Territory introduced legislation early in 2004 to permit adoption by gay or lesbian couples.[35]

---

[33] (1998) FLC 92–807. See, also, *Re Evelyn (No. 2)* (1998) FLC 92–187 where the High Court of Australia considered and dismissed the issue of appeal.

[34] (1993) FLC 92–807 at 85 106.

[35] An initiative promptly condemned by John Howard the then Australian Prime Minister. For evidence of a positive judicial approach to same sex parental care, see *Re Patrick: An Application Concerning Contact* (2002) FLC 93–096.

3.7. Open adoption

In the latter half of the 1970s most states and territories began to move away from the traditional or 'closed' model of adoption. The use of orders subject to contact conditions and the gradual recognition of post-adoption information rights contributed to the development of a more 'open' approach which first gained legislative recognition in Victoria with the introduction of the Adoption Act 1984. Thereafter, as has been said, "'openness' became the leitmotiv of the reformers".[36]

Open adoption, usually involving some form of contact between birth and adoptive families after a child is adopted, is now practiced in varying degrees throughout Australia. In New South Wales, following recommendations made by the Law Reform Commission (NSW), the provisions of the Adoption Act 2000 (NSW) enable the parties to jointly agree in advance of proceedings a plan for post-adoption contact and exchanges of information.[37] In Western Australia 'openness' is given legislative effect through similar provisions. In Victoria and the Australian Capital Territory while there is no requirement in relation to adoption plans, legislative provision does allow for the making of adoption orders subject to agreed conditions regarding information exchange and ongoing contact. Again, in Tasmania and the Northern Territory there is no provision for adoption plans but before making an order the court is required to be satisfied that any proposed arrangements for information exchange and/or contact have been taken into account. In South Australia there is provision for open adoption and for this and other matters with a bearing on a child's welfare interests to be formally agreed by the parties after the issue of an adoption order. Family group conferences have a legislative basis in South Australia, New South Wales and Queensland which facilitates openness in planning adoption or other form of permanency placement. In Queensland there is no legislative provision for information exchange or contact but every likelihood that this will shortly be introduced.[38]

4. OVERVIEW OF MODERN ADOPTION LAW AND POLICY

Adoptions in Australia peaked in 1971/2 at 9, 798 and have since, in common with all other western societies, decreased steadily. In the period 1997–98 a total

[36] See, Turner, J., 'Adoption or Anti-Adoption? Time for a National Review of Australian Law', 2 *JCULR* 43, 1995 at p. 45. Also, see, Barth, M., 'Risks and Benefits of Open Adoption', in *The Future of Children*, vol. 3, no. 1, 1993.

[37] See, Law Reform Commission Report 81, *Review of the Adoption of Children Act 1965 (NSW)*, (1997).

[38] Queensland Government, Dept of Families, *Public Consultation on the Review of the Adoption of Children Act 1964*, 2003, at chapter 4.

of 577 children were adopted including 178 who were born in Australia and adopted by non-relatives.[39] In 1998/99 the numbers had fallen back slightly to 543 of whom 127 were adopted by non-relatives (23%), 244 were intercountry adoptions (45%), 124 were adopted by step-parents or relatives (23%) and 48 were adopted by their carers (9%).[40]

4.1.   Adoption policy

Modern adoption law, policy and practice in Australia has been greatly influenced by the fact that all states and territories subscribed to the principles outlined in the Council of Social Welfare Ministers' National Minimum Principles in Adoption 1993 and subsequently to the UN Convention and the Hague Convention. The result has been a broad consensus among the states and territories as to the principles, policy and parameters of adoption law and a growing convergence in adoption practice. Throughout Australia, the policy issues arising for consideration during the different adoption law review processes were much the same. These include—

- Determining the objectives and principles underpinning contemporary, child focused adoption legislation.
- The development and application of the Aboriginal and Torres Strait Islander Child Placement Principle in adoption legislation and practice.
- The circumstances under which the making of an adoption order in favour of a relative or step-parent is warranted.
- Accommodating within any future legislative framework the Government's responsibilities in respect of intercountry adoption under the United Nations Convention on the Rights of the Child 1989 and the Hague Convention on Protection of Children and Co-operation in Respect of Intercountry Adoption.
- Provision for how and when consent is obtained, the counselling and information required before consent is given, who can or should give consent (ie, parents aged under 18, birth fathers, older children), and the revoking and dispensation of consent.
- The identification of reasonable and relevant eligibility criteria for selecting prospective adoptive parents that do not exclude people solely because of their age,[41] marital status, impairment or sexuality.
- Provision for birth parents' preferences when matching children requiring adoption with prospective adoptive parents, including circumstances where

---

[39]   See, *Adoption in Australia*, Report of the AIHW, 1998.
[40]   *Ibid*, 1998.
[41]   The National Minimum Principles in Adoption refer to a maximum age difference of 40 years between adopter and child for a first placement and 45 years for any subsequent placement (para 6(1)).

overseas adoption authorities have criteria regarding the placement of overseas born children with adoptive parents in Australia.

- Determining whether the legal process of adoption, including the making of adoption orders, should be governed by courts and tribunals or by an administrative body.
- The role of the state as provider of ongoing support services for adopted children, birth families and adoptive parents once an adoption order is made.
- Options for the future delivery of adoption services including provision of counselling and support services, the accreditation of non-government agencies to provide some adoption services, fees for and the cost of adoption services and data collection.

4.2.   Adoption law

In the late 1990s, all states and territories began the process of reviewing the 1960s statutory framework for adoption and introducing new adoption legislation to address the policy concerns listed above. The Family Law Act 1975 (amended in 1995), as administered by the Family Court of Australia, provides a framework for establishing principles and developing practice on a nationwide basis.

4.2.1.   CONTEMPORARY ADOPTION LEGISLATION

In 1997 the New South Wales Law Reform Commission published the Review of the Adoption of Children Act 1965 and followed up with the Adoption Act 2000. In Queensland the legislative authority for adoption, provided by the Adoption of Children Act 1964 and the Adoption of Children Regulation 1999, has been examined by the Adoption Legislation Review since 2000 and new legislation is imminent.

4.2.2.   THE INTERESTS OF THE CHILD

Section 63E of the Family Law Act 1975, as amended, requires the court to treat the best interests of the child as the paramount consideration; in so doing the court will have due regard to the wishes of that child. As was explained by the Family Court of Australia in *R and R: Children's Wishes*[42] where it was "clear that a court must take children's wishes into account, but is not bound by them".[43]

---

[42] (2002) FLC 93–108. 096 at 88.297.
[43] *Ibid, per* Nicholson, C.J., Holden, J. and Monteith J.

4.2.3.   INTERNATIONAL LAW

Adoption practice in all states and territories has been affected by Australia's ratification of both the United Nations Convention on the Rights of the Child which came into effect in 1991 and the Hague Convention on Protection of Children and Co-operation in Respect of Intercountry Adoption which has been implemented since 1998.

In each state and territory the legal framework for intercountry adoption is now provided by a combination of the Immigration (Guardianship of Children) Act 1946 together with the local adoption legislation and the relevant provisions of the UN Convention and the Hague Convention (see, further, Chap. 4). Australian states and territories can now arrange adoptions with the central authority of any of the 46 countries that have acceded to or ratified the UN Convention but the majority of intercountry adoptions continue to be arranged with countries with which Australia has negotiated adoption agreements.

5.   REGULATING THE ADOPTION PROCESS

Adoption, in all states and territories, is a modern statutorily regulated process. Although similar in many respects to that of the UK it is not so tightly regulated and lacks many of the formal mechanisms for monitoring standards and protecting the interests of the parties that have long been characteristic of adoption in the UK.

5.1.   Length and breadth of process

In order to manage waiting lists, many states and territories have now introduced 'an expression of interest' procedure and in effect the process does not start until an adoption agency receives such a notification. In New South Wales, South Australia, Western Australia and Queensland[44] the relevant agencies periodically issue a public invitation for prospective adopters to declare an interest and their names are then entered in an Expression of Interest Register. In due course those registered are usually offered an opportunity to attend an education and adoption awareness programme after which a formal assessment will be undertaken.

5.2.   Role of adoption agencies and other administrative agencies

The involvement of voluntary agencies in the adoption process began to fade in the mid-1970s and by 1978 only two remained—the Anglican and the Catholic.

---

[44]   This procedure was established in Queensland in July 2002.

Currently, in all states and territories, legislation requires an adoption agency to be approved and in practice these are invariably sited within the relevant government department. Only South Australia has approved a non-governmental body as an adoption (intercountry) agency.

5.2.1.   ADOPTION PANEL

Some agencies, such as those in Tasmania and Western Australia, now rely on an Adoption Panel to assist in the decision-making process prior to placement though most do not. This is under consideration in Queensland which currently uses a Children's Services Tribunal to review assessments and pre-placement decisions. In Western Australia an Adoptions Applications Committee decides on the approval or otherwise of prospective adopters. All other states and territories rely on adoption agencies internal procedures for pre-placement decisions and refer appeals to an external body.

5.3.   Role of the determining body

Initially, in all states and territories, adoption applications were determined by an administrative body. The current situation is that all except Queensland have relegated this function to the judiciary in courts of different levels. In New South Wales and the Australian Capital Territory the Supreme Court determines adoption applications. In other states and territories lower courts have jurisdiction. In Queensland applications are made to the office of the Director General for state welfare which issues all orders.

5.4.   Registrar General

In all states and territories, the Registrar General is required to maintain an Adopted Children Register into which must be entered the particulars of every adoption order issued. All access to the information recorded in this register and access to an original birth certificate is through the office of Registrar General.

6.   THRESHOLDS FOR ENTERING THE ADOPTION PROCESS: ELIGIBILITY AND SUITABILITY CRITERIA

In Australia, the essentially consensual nature of adoption is evident in the criteria determining entry to the process.

6.1.   The child

As elsewhere, there is a legislative requirement in all Australian adoption legislation that the child concerned must not have attained his or her 18th birthday. In the legislation of most states and territories there is a requirement that when considering adoption consideration must be given to a child's ethnic, religious, cultural and linguistic background.

All states and territories have endorsed the Child Placement Principle in an adoption context and the view that adoption of Aboriginal children should only occur in the most exceptional circumstances (see, further, Chap. 10).

6.1.1.   CONSENT

In New South Wales, South Australia, Western Australia and Queensland the consent of a child aged 12 years or more is a legislative requirement for his or her adoption. All other states and territories have no such legislative requirement in relation to consent but instead require the child's views and wishes to be ascertained and taken into account. In New South Wales, South Australia and Western Australia a court may dispense with a child's consent where satisfied that he or she lacks capacity to give a valid consent while in Queensland the child's welfare interests provide sufficient grounds for doing so but there is no legal requirement to ascertain the wishes of a child aged less than 12.

6.2.   The birth parent/s

In Australia, the voluntary relinquishment of a marital child for the purposes of adoption requires the consent of both parents. This is necessary even in circumstances where a spouse is not the birth parent of the child. However, this is not to imply that the law gives any particular preference to the *locus standi* of natural parent/s. As was explained by the Family Court of Australia in *Rice v Miller*[45]:

> ...while the fact of parenthood is an important and significant factor in considering which of the proposals best advance a child's welfare, the fact of parenthood does not establish a presumption in favour of a natural parent nor generate a preferential position in favour of that parent from which the Court commences the decision-making process.

6.2.1.   UNMARRIED MOTHER

The consent of such a mother is always a minimum legislative requirement for consensual adoption in Australia. In some states, notice of an unmarried mother's consent to the adoption of her child must be served on the child's father.

---

[45]   (1993) FLC 92–807 at 85 106.

6.2.2.   UNMARRIED FATHER

Whether the consent of unmarried father should be required has been the subject of a number of conflicting decisions in different jurisdictions, and has been a difficult question of interpretation. In all states and territories, except Queensland, there is now a legislative requirement that the consent of an unmarried father to the adoption of his child be either acquired or dispensed with. The recognition of such a father's *locus standi* in adoption proceedings was affirmed in New South Wales by the decision of the Family Court in *Hoye v Neely*[46] where it was ruled that he was a 'guardian' whose consent was required for the purposes of adoption.

In Western Australia the court may dispense with the consent of a father where he does not have day-to-day care responsibility, or a parental relationship and is unreasonably withholding consent. In Victoria, the Adoption Act 1984 gave such fathers the right to be informed of pending adoption proceedings and the right to intervene. By the early 1990s, most states had legislated to include birth fathers in the adoption process. They were required to be at least informed of the proposed adoption, their involvement was generally required and in many states their consent was necessary. In Queensland it remains unnecessary to obtain the birth father's consent nor is he required to be informed of prospective adoption proceedings.[47]

6.3.   The adopters; third party

The minimum eligibility criteria for adopters are invariably set out in the primary adoption legislation of the states and territories while criteria for assessing the suitability of prospective adopters are most often to be found in ancillary regulations. It is a legislative requirement that assessment of all third party applicants be undertaken by an approved adoption agency.

6.3.1.   ELIGIBILITY CRITERIA

Australia, in common with other modern western countries, specifies matters such as citizenship, residency, age,[48] marital status, health and period of care responsibility for the child concerned as constituting minimum eligibility criteria.

---

[46] (1992) 107 FLR 151. The relevant statutory provision being s 26(3) of the Adoption of Children Act (NSW) 1965.

[47] Arguably any such practice would be in breach of the Anti-Discrimination Act 1991 (QLD).

[48] In Australia the specified age limits are varied: South Australia, 18 to 55; New South Wales, at least 21 years of age or more than 18 years older than the child; in the Northern Territories, at least 25 years of age and more than 25 years older than the child and no more than 40 years older than the first adopted child and no more than 45 years older than any subsequently adopted child. See, also, the Council of Social Welfare Ministers, *National Minimum Principles in Adoption* at para 6.1 (1995) which requires a maximum age difference between adopters and adopted of 40 years for a first child and 45 years for subsequent children.

In some states and territories it is the duration of a couples' relationship that is important regardless of marital status.[49] It is also customary for the adoption legislation in Australia to specify infertility as among such criteria. Applicants are usually required to have had care responsibility for the child concerned for at least the 12 month period immediately prior to application.

Some eligibility criteria as stated in the Australian adoption legislation of the 1960s, such as Queensland's Adoption of Children 1964, are now incompatible with modern anti-discrimination prohibiting discrimination on grounds of age, marital status, impairment or sexuality. In Queensland, for example, single applicants are accepted only in exceptional circumstances or in relation to the adoption of special needs children.

6.3.2.   SUITABILITY CRITERIA

In Australia the review of 1960s adoption legislation has seen the transfer of some matters formerly listed under eligibility, such as health and infertility, to their current re-definition as suitability criteria. Other matters to be taken into account include criminal conduct, character references, child protection information and participation in adoption awareness programmes. In the case of Queensland, a corresponding transfer has occurred from primary to ancillary legislation as suitability criteria are now to be found in the Adoption of Children Regulation 1999. The latter, which is fairly representative of suitability criteria applied by other states and territories, requires the following to be considered in all assessments of adopters:

- quality, duration and stability of relationship;
- capacity to ensure a child's well-being; and
- capacity to provide for a child's emotional, physical, educational, recreational and social needs.

In addition, an assessment is required of each applicant's attitudes to and understanding of: children and their physical and emotional development; the responsibilities of parenthood; and the significance of adoption and the importance of birth parents and their families. Additional criteria apply in relation to intercountry adoption, or adoption of an Aboriginal child or a child with special needs.

Where a step-parent, or a relative, decides to commence adoption proceedings then the above eligibility and suitability criteria will broadly apply with additional requirements regarding duration of marriage and of care responsibility for the child concerned. The consents of both birth parents and of the child (age permitting) are usually required.

---

[49]   Victoria, the Northern Territory, Tasmania, New South Wales, Western Australia, the Australian Capital Territory and South Australia.

6.4.   Pre-placement counselling

In Australia pre-placement counselling is a legislative requirement in most states and territories. It is also provided even in those, such as Queensland, where there is no legislative requirement to do so. Australia, as a signatory of the UN Convention, is obliged to ensure that counselling must be provided to those whose consent is required. Consent is only legally valid if given by a mother after the birth of her child. The consequences of giving consent must be explained, it must not be induced by payment or compensation and it may be withdrawn.

6.5.   Placement decision

In Australia as elsewhere, the number of approved adopters far exceeds the number of children available. This normally results in approved adopters waiting for long periods before a child is placed with them,[50] though the waiting period is greatly reduced for applicants in respect of special needs children or those from overseas.

Most states now provide for 'open' adoptions. This allows the birth parent/s an opportunity to be involved in the process of selecting adopters.[51] Additionally, in most circumstances they may select the type and level of contact they want with their child during placement and following the issue of an adoption order. In some states, such as Victoria and Western Australia, open adoption arrangements form part of the adoption order and are legally enforceable whereas elsewhere they remain private and may be adjusted or terminated at the will of the parties.

Where the placement decision is taken by a registered adoption agency then adoption procedures require specified matching criteria to be applied.[52] Where the placement is respect of a proposed intercountry adoption then the decision is taken in accordance with the requirements of the Hague Convention.

6.6.   Placement supervision

In Australia there is a statutory requirement that prospective adopters complete a minimum period of direct care for the child concerned immediately before lodging an adoption application. In Queensland a 12 month care period is specified.

All children entering Australia for the purposes of intercountry adoption do so under the guardianship of the Commonwealth Minister for Immigration under

---

[50] For example in Queensland in March 2003 approved couples had been waiting 10 years for a placement.

[51] See, for example, the Adoption Act 2000 (NSW).

[52] In Queensland, for example, an amendment to the Adoption of Children Act 1964 effective from July 2002 specifies that the decision may only be made after consideration is given to matters concerning the needs of the particular child, the characteristics of the prospective adopters and the preferences expressed by the child's birth parents.

the Immigration (Guardianship of Children) Act 1946. An interim custody order is then issued in favour of the prospective intercountry adopters while the relevant government body gives effect to its guardianship duties by supervising the placement. Under the Hague Convention all states and territories are required to provide placement supervision in respect of intercountry placements and reports at periodic intervals to the relevant overseas authority.

In all states and territories except South Australia and Western Australia there is legislative provision for interim care orders to be made in respect of all children in adoption placements. Supervision, placement review procedures and powers to remove a child are generally available.

7.   THE HEARING AND ISSUE OF ORDER/S

The judicial hearing of an adoption application is favoured by all states and territories, except Queensland, because of the inherent focus of a court on procedural fairness, its independence from government policy and independence also from the decision-making processes of adoption agencies. Moreover, given the importance of the legal consequences for all parties concerned, it is considered more appropriate that adoption be a judicial rather than an administrative process.

7.1.   Consent

The principle that any consent must be informed, given in circumstances free from financial or other rewards and from duress, guides practice throughout Australia.[53]

7.1.1.   TIMING/VALIDITY

Issues most commonly arise in relation to those who are underage or suffer from mental illness or intellectual impairment when it is customary to ensure parental consent in respect of the former and independent representation for such other person whose needs require it. The witnessing of any such consent is a general legislative requirement in Australia. All states and territories have a legislative provision allowing for retraction of consent within a stated period during which an adoption order cannot be made.

---

[53] In Queensland, for example, the Adoption of Children Act 1964 permits maternal consent at any time after 5 days from giving birth but in practice the concern to ensure a reasoned and informed consent has resulted in no consents being sought until 10–14 days after birth. In New South Wales the Adoption Act 2000 specifies a period of 30 days after birth and a further period of 14 days to retract.

7.1.2.   UNAVAILABLE

All states and territories legislatively provide that consent may be judicially dispensed with in much the same sets of circumstances. In practice the following are the grounds most often relied upon:

- the person concerned cannot be found after reasonable inquiry;
- lack of capacity to give a valid consent;
- child conceived as a result of rape or incest; and/or
- where domestic violence by the father causes the mother to be fearful for the physical, psychological and emotional safety of herself and her child.

New South Wales, in the Adoption Act 2000, has reduced the grounds to the first two above together with an alternative criterion that it is justified by a serious concern for the welfare of the child and by his or her best interests. The latter is explicitly synchronised with grounds in child protection legislation; the focus is on a child's needs rather than on parental fault/failure.

8.   THRESHOLDS FOR EXITING THE ADOPTION PROCESS

In Australia, as elsewhere in most modern western jurisdictions, there is no general right to adopt or be adopted.

8.1.   The welfare interests of the child

The legislation in all states and territories now carries a requirement that the best interests of the child must be paramount in adoption which requires consideration of issues affecting their ongoing quality of life both at the time of making an order and later. In many states and territories there is a legislative requirement that an adoption order cannot be made unless the court is satisfied that this rather than any other order is best suited to further a particular child's welfare interests. Further, a statement of the principle that—adoption is a service for children rather than for adults seeking to acquire the care of a child—generally prevails.

8.1.1.   REPRESENTATION

The National Minimum Principles in Adoption agreed by the Social Welfare Ministers in 1993 recognise the child's right to independent representation throughout the adoption process. However, this principle has still to be fully implemented and it remains the case that Australian adoption law does not always provide for an independent child advocate in adoption proceedings.

In New South Wales and Western Australia the provision for representing a child's welfare and legal interests, involving a guardian *ad litem* and lawyer respectively, is fairly similar to that in the UK. In New South Wales, for example, there is provision under sections 122 and 123 of the Adoption Act 2000 for the interests of the child to be independently represented in court by a lawyer. In Queensland no such provision is available but prospective new legislation may introduce provision for such representation as is currently the case under s 110 of the Child Protection Act.

Only in the Northern Territory is the child a party to adoption proceedings.

9.   THE OUTCOME OF THE ADOPTION PROCESS

The outcome of a contemporary adoption application is no longer necessarily the granting of the order sought with its traditional permanent and absolute legal effects on all parties. The courts are now increasingly questioning the appropriateness of such applications and even when granted the traditional effects of the order may well be compromised by rights of others to contact and information.

9.1.   Adoption orders; third party applicants

In Australia, as elsewhere, consensual third party applications constitute a steadily decreasing proportion of total annual adoption orders. In this jurisdiction, the majority of such orders are in respect of intercountry adoptions. Non-consensual third party adoption orders are seldom made. This characteristic feature of the adoption process in Australia, which differentiates it from contemporary practice in the US and in the UK but corresponds with practice in Ireland, is due to the low level of child care adoptions.

9.2.   Adoption orders; parents and relatives

Modern statutory law in Australia generally treats an adoption application by a natural parent and spouse or by a relative as not necessarily in the best interests of the child. Applicants are usually required to show special circumstances and convince the court that none of the alternative orders available would be more appropriate.[54] In effect an adoption order cannot be made in favour of a step-parent or relative if a parenting order made by the Family Court of Australia can better serve the child's interests.

---

[54]   See, for example in Queensland where s 12(5) of the Adoption of Children Act 1964 (as amended) states that in such circumstances an adoption order shall not be granted unless "the welfare and interests of the child would be better served by such an order than by an order for guardianship or custody".

In Queensland, a number of challenges to adoption applications have been made by grandparents who have succeeded in persuading the Supreme Court to instead issue Family Court orders in their favour.

9.3.   Other orders

In non-consensual adoption applications, the courts in Australia have a well-established practice of preferring the less interventionist order of guardianship to the finality of adoption where circumstances permit. The Family Court of Australia, either in response to an application or of its own initiative in the course of adoption proceedings, now has the power to grant a parenting order instead of an adoption order. The court may make any of the following orders:

- **Residence order**
  Authorising a child to reside with a specified person, including shared parenting arrangements.
- **Contact order**
  Authorising contact between the child and other named person/s, including duration and location of contact.
- **Child maintenance**
  Directing that financial support be paid for the maintenance of a child.
- **Specific issues**
  Directing that a specified area of parental responsibility be undertaken in a specified manner, including matters such as day to day care, welfare and development, religion, education, sport or other such significant aspects of a child's upbringing.

These alternatives are very similar to those available in UK family proceedings.

9.4.   The effect of an adoption order

Whether consensual or otherwise and whether made in favour of parents, relatives or third parties, adoption orders are now quite likely to be influenced by the 'openness' ethos and be made subject to agreed contact arrangements.

9.4.1.   THE CHILD

In New South Wales in 1977, a test case involving the adoption of a 10 year old girl by her mother and step-father, established the legal precedent that a child has the right to know the facts relating to their adoption and to their birth family. In due course this right, available to those aged at least 18 and subject to prior counselling, accompanied by a 'contact veto' clause, was underpinned by legislation throughout Australia.[55] In Queensland, significant additional caveats were attached.[56]

9.4.2. NAME

The Adoption Act 2000 in New South Wales states as a principle that a child's given name should be preserved. It also requires that for a child aged more than 12 months, there should be no change to the first name unless special reason is shown to the court, a child aged 12 years or more must consent and before a court approves a change to either a first name or a surname it must ascertain and take into account the wishes of the child. In some other states a child's consent is required or their wishes must be ascertained and given due consideration.

9.4.3. THE BIRTH PARENT/S

The effect of an adoption order is, as always, to terminate the rights and duties of a birth parent but the consequences are no longer necessarily exclusive and permanent. Its absolute nature may now be compromised by implicit or explicit contact conditions while its permanent effects are subject to the information rights of other parties. In particular, the 'right to know' legislation has impacted upon birth parent/s by seriously compromising their traditional right to insist on permanent confidentiality. An adoption agency may now contact an adopted person aged 18 or older to inform, or confirm they have been informed, as to the identity of their birth parent/s. There has been some recent debate regarding the fairness of this legislative provision, which Queensland has failed to enact. However, in general, the 'right to know' issue has not generated anything like the same level of vigorous resistance that continues to polarise views in the US.

9.4.4. THE ADOPTERS

The traditional legislative intent, to fully vest the adopters with the rights of marital parents in respect of their adopted child, is broadly continued by contemporary legislation. Its essentially consensual character in this jurisdiction, however, coupled with the restrictions on its use, has allowed adopters to more freely accommodate aspects of 'openness' than is the case in other countries.

---

[55] Right to know legislation was introduced as follows: Victoria enacted legislation in 1984 and implemented it in 1985; New South Wales and Queensland in 1990 and 1991 respectively; the Australian Capital Territory in 1992 and 1993; and the Northern Territory in 1993 and 1994.

[56] Effective lobbying by the Queensland Adoption Privacy Protection Group, during the legislative process, succeeded in making this right subject to a condition enabling adopters to veto any divulging of information and any attempts by an adoption agency to contact an adopted person.

9.5.   Post-adoption support services

Traditionally, in keeping with the essentially private nature of adoption, the focus for service provision was on the pre-adoption stage; once an order was made then no further professional intrusion was generally either available or wanted. This has changed with the growing awareness that the interests of an adopted person need to be safeguarded and supported throughout their life.[57] Most states and territories now provide financial and/or other forms of support at least to adopters of children with special needs.

10.   INFORMATION DISCLOSURE, TRACING AND RE-UNIFICATION SERVICES

In Australia, the law governing information disclosure is, as Richard Chisholm has pointed out, "a highly complex topic, requiring a careful account of each Act: a tough topic to deal with".[58] However, following a series of legislative initiatives, it would seem that all states now provide some level of information services and related support provision. Adoption agencies, to a varying degree, are engaged in 'origins inquiries'.

10.1.   Information disclosure

On the one hand, there is no general right of unconditional access to identifying information contained in the records held by adoption agency, court or Registrar. On the other, a limited amount of non-identifying information has always been provided to the natural parent/s and adoptive parents prior to placement and at the time an adoption order is made.[59] Adult adopted people and birth parents may now usually obtain some level of non-identifying information at that time or later in circumstances of consensual adoption provided the other party has not registered an objection to such disclosure. In South Australia there is provision under the Adoption Act 1988 for open adoption and for this practice to be retrospectively legitimated; so all adoption records, regardless of when an adoption occurred, are available to all parties concerned. The only caveat is that the release of information is subject to a five year embargo, if a party has registered their veto. In New South

---

[57]   In Queensland it continues to be the case that there is no legislative requirement upon the state nor upon adoption agencies to offer any support services after the making of an adoption order to any of the parties concerned.

[58]   Letter to author, 7.10.04.

[59]   See, further, Harper, P., 'Adoption Law Reform: In Search of Self-Identity—Access to Information, 6 *Legal Service Bulletin* 52 (1981).

Wales, the Adoption Information Act 1990, which became fully effective on April 2, 1991, made original birth certificates accessible by right to adoptees.

10.1.1. CONDITIONAL ACCESS

Contact vetoes, whereby the birth parent may place on record their wish not to be contacted by the adoptee and to which the adoptee must comply or be subject to criminal penalties, were first introduced when New South Wales passed its Adoption Information Act of 1990. Queensland now has a similar veto law. Violating a contact veto in New South Wales carries financial penalties and the risk of imprisonment.

Usually, as in Queensland, the law tries to strike a balance between the concerns of those involved in adoption when it was a closed and confidential process and those who in recent years would have experienced it as a more open and informative process. The rights of the former group of participants are protected by legal provisions enabling access to identifying information only where other parties to the adoption in question have not registered an objection to disclosure and/or to contact. In contrast, all adult parties to an adoption dating from the early 1990s usually have an unqualified right to access identifying information as adoption records across Australia were then generally declared 'open' to the parties involved.

10.1.2. PROCEDURE

Where permitted, a party to an adoption can apply to the Registrar General for a certified copy of the adopted person's original birth certificate. He or she may then make application to the relevant adoption agency for disclosure of information on the circumstances of the adoption held on agency records. In New South Wales the Adoption Act 2000 makes provision for a complete record to be kept of birth and adoption information which can be accessed by adopted children, their birth parents and adopters.

10.1.3. THE ADOPTION CONTACT REGISTER

By the early 1990s such registers were established in most states and territories. They facilitate the reunion of adopted persons and birth parents following matched listings of registered wishes for contact.

10.2. Tracing and re-unification services

In some states and territories, agencies have been established to provide counselling and support services for adopted persons and birth parents seeking information but this remains an undeveloped level of national service provision. The Australian Institute of Health and Welfare Statistics reports that across Australia some 5,000 applications for identifying information are received annually. In Victoria, under the 1984 Act, some 24,000 applications (in relation to 64,000 adoptions) or a total of 37.5% had been received by the end of 1999 for identifying information. This contrasts with the experience in New South Wales (102,000 adoptions) where in the same period 19,000 applications had been received or 19% of the total. The majority of applicants, understandably, are adopted persons with only a minority of applications (at best a third) being from birth parents.

All states and territories, excepting Victoria and Tasmania, have some form of procedure for registering a veto against contact and in some cases also against the release of information. In New South Wales the veto must be lodged in person.

11.   CONCLUSION

The adoption process in Australia broadly conforms to that of other modern western societies which share a common law tradition; much the same issues of policy and practice are now being confronted by its legislators and judiciary. The Family Law Act 1975 (as amended in 1995) administered by the Family Court of Australia provides a framework for resolving adoption issues in accordance with established principles on a nationwide basis. Nonetheless and unsurprisingly, developmental progress is not proceeding at a uniform rate across the quite different cultures of the states and territories that constitute this vast continent. New South Wales, for example, tends to be in the forefront when it comes to legislative initiatives in the reform of adoption law and practice.

There are some interesting differences, largely of emphasis, in the Australian experience of adoption as viewed from the UK. Most noticeably, non-consensual adoption is comparatively rare. This is largely due to an established non-interventionist tradition in relation to family matters; other factors being equal, the state will favour the order that authorises least intervention.

This can be seen in the remarkably low rate of child care adoptions. The emphasis on family reunification, which seems out of step with current trends in the US and the UK, is perhaps in keeping with the earlier (and equally against the trend) experience of single mothers choosing to retain rather than relinquish their parental responsibilities. Moreover in Australia, unlike the US and the UK, the use of long-term foster care is encouraged for children with special needs which reduces the number available for child care adoption. The relatively low level of non-consensual adoption is also attributable to what appears to be a clearer and firmer policy in respect of family adoptions. Adoption by a birth parent and spouse or by a relative is generally viewed by the judiciary as being not necessarily in the best interests of the child concerned. Unlike the US, for example, there is a clear legislative presumption against adoption and a range of alternative orders has been made available. There is a presumption in favour of parenting orders and where 'step parent' adoption is proposed, leave to adopt must be obtained from courts exercising jurisdiction under the Family Law Act 1975. This diverts many would-be adoption applicants towards other proceedings.

The broadly consensual nature of adoption in this jurisdiction, perhaps also coupled with exposure to the experience of Indigenous people (see, further, Chap. 9), has facilitated the development of aspects of 'openness'. To a greater degree than most other countries and probably influenced by its neighbour New Zealand, an 'open' model of adoption is now practiced throughout Australia. This not only permits varying degrees of post-adoption contact between birth and adoptive families but often also allows the birth parent/s to be involved in the process of selecting adopters. This 'openness' has also permitted the introduction of legislation facilitating access to adoption information and the provision of related services.

Chapter 9

INTERCOUNTRY ADOPTION

1.   INTRODUCTION

Intercountry adoption, sometimes perceived as a rapidly growing modern social phenomenon, is in fact long established. It was and continues to be associated with the disruption to normal family life caused by war and civil unrest. The subjects are often orphans or refugees fleeing danger for sanctuary in any country offering safety and protection. This has recently been the experience of children in the Balkans following the violent breakup of Yugoslavia and is presently the case in Somalia, the Sudan and other parts of Africa. It does not necessarily involve the complete and permanent severance of a child's links with their culture and kinship networks as some may well be absorbed into the homes of displaced relatives or friends of their birth parents.

However, intercountry adoption is now most usually seen as a consequence of the demand led pressure to satisfy the parenting needs of infertile couples in modern western societies. While inevitably some of the children available will be the orphan victims of war, most will simply be from deprived backgrounds, abandoned in institutional care, with or without parental consent. The transfer of such children to adoptive homes invariably involves a total break with family and culture of origin.

Arguably, in both cases, intercountry adoption is a consequence of a failure in national politics. In the latter instance this failure might be seen as being further complicated by the political complicity of western nations choosing to facilitate the removal of children rather than resource the care and protection infrastructure in the child's country of origin.

Kerry O'Halloran (ed.), The Politics of Adoption, 263–289.
© 2006 *Springer. Printed in The Netherlands.*

This chapter begins by defining key aspects of this phenomenon, providing a brief historical background including a consideration of the role of the parties and countries involved and by tracing the emergence of an international legal response. It then outlines in turn, the policy and principles, the law and procedures and finally the practice of contemporary intercountry adoption.

2.   DEFINITIONS

Intercountry adoption is currently largely defined and regulated by The Hague Convention on Protection of Children and Co-operation in Respect of Intercountry Adoption 1993.

2.1.   Full and simple adoptions

'Adoption' in law may be either 'full' or 'simple': in the former the legal relationship between the birth parent/s and their child is terminated; in the latter this relationship is not completely severed. Countries such as the UK, the US, Australia and the Scandinavian countries recognise full adoptions while such others as France, Romania, Japan together with many countries in South America and Africa only recognise simple adoptions. Article 26 of The Hague Convention gives recognition to both forms and Article 27 empowers a receiving country to convert a simple adoption into a full adoption if the law of that country permits such a conversion and if the appropriate consents are available.

2.2.   Intercountry adoption

The Hague Convention on Intercountry Adoption states that an intercountry adoption occurs when:

> . . . a child habitually resident in one Contracting State ("the State of origin") has been, is being, or is to be moved to another Contracting State ("the receiving State") either after his or her adoption in the State of Origin by spouses or a person habitually resident in the receiving State, or for the purposes of such an adoption in the receiving State or in the State of origin.

An intercountry adoption can occur in one of three ways:

- adoption of a child from a Hague Convention State in accordance with the national legislation endorsing or incorporating The Hague Convention;
- adoption of a child in a country with "compatible" legislation; and
- adoption of a child from a non-Hague Convention State using other non-Hague Convention related national legislation and procedures.

In the UK, for example, adoption is defined as including a Convention adoption thereby giving automatic effect to the first while allowing for the possibility of granting recognition to adoptions arising by either of the other two methods.[1]

2.3. Overseas adoption

An 'overseas adoption' is one that has taken place in another country and falls outside the definition of a Convention adoption. The term refers to the associated legal difficulties in determining whether and to what effect such an adoption may be recognised by the court in the country where the issue of recognition has arisen. Most often it was an issue that occurred when immigrants sought recognition for an adoption order, granted in their country of origin, so that they could satisfy immigration/citizenship requirements in respect of their child. Essentially, 'overseas adoption' signifies national rules and procedures for managing a conflict of laws and was of particular importance in the years prior to the unrolling of The Hague Convention on Intercountry Adoption.

Nations independently legislated for the recognition of overseas adoption that occurred in a designated list of countries where adoption law and practice conformed to certain standards. In England and Wales there is legislative provision for overseas adoptions to be included within the definition of 'adoption' and provision for arrangements to be made for the recognition of overseas adoptions.[2] As Bridge and Swindells point out, the criteria for such recognition are likely to include.[3]

(a) confirming that the law in the overseas country ensures that the child has been freely given up for adoption and that this has not been induced by payment or compensation of any kind;

(b) confirming that the overseas country has made attempts to place the child in a family in that country;

(c) confirming that intercountry adoption is in the child's best interests;

(d) requiring that the domestic and intercountry adoption arrangements are the same; and

(e) ensuring that profit is not made from the process.

Currently, in many nations, the challenge in relation to overseas adoption is to ensure that it is used appropriately to supplement the procedures of The Hague Convention on Intercountry Adoption. In some countries the experience is that adopters are using the overseas adoption rules to circumvent Convention constraints by adopting children in countries that have not ratified it.

---

[1] See, s 66 of the Adoption and Children Act 2002.
[2] See, sections 66 and 87, respectively, of the Adoption and Children Act 2002.
[3] See, Bridge, C. and Swindells, H., *Adoption—The Modern Law*, Family Law, Bristol, 2003 at p. 314.

3.   BACKGROUND

The phenomenon of intercountry adoption has existed for a long time. It was evident, for example, in the practice of sending many tens of thousands of orphaned, abandoned and/or neglected children from the UK and Ireland to Australia, Canada and other British colonial and post-colonial countries in the late 19th and early 20th centuries. Its modern manifestation, however, signifying the movement of children from institutional care in impoverished or conflict ravaged countries into the middle-class homes of adopters in western societies, most probably dates from the aftermath of World War II. The 'child rescue' approach has its origins in a very practical and necessary humanitarian response to the plight of refugee children abandoned or orphaned in the many theatres of war.

3.1.   Needs

Intercountry adoption, as we now know it, was initially concerned with providing families for children orphaned by conflict. It most often took the form of adopters extending their family life and parental care to accommodate children additional to their own; the needs of infertile couples were not a particularly relevant factor. It has changed greatly in recent years in response to pressure from the needs of the different parties involved.

3.1.1.   CHILDREN

The modern interpretation of intercountry adoption, in terms of the geographic/cultural distances separating sending and receiving countries and the probable transracial component, first manifested itself in the international response to the physical and healthcare needs of the many young orphans of the Korean War. The children concerned were most probably orphans, not necessarily babies and their adopters may well have had children of their own.

As the role played by infertility as a motivating factor for adopters became the driving force in intercountry adoption so the needs of children abandoned or abused by parents, rather than simply orphaned, came to be seen as also appropriately met by such adopters. However, unlike their predecessors, these adopters were mostly interested in babies, preferably healthy and voluntarily relinquished, rather than children simply in need of a home. For sending countries, this switch in focus—from providing adopters with children in need of a home to instead providing babies to adopters in need of family life—has presented certain difficulties:

- firstly, it removes the most adoptable children from their own country, culture and kin and thereby exposes them to possible future difficulties in relation to matters of identity, racism and language;

- secondly, it pre-empts any possibility of meeting the needs of native adopters;
- thirdly, it leaves behind those children who are statistically less likely to be adopted and who will therefore probably be consigned to institutional care; and
- finally, because the market for intercountry adoption now places a higher value on young healthy babies, there is a correspondingly higher likelihood of market forces introducing profit motivated persons and agencies with potential to compromise the legality of the process.

3.1.2. BIRTH PARENTS

Maternal choice, to retain rather than relinquish a non-marital child, has played a significant role in reducing the number of children available for domestic adoption in modern western societies. The fading of the stigma traditionally attached to the role of unmarried mother, coupled with the availability of welfare benefits and other support services, has allowed parenting to become a feasible option for many such mothers. As indigenous adoption in some modern western societies changes from being consensual to coercive in nature, with the availability of children being determined more by the courts than by parental choice, the children involved have tended to be older and therefore to have needs for some level of ongoing contact with their birth parents. The latter are now much more likely to have a role in the lives of their adopted children and to attract the involvement of public service support that was the case up to the close of the 20th century.

Conversely, in many underdeveloped countries the lack of any support services and exposure to unremitting poverty increases the likelihood of parental relinquishment or abandonment of children. In some cases the benefit to poverty stricken birth parents in places such as South America and Africa derives not only from the ending of care responsibility and the comfort of knowing that their child will be better cared for by others, but from the direct or indirect payments made by intermediaries seeking to arrange adoption placements. To some this equation presents as just another instance of the west 'outsourcing' its production requirements to third world countries. For birth parents in sending countries, intercountry adoption can present certain difficulties:

- circumstances of poverty and hardship can make them vulnerable to pressure to relinquish a child for financial gain;
- the post-adoption opportunities for contact, access or for practicing 'open' adoption are seriously restricted; and
- whether or not financial gain is involved, they can be exposed to subsequent discriminatory attitudes from within their local communities.

3.1.3.   ADOPTERS

The key factor in the growth of intercountry adoption has been the motivation of prospective adopters. Whether driven by altruism or by personal need, they have sought to acquire elsewhere the babies unavailable in modern western society due to the fall in fertility rates and an increase in the efficiency and use of birth control techniques. There can be no doubt, however, that in many cases intercountry adoption is triggered by the compassionate altruistic response of prospective adopters to the plight of children, orphaned by war or abandoned to institutional care, in foreign lands.

For some prospective adopters, satisfying parenting needs within their country of origin may have been constrained by religious conviction or by prevailing national laws preventing recourse to such options as AID, GIFT or surrogacy arrangements that might otherwise have been available.[4] For others, particularly those resident in Sweden and Denmark, the fact that no children are available on a non-consensual basis from the public child care system has left intercountry adoption as the only possible means of acquiring a child.[5] Indeed in Sweden there are currently some 800–1,000 intercountry adoptions every year with a total of approximately 40,000 children adopted from overseas since 1969, mostly from Asia and South America. For all prospective adopters the likelihood of acquiring a baby as opposed to an older child is increased enormously by taking the intercountry rather than in-country adoption route.

Possibly, also, for some the attractions of intercountry adoption have increased as contemporary adoption embraces the principle of 'openness' and with it the probability of some degree of contact with a parent and/or other members of the adopted child's family of origin. The prospect of adopting a child born in a foreign land many thousands of miles away may carry with it assurances of privacy, anonymity and escape from any ongoing complicating entanglements. In fact, intercountry adoption may be attractive because it embodies many of the characteristics traditionally associated with 'closed' adoption in western society.

For adopters in receiving countries, intercountry adoption presents certain difficulties:

- achieving an appropriate and satisfactory match between their home circumstances and the needs of a child will necessarily involve a high degree of uncertainty;
- accessing verifiable information regarding parental consents, health and genetic background of the child etc can be problematic;

---

[4]   In Ireland, recourse to such options would be illegal.
[5]   In other countries, such as France and Ireland, the complete judicial termination of parental rights in respect of children in care is a rarity and consequently there is an established reliance on intercountry adoption.

- the costs will be considerable; and
- as they are often older than the average adopter, they can have problems coping with the complex adjustments that need to be made by their adopted child.

3.2. The countries

The socio-economic divide between countries of origin (the 'sending' countries) and countries of destination (the 'receiving' countries) for the children involved in intercountry adoption is unmistakable. The flow of children is invariably from the more undeveloped countries of the southern hemisphere to the modern western societies of the north.

3.2.1. THE SENDING COUNTRIES

The lack or collapse of the infrastructure of some third-world countries, for reasons of chronic poverty or socio-economic/political turmoil, has been a significant factor in generating the availability of children for adoption. The internal migration of people in search of food, security or employment led to a widespread breakdown in the traditional practice of relying on the extended family network to absorb child care needs. Instead, whether orphaned or abandoned, increasing numbers of children were admitted to institutional care. For the public health care systems of such countries, also victims of the prevailing social pressures and often unable to adequately cope with the increased workload, intercountry adoption seemed a provident solution. This is well illustrated by the experience of Korea which from 1956–1994 was by far the most significant single contributor to intercountry adoption[6] sending a total of some 150,000 children to adoptive homes in other countries. While initially the flow was stimulated by the plight of many children who as orphans or refugees were the casualties of war, this changed over time as government policy prioritised the use of revenues for industrialisation rather than for developing social and healthcare facilities.

The impact of poverty has itself been a significant factor in generating the availability of children. For example, the importance of Korea as a sending country rapidly declined in the early 1980s as national prosperity increased. The influence of politics can also produce the same result. The government decree in China that only one child per family should be the rule, coupled with the preference for male children, led to the current situation of many unwanted female children being absorbed by intercountry adoption. Again, in Romania under the Ceauseacu

---

[6] See, Hubinette, T., 'Adopted Koreans and the Development of Identity in the 'Third Space', in *Adoption & Fostering*, London, BAAF, vol. 28, no. 1, 2004, pp. 16–24 where the author refers to the resulting Korean adoption diaspora.

regime, the official policy that each family should have a minimum of four children resulted in many children being abandoned in orphanages because their parents could not provide for them.

3.2.2. THE RECEIVING COUNTRIES

In all modern western societies, the rapid decline in the number of children available for adoption, particularly healthy babies, generated a need now met by availing of those that are unwanted or cannot be coped with in their countries of origin.

Some countries have demonstrated a particularly strong and consistent interest in intercountry adoption. The US, for example, provided homes for two-thirds of all Korean children adopted outside their country of birth and received at least 2,000 children from Ireland during the 1960s. Europe in general and Scandinavia in particular has also over many decades accepted children from other countries for adoption placements. As noted by Hubinette.[7]

> The 45,855 adopted Koreans in Europe represent one out of three of all international adoptees on the continent. France is the leading country with about 11,000 individuals, but large numbers have been placed in Belgium, the Netherlands, Luxembourg and Scandinavia. Koreans constitute half of all international adoptess in Denmark and Norway and one-fifth in Sweden . . . Finally, there are altogether 5,000 adopted Koreans in Canada, Australia and New Zealand.

Further, as Hubinette has also pointed out,[8] where intercountry adoption arises from the circumstances of war then the outflow of children tends to be in the direction determined by the political allegiances of the war ravaged countries. So, following the Korean War, by far the majority of children from South Korea placed for intercountry adoption were adopted in the US with the remainder mostly going to adopters among South Korea's other wartime national allies in northern Europe. This pattern was repeated in the period following the wars in Europe and Vietnam.

The UK, unlike many other countries in Europe, does not have an established history of involvement in intercountry adoption; at least not as a receiving country. This may be partially attributed to its public policy of rigorously policing immigration in any form. It is also probable that unlike other countries, for example Ireland, the UK was able to divert the interests of prospective adopters towards children with special needs. Then there is the fact that the legal and professional framework was not conducive to intercountry adoption: adoption law prohibited non-agency placements; and local authority social work staff often treated assessment for foreign adoptions as a distraction from their mainstream work.

---

[7] See, Hubinette, T., 'Adopted Koreans and the Development of Identity in the 'Third Space', in *Adoption & Fostering*, London, BAAF, vol. 28, no. 1, 2004, p. 19.
[8] *Ibid*, at pp. 18–19.

3.3. The law: developments leading to an international framework

The early history of the law relating to intercountry adoption reveals a primary concern with the prevention of 'trafficking' in children.[9] This term refers not just to the age old practice of parents relinquishing their children for financial reward but also to the absence of an objective determination of the welfare interests of the child, the role played by any intermediaries, the validity of consents (including that of the child), irregular payments and the possible abuse of immigration rules and procedures.

3.3.1. THE COMMON LAW

The Court of Appeal in *Re Valentine's Settlement*[10] stated the general rule that, in keeping with the principle of international comity, recognition will be granted to an adoption made in another country when the adopters are domiciled (or, more recently, 'habitually resident') in that country. Denning LJ adding that the child also should be resident there at the time the order is made. For the purposes of the law in England and Wales, a foreign adoption will be treated as a common law adoption when it is not made in the British Isles, is not a Convention or an overseas adoption but is made within customary or common law rather than a statutory framework. In such cases, formal recognition of the validity of the order will be given by the High Court provided that recognition would not be contrary to public policy.

3.3.2. THE EUROPEAN CONVENTION FOR THE PROTECTION OF HUMAN RIGHTS AND FUNDAMENTAL FREEDOMS 1950

This Convention established a framework of international rights some of which have a bearing on intercountry adoption. Article 8, which states the right to respect for private and family life, has generated considerable adoption related case law with implications for international practice (see, further, Chap. 4).

3.3.3. THE UNITED NATIONS CONVENTION ON THE RIGHTS OF THE CHILD 1989

This Convention provides an agreed but aspirational body of principles rather than operational rules and procedures. It declares in its Preamble:

---

[9] A theme continued in the UN Convention (Article 11) and in the Hague Convention (the Preamble).
[10] [1965] 1 Ch. 831.

... that the family, as the fundamental group of society and the natural environment for the growth and well-being of all its members and particularly children, should be afforded the necessary protection and assistance so that it can fully assume its responsibilities within the community.

This is underpinned by Articles 18 and 20 which again reinforce the principle that the state should give priority to measures that keep children in their families and culture of origin and by Article 11(1) which requires measures to be taken to combat the illicit transfer and non-return of children abroad. These statements of principle, favouring state support to preserve the integrity of a child's family of origin, are counterbalanced by principles that distinguish the separate interests of children. For example, the Preamble also states that:

... the child, for a full and harmonious development, should grow up in a family environment, in an atmosphere of happiness, love and understanding ...

However, in circumstances where a child's family of origin is unable to meet the needs of that child, then Article 20 requires the state to "ensure alternative care for such a child".[11] Article 21 recognises that intercountry adoption may be considered as an alternative means of providing for a child's care but only after all other options for retaining the child within his or her country of origin have been exhausted. In that event, it requires the child's interests to be treated as of paramount importance (see, also, Chap. 4).

The steady increase in the number of signatories to this Convention has been accompanied by an increase in the volume of intercountry adoptions. It would seem, therefore, that the countries concerned are finding it necessary to protect and assist children through facilitating arrangements for substitute family care in other countries rather than through provision of the support services that would enable birth families to improve their caring capacity.

3.3.4.   THE HAGUE CONFERENCE ON PRIVATE INTERNATIONAL LAW

The increased mobility of families in the latter part of the 20th century was accompanied by ever more cross-jurisdictional disputes concerning matters such as marriage, divorce, child abduction and adoption. In an attempt to substitute international agreement for country to country negotiations on the rules and procedures for regulating such matters, The Hague Conference on Private International Law held a number of conferences to develop Conventions that would state the relevant agreed principles, standards and rules.[12] Eventually three Conventions

---

[11] Subject to the requirement that "due regard shall be paid to the desirability of continuity in a child's upbringing and to the child's ethnic, religious, cultural and linguistic background".

[12] See, for example, Dyer, A., *The Internationalisation of Family Law*, 30 UC Davis Law Review 625, (1997).

concerning children were produced including The Hague Convention on Protection of Children and Co-operation in Respect of Intercountry Adoption 1993.[13] The latter was a response to increased concern regarding trafficking in children, perhaps generated in particular by the international interest in rescuing children from the orphanages of post-Ceausescu Romania (see, further, below).

4. CONTEMPORARY INTERCOUNTRY ADOPTION: POLICY AND PRINCIPLES

The Hague Convention, other international Conventions and much national legislation now reveal an acceptance of permanency planning as a fundamental principle to be applied in the context of intercountry adoption in circumstances where children cannot be adequately cared for in their families and countries of origin. The entitlement of every child to safe family life is to prevail over all other considerations and this is to be furthered through a general policy that includes facilitating intercountry adoption in accordance with agreed standards of practice.

4.1. A controversial policy

The present harmonious convergence in national attitudes towards intercountry adoption has not been reached without a great deal of controversy. For the value systems of modern western nations—the legal structures of which are highly sensitised to issues of equality and non-discrimination as played out in matters of race, class etc—the phenomenon of intercountry adoption carries considerable baggage. For third world countries, coming to terms with the legacy of colonialism, this phenomenon resonates with earlier experiences of exploitation. Some of the more strident viewpoints have centred on political interpretations of intercountry adoption where the transfer of children is seen as a proxy manifestation of mercenary national interests.

4.1.1. THE 'COMMODIFICATION' OF CHILDREN

Intercountry adoption is seen by some as just another form of international trade in which children are the 'goods' to be traded.[14] They are necessarily objectified as neither 'buyer' or 'supplier' has any real understanding of each baby's singular needs and characteristics. In this analogy, the buyers are the middle class infertile couples of western society choosing to acquire babies as they would any

---

[13] The other two being the Convention on the Civil Aspects of International Child Abduction 1980 and the Convention on Jurisdiction, Applicable Law, Recognition, Enforcement, and Co-operation in Respect of Parental Responsibility and Measures for the Protection of Children 1996.

[14] See, further, Triseliotis, J., 'Intercountry adoption: global trade or global gift?', *Adoption & Fostering*, London, BAAF, vol, 24, no. 2, pp. 45–54, 2000.

other commodity. The suppliers are those in deprived countries relinquishing to foreigners, responsibility for the children for whom they cannot afford to care. The profit element is present in the release from care costs, the fees charged by intermediaries and in the opportunity to parent that would otherwise be denied.

The trading analogy is supported by evidence drawn from an assessment of the 'marketing position' of the supplier. As social stability has returned to countries such as Vietnam, Korea and Romania so their governments have moved to control the availability of the children by restricting or ceasing their involvement in intercountry adoption. Inevitably, this has resulted in western nations turning instead to other countries such as the Philippines, Cambodia and El Salvador to make up the shortfall. For some observers such as Hubinette, intercountry adoption carries "ugly parallels to contemporary trafficking of women and the historic transatlantic slave trade".[15]

4.1.2.   CULTURAL ASSIMILATION

The traditional 'closed' adoption system of western society has been predicated upon a perceived need to sever the child's links with the past, assimilate him or her within their new family and build a fresh identity that denies the child's origins. To a considerable extent, intercountry adoption has followed the same route. For the child involved, intercountry adoption has most usually entailed shedding the culture of their family of origin and substituting that of their adopters. Hubinette refers to this as a process whereby.[16]

> assimilation becomes the ideal as the adoptee is stripped of name, language, religion and culture, only retaining a fetishised non-white body, while the bonds to the biological family and the country of origin are cut off.

Denial and assimilation may occur despite the fact that in countries such as the UK, Adoption Panels invariably seek a commitment from prospective intercountry adopters that they will endeavour to instill and nurture in the adoptee a sense of their culture of origin and not restrict the latter to their own mono-cultural environment. The adopted child inevitably strives to 'fit in with' and assume the cultural characteristics of their parents.[17]

---

[15] *Op cit* at p. 19; citing Hermann Jr and Kasper, 1992; Triseliotis, 2000; Masson, 2001; Shiu, 2001.
[16] *Op cit* at p. 20.
[17] A considerable body of research testifies to the ability of transracial adoptees to assume the cultural characteristics of the receiving country; see, for example, Feigelman, W. and Silverman, A. *Chosen Children: New Patterns of Adoptive Relationships*, New York, Praeger (1983), and Saetersdal, B. 'What became of the Vietnamese "baby life children"?, Melbourne, paper in conference proceedings on *Permanence for Children*, (1989). However, this must be set against the evidence from adoptees transnational groups that adulthood often brings difficulties with cultural identity.

Intercountry adoptions are often also transracial and in such cases the scope for denial is clearly limited. However, there are those who suggest that perhaps some adopters are attracted by an obvious cultural difference; in fact, the more obvious the difference the stronger the attraction.

4.1.3. COLONIALISM

There are those who take the view that intercountry adoption is simply another modern manifestation of colonialism; seen as not dissimilar to the economic and commercial cultivation of dependent relationships of third world countries by modern western societies. Hubinette, for example, argues that this has certainly been the experience of Korea[18]:

> Continuous international adoption from Korea can thus be seen as a manifest symbol of Western dependency and the country's position as a client state in the world system, pointing to the persistence of colonial thinking and reflecting global racial hierarchies.

He adds that "many leading supply countries in the field of international adoption fall under the US sphere of influence or have been subjected to US warfare: Korea, Vietnam, Thailand and the Philippines in Asia, and Columbia, Chile and Guatemala in Latin America".

4.2. Some guiding principles

As intercountry adoption has become firmly established it has been possible to identify certain associated principles. While there is perhaps some truth in the above controversial interpretations placed on this phenomenon there is also much truth in the observation made by Silberman[19]:

> The other side of the adoption crisis is the tragic condition of unwanted children and the failure of any system to handle adoptions in a way that facilitates their placement. While critics of intercountry adoption view transnational and transracial placement of children as forms of imperialism and genocide, others argue that intercountry adoption offers the only viable opportunity for many of these children.

---

[18] *Op cit* at p. 19.

[19] See, Silberman, L., 'The Hague Children's Conventions: The Internationalization of Child Law' in Katz, S., Eekelaar, J. and Maclean, M. (eds.) *Cross Currents: Family Law and Policy in the United States and England*, Oxford, Oxford University Press, 2000, at p. 607; citing D'Amato, A., *Cross-Country Adoption: A Call to Action*, 73 Notre Dame Law Review 1239 and Bartholet, E., *International Adoption: Propriety, Prospect and Pragmatics*, 13 J Am Acad Matrim L 181 (1996).

4.2.1.   SUPPORTING THE WEAK SOCIAL INFRASTRUCTURE
          OF SENDING COUNTRIES

By definition, third world countries lack the sophisticated, flexible yet robust social infrastructure that can withstand political or socio-economic upheaval. In
particular their public child care services are often rudimentary and unable to
cope with a sudden influx of children requiring, for whatever reason, an alternative to parental care. Institutionalisation, often the only child care resource
available, offers a poor and damaging environment not conducive to nurturing
the physical, emotional and social development of children who may already be
traumatised on admission. They can often be poorly equipped and understaffed
'warehousing' facilities, with little professional child care expertise available, in
which children are contained until such time as they reach adulthood. The under-
standable altruistic response of western nations, with their comparatively refined
and well resourced child care services, is to facilitate child rescue by intercountry
adoption. However, as Triseliotis *et al* rightly point out[20]:

> Irrespective of the circumstances under which intercountry adoption takes place, it
> poses political, moral, empirical, policy and practical issues. From the policy and moral
> perspectives its practice gives rise to many similar questions to own-country adoption.
> In-country adoption in the West too has often come under criticism for involving the
> move of children mainly from poor to better-off families. The legitimacy of in-country
> or intercountry adoption will continue to be questioned until such time as adequate
> income maintenance schemes and preventative type services are developed to provide
> real choice for all birth parents.

The fact is that adoption, child care and foster care services are often so underdeveloped in such countries that intercountry adoption is an easier way of immediately securing the welfare interests of the children involved. Some western
nations, while facilitating intercountry adoption, are also investing resources in
building the services infrastructure in sending countries that in the long-term
will give the latter the capacity to cope with their own child care concerns and
make better choices to secure the best permanency placement for each child in
need.

4.2.2.   RELIEVING PRESSURE ON ADOPTERS IN RECEIVING COUNTRIES

In modern western nations both the fertility rates and the number of children available for adoption are steadily falling, which inevitably leads to increasing numbers of infertile couples joining the queue of prospective adopters. Intercountry

---

[20] See, Triseliotis, J., Shireman, J. and Hundleby, M., *Adoption Theory, Policy and Practice*, Cassell,
      London, 1997 at p. 181.

adoption is often the best option for those who desperately want to have their own family and virtually the only option if they want a healthy, 'normal' baby.

The pressures on prospective adopters are potentially harmful not just for them but for all parties involved in this process. Dealing with many officials in a foreign culture can prove to be a very expensive and uncertain business. The considerable costs entailed in acquiring a child can compromise the legality of the adopters' actions while the lack of information on the child can result in inaccurate data relating to his or her legal and health status. The officials with management responsibility for child care institutions can be tempted into putting undue pressure on unmarried mothers, can designate children as orphans when they are not and can receive financial benefits from discharging children into the care of adopters. In particular, needs driven adopters may not be as open to objectively considering whether they rather than anyone else are the best persons to promote the interests of a particular child who will be uprooted from their kin and culture and may also bring with them latent health disorders and associated complex care requirements.

In countries such as the UK, where there is a relatively high incidence of adoption from the public child care route and methods of assisting conception (e.g., AID, GIFT etc.) and surrogacy are legally available, there is also a low rate of intercountry adoptions. In countries such as Ireland the reverse is the case. It may be that every opportunity should be developed for adopters to meet their needs without having recourse to intercountry adoption, at least as a forced option.

4.2.3.   BALANCE IN ADDRESSING THE NEEDS OF CHILDREN

All western nations currently involved in intercountry adoption also have children in their public care systems whose needs could be more appropriately met by adoption. These children remain unadopted because of factors such as health and social care problems, age, lack of parental consent, lack of sufficient post-adoption support services and because they are in sibling groups. The likelihood of such children being adopted is reduced by the counter attraction to prospective adopters of securing a healthy 'normal' baby through intercountry adoption. Also, although clearly beneficial for almost all the children involved, intercountry adoption provides a context for 'trafficking' in children. The rights of some children in both receiving and sending countries are being endangered by intercountry adoption. Arguably, all receiving nations should be investing in facilitating the adoption of those children consigned to their child care systems for whom rehabilitation in their family of origin is not an option as well as in regulating intercountry adoption.

Again, in all sending countries there are potential carers such as relatives or perhaps foster parents who could be supported, financially and otherwise, to provide permanency through adoption for a child in the public care system. Intercountry adoption can obviate the need in sending countries to cultivate relevant local services. If such a country is unable to commit resources to this end then arguably there is a moral obligation on western nations to do so.

5. CONTEMPORARY INTERCOUNTRY ADOPTION: THE LAW AND PROCEDURES

Intercountry adoption has now become so complex that it requires to be regulated by its own body of international law. The Hague Convention on Protection of Children and Co-operation in Respect of Intercountry Adoption 1993[21] together with the United Nations Declaration on Social and Legal Principles relating to the Protection and Welfare of Children with Special Reference to Foster Placement and Adoption Nationally and Internationally 1986 (see, further, Chap. 4) provide the most directly relevant legislation. The European Convention on Human Rights, the European Convention on Adoption and of course the United Nations Convention on the Rights of the Child also contribute to the current framework for regulating intercountry adoption (see, further, above and also, Chap. 4). The Hague Convention, however, is of primary importance.

5.1. The Hague Convention on Protection of Children and Co-operation in Respect of Intercountry Adoption 1993

This Convention has the distinction of being the first truly international piece of regulatory legislation due to the near global reach of its provisions.[22] In its Preamble the Convention states that 'intercountry adoption may offer the advantage of a permanent home to a child for whom a suitable family cannot be found in his or her State of origin'. It declares in Article 1 the importance of establishing 'safeguards to ensure that intercountry adoptions take place in the best interests of the child and with respect for his or her fundamental rights as recognised in international law'. In Article 4(b) it provides that a Convention adoption 'shall only take place if the competent authorities of the State of origin have determined after the possibilities for placement within the State of origin have been given due consideration that intercountry adoption is in the child's best interests'. It gives effect to these principles through various provisions.

---

[21] In the UK, the Adoption (Intercountry Aspects) Act 1999, which received the Royal Assent on 28th July 1999, gives effect to the provisions of the Hague Convention (see, further, Chap. 5).

[22] Since it was concluded at The Hague on March 29 1993, some 60 countries have either signed, ratified it or acceded to it. The UK signed in 1994 and is due to ratify before September 2005. See, http://www.hcch.net/e/status/adoshte.html.

5.1.1. PROMOTING IN-COUNTRY CHILD CARE

Article 4(b) of the Hague Convention promotes the development of professional adoption services in 'donor' countries i.e. countries which for reasons of poverty and/or social instability are allowing children to be adopted by non-nationals. This is a significant moral stand. The 'child rescue' approach, with its attendant dislocation for human relationships and cultural identity, is not to be the preferred means of safeguarding welfare interests either locally or internationally. Priority is to be given to retaining a child in need within his or her family and social context of origin. Where consensually based retention is not feasible then foster care services should be provided which would permit a child to be placed as close as possible, in terms of geography and relationships, to his or her family/culture/community of origin. Resort to adoption should occur only when these options are not possible and then preference should again be given to maintaining the child within the cultural norms of his or her family of origin. The Convention views intercountry adoption as the final step in a continuum, to be taken when all others have been tried, when all the professional filters are in place and the adoption process is regulated to ensure that welfare interests are safeguarded. This approach very much echoes that embodied in Article 21(b) of the UN Convention.

5.1.2. BROAD APPLICATION TO DIFFERENT TYPES OF ADOPTION

The Hague Convention applies whenever a child habitually resident in a Convention compliant sending country has been, is being, or is to be moved for the purposes of adoption to another Convention compliant receiving country; it does not matter in which of the two countries the adoption takes place. It applies to both full and simple adoptions. Its broad application ensures that the Convention will eventually regulate the majority of intercountry adoptions.

5.1.3. A FRAMEWORK FOR REGULATING STANDARDS

The Hague Convention provides a framework of minimum standards for regulating intercountry adoption. In its Preamble the Convention declares that a Convention compliant country must 'prevent the abduction, the sale of, or traffic in children'.[23] It requires that receiving countries establish 'accredited bodies', which must be non-profit agencies, to carry out duties in relation to intercountry adoption; these 'accredited bodies' will most usually be approved adoption agencies though 'independent adoptions' remain permissible. Where unauthorised payments have been made the Convention permits the annulment of an adoption on the grounds that this constitutes a breach of public policy.

---

[23] A prohibition given effect in the 2002 Act by sections 83 and 92–97.

It also establishes a series of safeguards to ensure, for example, that:

- free and informed consent is sought from and given by birth parents and the child;
- that consent is not enduced by bribery;
- that the views of the child, where feasible, have been sought;
- that the adoptive parents have received such counselling as necessary and are suitable persons to adopt; and
- that the child's cultural heritage will be preserved (see, further, Chap. 4).

However, the fact remains that many of the sending countries do not have the resources to ensure that these safeguards are in place; in particular the obligation to ensure the provision of proper consents, uncompromised by financial irregularities, is often unrealisable in practice.

5.2.   Intercountry adoption procedure under The Hague Convention

The procedure for acquiring a foreign child for adoption under The Hague Convention can be briefly outlined.

5.2.1.   PROSPECTIVE ADOPTER/S

The person/s wishing to adopt must make application to the designated authority in the country where they are habitually resident. In the UK the 'authority', a registered adoption agency, will assign a professional social worker to undertake an assessment of the applicant/s eligibility and suitability to adopt and to compile a 'homestudy' report on their family background and a personal history for submission to the agency's Adoption Panel. The approved report will then be forwarded to the relevant authority in the country with an available child.

5.2.2.   SENDING COUNTRY

On receipt of the 'homestudy' report and other documentation attesting to the eligibility and suitability of the applicants, the appropriate authorities in the sending country will then make a preliminary determination as to whether or not the proposed placement is in the best interests of a particular child. In so doing the authorities are required, under Article 29 of the Convention, to give due consideration to the child's ethnic, religious and cultural background. A report on the child is then sent to the authorities in the receiving country together with evidence that all necessary consents have been obtained and the reasons for its 'best interests' determination in respect of the child. Article 16(2) provides for the withholding of identifying information regarding the child's birth parent/s where the authorities deem this to be necessary.

5.2.3. TRANSFER OF CHILD

When all administrative requirements have been satisfied, Article 17 of the Convention allows the child to be 'entrusted' (rather than placed) by the authorities in the sending country into the care of the prospective adopters. The responsibility for ensuring that the prospective adopters accept the transfer of the child rests with the authorities of the sending rather than the receiving country. Both sets of authorities, however, must agree to the proposed adoption and under Article 17(c) either may withhold consent if not satisfied that all legal requirements have been met.

5.2.4. ADOPTION ORDER

The adoption order may be made in either the sending or receiving country. The sending country bears responsibility for producing in court evidence that:

- intercountry adoption is in the child's best interests;
- all necessary consents have been obtained;
- the prospective adopters satisfy eligibility and suitability criteria; and
- the child is or will be authorised to enter and remain in the receiving country.

In some Hague compliant sending countries, such as China, the practice is to finalise the adoption order before the child leaves the jurisdiction.

5.2.5. INTERIM ADOPTION ORDER

Increasingly, some Hague compliant countries such as Russia are choosing to proceed by allowing the adopters to return home with their child under the authority of an interim adoption order. Thereafter, on return of six satisfactory consecutive monthly reports by the appropriate authority in the receiving country, the adoption order is automatically finalised.

5.3.   Effects of intercountry adoption under The Hague Convention

Article 26(1) of The Hague Convention states that a Convention compliant adoption order will terminate pre-adoption legal relationships (if permitted under the law of the sending country), vest parental responsibility in the adopter/s, establish a permanent legal parental relationship between adopter/s and the child and be recognised by the law of the receiving country and that of all other Convention countries.

5.3.1.   FULL AND SIMPLE ADOPTIONS

The subsequent legal standing of the birth parent/s in relation to the child will depend on whether the order made in the sending country is a 'full' or a 'simple' adoption order. In the former case the adoption order will then operate to wholly and permanently terminate the rights of the natural parent/s, whereas in the latter these rights are not completely extinguished. The statutory processes of some countries, such as the UK, have only ever provided for full adoption and that jurisdiction now provides for automatic recognition of both full and simple adoptions and for conversion of the latter.[24] Article 26(2) of the Convention provides that, in the case of full adoptions, a Convention compliant adoption order will have a legal effect equivalent to an order made under the statute law of the receiving country.

5.3.2.   ACCESS TO IDENTIFYING INFORMATION

Under Article 30(1) of the Convention, the sending countries are required to preserve information relating to the identity of natural parent/s and in particular to the child's personal and family history; this is to include information regarding the family's medical history. However, Article 30(2) leaves the issue of access to that information to be determined by the laws of the receiving country.

6.   CONTEMPORARY INTERCOUNTRY ADOPTION: PRACTICE

From about the mid-1970s, stimulated in part by the social dislocation in southeast Asia following the Vietnam War, intercountry adoption became a global phenomenon. It by then also embraced sending countries in South America and such receiving countries as Canada, Australia, the US and most of Western Europe. From the 1990s, it extended to include sending countries in Eastern Europe, most notably Romania. Although The Hague Convention now provides an international

---

[24] In England & Wales recognition is provided under s 66 of the 2002 Act and conversion under s 88 ensures that all Convention adoptions are treated as full adoptions. In order to deal with the diversity of national interpretations encountered in the context of intercountry adoption, s 88 of the 2002 Act also provides a procedure whereby those simple adoptions that are not amenable to conversion, perhaps because evidence of full and informed parental consent is not available, are sifted out and an alternative order is made.

regulatory framework its capacity to standardise and raise levels of practice is limited by the fact that a number of participants in intercountry adoption are not signatories to the Convention.

6.1.   The children

When intercountry adopters were motivated largely by altruism the children then transferred to receiving countries were often older, suffering from a disability and/or with pronounced social and healthcare needs. Contemporary practice, however, is driven by the needs of infertile couples in western societies.[25] This need is firmly directed towards healthy babies.

By the early years of the 21st century, intercountry adoption was continuing to grow in terms of the numbers of children involved as the deficit in babies available for adoption in modern western societies became more marked.[26] As Cretney has pointed out[27]:

> Now over 30,000 children from 50 countries are adopted outside their countries of origin each year. The USA is the main receiving country, the main countries of origin are Russia, China, Vietnam, Columbia and Guatemala.[28]
>
> Compared with the rest of Western Europe, the number of these adoptions in the UK is low; only approximately 300 orders are made each year.[29]

The age profile of the children involved is very revealing: two-thirds are less than one year old and only 16% are aged 3 years or older. Anecdotal evidence would suggest that very few children suffer from an obvious physical or mental disability though many are under-nourished, perhaps have a vitamin deficiency and some are eventually found to be HIV positive.

6.2.   Sending countries

The pool of countries prepared to make children available for intercountry adoption is continually changing. A number of former sending countries have now

---

[25] Research shows that this is the case in nine out of ten such adoptions; see, for example, Hoksbergen. R, Juffer, F. and Waardenburg, B., *Adopted Children at Home and at School*, Lisse, Sweets and Zeitlinger, (1987).

[26] In 1998 the rate of intercountry adoption, expressed per million of the population in the receiving country was: 116 in New Zealand; 52 in the Netherlands; 26 in Sweden; and 117 for Norway.

[27] See, Cretney, S., Masson, J. and Bailey-Harris, R., *Principles of Family Law*, London, Thomson Sweet & Maxwell, 2003 at p. 832.

[28] Citing, Selman, P., 'The demographic history of intercountry adoption' in Selman, P., (ed.) *Intercountry Adoption* (2000).

[29] Citing, *Second Report to the UN Committee on the Rights of the Child by the UK*, (1999), para 7.23.8.

either stopped or drastically restricted their involvement. Bangladesh, for example, recently prohibited the practice while Peru will only permit it on the basis of bilateral agreements. Other countries such as Korea, Romania[30] and India have developed laws to regulate it. While poverty is clearly a factor in determining whether or not a nation is or continues to be a sending country, politics also plays a role. In 'closed' totalitarian states, such as North Korea and formerly those in Eastern Europe, governments tend to prohibit intercountry adoption as they would any practice that might permit external involvement, indicate an inability to cope with indigenous social problems and present a risk of political 'loss of face'.

As some countries withdraw others take their place. For example, from the mid-1990s Russia and China were the lead suppliers of children for intercountry adoption while at present The Philippines has become a significant supply nation. Recently a number of countries in Latin America have come on-stream as sending countries including El Salvador, Guatemala, Honduras and Brazil.

6.3.   Receiving countries

The US has been a longstanding receiving country that in recent decades has absorbed 10,000 children a year through intercountry adoption while approximately the same number is distributed annually throughout northern and western Europe. Some European countries, notably those in Scandinavia, have developed a reliance on this form of adoption. Sweden and Holland receive approximately 2000 children a year as does Germany while 600 are adopted in Denmark. In the UK, some 300 intercountry adoption applications are currently processed annually while perhaps a further 100 bypass formal procedures.[31]

The key factor that now determines the involvement of a receiving country in intercountry adoption is the lack of indigenous children available to infertile couples. In all countries this is largely due to a sharp reduction in consensually relinquished children. In some countries this position is exacerbated by the non-availability of children through the public care system following judicial removal of parental rights. In Sweden and Denmark, for example, the non-availability of children through either consensual or compulsory means has led to a total reliance on intercountry adoption. Other countries, such as Ireland, are heavily though not exclusively dependent upon intercountry adoption for the same reasons. The US and more recently the UK have increased their capacity to make children available from their public care systems but still need to resort to intercountry

---

[30] In 1993 Britain and Romania signed a bilateral agreement which had the effect of practically ending the sending of Romanian children to the UK.

[31] Statistics cited in Triseliotis, J., Shireman, J. and Hundleby, M., *Adoption Theory, Policy and Practice*, Cassell, London, 1997 at p. 183.

adoption to meet demand. The considerable difference between the US and the UK as receiving nations is primarily due to independent and third-party adoption placements being permitted by the former but prohibited by the latter. Independent and third party adoptions are also allowed in countries such as Sweden, Germany, the Netherlands and France. The UK, in common with Norway and Finland, restricts adoptions to those arranged by approved agencies.

6.4.   Some issues in contemporary practice

A slow developmental process has seen the 1993 Hague Convention evolve from the work of The Hague Conference on Private International Law that commenced with The Hague Convention on Jurisdiction, Applicable Law and Recognition of Decrees Relating to Adoption 1965. It now provides a satisfactory framework for regulating intercountry adoption practice. Most of the serious issues that continue to threaten standards in modern practice arise from the fact that The Hague Convention does not apply to many countries currently participating in intercountry adoption.

6.4.1.   THE AVAILABILITY OF CHILDREN

The Hague Convention puts in place safeguards for ensuring that proper consents are provided in respect of children made available for intercountry adoption: every effort must be made to trace birth parents and to obtain their consent, including that of a birth father.[32] This allows for checks to be made as to a child's status as orphaned, abandoned, consensually relinquished or in respect of whom parental rights have been judicially terminated. It enables counselling services to be offered to birth parents to ensure that consents are informed and freely given; such services are not available in some sending countries such as Brazil. It requires professional medical checks and a proper standard of health and social care to be provided following parental relinquishment; as is the case in countries such as Thailand. It also requires that a child is only made available after a professional assessment has concluded that other preferred options are not feasible and that intercountry adoption is compatible with that child's welfare interests.

However, the fact remains that not all sending countries are Convention compliant and there is research evidence to show that many overseas adoptions involve children who are neither orphaned nor abandoned. In many cases the parental consent requirement is avoided by the claim that the parent/s cannot be found and there is little an authority in a receiving country can then do to satisfy itself that

---

[32] Subject to situations where the laws of a country such as Russia, prohibits the tracing of birth parents after a local adoption. See, *Re H; Re G (Adoption: Consultation of Unmarried Fathers)* [2001] 1 FLR 646.

every reasonable effort has been made to locate such a parent.[33] In other cases, where the consent of a 'guardian' rather than a parent is acceptable, the authorities in some sending countries offer the consent of an institution. Both types of response, not untypical of practice in countries such as Russia and Brazil, would breach the consent requirements of the Hague Convention.

6.4.2.   MATCHING CHILDREN WITH ADOPTERS

Matching the needs of a particular child with the attributes of available adopters is the key component to a successful adoption. This is unsatisfactory in intercountry adoptions and is often entirely missing in other overseas adoptions. In the UK and other receiving countries the careful assessment processes employed by adoption agencies will be applied in relation to intercountry adoption applicants. The assessment of a child's particular needs, however, and the matching process undertaken in the light of those needs, is left entirely to authorities in the sending country; excepting any broad conditions attached to the adopters approval by the authorities of the sending country. Whether or not Convention compliant, most sending countries have relatively weak social and health care infrastructures and are simply unable to dedicate the resources necessary to provide a matching service equivalent to that typically employed by UK Adoption Panels.

6.4.3.   COMMERCIALLY DRIVEN INDEPENDENT AGENCIES

Extreme poverty is most often the root cause of parents in third world countries making their children available for adoption. In that context the involvement of for-profit agencies in arranging adoption placements with couples from western societies carries the risk that this will invalidate the Convention requirement that consents be fully informed and be given free from either duress or financial inducement. Independent commercially driven agencies, often based in the US,[34] are frequently involved in facilitating the adoption placements of children from countries such as Brazil, elsewhere in South America and Russia. When the resulting adoption applications come before the courts, for example in the UK,[35] the standards of practice of such agencies are sometimes found to be in breach of Convention requirements. Overseas adoptions bypass the Convention and for

---

[33] See, for example, 'All God's Children, International'.

[34] See, for example, *Flintshire County Council v K* [2001] 2 FLR 476, the 'internet twins' case.

[35] See, for example, *Re M (Adoption: International Adoption Trade)* [2003] EWHC 219 (Fam), [2003] 1 FLR 1111 which concerned a white British couple who had adopted a baby from a black American couple after paying approximately £17,500 to an American adoption agency. The home study reports, prepared by a British social worker, were criticised by the court as "deeply flawed and inadequate documents" and it also referred to "the evil and exploitive trade" of buying and selling babies.

that reason attract the involvement of independent commercially driven agencies. It is important that the standards of protection, afforded to all parties under the Convention, are also applied to overseas adoptions.

6.4.4. FINANCIAL IMPROPRIETY BY INTERMEDIARIES

The profit motive is not confined to the involvement of independent commercial agencies. Anecdotal evidence, drawn from the experience of many adopters dealing with officials in sending countries, testifies to the considerable amount in fees that frequently have to be paid to a range of other intermediaries. Lawyers, doctors, officials in orphanages and/or in emigration, for example, may or may not require payment. For a particular intercountry adoption, as well as for practice in a sending country, to avoid any suggestion of complicit involvement in 'trafficking' it is clearly important that all costs are predictable and reasonable.

6.4.5. THE EFFECT OF INTERCOUNTRY ADOPTION

The most immediate effect of such an adoption is the removal of a child from their family, community and culture of origin. Despite the best intentions of all concerned, perhaps not always genuinely shared by the adopters and towards which the child concerned may be at least ambivalent, it often proves difficult to keep alive the links between the child and his or her cultural heritage. The practice whereby some sending countries, for example Korea, facilitate the setting up of culture-specific support groups for adoptees within receiving countries and also on a transnational basis, may well be an appropriate initiative for all participant countries to develop.

Some nations have traditionally treated intercountry adoption with suspicion on the grounds that it may be used to circumvent immigration rules and procedures; a suspicion that has not entirely been laid to rest. Currently, the UK and other countries such as the US and Sweden grant the adopted child residency status but not citizenship while others such as New Zealand grant citizenship. These inconsistencies need to be replaced by a standardised rule under the aegis of The Hague Convention.

6.4.6. POST-ADOPTION SUPPORT SERVICES

Most intercountry adoptions unfold satisfactorily for child and adopters. Some, however, do not. A number of children transferred to receiving countries are subsequently admitted to care, a few are severely abused and some even die at the hands of couples who had embarked on intercountry adoption with the best of intentions. The attraction that some find in this route to adoption, its essentially private nature carrying a promise of minimum involvement with public services, is arguably an area of weakness that leaves both child and adopter unnecessarily exposed to risk. Experience shows that intercountry adoptions are prone to their own specific type of vulnerability in addition to the risks inherent in all adoptions. The current practice in countries such as Russia to require annual post-adoption reports from receiving countries for three years is clearly sensible. It is important that all intercountry and overseas adoptions are subject to a structured, two-year minimum programme of monitoring and specialist support services and an optional ongoing programme thereafter.

6.4.7.   ACCESS TO IDENTIFYING INFORMATION

The fact that laws recognising rights and facilitating access to information exist in some receiving countries, such as the UK, is of no advantage in the context of intercountry adoption if they don't exist in the sending country.

Sending countries have established different practices in relation to making information available to the parties concerned in intercountry/overseas adoptions. In some the characteristics of 'closed' adoption, as traditionally practiced in western nations, are very much in evidence. Frequently, all arrangements are managed by designated intermediaries and in some countries, for example Thailand and India, no contact pre or post adoption is permitted between the parties. Other countries, such as Bulgaria, destroy birth records after an adoption order is made. The Hague Convention requirement, that birth and family of origin information is maintained by the authorities in sending countries, should clearly prevail in all overseas adoptions and rights of access to such information should be as outlined in the legislative provisions relating to in-country adoptions of the receiving country.

7.   CONCLUSION

Intercountry adoption is a rapid growth phenomenon that has developed to the point where it now involves some 50 countries and 30,000 children on an annual basis. It is clearly of the utmost importance that the related framework of law, policy and practice also evolves to safeguard the welfare interests of so many children. There is some way to go before we can be confident that this framework is compliant with Article 1 of the Hague Convention and provides "safeguards to ensure that intercountry adoptions take place in the best interests of the child and with respect for his or her fundamental rights as recognised in international law".

The politics of adoption are perhaps most apparent when viewed in an intercountry context. There is, for example, some evidence that a political dimension exists in the flow of children between countries. Also, some of the provisions of the Hague Convention seem to highlight the significance of domestic political choices. In particular, Article 4(b) states that intercountry adoption may be

considered as an alternative means of providing for a child's care but only after all other options for retaining the child within his or her country of origin
have been exhausted. This principle clearly places an obligation on both potential
sending and receiving countries to invest in the resource provision necessary to
retain a child within his or her country of origin as a first option. The principle
would also seem equally applicable to domestic child care adoptions. There are
real differences between countries, such as the UK and Sweden, in this regard.
The difference is ultimately attributable to a very different political choice made
on the issue as to whether government resources should be invested in providing
safe care for children within their families of origin or in providing alternative
permanency arrangements through non-consensual adoption.

The Hague Convention, as important as it undoubtedly is, provides only a
framework of minimum standards for regulating intercountry adoption. Even if
fully implemented by all countries engaged in intercountry adoption it would
still fall short of ensuring that optimal standards prevail in all instances for all
the children concerned. Currently, however, the main problem with the Hague
Convention is that it does not govern the practice of all relevant countries. This
in itself presents a significant political challenge if adoption is to safeguard and
promote the welfare interests of all children who enter the process.

Chapter 10

INTRACULTURE ADOPTION

1.   INTRODUCTION

Some modern western nations include within their borders distinct indigenous cultural groups, each established over many centuries and maintained in accordance with traditional customs that have survived relatively intact into the 21st century. This is the case, for example, with indigenous people in Australia, New Zealand, Africa, and North and South America. These indigenous cultural groups are, to a varying degree, coherent entities founded on rules and traditions governing relations within and between families and applying to the functioning of their social system as a whole. They co-exist alongside and in an uneasy relationship with the prevailing western culture; sharing time, territory and the necessities of life but often very little in the way of values, knowledge and social infrastructure.

The differences between indigenous and non-indigenous cultures are readily apparent in their respective sets of laws and customs governing the family. In particular the practice of adoption, which offers a fragmentary but revealing insight into the life of any culture, indicates the nature of differences in the value systems that now separate modern western society from its indigenous counterpart. This can be seen in the legal functions of adoption which in indigenous cultures are not quite the same as those of modern western societies. However the latter—having developed their present relatively recent, sophisticated, highly regulated and expensive models of adoption—are steadily assuming some of the characteristics of customary adoption. There is every reason to believe that this trend towards convergence will continue.

Kerry O'Halloran (ed.), The Politics of Adoption, 291–316.
© 2006 *Springer. Printed in The Netherlands.*

Customary adoption now exists alongside the statutory laws of adoption and there are frequent tensions between the two systems. To some extent the principles of international law, particularly the UN Convention on the Rights of the Child and the Declaration of Indigenous Peoples 1993, can offer a bridge when issues arise. The Preamble to the former, for example, includes a reference to "the importance of the traditions and cultural values of each people for the protection and harmonious development of the child".[1] Article 4 of the latter emphasises the right of indigenous peoples to maintain and strengthen their political, economic, social and cultural characteristics as well as their legal systems while Article 6 states that:

> Indigenous peoples have the collective and individual right to be protected against ethnocide and cultural genocide, including the prevention and redress for:
>
> (a) removal of indigenous children from their families and communities under any pretext.

As these principles suggest, the differences between the two systems have in the past caused real difficulties for indigenous people and to some extent will continue to do so in the future. However, they also present a challenge to the development of adoption in western societies.

This chapter examines the distinctive characteristics of customary adoption and its links with the statutory process. Its purpose is to identify the differences between the legal functions of both systems and to consider their significance in terms of law, policy and practice. It does so by examining in turn the experience of adoption among the Indigenous People of Australia, the Maori of New Zealand and the Inuit of Canada.

2.   AUSTRALIA: THE INDIGENOUS OR ABORIGINAL PEOPLE

2.1.   Background

The 'Aboriginal people of Australia' is an umbrella term that refers to a race that existed in Australia for at least 40,000 years before its discovery in 1788 by white Caucasians. At the time of its 'discovery' Australia was *terra nullius* according to its 'discoverers', meaning that it was either uninhabited or occupied only by nomadic people without any organised social systems. It was therefore available to be taken into the possession of the Crown.[2] The 'Aboriginal people

---

[1]   See, also, Articles 5, 20 (particularly 20.3) and 30.

[2]   In the 18th century, Captain Cook considered he was entitled to take possession of the continent and all its creatures and resources in the name of the British Crown. The full ownership of the

of Australia', now greatly eroded in number and cultural cohesion, is comprised of approximately 500 distinct communities from quite diverse cultural groups.

2.1.1. DEFINITIONAL MATTERS

The working definition[3] of an 'Aboriginal person' is one who:

(a) is either:
  (i) an Aboriginal person, meaning a person of the Aboriginal race of Australia; or
  (ii) a Torres Strait Islander, meaning a descendant of an indigenous inhabitant of the Torres Strait Islands;
  and
(b) identifies as an Aboriginal person or a Torres Strait Islander; and
(c) is recognised or accepted by an Aboriginal or Torres Strait Island community as a member of that community.

In particular a distinction can be made between the Torres Strait Island community and all other Aboriginal people.[4] In general terms, the population of the Torres Strait Islands differs from the Aboriginal population as a whole by having a more coherent community and culture, perhaps partially due to the extent to which they have subscribed to Christian principles while retaining traditional customs. According to the 1996 Census, Australia's Aboriginal and Torres Strait Islander population was then estimated to be 386,049, of which about 11% of were of Torres Strait Islander origin, representing 2.1% of the total Australian population.

2.2. Adoption as an imposed system

There are not many national examples of non-consensual[5] adoption being imposed as a matter of state policy upon the membership of an entire minority culture. This occurred in Australia where an invidious state policy, resulting in the trauma now referred to as the 'stolen generation', was applied by statute law to the Aboriginal people in the early years of the 20th century.

---

continent remained vested in Great Britain until transferred to the government of Australia when the latter acquired Dominion status.

[3] See, Department of Aboriginal Affairs, 1981. 'Aboriginal' or 'Indigenous' incorporates three distinct elements: descent, self-identification and community acceptance.

[4] Prior to 1971, Torres Strait Islanders were often classified as Polynesian or Pacific Islanders in official counts. The Commonwealth working definition was extended to include Torres Strait Islanders in 1972 but it was not until the 1996 Census that individuals could identify as both Aboriginal and Torres Strait Islander.

[5] There can be little doubt that very few Indigenous natural parents, even if some did sign certain papers, gave what would now be recognised as a full and informed consent.

2.2.1.   THE POLICY

This government programme was designed to accelerate racial assimilation by requiring the placement of all (except very dark skinned) Aboriginal children with non-Aboriginal families; no attempt was made to place children with Aboriginal families. It was explicitly intended that the children placed would lose their Aboriginal identity, assume the culture of their adopters and 'pass as white'. As has been explained[6]:

> This was part of a long-term government plan to assimilate Indigenous people into the dominant white community by removing the children from their families at as young an age as possible, preferably at birth, cutting them off from their own place, language and customs and thereby somehow bleaching aboriginality from Australian society."

It was a deliberate attempt to use adoption to engineer the long-term absorption of one racial group by another. Such a policy was prohibited by the International Convention on the Prevention and Punishment of the Crime of Genocide 1948 which includes within its definition of genocide "the forceful transferring of children of a group to another group.[7]

2.2.2.   THE LAW AND PRACTICE

The programme began in the Northern Territories with the Aboriginals Ordinance 1918 and continued until the legislative power to remove Aboriginal children was terminated in 1969; though the practice continued for some time on an informal basis. It was enforced by the Aborigines Protection Board which was established in every state and territory. In New South Wales, for example, the Board was empowered by the Aborigines Protection Act 1909 at first only to remove children who were neglected but by 1919 additional powers enabled the Board to pursue a policy of assimilation. As described by Behrendt[8]:

> The colour of a child's skin determined how the state would determine that child's future (highlighting the racist aspects of this policy). Fairer-skinned Indigenous children were more likely to be adopted into white families. Darker-skinned children were more likely to be institutionalised or sent out to work. Fairer-skinned children also tended to be removed at younger ages than darker-skinned children.

This practice was repeated across Australia.

---

[6] See, Bird, C., *The Stolen Children; Their Stories*, Random House, Australia, 1998, at p. 1.
[7] This Convention was ratified by Australia in 1951.
[8] See, Behrendt, L., *Achieving Social Justice*, the Federation Press, Sydney, 2003 at p. 68.

2.2.3. THE OUTCOMES

The enforced removal of countless children, from Aboriginal parents by the Child Welfare Department and their subsequent placement with approved white Caucasian foster parents or into institutional care was a disaster for the many thousands of Aboriginal families and the communities involved. It was probably also very stressful for the adopters whose care and dedication has never been in question. The very high incidence of placement breakdown in this context, when the children reached adolescence, testifies to the level of stress generated by transracial placements resulting from misguided motivation.[9]

As has since become evident from the close statistical correlation between placements and subsequent rates of suicide, imprisonment etc, the programme was particularly disastrous for the children concerned. The severance of a generation of children from their community and cultural roots, coupled with their indoctrination into non-Aboriginal cultural norms, caused serious dislocation to the continuance of traditional Aboriginal values and community cohesion.

2.2.4. THE BRINGING THEM HOME REPORT

An objective account of this policy and its long-term effects in terms of the incidences of suicide, mental illness and family breakdown etc are documented in the *Bringing Them Home* report by the Human Rights and Equal Opportunity Commission.[10] The government's response to the report was dismissive: refuting the claim that an entire generation were affected; and consigning the entire matter to history with the assertion that the policy had to be judged in accordance with the value context that prevailed at that time.[11] However, this policy of forcibly removing children from their Aboriginal parents has, in recent years, resulted in court cases[12] where applicants have claimed damages for the trauma they suffered.

---

[9]   See, for example, the report of the South Australian Aboriginal Child Care Agency which estimated that 95% of all ACCA adoption cases broke down and that:

> " ...this is reflected throughout the country ...65% of these breakdowns occurred in the adopted child's teenage years when their adoptive parents were unable to cope with their problems of alcohol abuse, offending behaviour, drug abuse, depression, self-destructive behaviour, emotional stress and identity crisis".

As cited in Marshall and McDonald, *op cit* at p. 155.

[10]   See, the Human Rights and Equal Opportunity Commission, *Bringing Them Home: A Guide to the Findings and Recommendations of the National Inquiry into the Separation of Aboriginal and Torres Strait Islander Children from their Families*, Australian Government Publishing Service, 1997 (http://www.austlii.edu.au/au/special/rsjlibrary/hreoc/stolen/). The factual basis of this report was memorably illustrated in the film *The Rabbit Proof Fence*.

[11]   See, the Federal Government submission to the Senate Legal and Constitutional References Committee on the *Inquiry into the Stolen Generation*, 1997.

[12]   See, for example, *Kruger v Commonwealth* (1997) 190 CLR 1 and *Cubillo v Commonwealth* (2000) 174 ALR 97.

2.3.   Contemporary adoption law and the Aboriginal People

For many Aboriginal communities the concept of adoption is itself rejected.[13] Such communities and Aboriginal agencies hold the view that children are 'free spirits' and cannot be 'owned' by anyone. For government legislators a legacy of 'the stolen generation' debacle is that it has become taboo to consider extending the statutory adoption process equally to aboriginal children; the earlier misguided political use of mandatory adoption for social engineering purposes negates the political possibility of now utilising it as a public service. Instead, although many Aboriginal children require permanent alternative care[14] they are now mainly accommodated in foster care arrangements, very few are adopted within the statutory process. For some Aboriginal children, alternative permanent care arrangements continue to be provided through the practice of customary adoption.

2.3.1.   THE STATUTORY ADOPTION FRAMEWORK AND THE ABORIGINAL PEOPLE

The different legislatures of Australia in their respective laws now pointedly recognise the place that customary adoption holds within Aboriginal culture. The level of recognition provided includes the following[15]:

- **New South Wales**

The New South Wales Adoption Act 1965, which allows Aboriginal children to be adopted by Aboriginal couples living in customary marriage, otherwise makes no specific provision for the adoptive placement of Aboriginal children.

- **Victoria**

The Victorian Adoption Act 1984 recognises Aboriginal rights to self-management and self-determination. It states that: in consensual adoption, a birth

---

[13] See, Queensland Government, *The Adoption Legislation Review: Public Consultation*, Department of Families, 2003 which notes that:

> "A key theme in the consultation forums with Aboriginal and Torres Strait Islander peoples throughout the State was that adoption, as conceived in the Adoption of Children Act 1964, is not a culturally appropriate care option for Aboriginal and Torres Strait Islander children" at p. 3.

[14] Aboriginal children are over represented in the public child care system. In June 1998, for example, 14.2 Aboriginal children per 1,000 aged between 0–17 years were in care; this was 5 times the rate for other children.

[15] See, further, the Law Commission, *Adoption and its Alternatives: A Different Approach and a New Framework*, Wellington, 2000 at paras H7–H18. Also, see, Ban, P., 'Slow Progress: The Legal Recognition of Torres Strait Islander Customary Adoption Practice', 4(7) *Indigenous Law Bulletin* 11 (1997).

parent has the right to declare a wish that their child be adopted within the Aboriginal community; in a non-consensual adoption, provisions approximating those of the Aboriginal and Torres Strait Islander Child Placement Principle must be applied. It also makes an adoption order conditional upon counselling by an Aboriginal agency being provided or offered and refused.

- **South Australia**

The Adoption Act 1988 makes an adoption order in respect of an Aboriginal child conditional upon there being no preferable order available to the court. It states a presumption that adoption within the child's Aboriginal community is in the child's best interests and where this is not possible provides a hierarchy of preferred placements. It permits a placement outside the Aboriginal community only in exceptional circumstances and when appropriate arrangements have been made to safeguard the child's Aboriginal identity.

- **Australian Capital Territory**

The Australian Capital Territory Adoption Act 1993 makes an adoption order conditional upon the court being satisfied that consideration has been given to the preference for Aboriginal adopters and to the importance of preserving contact between the child and the birth parents.

- **Northern Territory**

The Adoption of Children Act 1995 allows adoption by couples living in an Aboriginal customary marriage for more than two years. It makes an adoption order conditional upon the court first being satisfied that every effort has been made to place the child within his or her extended family or with other suitable Aboriginal persons. Failing that, placement should be in geographical proximity to the child's birth family and should be in keeping with parental wishes in relation to maintaining contact and cultural identity.

2.3.1(i). THE CHILD PLACEMENT PRINCIPLE

In broad terms, statutory child care in an Aboriginal context[16] is now underpinned by a fundamental principle that governs the relationship between the state and the family on such matters. The Aboriginal and Torres Strait Islander Child Placement Principle, formulated at the time of the Human Rights and Equal Opportunity Commission inquiry into the 'stolen generation' controversy, was a response to the associated public concern regarding the interventionist policies of an earlier era. It was endorsed in the Council of Social Welfare Ministers' National Minimum Principles in Adoption 1993 and by 1997 all states and territories had confirmed

---

[16] By the late 1970s, Aboriginal and Islander Child Care Agencies were established throughout most of Australia to control child care services for Aboriginal people.

their adherence to it.[17] This Principle states that when an Aboriginal child needs an alternative to parental care then the preferred placement is, in the following order of priority:

- within the child's extended family;
- within the child's Aboriginal community; and, failing that
- with other Aboriginal people.

The resulting practice is that the local Aboriginal community, organisations, and Aboriginal professionals in adoption agencies are now engaged when the issue of non-parental care for an Aboriginal child arises. The net effect is that a 'closed' form of culture specific adoption for the Aboriginal and Torres Strait Islander communities is now largely in place throughout Australia. However, while the Principle is informing practice everywhere in Australia it is most influential where given effect by legislation.[18]

2.3.1(ii). ABORIGINAL PLACEMENT

In Queensland's recent adoption law review[19] the Aboriginal respondents to the government's discussion document acknowledged that circumstances could arise requiring the permanent placement of an Aboriginal child in accordance with the provisions of the statutory adoption process. In such circumstances it suggested that the assessment of Aboriginal prospective adopters should be undertaken by or with Aboriginal assessors and should address matters such as[20]:

- the prospective adoptive parents' links with the particular child's community and where this has not been established, the parents' links with another Aboriginal or Torres Strait Islander community; and
- prospective adoptive parents' capacity to assist a child develop or maintain his or her cultural identity.

Thereafter, during the course of the placement, the continued involvement of representatives from the relevant Aboriginal community and agencies would ensure that the child's links with his or her culture are maintained.

---

[17] The Principle has received specific legislative endorsement in the Australian Capital Territory, South Australia and in Victoria. Note the resonance with US law: the Indian Child Welfare Act 1978 limits placement to the child's family, members of the tribe or other Native American families.

[18] The Report of the New South Wales Law Reform Commission (1997) examined the effectiveness of the Principle in placing Aboriginal children with Aboriginal people for foster care and adoption in all states and territories. It concluded that the Principle most strongly influences practice where it is incorporated into statute law.

[19] See, Queensland Government, *The Report: Public Consultation on the Review of the Adoption of Children Act 1964*, Department of Families, 2003.

[20] *Ibid*, at pp. 19–20.

2.3.1(iii). NON-ABORIGINAL PLACEMENT

In the above adoption law review the Aboriginal respondents accepted that there may be occasions when an Aboriginal child will have to be placed for adoption with a non-Aboriginal family. In such circumstances it was suggested that an Aboriginal counselling service should be offered to the birth parent/s before and after placement. It was further suggested that Aboriginal agencies should be required to approve any such placement and that an adoption plan should be drawn up to protect the cultural identity of the child and maintain links with his or her community of origin. This plan should include:

- a genealogical chart of the child's tribes/clans (mother and father); and
- all relevant cultural information such as kin names, clan groups, dreamings and stories.[21]

2.3.2. CUSTOMARY ADOPTION

The Aboriginal People view child rearing as a communal responsibility with no particular rights or duties reserved to birth parents. There is thus no natural cultural context for the practice of adoption. Customary adoption involves the placement of a child within the extended family group; only in exceptional circumstances is the child placed with 'strangers' or non-relatives. The birth parents maintain ongoing contact with their child and with the adopters throughout the placement. All information relating to the adoption is openly shared among the parties and among the extended family circle. This form of adoption tends to be bloodline specific and serves to strengthen and differentiate the kinship structures of tribal groups.

2.3.2(i). THE TORRES STRAIT ISLAND COMMUNITY

The Torres Strait Islanders have developed a somewhat different variation of customary adoption which resembles the foster care practice of western nations. The placement is often short-term and made with another related family, it may or may not extend for the duration of childhood and the child may return intermittently to the birth parents.

This practice, known as 'Kupai Omasker', has been explained in the *Bringing Them Home* report as a permanent transfer of parenting responsibilities which "serves to entrench reciprocal obligations within families thereby contributing to social stability".[22] It bears a strong similarity to some forms of adoption traditionally practiced in countries with homogenous cultures such as Ireland (see, further, Chap. 1). It is usually confined to kinship (i.e.determined by blood-link)

---

[21] *Ibid*, at p. 17.
[22] See, the Human Rights and Equal Opportunity Commission, *Bringing Them Home, op cit.*

but in recent years has extended to include relatives by marriage and even close family friends. It lies outside the legislative framework, is a form of customary adoption and is not recognised in Australian law.

The difference between adoption as practiced by Torres Strait Islanders and statutory adoption as practiced elsewhere in Australia is explained in the report by the New South Wales Law Reform Commission[23]:

> Adoption in Torres Strait Islander communities involves the permanent transfer of parental rights to adoptive parents. Further, there is a reluctance to tell children of their adoptive status. In contrast to Australian adoption law, however, adoption is almost always within the same blood lines, with members of the extended family or otherwise with close friends. Adoptive parents may be single or married, and may already have children of their own. Torres Strait Islander adoption also differs from Australian adoption in that, while there is a permanent transfer of rights, the adoption is characterized by notions of reciprocity and obligation.

The difference between customary adoption as practiced by Aboriginal People and by Torres Strait Islanders has been summarised by Marshall and McDonald[24] as follows:

> Customary adoption is accepted within Torres Strait Islander communities, and often arranged within families to preserve the blood line and family heritage and customs. It is similar to western adoption practice in its permanency but is almost always within the extended family. Customary adoption is not usually arranged by them outside their own culture. For Aboriginal peoples, however, adoption is a foreign and altogether alien concept. It would not have been conceived of in a functioning Aboriginal community.

By and large, Aboriginal communities are generally no longer independent and self-sustaining entities. The contemporary partial subjection of customary practice to the statutory adoption process is only one small part of the cultural concessions made by a race that had managed its own affairs for tens of thousands of years before the arrival of white Caucasians.

3.   NEW ZEALAND: THE MAORI

3.1.   Background

The Maori are the indigenous people of New Zealand. When Europeans first arrived they found a fully established society, developed over a thousand years, in possession of the islands. Initially, the 'newly discovered' New Zealand territory

---

[23]   See, New South Wales Law Reform Commission, *Research Report 81*, (1997) at chapter 9.
[24]   See, Marshall and McDonald, *op cit* at p. 148.

was administered by the colonial authorities in the Australian Colony of New South Wales. From the late 18th century, the Maori experienced the impact of successive but transient groups of Europeans who brought different kinds of influences. Not until the late 1830s did the islands become more permanently settled by non-indigenous people.

3.1.1. THE TREATY OF WAITANGI

This Treaty was the mechanism by which the British asserted sovereignty over New Zealand. It was signed on 6th February 1840 by Captain Hobson, the Lieutenant-Governor, and by many of the Maori chiefs.[25] The Treaty and the introduction of British rule was followed by settlers forcefully acquiring Maori land resulting in armed conflict especially in the 1860s, leading to generations of grievances, agitation, negotiations, inquiries and some settlements, and ultimately to the Treaty of Waitangi Act 1975 which established the Waitangi Tribunal. The Tribunal entertains claims by Maori that they have been prejudicially affected by conduct on the part of the Crown which was inconsistent with the principles of the Waitangi Treaty.

The Treaty of Waitangi is the founding constitutional document in New Zealand with its status as a compact between the Crown and Maori. It promised that:

- Maori cultural values would be respected and given effect (Article 11); and
- Maori would participate fully in the new society of New Zealand and its institutions (Article 11 reinforced by the Preamble to the Treaty).

The Treaty and the Constitution are best viewed as a composite set of basic principles that direct how all New Zealanders, Maori and non-Maori, are to be governed. However, as has been said: "the failure to acknowledge Maori status as tangata whenua, once the Treaty of Waitangi was signed is perhaps at the root of subsequent conflict and misunderstandings".[26]

3.1.2. THE MAORI POPULATION

The Maori currently total some 523,000 persons constituting approximately 15% of the population of New Zealand and are expected to represent nearly 20% of the population by the year 2031. The median age for Maori is around 22 years and 55% of the population is under 25 years compared with only 34.6% of non-Maori. More than half of all Maori live in the northern part of North Island,

---

[25] A retranslation of the Maori text of the whole Treaty can be found in the judgment of Cooke P in *New Zealand Maori Council v Attorney General* [1987] 1 NZLR 641, 662–3.
[26] See, Law Commission, Report 53, *Justice—the Experience of Maori Women*, Wellington, 1999; 'tangata whenua' literally means 'people of the land'.

mostly around Auckland (46%). In general, they have lower incomes and larger households than non-Maori and are more likely to be living in one-parent households. Relative to the non-Maori, they are disadvantaged by age, geographical distribution, by low standards of education and skills and by levels of unemployment.[27]

As a consequence of their status as Treaty signatories, this indigenous group has been able to preserve its cultural identity and coherence while, in recent years, it has exercised considerable influence over government policy in relation to issues affecting Maori interests.

3.1.3. THE MAORI CULTURE

The indigenous people of New Zealand have a well developed communal culture. The critical organisational construct is the tribe, an extended kinship organisation comprising sub-tribes and extended family groups. The tribal identity was and is the iwi. The tribal institutions of whanua (extended family or kin group), hapu (sub-tribe), hui (meeting of the iwi) and marae (ceremonial centre) remain key features of contemporary Maori culture. Maori belong to diverse communities: some identify with a particular iwi, hapu and whanau irrespective of where they reside; others identify with their tribal connections but do not know their ancestry or whakapapa; while others prefer to identify simply as Maori.

3.1.4. CUSTOMARY ADOPTION OR WHANGAI

For many centuries the Maori have had a practice known as whangai or atawhai[28] or customary adoption whereby a child is simply given to relatives for them to raise.

Whangai has few of the legal characteristics of adoption in western societies, is not recognised within the statutory adoption framework of New Zealand but is nonetheless still in use by the Maori.

Generally, a whangai placement was practiced within a hapu or iwi as a means of strengthening relations and had the advantage of ensuring that land rights were consolidated within the tribe; though placements were sometimes made with relatives by marriage. Because the severing of blood-ties was regarded as a betrayal of origins, a child from outside the whanau, hapu and iwi would seldom be adopted. Adoption by 'strangers', the foundation stone of practice in western societies, has been deliberately avoided in Maori culture.

---

[27] See, Statistics of New Zealand, *Census of Population and Dwellings*, Wellington, 1996.

[28] See, for example, Durie-Hall, D., and Metge, Dame J., 'Kua Tutu Te Puehu, Kia Mau Maori Aspirations and Family Law' in Henaghan, M., and Atkin W. (eds.) *Family Law Policy in New Zealand*, Oxford University Press, Oxford, 1992, pp. 54–82.

3.2. Legislative history

Initially, placements for the purpose of adoption were made informally, without recourse to law, by both Maori and non-Maori. Adoption in New Zealand, as a formal statutory process, commenced with the Adoption of Children Act 1895.

3.2.1. THE ADOPTION OF CHILDREN ACT 1895

This legislation introduced a process whereby any person in New Zealand could apply for an adoption order. The Maori were not required to use this statutory proceeding and did not do so, preferring instead to rely on whangai placements which were judicially recognised at the turn of the 19th century[29]:

> The right of the Maori to adopt according to his own custom is not interfered with by giving him a further right to adopt in the form and under the conditions provided by the Act.

However, the Maori approach to the statutory adoption process changed somewhat with the introduction of the Native Land Claims Adjustment and Laws Amendment Act in 1901. This directed that where Maori land disputes involved the claims of an adopted person then that person would have to produce evidence of their adoption in the form of a recorded entry in the register of the Native Land Court. Whangai placements, often made to secure or consolidate title to land, frequently led to court disputes. Adoption legislation provided a means for registering an adoption and gave the Maori an incentive to seek formal recognition of a whangai placement in case of a later necessity to produce such evidence in any land dispute proceedings.

3.2.2. THE NATIVE LAND ACT 1909

Maori compliance with the statutory adoption process was later enforced by the 1909 Act which sought to prohibit the use of whangai. The policy driving this legislation was quite explicit[30]:

> By this Bill, adoption by Native custom is abolished, and adoption by order of the Native Land Court is substituted.

Adoption orders were to be made by the Native Land Court in respect of Maori children while the same orders were made in Magistrates' courts (now the District court or the Family court) in respect of non-Maori children. The proceedings, however, were different: in the Native Land Court the hearing took place in open

---

[29] See, *Hineiti Rirerire Arani v Public Trustee* (1919) NZPCCI, *per* Phillimore LJ.

[30] Sir John Salmond's notes on the Bill as cited in the Law Commission report, *op cit*, at para 185.

court and the proceedings were published; in the Magistrates' court the hearing was in camera and the proceedings were not published. Since 1962 all statutory adoption proceedings, in respect of Maori and non-Maori children, have been held in Magistrates' courts. This policy was revised in 1927, when recognition was given to customary adoptions made before 1902, but only to be reinstated in 1931. From 1932 onwards a child subject to a whangai placement was denied recognition in law as an adopted child; the politics of the 1909 Act prevailed to displace customary adoption by the statutory process.

3.2.3.   THE ADOPTION ACT 1955

The policy of proscribing customary adoptions was consolidated by the 1955 Act which continues to state the law in New Zealand. In the words of the Law Commission[31]:

> The present Adoption Act confirms that Maori customary adoptions made after the introduction of the Native Land Act 1909 have no legal effect beyond the recognition accorded to such placements by Te Ture Whenua Maori Act 1993.

This approach reflected the assimilationist policies of the period by largely ignoring the Maori culture and value system. Legislation such as the Marriage Act 1955, the Adoption Act 1955, the Guardianship Act 1968 and the Matrimonial Property Act 1976 all directly or indirectly ignored Maori values relating to the structure and constitution of the family.[32]

3.3.   Contemporary adoption law and the Maori

In New Zealand the current statutory framework for adoption is intended for use equally by Maori and non-Maori applicants, though guardianship has always been more acceptable to the former. Alongside this statutory process, quite separate and independent from it, the Maori practice of whangai or customary adoption continues to operate.

3.3.1.   THE STATUTORY ADOPTION FRAMEWORK AND THE MAORI

The statutory adoption process, provided by the Adoption Act 1955 and the Adult Information Act 1985, is supplemented by certain national obligations arising under international Conventions. It occurs within a statutory child care context governed by the Children Young Persons and Their Families Act 1989 which

---

[31] See, the Law Commission report, *op cit*, at para 190. See, also, *Whittaker v Maori Land Court* [1996] NZ FLR 163.

[32] See, Durie-Hall, D., and Metge, Dame J., 'Kua Tutu Te Puehu, Kia Mau Maori Aspirations and Family Law' *op cit* pp. 54 and 59.

incorporates the family group conference as a decision-making mechanism for determining appropriate care arrangements (decisions can be challenged by the Children Young Persons and Their Families Service, a statutory body, but this seldom occurs). This legal framework has allowed New Zealand to pioneer the most 'open' adoption practice in the western world.[33] There is every reason to believe that this development within the modern statutory process is directly linked to the lessons learned from exposure to the age old Maori practice of customary adoption.

3.3.1(i). MAORI PLACEMENT

The 1989 Act rests on the assumption that children are best raised within their own cultural context and with their own people. It allows tribal elders to take an active leadership role in family group discussions and requires professional workers to observe—or at least not to ignore—cultural preferences and custom.[34] In recent years judicial notice has been taken of the importance of the Maori cultural context when determining issues of placement. For example, in the course of hearing an appeal by a grandmother against a decision by the Family Court to refuse her custody of her granddaughter, the court held that[35]:

> The welfare of the child can never be considered in isolation. The cultural background of a child is significant and the special position of a child within a Maori whanau, importing as it does not only cultural concepts but also concepts which are spiritual and which relate to the ancestral relationships and position of the child, must be kept in the forefront of the mind of those persons charged with the obligation of making decisions as to the future of the child.

However, the court added:

> ... the child's interests will not be subordinated to the interests of any member of the family or whanau, nor will the interests of the child be subordinated to those of the whanau as a whole.

The placement of a Maori child with Maori prospective adopters is facilitated by a Maori community representative appointed under the Maori Community Development Act 1962.

---

[33] See, for example, Ryburn, M. who has described New Zealand as "leading western practice with respect to openness" (1994).

[34] See, Law Commission, Report 53, *Justice—the Experience of Maori Women, op cit*, at para 90. Also, see, Ernst, 'Whanau Knows Best: Kinship Care in New Zealand', in Hegar, R.L. and Scannapieco, M., *Kinship Foster Care: Policy, Practice and Research*, Oxford University Press, 1999.

[35] See, *B v Director-General of Social Welfare*, [1997] NZFLR 642, *per* Gallen J and Goddard J.

3.3.1(ii).   Non-Maori placement

Section 321 of the Children Young Persons and Their Families Act 1989 requires the court to have regard to the principle that, where practicable, the relationship between the child or young person and his or her family, whanau, hapu, iwi, family groups and community group must be maintained and strengthened.

3.3.2.   Legal effects of statutory adoption

The issue of an adoption order has the same legal effect regardless of race: the child assumes the name of the adoptive parents; he or she inherits from the estate of an intestate adopter; and all legal ties to the birth parents are abolished. Access to identifying information is controlled by the provisions of the Adult Information Act 1985.

3.3.3.   Whangai or customary adoption

Whangai is characterised by openness, placement within the family and whaka-papa (identity within the context of family and culture) and whanaungatanga (the centrality of relationships to the Maori way of life). It does not require any partic-ular formalities, is a matter of public knowledge and is made with the express or tacit approval of the whanau or hapu (family or community group). As has been explained[36]:

> Maori customary adoption does not involve secrecy... The child has two sets of parents and recognises his or her relationship to them both. The child is aware of its birth parents and other family members and usually maintains contact with them. Once a child is accepted in this way, the adopter and child will frequently regard each other as parent and child for all significant purposes, as will the other members of the whanau ... placements are not necessarily permanent and it is not uncommon for such a child to later return to the birth parents.

3.3.4.   Legal effects of whangai

Under s 3 of the Te Ture Whenua Maori Act 1993 a "whatangi" is a person adopted in accordance with Maori law (this incorporates custom, values, traditional be-haviour and philosophy).[37]

The blood link is important to Maori culture and legal relationships, such as whangai, are not allowed to terminate or hide blood relationships or obscure cultural identity.

---

[36]   See, Law Commission, *Adoption and its Alternatives: A Different Approach and a New Frame-work*, Wellington, 2000 at para 180.

[37]   See, *In re Tukua and Maketu C2B Block* (10th March 2000, 116 Otorohanga MB 81) Carter J for a determination of whangai status.

3.3.4(i). PARENTAL RIGHTS

In the Maori culture a child is not viewed as the possession of parents but rather as the taonga (treasure) of the whanau, hapu and iwi.[38] Maori customary adoption does not, therefore, subscribe to the proposition, central to statutory adoption law in western societies, that the adopted child is legally severed from his or her birth parents and thereafter is to be treated in law as though born to them 'in lawful wedlock'. As the Law Commission has pointed out[39]:

> The fundamental difference in the way which the law, on the one hand, and Maori on the other, regarded adoption was that the law's adoption policy focused on the relationships which were created and the perceived advantages for members of the new family. No attention was given to the relationship between child and birth parent which was destroyed and the impact upon the child.

3.3.4(ii). SUCCESSION RIGHTS

Maori customary law varies as to whether whangai children may inherit from their adopters. Some iwi allow a whangai child to inherit only if the child is a blood relative. Whangai children can only succeed under the will of their adopting parent or by court order in the case of intestacy. The Maori Land Court is able to make provision for a whangai child when distributing an estate under Te Ture Whenua Maori Act 1993 and may determine whether a person is to be recognised as the whangai of a deceased landowner. When it decides in favour of such recognition the Court may order that the whangai's entitlement should be the same as if he or she was the birth child of the deceased. Where it decides against then it may order that the whangai either has no such entitlement or is entitled to a lesser extent that would have been the case if the deceased had been their birth parent.

Interestingly, there is provision for a European whangai adopted by Maoris to inherit Maori land.

4. CANADA: THE INUIT

4.1. Background

The Inuit are the indigenous people of Nunavut, a newly created territory in Canada. The total population of Canada is now almost 39 million, including a

---

[38] See, Durie-Hall and Metge, 'Kua Tutu Te Puehu, Kia Mau, Maori Aspirations and Family Law' in Henaghen and Atkin (eds.) *Family Law Policy in New Zealand*, Oxford University Press, Auckland, 1992.

[39] See, Law Commission, Report 53, *Justice—the Experiences of Maori Women*, Wellington, 1999, at para 83 citing Griffith, K.C., *New Zealand Adoption History and Practice, Social and Legal 1840–1996*, at para 9.

number of different indigenous groups. Nunavut, a territory of some two million square kilometers occupying almost one-fifth of the land mass of Canada, has a population of a mere 26,745 of which 82% are Inuit living in 28 villages.[40] In 1867, the confederation process initiated under the British North American Act made "Indians and Lands reserved for Indians" a federal responsibility within the new Dominion of Canada. This process included treaties with the Aboriginal peoples and led to the Indian Act 1876[41] under which all Aboriginal people were made wards of the federal government.

In keeping with the experience of indigenous people in Canada and elsewhere, the history of the Inuit also records abuse suffered at the hands of the non-indigenous population.[42] Government policies of assimilation or integration were often strategically directed towards children. Currently, the Stolen Generations project is researching the intergenerational effects of removing children from their ancestral homes, families and communities originating from the residential school experiences and the eventual removals in subsequent generations by the child protection laws that followed.[43]

4.1.1.   RESIDENTIAL SCHOOLS, ADOPTION, AND THE ABORIGINAL PEOPLE OF CANADA

In Canada, the first residential school for Aboriginal children was established in 1620 and the last closed in 1986. Throughout the intervening centuries, the collaboration between government and church saw residential school provision gradually extending across Canada. As has been noted[44]:

> What distinguishes the residential schools for Aboriginal children is that they were part of a policy of assimilation that was sustained for many decades.

This policy was consolidated by the Indian Act 1876, as amended, which pro-vided authority for the removal of many thousands of Aboriginal children from their homes, communities and culture to residential educational institutions. Non-attendance at school justified committal to one of the 54 boarding schools and

---

[40] See, Census statistics for 2001: the population of Nunavut has increased by 8.1% since the last census in 1996; a growth rate which is twice the national average.

[41] An Act to amend and consolidate the laws respecting Indians, S.C. 1876, c 18; amended to make attendance compulsory.

[42] See, for example, the *Royal Commission on Aboriginal Peoples: Looking Forward, Looking Back*, Ottawa, 1996.

[43] See, *Stolen Generations*, a local Aboriginal non-profit group, which in 2002 began a project dealing with the adoption process affecting Aboriginal people across Canada. The project is being funded by the Aboriginal Healing Foundation and sponsored by the Ma Mawi WI Chi Itata Centre Inc.

[44] See, the Law Commission of Canada, *Restoring Dignity: Responding to Child Abuse in Canadian Institutions*, 2000, at p. 51.

20 industrial schools that constituted residential school provision for some 5,347 Aboriginal children by the mid-20th century.[45] This was accompanied by other government strategies similarly directed towards racial assimilation. In particular, the Stolen Generations project now addresses one of the most significant issues arising in the aftermath of residential schools, namely the policy and practice of the adoption of Aboriginal children outside their inherent cultural groups.

As noted in the report by the *Aboriginal Justice Inquiry*[46]:

> ... between 1971 and 1981 alone, over 3,400 Aboriginal children were shipped away to adoptive parents in other societies, and sometimes in other countries.

4.1.2.   NUNAVUT

Nunavut came into being on April 1, 1999, through the division of the Northwest Territories, as a result of two agreements: the Nunavut political accord, and the Nunavut land claims agreement. The first laid the foundation for the Nunavut Act 1999, the federal law that serves as Nunavut's constitution. The Inuit in Nunavut control their own legislative assembly through a form of self-government under which non-Inuit residents are also guaranteed the right to participate in elections for the Nunavut legislative assembly and for Nunavut's 26 municipal governments. Although concentrated in Nunavut, the Inuit are by no means confined to that territory but in fact are spread over large areas of northern Canada.

4.2.   Contemporary adoption law and the Inuit

There are three types of adoptions in Nunavut: customary, private, and departmental. Although these parallel systems are in place, customary adoption currently predominates in Nunavut due to the continuing strength of this traditional practice among the Inuit. The prevalence of customary adoption is among the features that distinguishes Nunavut from the rest of Canada.

4.2.1.   ADOPTION

Adoption in Nunavut occurs when birth parents transfer all parental rights to adoptive parents through a permanent adoption order. Guardianship is transferred through adoption and, when finalisation occurs, the child becomes the legal child of the adoptive family and the child's birth and surname may be changed.

---

[45] *Ibid.*

[46] See, *Aboriginal Justice Inquiry*, 1999 at Chap. 14. The report also notes that "between 1971 and 1981, 70–80% of Manitoba's Aboriginal adoptions were in non-Aboriginal homes" at Chap. 14. See, also, the Law Commission report, *op cit* and Miller, J.R., *Shingwauk's Vision: A History of Native Residential Schools*, University of Toronto Press, Toronto, 1996.

4.2.1(i). CUSTOMARY ADOPTION

This is an arrangement for the care of a child between the birth parent(s) and the adoptive parent(s) who are usually relatives or members of the same community. Adoption is deemed to have taken place at the time of placement. Under the Aboriginal Custom Adoption Recognition Act 1994,[47] customary adoptions are processed by Adoption Commissioners in the various northern communities. As stated in the Preamble, this legislation "without changing aboriginal customary law respecting adoptions" sets out "a simple procedure by which a custom adoption may be respected and recognised and a certificate recognising the adoption will be issued". One or both birth parents and the adopting parents must be of Inuit, Dene or Métis descent and must be a resident of Nunavut or have some legitimate connection to the territory. Adoption certificates are completed by Commissioners and forwarded to the Supreme Court of Nunavut where they are certified by the Supreme Court Clerk.

4.2.1(ii). PRIVATE ADOPTION

These are regulated by the Adoption Act 1998 to protect the interests of all parties and to ensure the protection and well-being of the child. A private adoption occurs where the child to be adopted is not the subject of a care order. It can be arranged by birth parent(s) and adopting parent(s) as long as the requirements of the 1998 Act and the regulations have been met.

4.2.1(iii). DEPARTMENTAL ADOPTION

Departmental adoption placements are wholly governed by the legislative procedures, regulations, standards and policies relating to the Adoption Act 1998. They occur either on a consensual basis following parental relinquishment or on a compulsory basis following permanent care and custody of the child being vested in the Director of social services. When birth parent(s) consent to an adoption, 10 days must elapse after the day the child is surrendered before the parental consent is signed. When the parent(s) has signed a Voluntary Support Agreement form, the child is placed in an approved adoptive home and the placement is managed and supervised by appointed adoption workers. When a child is placed with a family prior to a court order, a pre-adoption acknowledgement is made with the approved adoptive parents, taking the best interests of the child and the possible risks into consideration. Prospective adoptive parents sign an acknowledgement that they understand that the child can be removed during a 30 day appeal period and that they are willing to accept a child under these conditions pending the making of a permanent adoption order.

---

[47] The Aboriginal Custom Adoption Recognition Act 1994, which came into effect on 30.09.95, was promulgated for the Northwest Territories.

4.2.2. THE STATUTORY ADOPTION FRAMEWORK AND THE INUIT

The current statutory framework governing adoption by Inuit and non-Inuit is provided by the Adoption Act 1998[48] which has a general application throughout the province and requires adoption proceedings to be commenced in court.

4.2.2(i). INUIT PLACEMENT

Before an aboriginal child can be placed for adoption, one of the three Inuit organizations in Nunavut (Kitikmeot Inuit Association, Kivalliq Inuit Association and Qikiqtani Inuit Association) must be informed. An exception is made for circumstances where the child is at least 12 years old or where one birth parent objects to any such involvement.

In considering the "best interests" of the child, consideration must be given to the aboriginal heritage of the child; his or her cultural, racial and religious background must be taken into account. An adoption order cannot affect any aboriginal or treaty rights of the child, nor can it affect any entitlement the child may have under the Indian Act.

4.2.2(ii). NON-INUIT PLACEMENT

Adoption within the Inuit culture, as elsewhere, often occurs within the context of the prevailing statutory child care framework. In such cases there is a statutory duty to try to place aboriginal children with members of their extended family or within their communities, if they must be placed in foster care. However, given the shortage of aboriginal foster parents, aboriginal children are often placed with non-aboriginal foster parents. There is then a requirement that kinship ties and the cultural identity of aboriginal children should be preserved, that aboriginal people should be involved in planning and delivering services to aboriginal children and families, and that the community should be involved in planning and providing services, in ways that are sensitive to the culture, racial and religious heritage of the families receiving them.

4.2.2(iii). LEGAL EFFECTS OF STATUTORY ADOPTION

Under the statutory process an adoption become final when a permanent adoption order certificate is granted to the adoptive parents, whereas under the customary process this occurs when the evidence that an adoption has occurred is registered in the Supreme Court. In both types of adoption the legal consequences are final and the birth parents relinquish their legal rights and responsibilities towards the child.

---

[48] c.9. In force November 01, 1998. SI-016-98.

4.2.3. CUSTOMARY ADOPTION

In Canada, customary adoption is an integral part of the life of all aboriginal societies, is common among the Inuit and is specifically recognised under the Indian Act. In addition to legislative recognition, customary adoption constitutes an aboriginal right within the meaning of s 35 of the Constitution Act, 1982 once it is established to be an integral part of the distinct culture of the aboriginal community.[49] The Aboriginal Custom Adoption Recognition Act 1994[50] formally recognised customary adoption in Nunavut[51] and now provides a statutory framework for it with an accompanying level of administration that was not formerly a part of customary adoption among the Inuit. It has now acquired a legal and institutional character.

4.2.3(i). CHARACTERISTICS OF CUSTOMARY ADOPTION

Customary adoption among the Inuit is a non-judicial process which has traditionally been viewed by them as essentially a family or community affair. It does have some administrative characteristics: the local customary adoption commissioner will record the parties intentions and keep information on file; there is no requirement that the commissioner be satisfied as to the merits of the adoption. The adoption is then registered in the Supreme Court and the commissioner will apply for an amended birth certificate in respect of the child. The features that distinguish customary from statutory adoption are:

- they are invariably open adoptions where everyone concerned, often the whole community, knows the exact nature of the relationships between the parties[52];
- most (but not all) customary adoptions occur between relatives;
- they only occur between Inuit; and
- mostly it is those who are relinquishing the child who initiate the process by approaching a relative or a friend who often lives in another Inuit community.

Customary adoption is an 'open' form of adoption. This is considered desirable because:

- the child generally knows he or she has been adopted;
- the child knows their birth parent/s; and
- open adoption enables the aboriginal child to maintain access with his or her family and aboriginal community.

---

[49] See, *Casimel v Insurance Corporation of British Columbia*, [1994] 2 C.N.L.R. 22 (C.A.).

[50] See, *Aboriginal Custom Adoption Recognition Act, S.K.K. v J.S.* in which a maternal grandmother who had adopted her granddaughter sought child support from the birth father.

[51] Since 1996: some 2000 customary adoptions have been formalised by the courts; approximately 40 departmental adoptions; and perhaps 35 private adoptions to non-Inuit.

[52] The term 'qiturngaqati' ('having the same child') refers to the fact that both birth parent and adopter share the same relationship with the child.

The Inuit practice allows for relationships to develop between the adopted child and the natural families throughout the child's life; originally the purpose was for the adopted child to return to the birth family, with which they had maintained a relationship, in the event of the death of their adoptive parents. Occasionally, in customary adoptions, a child returns to their family of origin and may be again placed for adoption with new adopters.

4.2.3(ii). THE PRACTICE

Each aboriginal community has its own process for giving effect to customary adoption. This differs in the three regions of Nunavut, and even within regions. In its most basic form, customary adoption among the Inuit simply rests on an agreement, usually verbal, whereby one family gives a child to be raised by another family. Evidence of an adoption properly executed by aboriginal custom would normally include the following[53]:

- the consent of the natural and adopting parents;
- the child's voluntary placement with the adopting parents;
- the adopting parents' aboriginal heritage or entitlement to rely on aboriginal custom; and
- the presence of a rationale for aboriginal custom adoption.

In addition, the relationship created by custom must have been intended to create fundamentally the same relationship as that resulting from an adoption order under the Adoption Act 1998. Where such evidence is presented, the court will then register the adoption without any requirement for a homestudy report.

The practice has given rise to problems. During the course of the recent inquiries conducted by the Nunavut Law Review Commission, or Maligarnit Qimirrujiit, into customary adoption the following issues were identified:

- agreement given during pregnancy but subsequently withdrawn by birth mother;
- adopters fears, sometimes well-founded, that birth parents will reclaim their child;
- concerns that birth fathers were not consulted prior to adoption;
- all information regarding birth fathers' should be recorded for every birth and that information should be available to an adopted child;
- concerns about people over the age of 65 adopting babies; and
- concerns that the traditional use of customary adoption, to assist infertile couples or to provide a home for an orphaned child, was now being seen more as a means of dealing with unwanted pregnancies.

---

[53] See, *Re: Tagornak Adoption Petition*, [1984] 1 C.N.L.R. 185 (N.W.T.S.C.).

4.2.3(iii). THE CHILD

For the purposes of adoption, a 'child' is a minor (less than 19 years) and the definition includes a child adopted in accordance with custom and amendments to the Indian Act which extended the entitlement of Indian status to children who are adopted by custom. An Inuit adopted child is known as "tiguaq".

4.2.3(iv). LEGAL EFFECTS OF CUSTOMARY ADOPTION

Under the Aboriginal Custom Adoption Recognition Act 1994, customary adoptions become legal when the adoptive parents assume responsibility for the child. A court order is unnecessary. Biological parents normally relinquish their rights and responsibilities towards a child when the government adoption certificate is issued and the adoptive parents assume full rights and responsibilities as legal parents of the child.

4.2.3(v). THE REGISTRAR

Application is made to the Registrar for a certificate of the registration of an adoption. Where this has been conducted in accordance with customary adoption then the Registrar responds by determining whether the eligibility criteria have been met. Affidavits from the natural parents, the adoptive parents, the band council, and elders usually accompany such an application. The affidavits state the particular form of customary adoption that was used and confirm that the applicant was adopted in accordance with that custom. Other supporting documentation may be required.

5.   CONCLUSION

The adoption processes traditionally and currently used by the Indigenous people of Australia, the Maori in New Zealand and the Inuit in Canada are illustrative of the type of customary practice to be found among indigenous cultural groups in other countries such as those of South America and Africa. The primary purpose served by adoption in an indigenous context is not fundamentally different from that in modern western nations. In both, adoption is essentially the most extreme means for giving effect to the common intention that total care responsibility for a child is transferred from the birth parent/s to approved other persons until such time as the child reaches adulthood. The goals address similar factors such as parental death, absence, relinquishment or abandonment, failed parenting, infertility, the need for an heir and the tidying up of re-formed family units. The legal functions, however, reflect significant differences in law, policy and practice.

Adoption within indigenous cultures is invariably a consensual process, governed more by practice than by policy or law. It has always been treated as a transparent and ongoing transaction between the parties, often following discussions involving the extended family, which require and receive the support of the community. It at least favours transactions that respect and maintain blood-link relationships. It emphasises the importance of ensuring that an adopted child is never in any doubt as to the identity of birth parents and members of their family of origin, with whom contact is maintained. It offers an assurance that the child will be reminded of their particular background, heritage etc and in general will be provided with all information necessary to form identity and maintain a sense of belonging to family and community. Insofar as there is a policy in this context, it could be said to be one of facilitating the harmonious reordering of parenting responsibilities in accordance with the wishes and needs of all concerned. The legal functions of adoption, redundant in terms of asserting or defending the rights of individuals, are appropriately minimal and non-interventionist serving mainly to endorse arrangements freely and openly entered into.

The politics of adoption can achieve a crude but revealing salience in the context of relations between indigenous people and their host society. As a non-consensual process, adoption is often imposed on indigenous cultures. This tends to occur in circumstances where indigenous parenting is judged to infringe standards required by the public child welfare law of modern western society. At its most extreme this can take the form of a discriminatory policy to use non-consensual adoption, perhaps in conjunction with institutional residential schooling, as a means to enforce the assimilation of indigenous children into non-indigenous society. Most usually, it occurs as a consequence of the non-discriminatory application of child welfare law that inevitably results in some indigenous children being drawn into the child care system and then entering the non-consensual adoption process. Non-consensual adoption in an indigenous context would seem to have the following implications for the law, policy and practice of modern western societies:

- involvement of parent/s, significant relatives, friends and/or community representatives in placement decision-making;
- first preference for long-term foster care, where permanency is required, if this better enables the child to maintain relationships with family/ community/culture of origin and revert to them on attaining adulthood;
- second preference for kinship placement, where adoption is necessary, to authenticate identity and maintain sense of belonging; and
- placement with 'strangers' or non-relatives only in exceptional circumstances, where adoption is necessary, and then to be in geographical proximity to the child's birth family, in keeping with parental wishes in relation to contact and accompanied by appropriate arrangements to safeguard the child's identity.

The hallmarks of secrecy, complete severance with birth family, agency mediation, total assimilation of identity and formal judicial endorsement that have always characterised adoption in modern western societies are now being increasingly challenged by the alternative approach of indigenous communities. Increasingly, western professionals are becoming attentive to the resonance of the indigenous experience as they review the appropriateness of established legal functions for contemporary adoption practice.

CONCLUSIONS

From the perspective of current fundamental change in the UK, *The Politics of Adoption* examined the law, policy and practice of other, largely common law, jurisdictions. Beginning with an historical account of the social role and emerging formative principles of adoption, this book identified the nature and effect of pressures for change and traced the path that led to the Adoption and Children Act 2002. It then conducted a comparative analysis of the adoption processes of England & Wales, Ireland, the US and Australia. It considered the impact of international developments on national law, policy and practice by focussing on the influence of Convention law and the phenomenon of intercountry adoption. It concluded by noting that alternative models of adoption, as practiced over many centuries within indigenous cultures, now offer useful guidance for the future development of adoption in modern western nations.

THE LAW

Adoption, evolving within countries sharing the common law tradition and drawing from the same pool of case law, would seem to have broadly retained much the same set of characteristics in each country. This, of course, is hardly surprising as the countries concerned shared the same colonial experience, taking the values, laws, institutions and many of the children from the heart of the British Empire to its constituent parts. These characteristics resonate with the concerns of Victorian England to maintain a structured society with a distinct value system as evidenced by a careful attention to matters of status. *The Politics of Adoption* used those characteristics to construct a template of typical legal functions which it applied to both differentiate the common law adoption process from that of other nations while also differentiating between the similar adoption processes of common law jurisdictions. It largely focussed on the latter task. The main conclusions to be drawn from that exercise may be grouped as follows.

EXISTENCE OF A SOPHISTICATED REGULATORY ENVIRONMENT

Adoption in all jurisdictions studied evolved from being largely concerned with third party or 'stranger' adoption into several distinct types (child care, step-parent, intercountry, kinship etc) each with associated bodies of regulations and involving a range of agencies and specialist professionals. Scope for independent decision-making by birth parents and voluntary bodies, characteristic of all adoption processes at an earlier stage, has virtually disappeared except in the US. The adoption process is invariably governed by statute and, with the notable exception of Ireland, is determined by a court. Among the common law nations, the UK now has the most centralised, professional, bureaucratic and government agency controlled system. It seeks to thoroughly and comprehensively regulate practice according to specified standards.

STATUTORY DEFINITION OF THE PARTIES RIGHTS

Statutory provisions define the eligibility of parties to enter the process, the terms on which they may engage in it and their post-adoption rights. The eligibility of some potential applicants, such as same gender couples, varies between jurisdictions but the rights of the parties, including those of an unmarried father, are similar. In the US, however, the birth parent/s in some states retain the statutory right to make or arrange a direct placement. In all jurisdictions, there is an absence of statutory provision for the independent assertion of children's rights as opposed to protection of their welfare interests. The rights and responsibilities of marital parents are accorded singular recognition in Ireland. Post-adoption financial and other support services are usually statutorily available but not yet in Ireland.

UPHOLDING AND APPLYING THE WELFARE OF THE CHILD PRINCIPLE

In all jurisdictions the legislation states the principle that the welfare interests of the child is the paramount concern in the adoption process. In the US and in England & Wales this principle determines a child's entry to the process from the public child care system and is the statutory determinant of adoption proceedings. In Australia and now in England & Wales the principle raises a statutory presumption that alternative orders will be more appropriate in the context of adoption applications by step-parents or relatives. In Ireland, this principle has less influence than in any other jurisdiction on the decision as to whether a child is available for adoption and if so whether he or she should be adopted. Professional representation of this principle is given greatest effect in the courts of the UK and least in Ireland. The right of a mature minor to consent or withhold consent to their adoption is most evident in US law.

THE STAGES OF THE ADOPTION PROCESS

The sequence of stages from pre-placement counselling to post-adoption information access is essentially the same in all jurisdictions, though there is considerable variation as regards statutory underpinning. In the UK all stages exist, are governed by statute, controlled by government bodies and are the subject of mandatory supervision in accordance with specific rules, regulations and standards. The US differs in that it permits the involvement of independent adoption agencies that may operate on a commercial basis. In Ireland there is no statutory provision for pre and post adoption services but these may be available from voluntary bodies. Australia is closer to Ireland than to the US or the UK in this respect.

THE ORDER MADE

In all jurisdictions an adoption order is the most likely outcome of adoption proceedings. Its legal effect is similar in all jurisdictions and the consequences for the parties in terms of a redistribution of rights, responsibilities and legal status are statutorily stated and clarified by a body of common case law. In Ireland there is least opportunity for an alternative private family order to be made and unlike the other jurisdictions there is no possibility of an adoption order being made subject to contact conditions. In England & Wales and in Australia alternative private family law orders are available together with a statutory requirement that they be used when appropriate instead of adoption. In the US the public law alternatives to adoption are now positively discouraged.

POST ADOPTION INFORMATION RIGHTS

In all jurisdictions the privacy rights of birth parents make the issue of an adopted person's right of access to identifying information contentious. Such statutory information rights are strongest in England & Wales, non-existent in Ireland and most hotly debated in the US. Where they exist, statutory rights are balanced by contact veto rights of varying rigour.

SUBJECT TO INTERNATIONAL CONVENTIONS

All jurisdictions studied subscribe at least to the United Nations Convention on the Rights of the Child 1989 (signed but not yet ratified or implemented by the US) and to the Hague Convention on Protection of Children and Co-operation in Respect of Intercountry Adoption 1993. All except the US have incorporated the European Convention for the Protection of Human Rights and Fundamental Freedoms 1950 into national legislation. The case law associated in particular with Article 8 of the European Convention is steadily introducing a uniformity of legal principle in relation to adoption practice. The case law also serves to benchmark standards against which national laws can be seen to be deficient. This would be the case, for example, in Ireland in relation to the non-availability for adoption of children from marital parents and in the US in relation to post-adoption information rights.

IMPLICATIONS FOR FAMILY LAW

Calibrating the fit between adoption law and other proceedings within a nation's body of family law and between that and the principles of Convention law is clearly a complex matter. The judiciary in common law jurisdictions, perhaps uniquely, have a proven capacity to use their discretionary powers to re-interpret principles and precedents in the light of changing social need. While this has facilitated the updating of domestic legal practice to ensure Convention compliance it has thereby accelerated and compounded tensions in the legislative balance traditionally held between private and public family law in each jurisdiction. The broadening use of adoption for private law purposes has displaced, if not absorbed, the functions once assigned to guardianship and wardship while fast becoming an optional extra following matrimonial proceedings. In public law the mainstreaming of adoption into child care provision threatens to transform the independent role of the state from 'guardian of last resort' to adoption agency, facilitating private family care arrangements.

England & Wales and Australia would seem to have achieved the preferable legislative reconfiguration of family law. Within an infrastructure of family oriented legislation, courts and proceedings they have strategically repositioned adoption closer to public law, provided more balance between adoption and alternative private law proceedings while allowing the permeation of Convention principles to maintain overall coherence within the body of family law. In the US adoption law would seem to have become essentially divided into two blocks, one dealing with proceedings relating to the public child care system and the other dealing with all other forms of adoption. This is in keeping with sharper divisions between the public and private, with a clearer emphasis on the rights of the individual, in US family law. Ireland is at present stuck, being unable to resolve the tensions between Constitution constraints and Convention requirements, with a body of family law that coheres around the central construct of the marital family unit.

THE POLICY

The law reform processes, currently underway or just concluded in all the jurisdictions studied, reflect a general awareness of the need to rethink adoption policy in the light of the pressures forcing rapid change in adoption practice. *The Politics of Adoption* identified and considered the pressures, their effect and the legislative response. The policies informing adoption law reform, outlined in preceding reports and discussion papers, were found to concern much the same matters though the legislative response often differed.

CHILD CARE ADOPTION

The US initiative to expedite the flow of children from the public care system into the adoption process, by substituting the welfare principle for the parental right to withhold consent, has been followed in England & Wales, but not in Australia and Ireland. It would seem to be predicated on a belief that public resources are more effective if invested in supporting permanent alternative care arrangements than in supporting failing parental care. This is a significant development that is set to establish a fundamental difference in adoption policy between common law nations and distance its adherents from such non-common law nations as Sweden, Denmark, Finland and France. It is also a policy that will have to be carefully managed if it is to avoid resulting in cases that breach the right to privacy of family life as protected by Article 8(2) of the European Convention. This requires evidence that support services or an alternative order would not be a more proportionate response and obviate the need to make such a draconian intervention as a non-consensual adoption order.

ADOPTION OF CHILDREN WITH SPECIAL NEEDS

The term 'special needs' is used differently in the jurisdictions studied; in the US it would seem to be synonymous with child care adoption. However, in Ireland and elsewhere among some modern western societies the term is used specifically in reference to children suffering from severe health and/or social care problems. Arguably, this sub-set of adoptable children should be differentiated from the broader class because the particular difficulties in facilitating their adoption require a correspondingly distinct policy emphasis. In the UK and Australia, unlike Ireland, such children are the focus of specialist and successful policies to establish appropriate adoption services.

STEP-ADOPTION

In England & Wales adoption policy has finally taken a stand against the previous fairly automatic granting of orders to step-parents. They are now required to show why adoption, rather than any other order, would be a better means of promoting the welfare of the child concerned. The fact that the law has been simplified by the removal of the legal anomaly requiring such an applicant to apply jointly with the birth parent, thereby permitting sole step-parent applications, is beside the point. Alternative permanency orders, including access to parental responsibility by agreement or court order, have been made available specifically for step-parents. In Australia the policy is similar, step-parents are required to show good reason why any other order or none would not better serve the welfare interests of the child. This is quite contrary to the approach in the US and in Ireland.

KINSHIP ADOPTION

In the US a policy of definite support for kinship adoption has recently emerged. Again this significant policy development led by the US presents a challenge to established practice elsewhere. It contrasts with present policy in England & Wales and in Australia, both of which favour diverting relatives and step-parents towards alternative orders. In Ireland the traditional policy of facilitating adoption by family members continues.

INTERCOUNTRY ADOPTION

This now appears to be an unstoppable phenomenon for all modern western nations, including those that were the subject of this study. It is accompanied by a common policy of acceptance coupled with a resolve to ensure that the welfare interests of children should be afforded no less protection in intercountry adoption than in domestic adoption processes. This policy is demonstrated by the fact that all jurisdictions had subscribed to The Hague Convention on Protection of Children and Co-operation in Respect of Intercountry Adoption 1993. However, this policy has not extended to the point of prohibiting adoption arrangements with non-Convention compliant countries nor does it effectively regulate the involvement of independent commercial agencies and it fails to grapple with the complexities of transracial placements and Convention requirements regarding the preservation of identity and culture. The policy deficit allows a continuation of practice that at times comes close to condoning 'trafficking in children' and where uncertainty regarding parental consent can give rise to concerns for the basic human rights of the birth parents and children involved.

AVAILABILITY OF ALTERNATIVES TO ADOPTION

Clearly a revealing indicator of a nation's policy in relation to adoption is the extent to which it makes available, or facilitates access to, alternative options for securing permanent care arrangements for children. Whether, if available, these are public or private family law options and what if any allowance is made for judicial choice, provides further clarification. *The Politics of Adoption* found significant jurisdictional differences in this area.

In public family law, the official US policy of discouraging the use of long-term foster care for children in respect of whom parental rights have been terminated has been followed in England & Wales and reinforced in both jurisdictions by a statutory entitlement to post-adoption allowances. In both, however, the introduction of guardianship orders is intended to provide a private law alternative to adoption for some foster parents. In Australia the policy of prioritising rehabilitation as the preferred option for children in the public care system has resulted in the development of specialist foster care services. In Ireland, the policy commitment to prioritising the use of long-term foster care in preference to adoption may at present be largely a forced choice, given constitutional constraints, but is reinforced by the absence of any statutory entitlement to post-adoption financial support.

In private family law, the absence of any specific alternative for step-parents in the US (a permanent legal guardianship order is intended for use by foster parents) reinforces the policy of at least not obstructing their continued access to adoption. This would also seem to be the case in Ireland. In Australia, as in England & Wales, the weight given to the alternative policy of discouraging step-adoptions is underpinned by the availability of a range of private law orders coupled with a requirement that such applicants show good reason as to why an adoption order would be more appropriate.

POST ADOPTION RIGHTS AND SERVICES

Post adoption support services are very largely viewed as specific to child care adoptions and policies regarding their statutory availability are thus pre-set by the priority given to that public family law option. In jurisdictions where the approach is to mainstream adoption into child care provision, a policy is emerging of extending the availability of post adoption support services to all parties in all types of adoption, public and private including intercountry. In England & Wales this policy is now given effect by provisions in the 2002 Act.

In all jurisdictions studied, the policies relating to post adoption rights of access to identifying information reflect a struggle to balance the rights of the parties involved. Although recent ECHR case law has been somewhat equivocal, it is probable that the combined effect of Articles 8 and 14 of the European Convention together with clear statements of similar principles in the UN and Hague Conventions will shape a future common policy. To ensure Convention compliance, such a policy will need to guarantee that an adopted person has access to sufficient information about his or her family background and cultural heritage to maintain or develop their cultural identity.

THE PRACTICE

The Politics of Adoption has highlighted the fact that reform of adoption law and revision of adoption policy has been driven by the range and pace of change taking place in adoption practice. The momentum generated by some aspects of this change process will continue into the foreseeable future. The experience of indigenous communities may then usefully inform adoption practice in western societies.

ASPECTS OF CHANGE

Any attempt to predict the likely drivers and direction of future change would be dangerously speculative. It is possible, however, to identify some features of contemporary practice that in all probability will be among those with a continuing significance for the adoption process.

• Parenting as a responsible choice

Developments in medical knowledge and skill in recent years have greatly enhanced the extent to which parenting is now a matter of choice, exercised largely by women. The law and policy of modern western nations have variously struggled to accommodate these developments. Some changes, such as in relation to the availability of effective contraception, methods of birth control and abortion, have clearly reduced the numbers of children available for adoption. Other changes, such as improved techniques for assisting conception and for improving survival rates for babies born prematurely and/or with complex health problems are reducing the number of potential adopters. Advances in medical skill, enabling surrogacy to be based on full embryo transplant, are now extending the range of parents by choice to include opportunities for same gender couples. Increased recourse to intercountry adoption will undoubtedly also increase the number of such parents.

An emerging trend with quite the opposite effect is the lowering of tolerance levels in some western countries for irresponsible parenting. Certainly in the UK and the US, the prospects for failing parents are now more likely than previously to include a high risk of proceedings resulting in their child being removed and placed with state approved responsible parents.

- **The European Convention**

Convention case law developments are a considerable force for change in practice. It is probably only a matter of time before the ECHR requires an adoption order to be conditional upon the prior consent of the child concerned unless good reason can be shown for this to be dispensed with. There are also strong indications that rights will be extended to non-resident parents, grandparents, foster parents and indeed to any carer who can show the existence of a meaningful relationship with a child.

Certain key principles emerging from Convention case law will serve to benchmark future practice. These include the paramount welfare interests of the child, proportionality in state intervention in family affairs and the right to access information necessary for identity. Others will undoubtedly emerge.

- **Role of the agencies**

A significant practice development in recent years has been the expansion of agency involvement in the adoption process accompanied by the broadening role of the professional. Pre and post adoption counselling, support services, intercountry assessments, tracing and reunion services etc have all added to the powerful position of the professional in modern adoption practice. It may be confidently predicted that the various adoption law reforms will see this trend continue and result in future practice being burdened with a greater weight of regulatory procedures. The distribution of responsibilities between agencies and the extent to which in each country they are government bodies, voluntary organisations or commercial companies will be revealing.

INDIGENOUS CULTURE AND OPEN ADOPTION

Certain characteristics of a more 'open' or simple form of adoption, as practiced for centuries within indigenous communities in accordance with established custom, are now finding their way into the adoption processes of modern western nations. This has had the effect of rapidly eroding several traditional hallmarks of the more 'closed' model developed in those jurisdictions.

- **Anonymity and confidentiality**
  Even if desired, these can no longer be guaranteed in any of the juris-dictions studied. The ready acceptance that ongoing contact arrangements were legally possible and often beneficial in both child care and family adoptions paved the way for acceptance of further compromise. While post adoption contact arrangements are now more likely than not, pre adoption information is also considered essential and contact at that stage is quite common. Increasingly, the birth parent/s are involved in the process of se-lecting adopters. This 'openness' is also apparent in the introduction of legislation facilitating access to information held by adoption agencies etc and the provision of tracing and re-unification services.

- **Eligibility and suitability**
  Such criteria, defined by legislation and applied by agency professionals respectively, are unknown in indigenous communities and are beginning to be questioned in western societies. As adoption by grandparents, single persons and same gender couples become more common so the usefulness of accepted strictures relating to adopters' age, health, residence, convic-tions, duration of relationship (where appropriate), income and infertility are now being queried. Once broad minimum criteria relating to motivation and capacity are satisfied, seeking further information may need advance justification in terms of its possible bearing on a specific welfare related issue. Similarly the relevance of an upper age limit in relation to the subject of adoption is open to question. The rationale for age limits as a factor in consensual adoptions, whether by persons with appropriate motivation and capacity or of children with dependency needs, may require further analysis.

- **Kinship adoption**
  Long practiced and often preferred among indigenous people, this is now emerging as a valued option for children in the public child care system. Its perceived strengths of maintaining family relationships and sense of conti-nuity with home environment were previously viewed in western societies as weaknesses. In the US, the recent increased reliance on kinship care and a higher tolerance for step-adoption would seem to indicate a greater readi-ness to use adoption to facilitate permanency through family care than has been evident in the UK.

- **Cultural identity**
  This has always been a much prized feature of upbringing in indigenous communities. Great importance is attached to ensuring that as children ma-ture they retain a sense of where they belong, an awareness of their cultural heritage and geographic locality. The value of such links for a child, in

promoting an authentic sense of personal identity through developing an orientation to their particular culture, is now strongly endorsed for use in the adoption processes of western societies by the provisions of international Conventions and national legislation. Such recognition, however, is at variance with the practice of intercountry adoption.

- **Community knowledge and support**
  Again, this has long been a key feature of adoption among indigenous people. It is now becoming accepted in western societies as adoption orders are increasingly accompanied by financial assistance, the ongoing involvement of a range of different professions and various forms of service provision.

The challenge presented by the characteristics of 'open' adoption in indigenous communities is evident not only in the erosion of the above traditional hallmarks. It also raises some more fundamental questions regarding the more 'closed' model of the adoption process in western societies with its abiding concern for incidences of status.

- **A highly legalistic and regulated process**
  The statute based, professionally administered and judicially determined adoption process typical of western society, stands in complete contrast to that still practiced within indigenous cultures in accordance with traditional customs rather than prescriptive laws. While a regulated approach is clearly necessary in relation to non-consensual and intercountry applications and in any set of circumstances giving rise to particular concerns for the welfare of a child, it is open to question whether this is equally applicable to all other adoptions. A professional filter, in terms of a completed home study report addressing motivation and capacity, confirming consents and identifying any welfare related matters, will often provide all information necessary for assessment. In the absence of legal issues, it may that a body similar to the Adoption Panel in the UK could then satisfy itself as to the capacity of the parties and determine whether or not adoption would be in the best interests of the child concerned. Such a body would be broadly constituted and representative, as in indigenous communities, but would include some professionals with relevant specialist expertise. It would hear directly from the principal parties and from anyone else who wished to be heard. Approval by that body would be subject to formal authorisation and registration by the Registrar on submission of appropriate documents. Arguably, most adoptions could be processed in that way.

- **Adoption as option of last resort**
  In indigenous communities formal adoption is viewed as an extreme option. Other, if possible informal, care arrangements that help a child to retain their sense of place in terms of relationships, culture and locality are preferred. This option of least intervention also has firm Convention endorsement.

Where safe reunification with parents or relatives is not feasible, there is much to be said for consolidating the care arrangement that maintains most links with family and environment of origin. If this can be achieved through long-term foster care and/or by guardianship or by any other public/private family law orders, then perhaps good reason needs to be shown before preference is given to adoption.

- **Adoption as a stand alone process**
  Finally, and intimately linked to the above, there is the fact that it is no longer possible nor desirable to continue viewing adoption as it has been for most of its statutory existence in western societies. It has long ceased to be the most private, discrete and detached of all the family law proceedings. For some decades it has largely functioned as an adjunct to matrimonial proceedings and now, particularly in the US and the UK, it is increasingly doing so in relation to child care proceedings. In indigenous communities, where the private/public distinction and incidences of status are less relevant, adoption avoided the degree of preciousness it acquired in western societies. As the concept of 'family' becomes more fluid and indeterminate in those societies, with serial parenting arrangements and ever more intrusive public service intervention (benign and coercive), so it is losing its insularity and assuming the more flexible characteristics associated with indigenous communities. It is highly probable that the functions of the adoption process in western societies will adapt accordingly, will continue to develop features of 'openness' and will find a more central place in family law.

Index

334